CREDITOR PROTECTION IN PRIVATE COMPANIES

Limited liability companies form the backbone of our modern economy. However, there is a persistent risk of moral hazard on the part of directors and shareholders, particularly in closely held or private companies. Like all developed legal systems, both English and German law provide mechanisms designed to protect creditors from such risks. This book investigates some of these mechanisms, including the avoidance of pre-insolvency acts, capital maintenance and creditor-regarding duties of directors. By analysing the different conceptual and doctrinal perspectives inherent in the English and German systems, this book seeks to advance a discourse between audiences with different legal backgrounds. It will be an invaluable guide for those wishing to understand how the protective mechanisms operate and interact with each other, and how they do so in quite different ways in the two jurisdictions.

THOMAS BACHNER is Assistant Professor at WU (Vienna University of Economics and Business).

CREDITOR PROTECTION IN PRIVATE COMPANIES

Anglo-German Perspectives for a European Legal Discourse

THOMAS BACHNER

CAMBRIDGE
UNIVERSITY PRESS

CAMBRIDGE UNIVERSITY PRESS
Cambridge, New York, Melbourne, Madrid, Cape Town, Singapore, São Paulo, Delhi

Cambridge University Press
The Edinburgh Building, Cambridge CB2 8RU, UK

Published in the United States of America by Cambridge University Press, New York

www.cambridge.org
Information on this title: www.cambridge.org/9780521895385

First published 2009

Printed in the United Kingdom at the University Press, Cambridge

A catalogue record for this publication is available from the British Library

Library of Congress Cataloguing in Publication data
Bachner, Thomas.
Creditor protection in private companies : Anglo-German perspectives for a
European legal discourse / by Thomas Bachner.
p. cm.
Includes bibliographical references and index.
ISBN 978-0-521-89538-5 (hardback)
1. Corporations–Finance–Law and legislation–Germany. 2. Debtor and
creditor–Germany. 3. Corporation reserves–Law and legislation–Germany.
4. Directors of corporations–Legal status, laws, etc.–Germany. 5. Corporations–
Finance–Law and legislation–Great Britain. 6. Debtor and creditor–Great Britain.
7. Corporation reserves–Law and legislation–Great Britain. 8. Directors of
corporations–Legal status, laws, etc.–Great Britain.
I. Title.
K1330.B33 2009
346.07′7–dc22 2008053262

ISBN 978-0-521-89538-5 hardback

CONTENTS

PREFACE

This book represents a thoroughly revised and updated version of my Ph.D. thesis approved by the Law Faculty at Cambridge University in 2006. The entire process that has led to this book has occupied the better part of a decade, and the end result is a far cry from the original plan. The book is an attempt – and it cannot be more than that – to write about German law and English law in a manner designed to make the exposition accessible to readers from each of the two jurisdictions by taking account of their respective conceptual and terminological background. My own status as an outsider, being neither German nor English, will hopefully have contributed to a fair balance between the two. Obviously, my legal education and academic roots in Austria, with its proximity to Germany especially in the field of company law, meant that the true voyage of discovery for me started only when I was given the fascinating opportunity to explore English law at Cambridge University.

I owe a sincere debt of gratitude to Eilís Ferran, who took on the charge of being my Ph.D. supervisor – and a charge it must have been with a supervisee constantly venturing off to do things he was not supposed to do – and who subsequently masterminded the publication of the book with Cambridge University Press. I also owe an intellectual debt to Simon Deakin and Brian Cheffins, each of whom taught me in his own manner and style that there is more to company law than I had hitherto thought. Thanks must go to Roderick Munday, Tony Weir and Pippa Rogerson for instilling in me an enthusiasm for the Common Law. Upon the introduction by Eva Micheler, Sarah Worthington and Paul Davies entrusted me with teaching their undergraduate classes at the London School of Economics on company law for two consecutive years (2001–2002 and 2002–2003). It turned into an immensely valuable experience for me, because it forced me to come to terms with English law in a very direct and almost brutal manner. Subsequent to the submission of the thesis, John Armour and Heribert Hirte, being the examiners for the Ph.D., as well as one anonymous German referee made valuable suggestions for the improvement of the text. Over the years all these influences have come together and shaped this book into something I could not have imagined at the outset of the process. In the run-up to publication Vanessa Wilcox, Laurence Marsh and Donna Stockenhuber critically examined the whole text, while Christina Gasser, Olga Horwath, Veronika Korom, Helena Nejedlá and Felix Prechtl provided technical support. Naturally, I am solely responsible for all mistakes that remain.

In order to carry out my research at Cambridge I was on leave from the University of Economics and Business Administration in Vienna during the years 2000 to 2004. This would not have been possible, first, without the understanding of my academic mentor Peter Doralt, who greatly encouraged me to go abroad. It would also not have been possible without generous funding from a number of sources. The Austrian Science Fund (FWF), the Austrian Federal Ministry of Education and the Emil-Boral-Stiftung, Zurich provided living allowances at various stages. Smaller grants were made available by the University of Economics and Business Administration (from its OeNB-Förderpreis), the Cambridge European Trust, the Helmuth H. Merlin-Stiftung, the Graf Hardegg'sche Doktoren-Stiftung and the Walther Kastner-Stiftung. I am grateful to all of them.

Last, but not least, I wish to thank the team at Cambridge University Press for their valuable advice and for their patience in the face of numerous postponements of submission.

I have endeavoured to present the law as it was available to me on 6 April 2008. The book takes full account of the Companies Act 2006, notwithstanding that some of the new provisions may not yet be in force by the time of its publication. References in the text or in the footnotes guide readers to the respective provisions in the Companies Act 1985 and in earlier Companies Acts, where appropriate, thereby facilitating the work with secondary literature on the old and the new law. Moreover, the book already takes account of the German Gesetz zur Modernisierung des GmbH-Rechts und zur Bekämpfung von Missbräuchen (MoMiG), which entered into force on 1 November 2008. All references to websites were last checked as live on 6 November 2008.

Thomas Bachner
Vienna, November 2008

TABLE OF ABBREVIATIONS

Names in '. . .' designate journals (which also function as case reports in Germany).

ABGB	Allgemeines bürgerliches Gesetzbuch – the Austrian Civil Code
AC	Appeal Cases (The Law Reports – House of Lords and Judicial Committee of the Privy Council)
ACLC	Australian Company Law Cases
AcP	'Archiv für die civilistische Praxis'
ACLR	Australian Company Law Reports
AG	Aktiengesellschaft – the German Joint Stock Company; 'Die Aktiengesellschaft'
AktG	Aktiengesetz – the German Joint Stock Companies Act
All ER	[The] All England Law Reports
AnfG	Anfechtungsgesetz – the German Act on the Avoidance of Legal Acts of a Debtor outside Insolvency Proceedings
App.Cas.	Law Reports, Appeal Cases [Second Series, 1875–1890]
Art., art.	Article, article
BayObLG	Bayerisches Oberstes Landesgericht – the Bavarian Superior Court of Appeal [now abolished]
BB	'Der Betriebsberater'
BCC	British Company Cases
BCLC	Butterworths Company Law Cases
BGB	Bürgerliches Gesetzbuch – the German Civil Code
BGBl.	Bundesgesetzblatt – Federal Law Gazette
BGH	Bundesgerichtshof – the German Federal Court of Justice
BGHZ	Entscheidungen des Bundesgerichtshofs in Zivilsachen – the official law reports of the German Federal Court of Justice in civil law matters
BPIR	Bankruptcy and Personal Insolvency Reports
CA	Companies Act; Court of Appeal

ch.	chapter(s)
Ch.	The Law Reports – Chancery Division
ChD	Chancery Division (of the High Court); Law Reports, Chancery Division [Second Series, 1875–1890]
CFILR	Company Financial and Insolvency Law Review
CJ	Chief Justice
CLJ	'Cambridge Law Journal'
CMLR	Common Market Law Reports
CoLaw	'[The] Company Lawyer'
DB	'Der Betrieb' (Germany)
DStR	'Deutsches Steuerrecht'
DTI	Department of Trade and Industry
EBLR	'European Business Law Review'
EBOR	'European Business Organization Law Review'
ECFR	'European Company and Financial Law Review'
ECR	European Court Reports
ed.	editor(s)
edn	edition
EGBGB	Einführungsgesetz zum Bürgerlichen Gesetzbuch – the 'Introductory Act' to the German Civil Code (a statute containing transitional and supplementary provisions, including the rules on the conflict of laws)
EuZW	'Europäische Zeitschrift für Wirtschaftsrecht'
EWCA Civ	England and Wales Court of Appeal (Civil Division)
EWHC	England and Wales High Court
EWiR	'Entscheidungen zum Wirtschaftsrecht'
EWS	'Europäisches Wirtschafts- und Steuerrecht'
f., ff.	and subsequent [page(s), paragraph(s) etc.]
fn.	footnote(s)
GmbH	Gesellschaft mit beschränkter Haftung – the German Limited Liability Company
GmbHG	Gesetz betreffend die Gesellschaften mit beschränkter Haftung – the German Limited Liability Companies Act
GmbHR	'GmbH-Rundschau'
HGB	Handelsgesetzbuch – the German Commercial Code
HL	House of Lords
IA	Insolvency Act
ICCLJ	'International and Comparative Corporate Law Journal'
ICCLR	'International Company and Commercial Law Review'
ICLQ	'International and Comparative Law Quarterly'

IIR	'International Insolvency Review'
IL&P	'Insolvency Law & Practice'
InsO	Insolvenzordnung – the German Insolvency Code
J	Justice
JBL	'Journal of Business Law'
JCLS	'[The] Journal of Corporate Law Studies'
JuS	'Juristische Schulung'
JW	'Juristische Wochenschrift'
JZ	'Juristenzeitung'
KG	Kammergericht – a traditional designation for the OLG Berlin
KO	Konkursordnung – the Austrian Bankruptcy Act
KTS	'Zeitschrift für Insolvenzrecht – Konkurs, Treuhand, Sanierung'
LC	Lord Chancellor
LJ, LJJ	Lady Justice/Lord Justice, Lord Justices
LG	Landgericht – a regional court of first instance in Germany
LMCLQ	'Lloyd's Maritime and Commercial Law Quarterly'
LR	Law Reports [First Series, 1865–1875]
LR Ch.App.	Law Reports, Chancery Appeal Cases
LR Eq.	Law Reports, Equity Cases
LR Ex.	Law Reports, Court of Exchequer
LR HL	Law Reports, English & Irish Appeals
MDR	'Monatsschrift für Deutsches Recht'
MLR	'Modern Law Review'
mn.	marginal number – Randzahl, Randziffer
MoMiG	Gesetz zur Modernisierung des GmbH-Rechts und zur Bekämpfung von Missbräuchen – Act to modernise the law governing private companies and to combat abuses (Germany)
n.	note; number – Nummer (in German statutes)
NJW	'Neue Juristische Wochenschrift'
NJW-RR	'Neue Juristische Wochenschrift – Rechtsprechungsreport'
NSWLR	New South Wales Law Reports
NZG	'Neue Zeitschrift für Gesellschaftsrecht'
NZI	'Neue Zeitschrift für das Recht der Insolvenz und Sanierung'
ÖBA	'Österreichisches Bankarchiv' (Austria)

OGH	Oberster Gerichtshof – the Austrian Supreme Court
OJ	Official Journal of the European Communities/of the European Union
OLG	Oberlandesgericht – a regional appellate court in Germany
OLGZ	Entscheidungen der Oberlandesgerichte in Zivilsachen
p.	page(s)
para.	paragraph(s)
PC	Privy Council
QB	The Law Reports – Queen's Bench Division
QBD	Queen's Bench Division (of the High Court)
r., rr.	rule, rules
RabelsZ	'Rabels Zeitschrift für ausländisches und internationales Privatrecht'
RG	Reichsgericht – the German Imperial Court (until 1945; see now BGH)
RGBl.	Reichsgesetzblatt – Imperial Law Gazette (until 1945; see now BGBl.)
RGZ	Entscheidungen des Reichsgerichts in Zivilsachen – the official law reports of the German Imperial Court in civil law matters
RIW	'Recht der internationalen Wirtschaft'
s., ss.	section, sections
SI	Statutory Instrument
SLT	Scots Law Times
SZ	Entscheidungen des österreichischen Obersten Gerichtshofes in Zivilsachen – the official law reports of the Austrian Supreme Court in civil law matters
UKHL	United Kingdom House of Lords
vol.	volume
WLR	[The] Weekly Law Reports
WM	'Wertpapier-Mitteilungen'
ZEuP	'Zeitschrift für Europäisches Privatrecht'
ZGR	'Zeitschrift für Unternehmens-und Gesellschaftsrecht'
ZHR	'Zeitschrift für das gesamte Handelsrecht und Wirtschaftsrecht'
ZIP	'Zeitschrift für Wirtschaftsrecht', formerly 'Zeitschrift für Wirtschaftsrecht und Insolvenzpraxis'
ZPO	Zivilprozessordnung – the German Civil Procedure Code

TABLE OF LEGISLATION

European Community

England

Other Commonwealth jurisdictions

Germany

Austria

TABLE OF CASES

European Court of Justice

England

Lagunas Nitrate Co v Lagunas Syndicate [1899] 2 Ch. 392 (ChD, CA) 230
Lands Allotment Co [Re] [1894] 1 Ch. 616 (ChD, CA) 161–162, 167
Leyland Daf Ltd [Re] – see Buchler v Talbot
Lipkin Gorman (a firm) v Karpnale Ltd [1991] 2 AC 548; [1991] 3 WLR 10; [1992] 4 All ER 512 (HL) 177
Liquidator of Marini Ltd v Dickenson [2003] EWHC334 (Ch); [2004] BCC 172 (ChD) 119, 173
London & General Bank [Re] [1895] 2 Ch. 166 (CA) 163
Lord (Liquidator of Rosshill Properties Ltd) v Sinai Securities Ltd [2004] EWHC 1764 (Ch); [2004] BCC 986; [2005] 1 BCLC 295; [2004] BPIR 1244 (ChD) 73
MacPherson v European Strategic Bureau Ltd [2002] BCC39; [2000] 2 BCLC 683 (CA) 121, 123, 125–126, 129–130
MC Bacon Ltd [Re] [1990] BCC 78; [1990] BCLC 324 (ChD) 52–55, 73–74, 91, 221
MC Bacon Ltd (No 2) [Re] [1991] Ch. 127; [1990] 3 WLR 646; [1990] BCC 430; [1990] BCLC 607 (ChD) 220–224, 240
MDA Investment Management Ltd [Re], Whalley v Doney [2003] EWHC 2277 (Ch); [2005] BCC 783; [2004] 1 BCLC 217; [2004] BPIR 75 (ChD) 88
MDA Investment Management Ltd [Re], Whalley v Doney (No 2) [2004] EWHC 42 (Ch); [2005] BCC 783 (ChD) 170
Menzies v National Bank of Kuwait SAK [1994] BCC 119; [1994] 2 BCLC 306 (CA) 53
Montagu's Settlement Trusts [Re], Duke of Manchester v National Westminster Bank Ltd [1987] Ch. 264; [1987] 2 WLR 1192; [1992] 4 All ER 308 (ChD) 176
Morris v C W Martin & Sons Ltd [1966] 1 QB 716; [1965] 3 WLR 276; [1965] 2 All ER 725 (CA) 28
National Funds Assurance Co [Re] (1878) 10 ChD 118 (ChD) 166
National Westminster Bank plc v Jones [2001] 1 BCLC 98; [2000] BPIR 1092 (ChD); affirmed [2001] EWCA Civ 1541; [2002] 1 BCLC 55; [2002] BPIR 361 (CA) 64–65, 91
Norman v Theodore Goddard (a firm) (Quirk, third party) [1992] BCC 14; [1991] BCLC 1028 (ChD) 168, 230–231
Nurkowski [Re] – see Hill (as Trustee in Bankruptcy of Nurkowski) v Spread Trustee Co Ltd
Oasis Merchandising Services Ltd [Re], Ward v Aitken [1995] BCC 911; [1995] 2 BCLC 493 (ChD); [1998] Ch. 170; [1997] 2 WLR 764; [1997] 1 All ER 1009; [1997] BCC 282; [1997] 1 BCLC 689 (CA) 216–218, 223–226, 228
Orleans Motor Co Ltd [Re] [1911] 2 Ch. 41 (ChD) 51
Pantmaenog Timber Co Ltd [Re] [2003] UKHL 49; [2004] 1 AC 158; [2003] 3 WLR 767; [2003] 4 All ER 18; [2003] BCC 659; [2003] 2 BCLC 257; [2004] BPIR 139 (HL) 207
Pantone 485 Ltd [Re], Miller v Bain [2002] 1 BCLC 266 (ChD) 238, 243–244

Other Commonwealth jurisdictions

Australia

Brunei

New Zealand

Scotland

Germany

Reichsgericht, Bundesgerichtshof

Bayerisches Oberstes Landesgericht (Bavarian Superior Court of Appeal)

Oberlandesgerichte (regional courts of appeal)

Austria

TERMINOLOGY

The terms listed below are printed in **bold** on the pages referred to, where issues of terminology are discussed in the respective legal context. ~ denotes a vague correspondence requiring an explanation.

Außenhaftung (external liability), 186
bedingter Vorsatz, dolus eventualis (~ recklessness), 69
besondere Insolvenzanfechtung (special avoidance in insolvency), 45
Deckungsanfechtung (avoidance of cover), 56
Deutscher Juristentag (German Jurists' Convention), 14
eigenkapitalersetzender Gesellschafterkredit (equity-substituting shareholder credit), 138
Europäische Rechtswissenschaft (~ European legal discourse), 19
Gläubigerschutz (creditor protection), 8
inkongruente Deckung (incongruent cover), 79
Innenhaftung (internal liability), 186
Insolvenzanfechtung (avoidance in insolvency), 39
Insolvenzverschleppungshaftung (liability for delayed filing for insolvency) (formerly *Konkursverschleppungshaftung*), 181
Insolvenzverwalter (insolvency administrator, office-holder), 43
Kapitalaufbringung (raising of capital), 100
Kapitalerhaltung (capital maintenance), 97
Kapitalschutz (capital protection), 100
kongruente Deckung (congruent cover), 79
massearme Insolvenzen (asset-starved insolvencies), 205
Neugläubiger (new creditor/creditors), 196
Quotenschaden, Quotenverringerung (damage to/diminution of the quota), 196
Rechtsgeschäft (~ legal transaction), 60
Rechtshandlung (~ legal act), 57
Rechtswidrigkeit (unlawfulness), 154
Schutzgesetz (protective norm), 187
Sorgfaltspflicht (duty of diligence), 154
Treuepflicht (duty of loyalty), 149
verdeckte Gewinnausschüttung (concealed distribution of profits [a misnomer]), 105
Verkehrsschutz (commercial certainty), 78
Verschulden (culpability), 154
Vertrag (contract), 86
Vorsatz (intent), 69
Zahlungsunfähigkeit (illiquidity), 47

1

Introduction

A. Creditor protection – a focal point of current developments

1. The Centros *case: from Denmark to Delaware*

In any future account of the history of European company law the *Centros* case[1] will take a pride of place as one of those cases that deserve the epithet 'seminal'. The case concerned a Danish couple who wanted to set up a business in Denmark, but did not want to use a Danish corporate vehicle. Instead they bought a shelf-company registered in England. When the Danish authorities refused to register their (single) place of business as the Danish branch office of the English company, the couple appealed successfully to the European Court of Justice. The Court accepted the argument that a company formed under the laws of one Member State with a view to carrying on its business exclusively in another Member State had a right to do so under the principle of freedom of establishment enshrined in Articles 43 and 48 of the EC Treaty.

The *Centros* decision came as a surprise to many lawyers in Germany, and for a short time it engendered an intense debate whether or not it would force them to abandon a doctrine of German domestic law known as the 'theory of the real seat'.[2] Its conformity with Community law had previously been widely assumed on the basis of an earlier decision by the European Court of Justice in *The Queen v HM Treasury, ex parte Daily Mail and General Trust plc.*[3] Against the seemingly unassailable authority of that case, even scholars who had previously

[1] *Centros Ltd v Erhvervs- og Selskabsstyrelsen* [1999] ECR I-1459.

[2] Initial conclusions about the implications of the case on German law ranged from 'straightforward abolition of the theory of the real seat' (*Wienand Meilicke* in a case note on *Centros*, DB 1999, 627) to 'irrelevant for Germany, because Denmark's domestic law does not follow the theory of the real seat' (*Peter Kindler*, 'Niederlassungsfreiheit für Scheinauslandsgesellschaften? – Die 'Centros'-Entscheidung des EuGH und das internationale Privatrecht', NJW 1999, 1993). The German discussion is summed up by *Werner Ebke*, '*Centros* – Some Realities and Some Mysteries', 48 American Journal of Comparative Law 623 (2000).

[3] [1988] ECR 5483.

thought that the theory of the real seat was incompatible with Community law felt reluctantly that the European Court had decided otherwise.[4] Arguably, however, the near-universal German understanding of *Daily Mail* as confirming the theory of the real seat was coloured by a slightly misleading German translation of that judgment, and by the fact that German lawyers were all too willing to read the case through their specific doctrinal lens, which had been shaped by the previous debate in Germany.[5] Before *Centros*, German courts had been confronted with similar cases involving companies incorporated under English law, but carrying on business in Germany, and they had used these cases as opportunities to reinforce their doctrine of the real seat, while refusing to refer the issue to the European Court of Justice.[6] After *Centros*, a reference from a German court would only be a matter of time. It duly came with *Überseering BV v Nordic Construction Company Baumanagement GmbH*.[7] Although this decision did not outlaw the theory of the real seat as such, arguably allowing Member States to prevent the cross-border movement of companies formed under their own law,[8] the European Court of Justice put an end to all reasonable doubt that Member States cannot normally invoke the theory to stave off companies registered elsewhere within the European Union. Moreover, attempts to interpret *Überseering* restrictively as requiring only the recognition of the existence, status and capacity of the foreign company, but leaving the host Member State free to impose its own law on the

[4] Cf. in particular the article by *Peter Behrens*, 'Niederlassungsfreiheit und Internationales Gesellschaftsrecht', RabelsZ 52 (1988), 498, notably at 517 ff., with his later comment 'Sind Gesellschaften Niederlassungsberechtigte minderen Rechts?', EuZW 1991, 97; see also *Otto Sandrock*, 'Sitztheorie, Überlagerungstheorie und der EWG-Vertrag: Wasser, Öl und Feuer', RIW 1989, 505 at 511; *Brigitte Knobbe-Keuk*, 'Umzug von Gesellschaften in Europa', ZHR 154 (1990), 325 at 332.

[5] *Harald Halbhuber*, Limited Company statt GmbH? – Europarechtlicher Rahmen und deutscher Widerstand (2001), 29 ff.

[6] BayObLG 21.3.1986, NJW 1986, 3029 (denying an obligation to refer the case to the ECJ on the basis of *CILFIT Srl v Ministro della Sanità* [1982] ECR 3415); OLG Oldenburg 4.4.1989, NJW 1990, 1422; KG (OLG Berlin) 13.6.1989, NJW 1989, 3100.

[7] [2002] ECR I-9919.

[8] Cf. *Überseering* (fn. 7), para. 66–70 and 81, citing *Daily Mail* [1988] ECR 5483, para. 19–20 and 23. Reading the judgment to this effect was promoted by some German commentators, e.g. *Stefan Leible / Jochen Hoffmann*, '"Überseering" und das (vermeintliche) Ende der Sitztheorie', RIW 2002, 925 at 930 ff.; yet doubted by others, e.g. *Daniel Zimmer*, 'Wie es Euch gefällt? Offene Fragen nach dem Überseering-Urteil des EuGH', BB 2003, 1. The compatibility of such restrictions with the freedom of establishment is called into question in a case currently before the ECJ: C-210/06 (*Cartesio*).

internal and external relations of the company via its choice of law rules,[9] were hard to maintain after the subsequent decision of the European Court of Justice in *Kamer van Koophandel en Fabrieken voor Amsterdam v Inspire Art Ltd*,[10] where the Court held that a Dutch statute applying the domestic rules on minimum capital and directors' liability to a company registered in the United Kingdom, while recognising the legal personality granted by the law of incorporation, was nevertheless incompatible with the freedom of establishment guaranteed by Articles 43 and 48 of the EC Treaty.

What was it that German lawyers had found so appealing about the theory of the real seat? In essence, the theory is a rule of private international law that a company will be treated according to the law of its central place of management (the 'real seat'), notwithstanding that it may have been incorporated in a different jurisdiction. If the company has not complied with the formal requirements of registration in the jurisdiction of its real seat, it will normally lack the quality of a legal person there. The aim of the theory is to preserve national company law as a policy instrument in areas like creditor protection, by imposing a blanket ban on 'pseudo-foreign companies', i.e. companies doing business mainly or exclusively in one jurisdiction, but evading local regulation there by incorporating abroad. Hence, as long as Germany was allowed to shield behind the theory, German entrepreneurs wishing to set up a business in Germany had to accept whatever strings were attached to forming a company under German law.

Now, the freedom of establishment enshrined in the EC Treaty requires all Member States to accept as a rule of private international law what is known as the 'theory of incorporation', under which the law applicable to a company is the law of its (chosen) jurisdiction of incorporation. In many respects this new development within the European Union resembles a system which has long been in operation within the United States. It opens up the possibility of a 'market for incorporations', where entrepreneurs can shop around Europe to choose whatever legal regime they like best for setting up their company.[11]

[9] *Kurt Lipstein*, 'The Law relating to the movement of companies in the European Community', in: Festschrift für Erik Jayme (2004), 527 at 530; *Peter Kindler*, 'Auf dem Weg zur Europäischen Briefkastengesellschaft?', NJW 2003, 1073 at 1077–1078.

[10] [2003] ECR I-10155.

[11] See already *Brian Cheffins*, Company Law (1997), 421 ff. (describing the situation in the US) and 426 ff. (pondering portability to the EU).

Consequently, 'regulatory competition' ('*Wettbewerb der Rechtsordnungen*', as it is put in German) has become a much debated topic.[12]

However, the choice element inherent in such a system has also made it the target of vocal criticism, which, as far as the American discourse is concerned, is indelibly associated with the name of William Cary. In a 1974 article,[13] which was to become one of the most-cited articles in the history of the Yale Law Journal[14] and said to have had 'the impact of a firecracker in a hornets' nest',[15] he coined the phrase 'Delaware syndrome' and called it a 'race for the bottom', arguing that state legislators were undercutting each other in a competition to please corporate decision-makers to the detriment of other interest groups. His article has sparked an ongoing debate in the United States about the virtue or vice of, respectively, uniform corporate law rules (advocated by Cary) and its opposite, federalism, where the states retain the power to legislate on matters of corporate law. Cary's argument and most of the American debate ever since has centred on the conflict of interest between shareholders and managers in large publicly quoted companies, and issues of creditor protection hardly come to the fore.[16] In the aftermath

[12] See generally *Daniel C. Esty / Damien Geradin* (eds.), Regulatory Competition and Economic Integration – Comparative Perspectives (2001), and more specifically the article in this volume by *Simon Deakin*, 'Regulatory Competition versus Harmonization in European Company Law', at p. 190; *Eva-Maria Kieninger*, Wettbewerb der Privatrechtsordnungen im Binnenmarkt (2002); *idem*, 'The Legal Framework of Regulatory Competition Based on Company Mobility: EU and US Compared', 6 German Law Journal 741 (2005), available at www.germanlawjournal.com/article.php?id=590; *John Armour*, 'Who Should Make Corporate Law? EU Legislation versus Regulatory Competition' (2005) 58 Current Legal Problems 369; *Robert Drury*, 'A European Look at the American Experience of the Delaware Syndrome' [2005] JCLS 1; *Martin Gelter*, 'The Structure of Regulatory Competition in European Corporate Law' [2005] JCLS 247; *Horst Eidenmüller*, 'Die GmbH im Wettbewerb der Rechtsformen', ZGR 2007, 168; for a German contribution before *Centros* see *Hanno Merkt*, 'Das Europäische Gesellschaftsrecht und die Idee des "Wettbewerbs der Gesetzgeber"', RabelsZ 59 (1995), 545, whose analysis is, however, severely criticised by *Halbhuber* (fn. 5.) 183 ff.

[13] 'Federalism and Corporate Law: Reflections Upon Delaware', 83 Yale Law Journal 663 (1974).

[14] *Fred R. Shapiro*, 'The Most-Cited Articles from *The Yale Law Journal*', 100 Yale Law Journal 1449 (1991), ranking the article as ninth in citations between January 1985 and August 1989 (at 1464), even though by then more than ten years had passed since its publication.

[15] Commentary by *John C. Coffee, Jr.* (fn. 14, at 1498).

[16] Some believe that there is no need at all for legislative protection of creditors, see *Frank Easterbrook / Daniel Fischel*, 'The Corporate Contract', 89 Columbia Law Review 1416 (1989): 'For debt investors . . . everything (literally) is open to contract' (at 1418). In contrast *Lucian Bebchuk*, 'Federalism and the Corporation: The Desirable Limits on State

of *Centros*, however, the powerful image of the 'race for the bottom' has been taken up in Europe, as fears about an erosion of standards of creditor protection, in particular, have been voiced – especially in Germany.

An obvious difference between English company law on the one hand and German company law on the other is that the former has never known a minimum capital requirement for private companies.[17] This appears to be attractive for some entrepreneurs, and in *Centros* the applicants left no doubt that their reason for choosing England as the jurisdiction of incorporation was to avoid Danish rules on minimum capital. In terms of policy, minimum capital rules may not be all that important as an instrument of creditor protection. It has been said that 'the symbolic significance of this issue for the (supposed) modernisation of corporate law far exceeds its economic relevance'.[18] Yet it seems that precisely this symbolic value of a 'headline figure', easy to grasp for lawyers, business people and politicians alike, has been the main driver behind the debate about competition among the Member States in the field of company law.

2. *The European regulation on insolvency proceedings*

In a curious twist of legal history, at around the same time as the European Court of Justice demolished the theory of the real seat, efforts were under way to adopt a new piece of EC legislation in a closely related field, viz. the Insolvency Regulation.[19] Nothing indicates that the contemporaneous development in the case law had any direct impact on the drafting of the Regulation. On the contrary, the Regulation took over, more or less without any substantive changes, the text of the failed

Competition in Corporate Law', 105 Harvard Law Review 1435 (1992) argues against state competition in respect of creditor protection (at 1489–1490) and points out that the federal Bankruptcy Act, i.e. corporate insolvency law, provides rules that protect the interests of creditors (at 1495).

17 The minimum capital requirement of £50,000 in s. 763 CA 2006 only relates to public companies; it is a requirement under Article 6 of the Second Company Law Directive (77/91/EEC), OJ L 26 of 31.1.1977, p. 1. This directive has never been extended to private companies, not least due to resistance from the UK: *Vanessa Edwards*, EC Company Law (1999), 53–55.

18 *Horst Eidenmüller / Barbara Grunewald / Ulrich Noack*, 'Minimum Capital in the System of Legal Capital', in: *Marcus Lutter* (ed.), Legal Capital in Europe (2006), 17 at 30.

19 Council Regulation (EC) 1346/2000 of 29 May 2000 on insolvency proceedings, OJ L 160 of 30.6.2000, p. 1.

European Insolvency Convention,[20] which goes back to a time when it seems to have been unchallenged wisdom among European lawmakers that the theory of the real seat was here to stay. So entrenched was the defence of the theory in some Member States, and the belief in its compatibility with primary Community law, that even as late as April 1998 (less than a year before *Centros*), a senior official from the European Commission informed the audience at a conference in Bonn that the Commission had no plans to introduce legislation with a view to forcing Member States to relinquish it.[21]

Under the Insolvency Regulation, insolvency proceedings are governed by the law of the insolvency forum (Article 4), and the insolvency forum is determined according to the 'centre of a debtor's main interests' (Article 3). This 'centre of a debtor's main interests' or COMI (as it is known colloquially) represents a kind of re-incarnation of the old idea of the 'real seat',[22] albeit with a rebuttable presumption that the centre of a company's main interests is situated at its registered office. Concerns have been voiced about the ambiguity of the COMI standard.[23] Moreover, there appears to be some scope for forum shopping, notwithstanding that the Regulation aims at preventing it.[24]

Still, taken together, the case law under Articles 43 and 48 of the EC Treaty and the Insolvency Regulation create an intriguing bifurcation as regards the private international law framework for creditor protection. On the one hand, freedom of establishment, as interpreted by the European Court of Justice, requires all Member States to accept the law of the Member State of incorporation in matters properly characterised as company law, including, arguably, capital maintenance and directors' duties.[25] On the other hand, in all matters properly characterised as

[20] Convention on Insolvency Proceedings of 23 November 1995 (Council Document CONV/INSOL/X1), reprinted as Appendix 2 in *Paul Omar*, European Insolvency Law (2004).

[21] *Giuseppe Di Marco*, 'Der Vorschlag der Kommission für eine 14. Richtlinie', ZGR 1999, 3 at 4–6.

[22] Recital 13 of the Regulation; Virgos/Schmidt-Report on the Insolvency Convention para. 75 (with reference to the company's 'head office').

[23] *John Armour*, 'Who Should Make Corporate Law? EU Legislation versus Regulatory Competition' (2005) 58 Current Legal Problems 369, at 404.

[24] *Horst Eidenmüller*, 'Free Choice in International Company Insolvency Law in Europe' [2005] EBOR 423, at 428; *Luca Enriques / Martin Gelter*, 'Regulatory Competition in European Company Law and Creditor Protection' [2006] EBOR 417, at 436 ff.

[25] Cf. the ECJ's reference to the 'functioning' of the company in *Überseering* [2002] ECR I-9919, para. 81. For the position of English law see *Arab Bank Plc v Merchantile Holdings Ltd* [1994] Ch. 71, holding that s. 151 CA on the prohibition of financial assistance by a

insolvency law (of which Article 4 of the Regulation contains a non-exhaustive list), the Insolvency Regulation allows and indeed requires each Member State to apply its domestic law to all companies which have their 'centre of main interests' within its territory, even though a company may have been incorporated in another Member State. While, under EC rules, the distinction between company law and insolvency law has been elevated to a question of law, the substantive national rules on creditor protection have typically evolved in response to domestic fact situations, and as long as Member States could rely on the theory of the real seat, they did not have to worry about whether protection would be effected through mechanisms of company law or insolvency law. Thus, the newly established European framework for the conflict of laws may upset delicate balances between company law and insolvency law. Moreover, notwithstanding the list of insolvency law matters in Article 4 of the Insolvency Regulation, there remains a grey area with anything but general agreement among the Member States on where to draw the line between company law, insolvency law, and possibly other categories such as the law of delict: English-style wrongful trading and its German counterpart, *Insolvenzverschleppungshaftung* (liability for delayed filing for insolvency), present an excellent illustration, on which more will be said in chapter 5.

3. *The interconnectedness of company law and insolvency law*

Whereas the new European legal framework clearly creates some difficulties with respect to delineating the realms of company law and insolvency law, it is equally important to bear in mind that company law and insolvency law go hand in hand and complement each other with a view to protecting the creditors of limited liability companies.[26] Company law and insolvency law do not operate as two islands with no bridges between them. Yet if one takes a parallel look at the landscapes mapped out by the respective legal discourses in England and Germany, one cannot help but realise that the islands appear markedly different in size. As a preliminary point to this, it is pertinent to enquire into the

subsidiary company does not extend to a subsidiary company incorporated abroad; *Dan Prentice*, 'The Incorporation Theory – The United Kingdom' [2003] EBLR 631; *Harry Rajak*, 'The English Limited Company as an Alternative Legal Form for German Enterprise', EWS 2005, 539 at 544; *Dicey, Morris & Collins*, Conflict of Laws (14th edn 2006), ch. 30.

26 On 'unbundling' and 'packaging' company and insolvency law in the context of choice of forum see *Horst Eidenmüller*, 'Free Choice in International Company Insolvency Law in Europe' [2005] EBOR 423, at 434 ff.

respective usage of the notions of '**creditor protection**' and '**Gläubigerschutz**', and to reflect on whether the use of the English term 'creditor protection', as the literal translation of '*Gläubigerschutz*', provides a sufficiently neutral ground.

'*Gläubigerschutz*' has long been a standard topic in the analysis of company law in the literature of German-speaking countries. A search in two databases[27] reveals that within the present decade at least twenty-six monographs have been published in Germany which carry the word '*Gläubigerschutz*' in their main title and discuss the topic in the context of company law.[28] A German textbook refers to '*Gläubigerschutz*' as a 'classic task' of company law.[29]

[27] At www.buchhandel.de (a search engine provided by German publishing companies) and at www.obvsg.at/kataloge/verbundkataloge (the electronic catalogue of the Austrian university libraries).

[28] In chronological order: *Andreas Lenz*, Gesellschafter- und Gläubigerschutz bei dem Formwechsel einer OHG in eine GmbH (2000); *Miriam A. Parmentier*, Gläubigerschutz in öffentlichen Unternehmen (2000); *Lars Franken*, Gläubigerschutz durch Rechnungslegung nach US-GAAP (2001); *Krzysztof Oplustil*, Gläubigerschutz durch reale Kapitalaufbringung im deutschen und polnischen Recht der Kapitalgesellschaften (2001); *Jens Petersen*, Der Gläubigerschutz im Umwandlungsrecht (2001); *Thomas Theißen*, Gläubigerschutz bei der Spaltung von Gesellschaften nach dem Umwandlungsgesetz (2001); *Alexander Veith*, Der Gläubigerschutz beim Formwechsel nach dem Umwandlungsgesetz (2003); *Edward Renger*, Gläubigerschutz durch § 32a GmbH (2004); *Tobias Schönbeck*, Bankenrechnungslegung nach IAS/IFRS – Gläubigerschutz durch Information? (2004); *Tobias Böckmann*, Gläubigerschutz bei GmbH und close corporation (2005); *Helke Drenckhan*, Gläubigerschutz in der Krise der GmbH (2005); *Markus E. Krüger*, Mindestkapital und Gläubigerschutz (2005); *Alexander Müller*, Gläubigerschutzkonzepte bei Sachgründung und Umwandlungsgründung einer GmbH (2005); *Ellen Reinbach*, Gläubigerschutz gegen den Mißbrauch einer private limited company – Eine Darstellung anhand einer Gesellschaft des englischen Rechts mit Sitz in Deutschland nach Inspire Art (2005); *Oliver Böttcher*, Gesellschafter- und Gläubigerschutz beim Formwechsel aus der Personen- in die Kapitalgesellschaft (2006); *Truls Hebrant*, Beihilferechtswidrige Gesellschaftsbeteiligungen und Gläubigerschutz (2006); *George Jugeli*, Der Gläubigerschutz bei der Umwandlung juristischer Personen (2006); *Claus M. Mössle*, Gläubigerschutz beim Zuzug ausländischer Gesellschaften aus der Sicht des englischen Rechts (2006); *Eike Th. Bicker*, Gläubigerschutz in der grenzüberschreitenden Konzerngesellschaft (2007); *Christian Gloger*, Haftungsbeschränkung versus Gläubigerschutz in der GmbH (2007); *Tobias Nikoleyczik*, Gläubigerschutz zwischen Gesetz und Vertrag (2007); *Katharina Röpke*, Gläubigerschutzregime im europäischen Wettbewerb der Gesellschaftsrechte (2007); *Holger Seeberg*, Der Gläubigerschutz bei (Schein-)Auslandsgesellschaften mit Verwaltungssitz in Deutschland am Beispiel der Private Limited Company by Shares aus Irland (2007); *Beate Stirtz*, Gläubigerschutz bei der englischen Limited im Vergleich zur GmbH (2007); *Andreas Stoll*, Garantiekapital und konzernspezifischer Gläubigerschutz (2007); *Stefan Weiß*, Aktionärs- und Gläubigerschutz im System der echten nennwertlosen (Stück-)Aktie (2007).

[29] *Friedrich Kübler / Heinz-Dieter Assmann*, Gesellschaftsrecht (6th edn 2006) § 14 III 2 b (p. 179): '*klassische Aufgabe*'.

In contrast, the terms 'creditor protection' or 'protection of creditors' have been less prominent in England. A similar search in the on-line catalogue of the Squire Law Library at Cambridge University yielded not a single hit, and a search in the on-line catalogue of the Oxford Libraries Information System came up with a book published in the United States in 1912[30] and a recent Ph.D. thesis by a Greek scholar.[31] Most textbooks do not feature a separate chapter on the topic,[32] and many do not even carry the term in their subject index. Company lawyers tend to discuss the matter under various separate headings such as 'directors' duties owed to creditors',[33] 'maintenance of capital',[34] and 'company charges'[35] (an issue which German lawyers never discuss as part of company law, but as part of property law, the law being the same for companies and for individuals). Thus, for 'creditor protection' to be the core notion in this book might be seen as already tilting the scales slightly towards the German side. Recent scholarly writing in English has, however, accentuated the idea of 'creditor protection' as a subject worthy of inquiry in its own right,[36] although the term is still not used nearly as widely as in the German discourse. Nevertheless, the present study relies on this development to argue that creditor protection, which will be used from now on without giving the German word in brackets, can be seen as a sufficiently neutral term.

The prominent role that the topic of creditor protection has traditionally occupied in German company law scholarship goes hand in hand with a curious disregard for insolvency law. In retrospect, it is amazing how many volumes – quite literally – German company lawyers have managed to write on creditor protection without ever touching on the subject of insolvency law. Several observations are pertinent here.

30 *Arthur K. Kuhn*, A Comparative Study of the Law of Corporations: With Particular Reference to the Protection of Creditors and Shareholders (New York: Columbia University, 1912).

31 *Dimitrios Ph. Christodoulou*, The Single Ship Company: The Legal Consequences From Its Use and the Protection of its Creditors (Athens: Ant. N. Sakkoulas, 2000).

32 For an exception see *Paul Davies*, Gower's Principles of Modern Company Law in its 6th edition, Part Six of which was entitled 'Shareholder and Creditor Protection'; but this has disappeared since the 7th edition.

33 See, for instance, *Gower & Davies*' Company Law (7th edn 2003), 372–374. With the arrival of the Companies Act 2006, this discussion has moved into a slightly different context, viz. the directors' duty to promote the success of the company (s. 172); see now *Gower & Davies*' Company Law (8th edn 2008), 519–523.

34 Ibid. 8th edn 2008, ch. 13. 35 Ibid., ch. 32.

36 *Brian Cheffins*, Company Law (1997), ch. 11; *Paul Davies*, Introduction to Company Law (2002), ch. 3 and 4; *Kraakman et al.*, Anatomy of Corporate Law (2004), ch. 4.

In England, the connection between company law and corporate insolvency law has long been evident, not least in the legislative history. The 'Insolvency Act 1986', despite this being its official short title (s. 444 IA), does not only apply to insolvencies; it is an 'Act to consolidate the enactments relating to company insolvency and winding up (including the winding up of companies that are not insolvent, and of unregistered companies)'. The combination of the 'winding up' (compare the German term '*Abwicklung*') of both solvent and insolvent companies goes back to the earliest 'Companies Winding Up Acts' of the mid-nineteenth century,[37] which were consolidated, for the first time, in the Companies Act 1862. The provisions on company insolvency remained part of subsequent Companies Acts,[38] before the Insolvency Act 1986 took over all the provisions on company insolvency from the Companies Act 1985. At the same time, the insolvency of individuals, i.e. natural persons, was treated entirely separately.[39] This explains why, in contrast to the terminology in the United States, the term '**bankruptcy**' in English legal parlance is strictly limited to the insolvency of individuals. Unsurprisingly, the linkage of company law and insolvency law is reflected in the legal literature. Standard texts on company law invariably deal with wrongful trading (s. 214 IA),[40] and many carry chapters outlining corporate insolvency.[41] Numerous company lawyers have also written on insolvency law,[42] whereas recent

[37] The first such act was 7 & 8 Vict. c. 111, passed on the same day in 1844 as the famous act which introduced the incorporation of companies through registration.

[38] Companies (Consolidation) Act 1908; Companies Act 1929; Companies Act 1948; Companies Act 1985.

[39] Bankruptcy Act 1869; Bankruptcy Act 1883; Bankruptcy Act 1914. There were occasional cross-references from the company insolvency regime to the bankruptcy regime for individuals, notably s. 320 of the Companies Act 1948, whose effect it was to make the rules on fraudulent preferences laid down in s. 44 of the Bankruptcy Act 1914 applicable to company insolvencies as well.

[40] E.g. *Gower & Davies* (fn. 33, 8th edn 2008), 217–224; *Pettet*, Company Law (2nd edn 2005), 33–37.

[41] E.g. *Sealy / Worthington*, Cases and Materials in Company Law (2007), ch. 14; *Hannigan*, Company Law (2003), whose Part VII on 'Corporate Insolvency and Rescue' runs to five chapters with more than 160 pages.

[42] *Robert Pennington* has produced textbooks on both subjects: 'Pennington's Company Law' (8th edn 2001) and 'Pennington's Corporate Insolvency Law' (2nd edn 1997); *Len Sealy* is the author of 'Cases and Materials in Company Law' (7th edn 2001; 8th edn 2007, together with *Sarah Worthington*) and, together with *David Milman*, of an 'Annotated Guide to the Insolvency Legislation' (10th edn 2007); the title and location of *Dan Prentice's* article 'The Effect of Insolvency on Pre-Liquidation Transactions', in: *Ben Pettet* (ed.), Company Law in Change (1987) is in itself testimony to this cross-over thinking. Other writers with publications on both subjects include (without any claim to

works on transaction avoidance in insolvency take into account parallels and overlaps with rules and remedies of general company law.[43]

In contrast, lawyers in Germany are trained to put company law and insolvency law into different intellectual compartments. The two subjects are invariably taught in different undergraduate courses, reflecting long-established boundaries of academic disciplines. Very few German academics have a track-record of writing on both subjects – although there are notable exceptions.[44] Traditionally, insolvency law has not been seen as a matter attached to (substantive) commercial law or company law, but as an annex to civil procedure.[45] Standard German textbooks combine the execution of judgments and insolvency as two sides of one coin.[46] Here too, legislative history offers further pointers. Modern German insolvency law goes back to the Konkursordnung of 1877, which was part of a legislative package that included a uniform court system and civil procedure rules for the newly created German Empire.[47] As a corollary, German law has never had a reason to

exhaustiveness): *John Armour, Eilís Ferran, Vanessa Finch, Andrew Hicks, Andrew Keay, Richard Nolan, Harry Rajak, Adrian Walters* and *Sally Wheeler*.

43 *Rebecca Parry*, Transaction Avoidance in Insolvencies (2001), chs. 18 and 19; *John Armour/Howard Bennett* (eds.), Vulnerable Transactions in Corporate Insolvency (2003), especially ch. 7 on 'Avoidance of Transactions as a "Fraud on Creditors" at Common Law' by *John Armour*.

44 First to the fore is *Karsten Schmidt*, whose distinguished writing career of many decades has sought to integrate company law and insolvency law: e.g. 'Insolvenzordnung und Gesellschaftsrecht', ZGR 1998, 633; most recently: 'GmbH-Reform, Solvenzgewährleistung und Insolvenzpraxis – Gedanken zum MoMiG-Entwurf', GmbHR 2007, 1; 'Reform der Kapitalsicherung und Haftung in der Krise nach dem Regierungsentwurf des MoMiG', GmbHR 2007, 1072. A few other scholars have also begun to explore this path including (again, without any claim to exhaustiveness): *Ulrich Ehricke*, Das abhängige Konzernunternehmen in der Insolvenz (1998), dealing with capital maintenance and avoidance remedies in group insolvency situations; *Heribert Hirte*, whose publications include a textbook on company law (Kapitalgesellschaftsrecht, 5th edn 2006) and the commentary on the avoidance provisions of the Insolvency Code in *Uhlenbruck*, InsO[12] §§ 129 to 147; *Horst Eidenmüller*, *Ulrich Haas* (see the bibliography and the passage below, text accompanying fn. 62).

45 See, for instance, the path in the 'German Law Archive' at www.iuscomp.org/gla (Statutes > Civil Procedure Law Statutes).

46 *Wolfgang Grunsky*, Grundzüge des Zwangsvollstreckungs- und Insolvenzrechts (5th edn 1996); *Othmar Jauernig/Christian Berger*, Zwangsvollstreckungs- und Insolvenzrecht (22nd edn 2006); cf. *Christoph Paulus*, 'Claw-back Rules and Creditors' Protection', in: *Marcus Lutter* (ed.), Legal Capital in Europe (2006), 325, speaking of 'the law of enforcement and the insolvency law' (at 326).

47 Gerichtsverfassungsgesetz vom 27.1.1877, RGBl. p. 41; Zivilprozessordnung vom 30.1.1877, RGBl. p. 83; Konkursordnung vom 10.2.1877, RGBl. p. 351. All three acts were brought into force jointly on 1 October 1879.

distinguish corporate insolvency from individual bankruptcy in the way English law does.[48]

These insights into perceptions about how legal subjects are connected provide a first partial explanation of why German lawyers were so appalled at the *Centros* decision. To many of them, 'creditor protection' had been more or less synonymous with 'creditor protection through company law'. Chapter 3 will demonstrate how German law has developed capital maintenance into an elaborate structure, much of which is not actually spelt out in the relevant statutory provisions, §§ 30 and 31 GmbHG, but has been built over many decades by a continuous process of judicial law-making and scholarly writing. *Centros* appeared to bring the whole edifice crashing down in one sweep.

It is submitted that any proper analysis of creditor protection must take into account at least some instruments that would traditionally be seen as belonging to the field of insolvency law. Indeed, any such separation of company law and insolvency law may be more of an artificial barrier erected by academics. Practitioners are acutely aware that any advice to clients on capital maintenance rules must also take account of the possibility that the company might subsequently become insolvent. Still, to what extent the impact of *Centros* will lead to a fundamental rethinking of the systematic place of creditor protection in the perception of German lawyers remains one of the most intriguing questions raised by that case – with far-reaching implications for our ability to ever agree on a common legal framework in this field.

4. *Recent developments in a nutshell*

Germany

Centros lit a fuse in German company law. *Überseering* detonated the charge. What followed can only be described as publication frenzy. Scores of German writers, academics and practitioners alike, set about exploring English company law and investigating the legal consequences for foreign, mainly UK-registered, companies operating in Germany.[49]

[48] However, modern German insolvency law does make special provision for the insolvency of individuals who are not (or no longer) engaged in business activities (*Verbraucherinsolvenz*).

[49] Besides countless journal articles, books on the subject include *Horst Eidenmüller* (ed.), Ausländische Kapitalgesellschaften im deutschen Recht (2004); *Marcus Lutter* (ed.), Europäische Auslandsgesellschaften in Deutschland (2005); *Heribert Hirte / Thomas Bücker* (eds.), Grenzüberschreitende Gesellschaften – Praxishandbuch für ausländische

The spectrum of opinions included every conceivable attitude from reassuring German lawyers that things would be alright, if only such companies were left to be governed by their law of incorporation,[50] to lamenting the new possibilities for setting up letter-box companies in foreign jurisdictions in terms of a Shakespearean tragedy.[51] The debate in the literature has been fuelled by a growing number of German court decisions involving English companies set up to run a business in Germany, including two decisions from the Bundesgerichtshof[52] and a further decision from the European Court of Justice upon reference from a German court.[53] At the time of finishing the manuscript for this book, at least 70 such cases have been reported in German law journals.[54]

No-one knows exactly how many English-registered companies currently operate in Germany. One empirical study suggests well over

Kapitalgesellschaften mit Sitz im Inland (2nd edn 2006); *Clemens Just*, Die englische Limited in der Praxis (2nd edn 2006); *Sabine Otte*, Das Kapitalschutzsystem der englischen private limited company im Vergleich zur deutschen GmbH (2006); *Simon Schilling*, Insolvenz einer englischen Limited mit Verwaltungssitz in Deutschland (2006); *Tobias Wilms*, Die englische Ltd. in deutscher Insolvenz (2006); *Thomas Buchmann*, Die Insolvenz der englischen Limited in Deutschland (2007); books by *Reinbach*, *Mössle*, *Seeberg* and *Stirtz* cited in fn. 28; the most comprehensive German presentation of English company law as regards private companies is provided by *Sabine Ebert / Christian Levedag*, 'England', in: *Rembert Süß / Thomas Wachter* (eds.), Handbuch des internationalen GmbH-Rechts (2006), 573–728.

[50] *Alexander Schall*, 'Englischer Gläubigerschutz bei der Limited in Deutschland', ZIP 2005, 965; *idem*, 'The UK Limited Company Abroad – How Foreign Creditors are Protected after Inspire Art (Including a Comparison of UK and German Creditor Protection Rules)' [2005] EBLR 1534. While a thorough understanding of the English approach to creditor protection is of doubtless importance for a constructive handling of the situation created by the jurisprudence of the ECJ, there are limits as to the extraterritorial reach of this approach, notably when it comes to directors' disqualification; see *Thomas Bachner*, Die Limited in der Insolvenz (2007).

[51] *Gerhard Kegel*, 'Es ist was faul im Staate Dänemark. . .', EWS 1999, issue 8 (editorial). The title is a line from Shakespeare's 'Hamlet', Act 1, Scene 4: 'Something is rotten in the state of Denmark.'

[52] BGH 14.3.2005, NJW 2005, 1648; BGH 7.5.2007, NJW 2007, 2328; concerning Liechtenstein (EEA Member State): BGH 19.9.2005, BGHZ 164, 148.

[53] *Re innoventif Limited* [2006] ECR I-4929.

[54] A list of the cases is on file with the author. In order to put the number into perspective for English readers, one should add that many of them concern legal questions that have arisen in connection with the registration of a branch office in the German commercial register. Unlike company registration in the UK, registration in Germany is a judicial process so that even at first instance a denial of registration or an instruction to the petitioner to supply further information or evidence produces a fully-reasoned decision fit for reporting in a law journal.

40,000 incorporations until the end of the year 2006.[55] Go Ahead, the market leader for UK company registration services in Germany, claims that it helped to set up 30,000 companies and that one in four of all newly established businesses in Germany now opts for an English-registered private limited company.[56] Whatever the precise figures, the scale of the phenomenon and the intensity of the public debate it generated inevitably propelled the issue into the political sphere.

At this point, many non-German readers will have their first encounter with a peculiar element of German legal culture, viz. the **Deutscher Juristentag.** If there has to be a translation of this proper name, one might choose 'German Jurists' Convention'[57] so as to convey a sense of its main purpose, which is to organise a biennial conference – although a recent off-spring, the Europäischer Juristentag, has styled itself 'European Jurists' Forum' in English ('Journée des Juristes Européens' in French).[58] Legally, the Deutscher Juristentag is no more than a private association with a voluntary membership consisting of lawyers from all areas of practice and academia. However, in terms of its prestige, it ranks as one of the most venerable non-governmental institutions in the field of law, with a history going back to 1860, when the first convention was held in Berlin to promote legal unity between the German states (then linked only by the weak constitutional bond of the German Confederation). Today, the larger part of every convention is organised in parallel streams or 'sections' (*Abteilungen*), and one of the sections has traditionally been devoted to commercial law, including company law. Proceedings at the convention are always oriented towards law reform and legal policy.[59] At the end of the debate, which lasts for about two days, the members present at the convention vote on formal recommendations directed at the legislator, and these recommendations do in fact carry a certain weight when it comes to actual legislation.

55 *Marco Becht / Colin Mayer / Hannes F. Wagner*, 'Where Do Firms Incorporate?', ECGI-Working Paper No. 70/2006 (revised August 2007), available at http://papers.ssrn.com/sol3/papers.cfm?abstract_id=906066.

56 On its company website at www.go-limited.de (as of 31 January 2008).

57 *Reinhard Zimmermann* renders it as 'Meeting of the Association of German Lawyers', but prefers to use the German term in his text: The New German Law of Obligations (2005), 30.

58 The European Jurists' Forum also organises conferences at biennial intervals: Nuremberg 2001, Athens 2003, Geneva 2005, Vienna 2007 and Budapest 2009.

59 As for the involvement of the Juristentag in the reform of the law of obligations, see *Zimmermann* (fn. 57), 30–33.

Not surprisingly, given the heightened attention for the topic in the wake of *Centros*, the 66th Juristentag, held in Stuttgart in September 2006, devoted its commercial law section to the 'reform of creditor protection in company law' ('*Reform des gesellschaftsrechtlichen Gläubigerschutzes*'), a choice of topic that reflects the conviction, deeply ingrained among German lawyers, that company law is the primary place to regulate creditor protection.[60] Interestingly, though, the organisers enlisted Ulrich Haas, an insolvency lawyer who has his academic roots in civil procedure law,[61] to deliver the main opinion (*Gutachten*) on the topic, which is published in advance of the conference in order to stimulate the debate, together with conclusions (*Thesen*) that form the nucleus of the recommendations to be adopted at the end of the conference.[62] Heribert Hirte, one of the discussants invited to speak at the beginning of the conference, presented even more far-reaching conclusions for a reform of the law.[63] In the end, however, the conservative attitudes prevailed. The members of the Juristentag participating in the commercial law section voted in favour of preserving the requirement of a minimum share capital as the *quid pro quo* for obtaining the protection of limited liability by 166 to 14 votes, and even the proposal to reduce the minimum share capital below the existing level of €25,000 was rejected by a comfortable margin of 112 to 58 votes.[64]

Yet the dynamics at work in the political arena were unimpressed by this advice. In May 2007, the Federal Government laid a bill before parliament known by the acronym 'MoMiG', which stands for 'Gesetz zur Modernisierung des GmbH-Rechts und zur Bekämpfung von Missbräuchen', i.e. an 'Act to modernise the law governing private companies and to combat abuses'.[65] The bill was passed into legislation

60 For another brief account of the proceedings in English see *Anja Strüve*, 'Deutscher Juristentag 2006', Legal Latitudes – Newsletter for the Transatlantic Business and Law Community, vol. 1 no. 1 (2007).

61 Professor Haas then held a chair for Civil Procedure Law and Civil Law at the Johannes Gutenberg-Universität Mainz. He has since moved to the University of Zurich.

62 *Ulrich Haas*, 'Reform des gesellschaftsrechtlichen Gläubigerschutzes', Gutachten E zum 66. Deutschen Juristentag Stuttgart 2006.

63 *Heribert Hirte*, 'Reform des gesellschaftsrechtlichen Gläubigerschutzes', Referat am 66. Deutschen Juristentag Stuttgart 2006, in: Verhandlungen des 66. Deutschen Juristentages, vol. II/1.

64 Altogether the commercial law section voted on 28 resolutions. Results are published at www.djt.de/files/djt/66/66_DJT_Beschluesse.pdf.

65 Reference number: Bundestags-Drucksache 16/6140. The bill and the accompanying explanatory notes are available at the website of the Federal Ministry of Justice at www.bmj.bund.de. Note that the article by *Ulrich Seibert*, 'Close Corporations – Reforming

in October 2008.[66] The general thrust of the bill is an extensive technical overhaul designed to facilitate and accelerate the formation of companies and to resolve a number of practical issues that have arisen over the last few years, while the underlying fabric of the corporate form of the Limited Liability Company (GmbH) is left largely unaltered. There are, however, two changes which must be characterised as a new departure in German company law.

First, the MoMiG abolishes the legal requirement of a minimum share capital for incorporating a business with limited liability. Technically, this is achieved by virtue of a new variant of the Limited Liability Company (GmbH), regulated in a single paragraph (section) inserted into the existing statute, viz. § 5a GmbHG. In order to distinguish this lesser corporate form, it will not be called by the name 'GmbH' (though treated as a GmbH in all other respects), but by the evocative name '*Unternehmergesellschaft (haftungsbeschränkt)*', meaning 'entrepreneurial company with limited liability'. As a tribute to the enduring German enthusiasm for capital maintenance the bill provides that one quarter of the annual surplus of an 'entrepreneurial company' shall be excluded from distribution to the shareholders and appropriated to a compulsory reserve account, perhaps in the hope that companies will thus build up the legal capital required to become a 'regular' GmbH in due course. However, contrary to the government proposal in the bill, the MoMiG did not reduce the minimum share capital for the 'regular' GmbH to €10,000, but left it unchanged at €25,000.

The second fundamental change concerns the straightforward abolition of a vast complex of regulation known to German lawyers by the term '*eigenkapitalersetzendes Gesellschafterdarlehen*' (equity-substituting shareholder loan). The concept will be explained in a brief excursus towards the end of chapter 3. The MoMiG will replace this sprawling body of law with a comparatively simple rule in the Insolvency Code providing for the general subordination of all shareholder loans in the insolvency of the company.

Private Company Law: European and International Perspectives' [2007] EBOR 83 refers to an earlier draft of the MoMiG bill (published in May 2006), which has partly been overtaken by subsequent events, for instance in relation to the new 'entrepreneurial company' (not yet mentioned in the article); this may also be the case with the relevant passage in the article by *Daniela Weber-Rey*, 'Effects of the Better Regulation Approach on European Company Law and Corporate Governance' [2007] ECFR 370, at 413–414.

66 BGBl. 2008, Part I, p. 2026.

From a long list of further amendments contained in the MoMiG, two are linked with topics analysed in this study. One point is mainly concerned with the reversal by the legislature of a decision from the Bundesgerichtshof treating the widespread practice of cash pooling within a group of companies as a violation of capital maintenance principles.[67] The other change concerns the statutory duty of the company directors to request the opening of insolvency proceedings, which will be discussed in some detail in chapter 5.

United Kingdom

German reform efforts of recent years look pale in comparison with the reformatory zeal that swept through English company law after the Labour Government came to power in 1997. In March 1998, the Department of Trade and Industry (DTI) – which was renamed in 2007 to become the Department for Business, Enterprise and Regulatory Reform (BERR) – launched a wide-ranging consultation exercise entitled programmatically 'Modern Company Law for a Competitive Economy'. The project, which came to be known as the 'Company Law Review', was set out on a grand scale to run for a period of three years with an elaborate institutional structure comprising a Steering Group, a Consultative Committee, a dozen Working Groups and external experts to whom in-depth research on several issues was contracted out. During the process the Steering Group published a series of consultation documents, colloquially known as 'green bricks' on account of their colour and weight.[68] In June 2001, the Company Law Review Steering Group duly presented its two-volume Final Report.[69] A year later, in July 2002, the DTI published a White Paper

[67] BGH 24.11.2003, BGHZ 157, 72 = NJW 2004, 1111; for a concise introduction on how the problem arose and the solution proposed by the MoMiG see *Karsten Schmidt*, 'Reform der Kapitalsicherung und Haftung in der Krise nach dem Regierungsentwurf des MoMiG', GmbHR 2007, 1072 at 1074–1075; a closer analysis is provided by *Tim Drygala / Thomas Kremer*, 'Alles neu macht der Mai – Zur Neuregelung der Kapitalerhaltungsvorschriften im MoMiG', ZIP 2007, 1289; this point will not be dealt with further in the present study.

[68] 'The Strategic Framework' (February 1999); 'Developing the Framework' (March 2000); 'Completing the Structure' (November 2000); shorter consultation documents referring specifically to capital maintenance were published in October 1999 and June 2000; the complete list of documents (with publication references, where applicable) can be found at p. 305.

[69] URN 01/942 and URN 01/943. At the time of writing, unfortunately, these two documents are no longer on-line at www.berr.gov.uk (although the documents mentioned in the previous footnote are), but they are available in print from the Department for Business, Enterprise and Regulatory Reform.

'Modernising Company Law',[70] which contained proposals and even draft clauses for legislation in the wake of the Company Law Review. There then followed a conspicuous pause until, in March 2005, the DTI published a new White Paper 'Company Law Reform',[71] which was followed by the Company Law Reform Bill introduced in the House of Lords on 1 November 2005.

The final achievement of this extended process is the Companies Act 2006, which received Royal Assent on 8 November 2006. It is thought to be the biggest bill ever to have gone through the UK Parliament, with 1,300 sections and 16 schedules.[72] The Companies Act 2006 recasts the entire body of company law previously contained in the Companies Act 1985, and although many provisions of the 2006 Act do little more than restate the previous law (sometimes with minor amendments), the Act produces significant changes across all areas of company law. Moreover, the Companies Act 2006 introduces comprehensive regulation in areas that were hitherto governed largely or exclusively by common law rules. In terms of the scope of this book, the most important changes concern the rules on capital maintenance,[73] which will be dealt with in chapter 3, and the codification of the general duties of directors,[74] which will be considered in chapter 4. In addition, a single provision tucked away in the 'Miscellaneous Provisions' of the Companies Act 2006 contains a modification of the Insolvency Act,[75] which will be examined in detail in chapter 5.

The mass of new legal material that needs to be digested involves an intricate schedule for bringing the Act into force. In accordance with the usual practice in the United Kingdom – and quite astonishing by German standards on the constitutional separation of powers – the statute adopted by Parliament does not determine when its provisions come into force,[76] but leaves it to the Secretary of State to appoint the commencement date by way of secondary legislation.[77] To this end, no

[70] Cm. 5553 (2 vols.). [71] Cm. 6456.

[72] Comprehensive coverage is provided, inter alia, by *Hannigan & Prentice*, Companies Act 2006; *Scanlan et al.*, Companies Act 2006; *Steinfeld et al.*, Blackstone's Guide to The Companies Act 2006.

[73] In particular CA 2006, Part 17, Chapter 10, ss. 641 to 653 (reduction of share capital) and Part 23, ss. 829 to 853 (distributions).

[74] CA 2006, Part 10, Chapter 2, ss. 170 to 181.

[75] CA 2006, s. 1282, inserting a new s. 176ZA into the Insolvency Act 1986.

[76] With a few limited exceptions: CA 2006, s. 1300 (1). [77] CA 2006, s. 1300 (2).

fewer than eight Statutory Instruments have been adopted,[78] which provide for the various parts of the Act to come into force in stages until 1 October 2009.[79] The main reason for this protracted course of action is that the Act does not stand on its own, but is accompanied by a raft of secondary legislation on a multitude of substantive issues.[80]

B. Comparative legal methodology and the quest for a European legal discourse

1. *'Europäische Rechtswissenschaft'*

The European developments in relation to creditor protection are part of a bigger picture. For several decades the European Union has adopted harmonisation measures with a view to reducing the diversity of laws within its borders, which is perceived as an obstacle to the optimal functioning of the single market. This legislation has influenced national systems of private law in the Member States, and with it legal writing and scholarship even where the subject of enquiry is not Community law as such. Indeed, the prospect of a future European private law has created an immensely rich academic discourse.

Thus, at the beginning of the 1990s some German academics started to write about an emerging '**Europäische Rechtswissenschaft**'.[81] In German it is a very catchy formula, but finding an English equivalent turns out to be tricky. One possibility is to translate it as 'European legal science', just as Tony Weir has chosen to translate '*Rechtswissenschaft*' as

[78] Companies Act 2006 (Commencement No. 1, Transitional Provisions and Savings) Order 2006, SI 2006/3428; Companies Act 2006 (Commencement No. 2, Consequential Amendments, Transitional Provisions and Savings) Order 2007, SI 2007/1093; Companies Act 2006 (Commencement No. 3, Consequential Amendments, Transitional Provisions and Savings) Order 2007, SI 2007/2194; Companies Act 2006 (Commencement No. 4 and Commencement No. 3 (Amendment)) Order 2007, SI 2007/2607; Companies Act 2006 (Commencement No. 5, Transitional Provisions and Savings) Order 2007, SI 2007/3495; Companies Act 2006 (Commencement No. 6, Saving and Commencement Nos. 3 and 5 (Amendment)) Order 2008, SI 2008/674; Companies Act 2006 (Commencement No. 7, Transitional Provisions and Savings) Order 2008, SI 2008/1886; Companies Act 2006 (Commencement No. 8, Transitional Provisions and Savings) Order 2008, SI 2008/2860.

[79] A concise timetable is available at www.berr.gov.uk/files/file48793.pdf.

[80] Further information on these Orders and Regulations can be found at www.berr.gov.uk/whatwedo/businesslaw/co-act-2006/index.html.

[81] Early references to the term include *Helmut Coing*, 'Europäisierung der Rechtswissenschaft', NJW 1990, 937 at 940; *Oliver Remien*, 'Europäische Rechtswissenschaft – Voraussetzung oder Folge europäischer Rechtsangleichung?', in: *Klaus Hopt* (ed.), Europäische Integration als Herausforderung des Rechts (1991), 124.

'legal science' throughout his translation of the 'Introduction to Comparative Law' by Konrad Zweigert and Hein Kötz.[82] Indeed, many German lawyers consider the subject of law as a 'science', though English lawyers, on the whole, do not. The difficulties are compounded by the fact that the German word '*Wissenschaft*' is wider than 'science' and covers humanities as well as natural and social sciences. I prefer to speak of a '**European legal discourse**'.

The existence of such a discourse could radically alter perceptions like the following, which sums up the status quo: 'As far as the domestic debate in Great Britain is concerned, we are obviously limited to the role of an interested observer. But to the extent that English letter-box companies operate on German markets the protection of local contracting parties and creditors from such "guests" becomes a German affair as well.'[83] In a truly European legal discourse this dichotomy of 'us' and 'them' would be overcome by a shared sense of commonality and diversity across the legal systems of the Member States. This book seeks to contribute to the development of such a discourse. But it is doubtful whether the hitherto predominant functional approach to comparative law provides the right tool for this endeavour, and this book therefore employs a decidedly doctrinal approach.

2. *A functional approach to creditor protection*

The functional approach is a well-established and perhaps the most widely used method in comparative legal scholarship today.[84] The basic idea of the functional method is to construct a function that is deliberately decoupled from the doctrinal structures of the legal systems to be

[82] *Konrad Zweigert / Hein Kötz*, Einführung in die Rechtsvergleichung (3rd edn 1996); translated into English as 'Introduction to Comparative Law' by Tony Weir (3rd edn 1998). All subsequent references are to the English edition.

[83] 'Soweit es um die Binnendiskussion in Großbritannien geht, bleibt uns selbstverständlich nur die Rolle eines interessierten Beobachters. In dem Maße aber, in dem sich englische Briefkastengesellschaften auf deutschen Märkten bewegen, wird der Schutz örtlicher Vertragspartner und Gläubiger vor solchen "Gästen" auch zu einer deutschen Angelegenheit.' From *Holger Fleischer*, 'Gläubigerschutz in der kleinen Kapitalgesellschaft: Deutsche GmbH versus englische private limited company', DStR 2000, 1015 at 1020.

[84] See generally *Michele Graziadei*, 'The functionalist heritage', in: *Pierre Legrand / Roderick Munday* (eds.), Comparative Legal Studies: Traditions and Transitions (2003), 100; *Ralf Michaels*, 'The Functional Method of Comparative Law', in: *Mathias Reimann / Reinhard Zimmermann* (eds.), Oxford Handbook of Comparative Law (2006), 339.

investigated, so as to allow for an 'external' vantage point that is neutral in relation to each of the systems.

In analysing creditor protection from a functional perspective, one needs to establish why creditors need to be protected.[85] The short answer is that the creditors need to be protected against a class of actors on the corporate scene who may be called the 'controllers' of the company. The term is largely self-explanatory. The controllers are those persons who have the power to take decisions on the company's actions. The most obvious controllers of a company are its directors. Typically they are vested with the power to take decisions on behalf of the company, and they are also the company's agents in a legal sense, having power to bind the company to transactions with third parties. But the idea of a company's controllers is not confined to the directors. In many ways the shareholders also act as controllers, and this is true, in particular, of private companies, to which the present analysis is confined. In this type of closely-held company, shareholders will frequently appoint themselves as directors ('owner-managers'), and even where this is not the case the shareholders will often be closely involved in decision-making, at least in transactions of major importance, or in a situation where the company is in financial difficulties. Often shareholders and directors, to the extent that they are not the same persons, will be linked by informal bonds, especially family ties, allowing them to share information in ways not accessible to outsiders, and enabling the shareholders to monitor the directors' performance informally, yet quite effectively.

Although the company is a separate entity in law,[86] the controllers may enlist it to serve their own economic or financial purpose. The most extreme, yet by no means unusual situation is that of a company with a single shareholder who is also its sole director. Many of these companies are run with little or no regard to anyone else's interests. The flip-side of this power is that the controllers have it in their hands to use the company opportunistically to the prejudice of other actors whose interests depend on the economic fortunes of the company but are not aligned with the interests of the controllers – including the creditors of the company.

[85] See, for instance, *Brian Cheffins*, Company Law (1997), ch. 11; *Kraakman et al.*, Anatomy of Corporate Law (2004), ch. 2 and 4; for a theoretical analysis that takes a critical view of the prevailing law and economics approach see *Andrew Keay*, Company Directors' Responsibilities to Creditors (2007), ch. 18 ff. (Part E).

[86] *Salomon v Salomon & Co Ltd* [1897] AC 22; § 13 (1) GmbHG.

Every creditor's main risk is that the debtor will not have sufficient funds when payment is due. But for creditors of a limited liability company the risk is aggravated by the potential for 'moral hazard' on the part of the controllers of the company. As long as the company remains profitable the controllers have an incentive to see to its success. But when the company's financial situation turns precarious, a conflict of interests arises which bears all the hallmarks of a principal-agent relationship. Three additional risks to creditors can be identified:

(i) The controllers of the company carry on the business to gamble their way out of the crisis by embarking on a high-risk business strategy. If the gamble pays off, the controllers will have saved their company. But if it fails, the resulting additional losses will only make the creditors worse off. This is the quintessential problem of wrongful trading, but it may also be addressed by directors' general duties and, under German law, by general principles of the law of delict.

(ii) The controllers of the company siphon off company assets into their hands. Here the recipients are enriched at the company's expense, i.e. the company itself is made 'poorer'. At the same time, the creditors suffer a detriment because of the reduced chances for them to be paid out of the reduced company assets. This is the problem that stands behind the concept of transactions at an undervalue, but also behind that of concealed distributions in contravention of capital maintenance rules.

(iii) The controllers make payments to certain creditors (especially themselves) in preference over other creditors. Here the company does not actually suffer – its net asset position remains unchanged – but the unsatisfied creditors suffer a reduction in their dividend. This is mainly covered by avoidance provisions against preferences, but directors' duties also come into play.

The functional approach to creditor protection would appear to be especially suitable for a comparative analysis. Comparing laws, like any comparison, requires a *tertium comparationis*, a common yardstick. One possibility for such a yardstick is to use paradigms from the economic analysis of law,[87] such as the welfare-reducing effects of a principal-agent relationship and the efficiency of legal instruments to counteract them. Economic analysis is highly functional in its understanding of the

[87] *Ugo Mattei*, Comparative Law and Economics (1997).

law. It sees the law as a tool to maximise aggregate social welfare. A recent major study of company law in an avowedly comparative and functional perspective is based on this methodology.[88] A research programme on these lines would look at legal systems with a view to establishing how far they achieve this goal by eliminating welfare-reducing behaviour of controllers of companies and would typically conclude with proposals for law reform where one jurisdiction has been found wanting by performing significantly less well than others.

3. *Beyond functionalism*

Functionalism in comparative law is not confined to a comparison of legal systems through the lens of economic analysis of the law because it accepts a wider range of possible social functions for the law than maximising aggregate social welfare. However, what all functionalist yardsticks for comparison have in common is their extra-legal character. The law is seen 'functionally as a regulator of social facts'.[89] In other words, the law is reduced to an input factor in a comparative operation which is less interested in legal thinking as a way to determine the contents of the law and more in the impact of any given law on real-life human actors, which requires a wholly different methodology in order to obtain valid data on empirically observable human behaviour.

This book does not present an economic or otherwise functionalist analysis of the law, but a doctrinal analysis, yet one that undertakes to build a bridge between two legal systems as different as English law and German law. For this purpose the functional problems set out above provide no more than the starting point for any meaningful discourse on the subject of creditor protection. Given the social and economic similarities between the various societies that make up Europe (and the industrialised world in general), it will always be possible to find functional equivalents at some level of abstraction. This observation lies at the heart of what Konrad Zweigert and Hein Kötz, in their 'Introduction to Comparative Law', a book widely regarded as a standard work on the subject, call the *praesumptio similitudinis*, a presumption that the practical results achieved in different legal systems are similar as

[88] *Kraakman et al.* (fn. 85), where the authors state in the preface: 'The corporate form, and the law to which it gives rise, are utilitarian institutions, which must be understood in the first instance in the light of their economic contributions to business life.'

[89] *Zweigert / Kötz* (fn. 82), 46.

long as the social and economic structures are also similar.[90] However, the danger starts when those making the comparison claim that the exercise of finding functional equivalents is all that matters, because the differences between national laws falling by the wayside in the course of this process are accidental and irrelevant, unless they are attributable to the political, moral, or social qualities of the different nations.[91]

This book does not seek to refute the functional methodology of comparative law as such. The method may serve a number of valid and important intellectual goals. But its inherent reductionism makes it unsuitable to lead towards a truly European legal discourse, because it fails to capture important aspects of the law. There is more to law than a set of straightforward rules creating incentives for human actors to behave or not to behave in a certain way. One striking feature of many comparative studies is their sense of certainty with regard to the national laws under comparison. Their national reports often present the law as so tidy as to be almost sterile, with little or no evidence of the debates which doctrinally oriented lawyers constantly have about what their law actually is.

That goes hand in hand with some scholars confessing to a striking distaste for the doctrinal analysis of the law. Zweigert and Kötz contemplate that, perhaps, 'the mere interpretation of positive rules of law in the way traditionally practised by lawyers does not deserve to be called a science at all, whether intellectual or social'.[92] They go on to denounce 'the hollowness of the traditional attitudes – unreflecting, self-assured, and doctrinaire', and then praise the virtues of comparative law, which 'not only shows up the emptiness of legal dogmatism and systematics but, because it is forced to abandon national doctrines and come directly to grips with the demands of life for suitable rules, it develops a new and particular system, related to those demands in life and therefore functional and appropriate'.[93] This is the credo of the functional method of comparative law.

The difficulties arise a few pages later, where Zweigert and Kötz remind us that 'the comparatist must treat as a source of law whatever moulds or affects the living law in his chosen system, whatever the lawyers there would treat as a source of law, and he must accord those sources the same relative weight and value as they do. He must attend, just as they do, to statutory and customary law, to case-law and legal writing, to standard-form contracts and general conditions of business,

[90] Ibid., 40. [91] Ibid., 3. [92] Ibid., 4. [93] Ibid., 33–34.

to trade usage and custom.'[94] There is no denying that we are faced here with a problem of circularity: we are invited to denounce the 'emptiness' of traditional legal doctrine, but at the same time we must rely on it to tell us what the law, which we seek to compare, actually is.

Alan Watson has warned of the dangers of taking the investigation into the foreign law lightly: 'To begin with, Comparative Law is superficial. . . . This peril of Comparative Law is then compounded with another, even more serious, getting the foreign law wrong.'[95] To be sure, nothing can justify 'getting the foreign law wrong', but Watson appears more understanding towards being superficial in researching the foreign law. He accepts that even a superficial knowledge of a foreign legal system may be useful, for instance where a legislator is seeking inspiration for national law reform. Of course, such comparisons can sometimes be useful, but a higher standard is called for where the aim is to achieve a European legal discourse. If this discourse is to get off the ground, it should not remain the preserve of a priestly caste of comparative lawyers, who have developed their own 'functional' terminology which separates them from 'traditional' lawyers. The danger here is that their engagement with national law is so superficial that it can easily be dismissed as irrelevant by the 'traditional' lawyers.

4. Understanding foreign law – from Auslandsrechtskunde *to a European legal discourse*

At its heart, this book is about better ways to reach an understanding of foreign law. It is a subject for which German lawyers have coined the term '*Auslandsrechtskunde*', but which is not perceived as an academic discipline in its own right. The study of the actual contents of foreign legal systems in terms of their rules is sometimes viewed as a lesser art.[96] It has been said that new information technologies make it even less important as a special field of study.[97] Yet a database or the internet delivers no more than a string of characters that needs human intellect to turn it into meaning, and the meaning which, say, a continental

[94] Ibid., 35–36. [95] *Alan Watson*, Legal Transplants (2nd edn 1993), 10.

[96] See, for instance, *Franz Mänhardt / Willibald Posch*, Internationales Privatrecht – Privatrechtsvergleichung – Einheitsprivatrecht (2nd edn 1999), para. 5/5.

[97] *Ralf Michaels*, 'Im Westen nichts Neues? 100 Jahre Pariser Kongreß für Rechtsvergleichung – Gedanken anläßlich einer Jubiläumskonferenz in New Orleans', RabelsZ 66 (2002), 97 at 113.

reader attaches to the words and phrases in an English judgment may not be the same as the meaning given to them by the judge.

Even before the *Centros* case, German writers had started to develop an interest in English law, as is demonstrated by a number of monographs, often published doctoral dissertations, on English company law[98] and insolvency law.[99] After *Centros* this interest increased dramatically and has led to the emergence of a whole new body of literature dealing specifically with foreign, i.e. mostly English-registered, companies operating in Germany.[100] Such interest is surely a positive indication of the richness and openness of legal scholarship in Germany.[101] In contrast, there is very little writing by English scholars on German company and insolvency law beyond a few book chapters or articles[102] and two edited volumes produced by the Oxford Anglo-German Law Conference some years ago.[103] Apparently there is not a single monographic work written by an English lawyer on German company law or insolvency law.

98 E.g. *Carsten Bödecker*, Die Kapitalerhaltung im englischen Gesellschaftsrecht (1994); *Martin Wolf*, Konzernhaftung in Frankreich und England (1995); *Ernst-Markus Schuberth*, Konzernrelevante Regelungen im britischen Recht – Ein Beispiel für die Bewältigung konzernrechtlicher Fragestellungen durch Regeln des allgemeinen Gesellschafts-, Kapitalmarkt- und Insolvenzrechts (1997); *Henning Bloß*, Die Unternehmensgruppe im englischen und deutschen Recht der Kapitalgesellschaften (1999).

99 E.g. *Matthias Florian*, Das englische internationale Insolvenzrecht (1989); *Susanne Perker*, Das Reorganisationsverfahren im englischen Insolvenzrecht im Vergleich zur geplanten deutschen Insolvenzordnung (1994); *Klaus Kamlah*, Die Anfechtung in der Insolvenz von Unternehmen – Dargestellt am deutschen und englischen Recht (1995).

100 See above, fn. 49 and accompanying text.

101 Indeed, as early as 1926, a prominent German law professor put forward the question: 'Should a future reform of company law bring about an approximation towards the Anglo-American law on fundamental questions?' – *Julius Lehmann*, 'Soll bei einer zukünftigen Reform des Aktienrechts eine Annäherung an das englisch-amerikanische Recht in grundlegenden Fragen stattfinden?' Gutachten zum 34. Deutschen Juristentag (1926). In 1929, within a few months, the UK Companies Act of the same year appeared in a German translation, together with a 100-page introduction, by *Arthur Curti*, Die Englische Aktien-Gesellschaft nach neuem Recht – Systematische Darstellung und Gesetz vom 10. Mai 1929 (1929).

102 E.g. *Robert Drury / Peter Xuereb* (eds.), European Company Laws: A Comparative Approach (1991); *Frank Wooldridge*, 'Aspects of German Law Governing Private Limited Liability Companies', in: *David Feldman / Frank Meisel* (eds.), Corporate and Commercial Law: Modern Developments – Published in Honour of Professor R.R. Pennington (1996) 33; *Paul Davies*, 'Board Structure in the UK and Germany – Convergence or Continuing Divergence?' (2000) 2 ICCLJ 435; *Frank Wooldridge*, 'Duty of Care and Liabilities of Members of the Two Boards of German Public Companies', [2006] EBLR 109.

103 *Eva Micheler / D.D. Prentice* (eds.), Joint Ventures in English and German Law (2000); *Jennifer Payne* (ed.), Takeovers in English and German Law (2002).

If readers feel that German writers come in for harsher criticism in this book than their English counterparts, they should bear in mind that English scholars have by and large avoided Alan Watson's perils of comparative law by not writing much about German law in the first place. On the other side, German writers occasionally put forward statements and propositions about English law in the most confident language, which English lawyers would probably find rather bewildering. We shall come across more than one such instance, and I should like to emphasise that my aim with the discourse analysis in this book is not to belittle the efforts of others or to mete out personal criticism, but to warn of errors and misunderstandings, which might otherwise congeal into entrenched wisdom.[104]

Apart from occasionally 'getting the foreign law wrong', the German literature on English law provides evidence of a much deeper and more general problem. Writing about a legal system in a language other than its own presents a serious challenge. It is often difficult to convey every nuance of a word's meaning in translation. Moreover, terms that carry a well-defined meaning in one's home system may be misleading, because the reader is led to believe that the meaning in the foreign legal system is the same. Legal language, properly used, is a precisely calibrated language which can convey a lot of meaning in comparatively few words. This raises problems for comparative legal studies – and for European law-making – which, although perhaps not a novel insight in theory, are all too often woefully ignored in practice.

In its attention to detail this book takes some encouragement from Basil Markesinis, who writes that to those comparative works which look at the big picture 'one can – and should – add a more focused effort to understand a foreign system and piece by piece come to terms with its complexity'.[105] However, Markesinis then goes on to discuss what he calls 'The Problem with Concepts' for, in his words, 'the comparison of systems through their concepts can lead to confusion and inaccuracies. For different concepts may conceal similar solutions and philosophies; and similar concepts may hide differences, which flow from other structural differences.'[106] The cure, he submits, is to compare legal systems through their case law in relation to

[104] For a less clement account of observations to this effect see *Harald Halbhuber*, Limited Company statt GmbH? – Europarechtlicher Rahmen und deutscher Widerstand (2001), ch. 8, with a stinging rebuke of some German views about English company law.

[105] *Basil Markesinis*, 'Unity or Division: The Search for Similarities in Contemporary European Law' (2001) 54 Current Legal Problems 591, at 592.

[106] Ibid., 595.

factual equivalents, which reveals not only a considerable similarity of factual litigated instances, but also policy debates which show a remarkable degree of duplication of ideas once the researcher has penetrated through the differences of concepts and reasoning.[107] There can be no doubt at all about the usefulness of analysing cases.[108] However, one wonders whether 'concepts and reasoning' should be skated over so quickly.

For what matters to lawyers is not just the practical results of a number of standard fact patterns, but how these results can be derived from authoritative sources through a process of reasoned argument. As Andrew Burrows lucidly observed:

> Everyone, to some extent, uses categories to make facts or ideas comprehensible and manageable. For lawyers, categorisation is particularly important because it is through categorisation – or as one might otherwise label it 'principled reasoning' – that we attempt to adhere to that essential requirement of the rule of law that like cases should be treated alike. . . . [T]o reject the discipline of clarity and rationality imposed by categorisation is to slide from the rule of law into a potentially disastrous regime of decision-making by pure intuition.[109]

Principled reasoning admits of plurality of opinions and does not exclude the possibility of dissent. Lord Justice Diplock once memorably said: 'I agree that this appeal should be allowed although the legal route which has led me to this conclusion is not at all points identical with that traversed by the Master of the Rolls. After all, that is the beauty of the common law; it is a maze and not a motorway.'[110] With respect, it is not just the beauty of the common law – it is the beauty of the law as such. Statutes are not immune to ambiguity and thus lend themselves to argument. At this point, traditions and methods may differ between England and Germany, although Stefan Vogenauer, in his massive two-volume study,[111] has argued that the canons of interpretation for statutes are much more similar in England and on the Continent than is generally assumed and perhaps do not display any disparities of great relevance at all. The present book is not the proper place to dispute such

[107] Ibid., 607–608.

[108] German readers might wish to look at *Basil Markesinis*, 'Zur Lehre des Rechts anhand von Fällen: Einige bescheidene Vorschläge zur Verbesserung der deutschen Juristenausbildung', in: Festschrift für Peter Schlechtriem (2003), 119.

[109] *Andrew Burrows*, Understanding the Law of Obligations – Essays on Contract, Tort and Restitution (1998) 16.

[110] *Morris v C W Martin & Sons Ltd* [1966] 1 QB 716, at 730G.

[111] Die Auslegung von Gesetzen in England und auf dem Kontinent (2001).

a copious scholarly work in any detail, but it is pertinent to draw attention to one particular aspect. By and large, the study by Vogenauer has little to say about the differences in drafting between English and continental statutes, and German statutes in particular, although one would have thought that the way in which any given text is written must have some bearing on how it is interpreted.

A glance at the statutes reprinted (and translated) in the Appendix reveals formidable differences in the style of legislative drafting between England and Germany. English statutes often deploy long-winded enumerations, multiple repetitions and minute cross-references as if to foresee and exclude even the most perverse misreading of the text. It is no surprise to find a German lawyer complaining about the 'intricacy' (*Kompliziertheit*) and 'inacessibility' (*Unzugänglichkeit*) of English statutes.[112] German statutes are also drafted with great attention to their inner structure and coherence, but this expresses itself more subtly, and the draftsman seems less troubled by the idea that certain connections and conclusions are left to be spelt out by commentators. Moreover, German lawyers invariably understand all their statutes as one coherent body, with the Civil Code at its heart. Terms and concepts defined in the Civil Code are routinely used in other statutes without any need for cross-references. This, after all, is the essence of having a codified system of private law. Reading German statutes demands skills in textual analysis distinct from those required for reading English statutes, and both need a fair amount of training. The different drafting styles match a difference in the way the statute is, and is meant to be, applied: English lawyers construe their statutes, German lawyers interpret theirs. Incidentally, judicial law-making is by no means the sole preserve of the common law. Time and again, the Bundesgerichtshof has shown itself remarkably willing to engage in the creative interpretation of statutes, not least because the drafting of statues in Germany allows, and in fact presupposes, considerable latitude of interpretation.

Lawyers are sometimes criticised for their use of language, especially by non-lawyers. Indeed, doctrinal legal language should never form an excuse for either bad style or an attempt at mystery-mongering with a view to disenfranchising laypersons. But at a fundamental level the law employs its doctrinal language for a necessary purpose. Gunther Teubner reminds us that law, like art, is an 'imaginary world', which makes things thinkable that could not be thought otherwise: 'Reconstructing a conflict

[112] *Volker Beissenhirtz*, Insolvenzanfechtung in Deutschland und England (2003), 229.

in the language of legal doctrine, raising the *quaestio juris*, factorising it into a sequence of questions of fact and questions of law, allows for inventing new arguments, new criteria, new rules which would not be possible at all did legal doctrine not exist.'[113] In a similar vein, Geoffrey Samuel has emphasised the epistemological difference between mere legal rules or propositions and legal or doctrinal notions which 'are not really rules [but] are focal points through which one moves from the world of fact to the world of law and vice versa'.[114] Doctrinal language is not irrelevant – it is the only proper language for lawyers to use. Crucially, different legal systems have different doctrinal languages and therefore different arguments and criteria, which they use in their discourse. The real challenge of writing about a legal system operating in a foreign language is to keep the loss of information to a minimum while producing a text that is readable and accessible for lawyers from another system.

Markesinis is certainly right that 'similar concepts may hide differences, which flow from other structural differences', but instead of resigning to a position that 'concepts can lead to confusion and inaccuracies',[115] this book suggests taking the bull by the horns. Each of its four main chapters will include reflections on expressions which seem concordant at first, yet the analysis will reveal not only important differences in meaning and scope, but errors and misunderstandings that have followed, or are likely to follow, from a superficial translation. It has been said, with some justification, that comparison precedes translation because the translation reproduces the results of the comparison.[116] Better still perhaps is the view that there is no simple relationship of A followed by B in either direction, but an iterative process of preliminary translation, without which no comparison can get under way, improved understanding and subsequent refining of the translation, a process which may not only go through several loops, but may have no definite endpoint at all. Yet none of this provides an excuse for burying one's head in the sand. The very first aim of any European legal

[113] *Gunther Teubner*, 'Alienating Justice: On the Surplus Value of the Twelfth Camel', in: *Jiří Přibáň / David Nelken* (eds.), Law's New Boundaries – The Consequences of Legal Autopoiesis (2001) 21, at 25–26.

[114] *Geoffrey Samuel*, Law of Obligations and Legal Remedies (2nd edn 2001), 7.

[115] Above, fn. 106.

[116] 'La comparaison précède, la traduction suit; car la traduction juridique est la reproduction des résultats de la comparaison' – *Rodolfo Sacco*, 'Souvenirs d'un vieux comparatiste', ZEuP 2002, 727 at 734.

discourse must be to ensure our mutual understanding, notwithstanding our use of different languages.

C. The scope and aims of this book

The discussion of creditor protection in the present book is built around four topics that have been selected with a view to their suitability for the purpose of this study, and one chapter of the book will be devoted to each of them. Chapter 2 deals with the avoidance of pre-insolvency acts that are detrimental to creditors, a body of law known colloquially to English lawyers as 'transaction avoidance' and to German lawyers as '*Insolvenzanfechtung*' (literally 'avoidance in insolvency'). Chapter 3 looks into capital maintenance (*Kapitalerhaltung*) with a particular emphasis on unlawful distributions and legal remedies to reverse them in favour of the company and its creditors; in particular, it will be shown how German law has managed to develop a rather terse statutory provision on capital maintenance (§ 30 GmbHG) into a system of creditor protection performing functions that English lawyers would perhaps rather entrust to insolvency law. Chapter 4 complements this by analysing the personal liability of company directors for making dispositions of company assets in breach of capital maintenance rules. Chapter 5 investigates the personal liability of company directors arising from their specific responsibility to protect the interests of creditors when the company operates in the vicinity of insolvency, including German *Insolvenzverschleppungshaftung* (liability for delayed filing for insolvency) as well as wrongful trading and related aspects of directors' duties in English law.

The aim of what may be called the descriptive aspect of this book is to demonstrate how these components of creditor protection operate and interact with each other, and how they do so in quite different ways in the two jurisdictions. In doing so, the book presents a number of findings that may hold insights for the application of foreign law in an Anglo-German cross-border situation, which has become a widespread concern given the increasing number of German businesses incorporated as private limited companies in England. This, however, is not the main thrust of the book. Were it so, German readers might, with some justification, expect the inclusion of further topics they consider important to creditor protection such as the doctrine of equity-substituting shareholder credit (*eigenkapitalersetzender Gesellschafterkredit*)[117]

[117] See the brief excursus in chapter 3 D.

or shareholder liability by way of piercing the corporate veil (*Durchgriffshaftung*) – only that in England, the former simply does not exist (nor do any similar restrictions on debt finance provided by shareholders),[118] and the latter has not received anything close to the elaborate doctrinal analysis that can be found in Germany.[119] Conversely, a comprehensive account of creditor protection would need to include some discussion of security interests, notably with regard to the floating charge and contractual receivership as peculiar self-help remedies under English law, which used to be of great importance, although the Enterprise Act 2002 all but abolished this mechanism; however, the floating charge will appear as historic background in chapter 5.

Returning to the four topics that are covered in this book, apart from their connection with the general topic of creditor protection, the thread that binds them together is the fact that each of them provides ample material in both legal systems for the kind of analysis that lies at the heart of this book. The manner in which the argument in this book is structured delivers the most striking results if it can build on a sufficiently deep doctrinal discourse on either side, making it all the more difficult for outsiders to understand and follow events as they unfold. At the same time, the book builds on existing comparative writing, mostly from the German side, with a view to learning from the difficulties which seem to have been regularly encountered in this respect. The overarching purpose of the present study is the advancement of a legal discourse between two audiences – one English, the other German – both deeply imbued with the doctrinal language and conceptual order in their respective home jurisdiction, yet increasingly aware of a need to master a foreign legal system of equivalent complexity. Four themes follow from this, which run through the whole of this book.[120]

[118] Cf. the seminal case *Salomon v Salomon & Co Ltd* [1897] AC 22, which involved a loan from Mr Salomon to his company. The Cork Report ('Insolvency Law and Practice: Report of the Review Committee'), Cmnd. 8558 (1982) made recommendations on the deferment of inter-company indebtedness (para. 1958 to 1965), but these have not been implemented: *Eilís Ferran*, Company Law and Corporate Finance (1999) 39.

[119] *Sealy / Worthington* (fn. 41), 53: 'The topic of "lifting the veil" persists in company law textbooks (as in this one), yet all the signs are that, after a brief flurry of interest some decades ago, there is now little potential for it to develop into a doctrine of any substance.'

[120] For a somewhat similar approach to comparative methodology see *Mitchel Lasser*, 'The question of understanding', in: *Pierre Legrand / Roderick Munday* (eds.), Comparative Legal Studies: Traditions and Transitions (2003), 197.

(i) Language and terminology

First, the existing German literature on English law is proof that it is dangerous to approach any foreign law simply on the basis of a general knowledge of the foreign language. The corollary throughout the book is a consistent concern for terminology and translation. Lawyers cannot help but resort to human language, yet by employing a professional terminology, which sets their discourse apart from others within society, they have developed a powerful tool for precise and efficient communication. As soon as the familiar domestic discourse is left behind, this use of language requires deeper reflection, especially in relation to communicating between two legal systems operating in different languages, where the problem of understanding foreign legal terminology is central, but cannot be solved by dictionary-style translations. The self-referential character of the law means that even simple definitions may refer to other terms needing just as much explanation. There are practical limits to what can be achieved in a single book, but the aim is clear. The foreign law can and should be presented through a process of discovery which starts from the terminological and conceptual premises of the observer's own law and leads to an understanding of the foreign law tuned in as closely as possible with the terminological and conceptual connotations of the indigenous, foreign lawyers.

On the point of language, the relevance of the approach advocated by this book extends beyond the two jurisdictions directly concerned. The reason for this lies in a combined effect of German law and English language. Historically, German private law, and German company law in particular, was very influential in other parts of Europe, especially in the Central-Eastern region of the Continent. In these countries, German as a foreign language was widely understood, which supported the reception of German law. Take the example of Poland. Personally, I do not read Polish, but whenever I open my bilingual Polish–English edition of the Polish Companies Act,[121] I can see the German law shimmering through on virtually every page. In fact, anyone familiar with German company law will immediately find his or her way through the company laws of half a dozen jurisdictions between the Baltic Sea and the Adriatic. In comparison, the UK Companies Act is a wholly different

[121] Code of Commercial Companies – Kodeks spółek handlowych, translated by Renata Bem, Ewa Kucharska, Joanna Marynowicz and Agnieszka Mączka, published by Zakamycze (2004).

universe. However, for obvious reasons, knowledge of German as a foreign language declined sharply in Eastern Europe after World War II, and the process has accelerated since 1989, when the fall of communism removed all reservations against English, which is now firmly established as the first foreign language in all these countries. It follows that the vast majority of lawyers from these jurisdictions will prefer to communicate with their German colleagues in English, notwithstanding that their respective laws have a lot more substance in common with each other than either has with English law.

I am aware that several Member States with a proud legal history do not appear in this equation. For them it may come as a consolation to think of English as the lowest common denominator in a double sense. On the one hand, the English language is probably the only common denominator Europeans are going to find for all-party communication in the foreseeable future. The informal practice in Brussels today is overwhelming evidence for this. On the other hand, communicating in the language of English law creates its own problems when it comes to a discourse among the majority of the EU Member States that do not follow the traditions of the common law, as the requisite terminology is often developed in a haphazard way. Moreover, there is a risk that British lawyers and lobbyists promote their law through the use of their language without everyone being fully aware of the consequences. The story of 'wrongful trading', which captured the German imagination as a handy phrase and almost made it into a European directive, is a case in point. One of the aims of this book is to initiate a discourse on the often ill-reflected use of the English legal language in the multi-lingual setting, which the EU is. That might reconcile the Anglo-sceptics with this book.

(ii) Stereoscopic view

From the goal of fostering mutual understanding follows another aspect of this book in which I beg to disagree with Zweigert and Kötz. In discussing the contribution of comparative law to the emergence of a European private law they demand 'a body of legal literature which presents the different areas of law from a European perspective, not focusing on any particular legal system or its systematics and not addressed to readers of any particular nation'.[122] It may be a desideratum for the future that such publications be understood by every European

[122] *Zweigert / Kötz* (fn. 82), 30.

reader in more or less the same way. The reality today is that every European lawyer has a far better knowledge of his home system than of any other system. German writing on English law makes it abundantly clear just how difficult it is to dissociate oneself from one's own legal background. And even if German writers publish their arguments in English, does that guarantee that English readers fully comprehend their meaning as intended by the authors? This has been a particular concern throughout the work on this book. The answer, I submit, lies not in the kind of detached writing advocated by Zweigert and Kötz. Instead, what is needed is precisely a body of literature that engages with its readership and takes into account that readers from two different jurisdictions will look at the text from different angles. This book represents a deliberate attempt to write about German law and English law in a manner that makes the exposition accessible to readers from each of the two jurisdictions by taking account of their respective conceptual and terminological background. As a consequence the presentation will frequently switch between the perspectives of an English lawyer and a German lawyer. The idea can be compared with that of a stereoscopic camera which produces two slightly different images of the same object, taken from different angles, which are then combined to allow for a better, namely a three-dimensional image of the object. Too many comparative studies nowadays focus on superficial similarities and ostensible functional equivalents, with a serious risk of underestimating the complexity of legal systems. By looking systematically at differences between legal systems one can tease out more information on both of them, delivering a more vivid image of the law. This book focuses on difference and diversity not for their own sake, but in order to improve our understanding of, and our communication with, the 'other'.

(iii) Discourse analysis

The third theme is that the legal discourse itself becomes a legitimate, and even necessary, subject of enquiry. This explains the bulky footnotes which occasionally feature in this text and which English readers may consider unattractive; their purpose will, hopefully, become clear from their respective context. In every investigation of a foreign legal system a concern which may seem trivial in the domestic debate moves centre stage. One cannot seek to answer the question 'What is the (foreign) law?' without reflecting on the question 'How do we know what the (foreign) law is?'. There is a vast volume of comparative literature

law of the Member State of the opening of proceedings (known as the *lex concursus*). According to Article 3 of the Regulation, this will normally be the Member State within the territory of which the centre of a debtor's main interests is situated.[6] The focus of the Regulation on the centre of a debtor's main interests brings the German legislator back into play in relation to the classic *Centros*-type companies, which are incorporated in England with a view to evading German company law. A well-developed domestic armoury of avoidance laws could do much to assuage German fears about an erosion of standards of creditor protection. Yet recent developments in Germany, notably the deliberations at the Juristentag in September 2006 and the MoMiG in 2008, show no more than timid signs of a re-orientation in this respect. Only in one particular field, viz. the rules on mandatory subordination of equity-substituting shareholder credit (*eigenkapitalersetzender Gesellschafterkredit*),[7] has the focus now clearly shifted onto insolvency law, whereas the thrust of the argument in this and the following chapter has remained intact.

One peculiar feature makes the treatment of avoidance remedies in the Insolvency Regulation more complex. Article 13 contains a crucial limitation on the application of the *lex concursus*. It provides that Article 4 (2) (m) shall not apply where the person who benefited from an act detrimental to all the creditors provides proof that the said act is subject to the law of a Member State other than that of the State of the opening of proceedings, and that that law (known as the *lex causae*) does not allow any means of challenging that act in the relevant case. The rule has been criticised.[8] The parties in a contractual relationship may choose the

[6] Subject to the important qualification that once insolvency proceedings have been opened in one Member State, the priority rule contained in Article 16 (1) of the Regulation prevents the courts of all other Member States from reviewing the jurisdiction of the opening court on the ground that the COMI is not situated in that Member State: *Eurofood IFCS Ltd* [2006] ECR I-3813; for a detailed analysis of the manifold aspects of this case see *Thomas Bachner*, 'The Battle over Jurisdiction in European Insolvency Law' [2006] ECFR 310. See already chapter 1, text accompanying fn. 23 and 24, as regards certain difficulties with the determination of the COMI.

[7] Excursus in chapter 3 D.

[8] Even judicially, by the Bundesgerichtshof: BGH 30.4.1992, BGHZ 118, 151 at 169 = NJW 1992, 2026 at 2030; *Hans Hanisch*, 'Report for Germany', in: *Ian Fletcher* (ed.), Cross-Border Insolvency: National and Comparative Studies (1992), 104 at 120–122 ('the worst of all possible solutions'); *Stefan Reinhart*, Germany's Insolvency Bill and its Cross-Border Provisions (1993) 2 IIR 187, at 196–197; *Sebastian Zeeck*, Das Internationale Anfechtungsrecht in der Insolvenz (2003), 55–68.

applicable law under Article 3 of the Rome Convention[9] and thereby reduce the risk of subsequent avoidance through choice of a legal regime that is less strict in relation to avoidance remedies in insolvency, notably by having shorter 'twilight periods'. Moreover, whenever the *lex causae* of a legal act differs from the *lex concursus*, the rule requires the analysis of the case under two different laws. Whatever opinion one has of the pertinency of the rule, its existence moves mutual comprehension and a shared legal discourse centre-stage, these being the principal themes of this book. Whether the problem is one of planning a transaction or of litigation, it forces lawyers to think in two different dimensions, which may be as diverse as English and German avoidance laws.

Notwithstanding the vast differences, there are common structural features which may serve as initial points of reference. Section B starts from the observation that neither jurisdiction limits avoidance remedies to insolvency proceedings, although each provides for a wider range of avoidance grounds in the latter. Typically, these additional grounds rely on the debtor's factual insolvency at the time of the impugned act, and are limited to events occurring within defined 'twilight periods' before formal insolvency. However, that common ground is already left behind by the different ways in which the two jurisdictions combine these structural elements.

Section C goes to the heart of avoidance laws. What is it that characterises a transaction so flawed as to justify its ex post unravelling in order to augment the assets available for the satisfaction of the creditors? The proposition in the Insolvency Regulation that such acts are 'detrimental to all the creditors' merely begs the afore-posed question. A closer look reveals that this phrase may have little resonance with domestic English rules, but it demonstrates a striking correlation with the manner in which German law approaches the issue. Once it is clear just how general the German concept of 'detriment to creditors' actually is, the reader will understand that balancing creditors' interests with the need for commercial certainty is of paramount importance for German law.

From there it is only a small step to discussing the different roles of subjective or mental elements in relation to avoidance remedies in section D. In English law, these appear more as the result of discrete policy decisions made, and capable of being reversed, by the legislator as

[9] Convention on the law applicable to contractual obligations (80/934/EEC), OJ L 266 of 9.10.1980, p. 1 (as amended); implemented in Germany by virtue of Article 27 EGBGB and in England by virtue of the Contracts (Applicable Law) Act 1990.

it sees fit. Numerous academic writers have indeed put forward reform proposals in this respect. The way in which German law relies on mental elements is not only different in its substantive rules, but is also a function of how German law balances the interests of creditors and commercial certainty, so that – absent root-and-branch changes – it probably cannot operate entirely without them. Section E rounds off the chapter with an investigation into the respective roles for the concept of 'connected persons' in both systems of avoidance law.

This chapter may sound a wake-up call to company lawyers in Germany to look more closely at avoidance remedies as an instrument of creditor protection. English readers in turn will find out about fundamental structural principles built into German avoidance law, which, if contrasted with capital maintenance rules, may go some way towards explaining why German lawyers are so keen to preserve the latter. The analysis will pick up on this last point in chapter 3, where capital maintenance will be analysed as an alternative to the avoidance of transactions at an undervalue. The issue of preferences, on the other hand, will re-appear in chapter 5 in connection with remedies resulting from directors' breach of duty and wrongful trading.

Initial terminological observations

Linguistically, the German word '***Anfechtung***' and the English word '**avoidance**' are not exactly congruent terms. The German '*Anfechtung*' presupposes an action brought by the office-holder and becomes effective only upon the decision of the court. Hence, an automatic invalidation of a pre-insolvency act by operation of law does not strictly fall within this concept.[10] English lawyers, on the other hand, see no problem in including such an automatic invalidation within their concept of 'avoidance', as the title and content of s. 245 IA ('Avoidance of certain floating charges') confirms. As a matter of plain language, '*Anfechtung*' corresponds more to 'challenge' in the sense of 'taking an active step to make something void or invalid', whereas 'avoidance' is wider than that. This may explain why one German translator has chosen the English word 'contest' as translation for the noun '*Anfechtung*' and for the respective verb '*anfechten*'.[11] However, with the above caveat,

[10] *Volker Beissenhirtz*, Die Insolvenzanfechtung in Deutschland und England (2003), 141.
[11] *Peter de Bra* in *Braun* (ed.), Commentary on the German Insolvency Code § 129 and subsequent provisions.

translating '*Anfechtung*' as 'avoidance' makes sense as it saves the text from unnecessary complications.

'**Office-holder**' is the generic English term comprising the liquidator in an insolvent winding up and the administrator in administration proceedings. Its counterpart in the unitary procedure under the German Insolvency Code is called the '***Insolvenzverwalter***' ('insolvency administrator'). Contrary to the UK terminology, the Insolvency Regulation, in Article 2 (b), defines '**liquidator**' more broadly as 'any person or body whose function is to administer or liquidate assets of which the debtor has been divested or to supervise the administration of his affairs'. In view of this potentially misleading terminology, it seems preferable to use the neutral term 'office-holder', unless the context specifically refers to either English or German law.

B. The relevance of insolvency and 'twilight periods'

1. *Avoidance remedies outside insolvency proceedings*

It is not a defining element of avoidance remedies that the debtor must have become subject to formal insolvency proceedings, nor, for that reason, that only an office-holder can invoke avoidance mechanisms. English law and German law both recognise especially severe circumstances where an individual creditor may take action with a view to having a prior legal act or transaction of the debtor set aside in order to achieve satisfaction for his claim. In Germany, avoidance provisions that operate outside insolvency proceedings are contained in a separate enactment known as the Anfechtungsgesetz (literally Avoidance Act).[12] In England, the relevant statute is s. 423 of the Insolvency Act, which may be invoked whether or not the person who entered into the transaction has been declared formally insolvent.

The direct equivalent to s. 423 IA is to be found in § 3 Anfechtungsgesetz (AnfG). Both provisions are built on the premise that where a debtor acts voluntarily with a view to defeating the claims of his creditors by frustrating their (contingent) right to satisfy their claims out of his assets, the law will not tolerate this. Notwithstanding the common underlying idea, the two laws, being based on different languages, necessarily define the mental element in different terms. The

12 Gesetz über die Anfechtung von Rechtshandlungen des Schuldners außerhalb des Insolvenzverfahrens (Anfechtungsgesetz, AnfG), BGBl. 1994, Part I, p. 2911; the statute re-enacts (with modifications) the Anfechtungsgesetz of 1879, RGBl. p. 277.

substance of these terms and their relation to each other will be discussed in some detail later in this chapter.[13]

In any case the two laws differ greatly on the combination of further elements that are seen as justifying the grave measure, which is the avoidance of a previous legal act or transaction. They thereby reveal in a nutshell some of the salient features of the two systems of avoidance remedies which will form the core of this chapter and the substance of the more detailed analysis that will follow. English law, in s. 423 IA, requires an objective imbalance, viz. that the transaction is for a consideration the value of which, in money or money's worth, is significantly less than the value of the consideration provided by the debtor, but without any reference to a mental element on the part of the counterparty in the transaction. In stark contrast, § 3 AnfG is not restricted to a direct detriment resulting from an imbalance between the value of what the debtor has given and the consideration he has received, but it covers any kind of detriment to creditors, including what German lawyers know as indirect detriment.[14] The far-reaching scope of this concept of detriment could have devastating effects on commercial certainty, were it not for the counterbalance created by the requirement of a mental element, as the counterparty is vulnerable only if it had (actual) knowledge of the debtor's intent to prejudice creditors. In order to alleviate the restrictions imposed by the subjectivity of this avoidance mechanism, § 4 AnfG adds a strictly objective avoidance mechanism for gifts or other gratuitous dispositions made within the last four years.[15] This separate ground for avoidance requires neither a subjective element on the part of the debtor, nor on the part of the counterparty (the donee). It testifies to a very robust German application of the maxim 'that persons must be just before they are generous, and that debts must be paid before gifts can be made'.[16] In contrast, whereas s. 423 (1) (a) IA mentions gifts and other transactions for no consideration separately,

[13] Below D.1. [14] More on this in section C.5.

[15] § 3 AnfG operates on transactions up to ten years in retrospect. In England claims under s. 423 IA are subject to the general limitation periods, i.e. twelve years where the relief claimed is to set aside a transaction: *Hill v Spread Trustee Co Ltd, Re Nurkowski* [2006] EWCA Civ 542 = [2007] 1 WLR 2404.

[16] *Freeman v Pope* (1870) LR 5 Ch.App. 538, at 540 (Lord Hatherley LC). German lawyers tend to formulate such maxims in a much more abstract manner, speaking, in this context, of the '*geringere Schutzwürdigkeit des unentgeltlichen gegenüber dem entgeltlichen Erwerb*', i.e. a gratuitous acquisition being less worthy of protection than an acquisition for value: *Volker Beissenhirtz* (fn. 10), 34; similarly *Reinhard Bork* (fn. 3), ch. 6 para. 2. It is hard to imagine an English lawyer coming to court with a phrase exactly like this.

the requirement of a purpose to prejudice creditor interests must also be satisfied in this case. This interlocking between elements that define an objective imbalance inherent in a transaction or legal act and mental elements for the parties involved will continue to run throughout this chapter.

All the provisions referred to so far apply irrespective of whether, at the time of the act, the debtor was solvent or not, which dovetails with the rule that the debtor need not have been declared formally insolvent at any time for the provisions to operate. Obviously, where the law allows for the avoidance of such transactions or legal acts outside insolvency proceedings, the only sensible solution is to provide for the same mechanism after the commencement of insolvency proceedings as well. By virtue of s. 424 (1) (a) IA, the scope of application of s. 423 IA extends to a debtor company that is being wound up in an insolvent liquidation. German law achieves the like result by including provisions in the Insolvency Code, viz. § 133 InsO (intentional prejudice) and § 134 InsO (gratuitous dispositions), which mirror § 3 and § 4 AnfG. However, as will become clear at the next stage of the analysis, § 133 InsO has a much larger role to play in German insolvencies than s. 423 IA has in English insolvencies.

2. *Additional grounds for avoidance in insolvency*

To the aforementioned armoury against fraudulent activities or gratuitous dispositions by the debtor, both legal systems add further grounds that are only available in formal insolvency proceedings. For these, German lawyers have coined the term '***besondere Insolvenzanfechtung***', which translates best as 'special avoidance in insolvency'. Its background is formed by a threefold presentational scheme adopted more or less universally by writers[17] to categorise avoidance remedies, and mirrored in the arrangement of the statute, viz. (1) avoidance of acts committed by the debtor with intent to prejudice its creditors (§ 133 InsO); (2) avoidance of gratuitous dispositions (the objective test, § 134 InsO); and (3) 'special avoidance in insolvency' (§§ 130, 131, 132 InsO). What is 'special' about the latter is the fact that avoidance on these grounds is only available where a debtor has been formally declared insolvent, but not where the assets are otherwise insufficient to

[17] E.g. *Reinhard Bork*, Insolvenzrecht (4th edn 2005), 114–119; *Othmar Jauernig / Christian Berger*, Zwangsvollstreckungs- und Insolvenzrecht (22nd edn 2006), 198–202.

meet the claims of creditors. As a corollary, this type of avoidance mechanism is only available to the office-holder.

As regards the substantive relevance of insolvency, one characteristic feature, albeit not strictly a defining element of 'special avoidance in insolvency', is the requirement of the debtor's factual insolvency prior to the commencement of formal insolvency proceedings at the very time when the impugned act happened.[18] This testifies to the theoretical concept behind the rules on 'special avoidance in insolvency'. Their purpose is to move forward the point in time when the treatment of creditors should follow the regime of the insolvency process, by ensuring their collective and rateable satisfaction, even though that process has not yet been formally launched.[19] In contrast, avoidance of acts committed by the debtor with intent to prejudice its creditors and avoidance of gratuitous dispositions cannot be said to be governed by the same philosophy, as they can be invoked irrespective of whether the debtor was in a state of factual insolvency at the time of the impugned act, and indeed irrespective of whether the debtor ever reached such a state of insolvency.[20]

In this light, English law clearly has its own version of what might be called 'special avoidance in insolvency' from a German vantage point.[21] Characteristically, apart from s. 423 IA, the other avoidance provisions in s. 238 IA (transactions at an undervalue), s. 239 IA (preferences) and – partly[22] – s. 245 IA (avoidance of certain floating charges) can only be invoked by the office-holder after the commencement of insolvency proceedings and only if, at the time of the transaction, the company was unable to pay its debts, within the meaning given to this term in s. 123 IA, or became unable to pay its debts in consequence of the transaction. This leads to a brief look at the grounds of insolvency.

[18] § 131 (1) n. 1 and n. 3 InsO stand out as the only grounds of 'special avoidance in insolvency' operating irrespective of this requirement. The nature of the latter provision is not free from doubt; see *Heinrich Schoppmeyer* in Handbuch des Insolvenzanfechtungsrechts (2006), ch. 8 paras. 135–137; contra *Hans-Peter Kirchhof* in Münchener Kommentar InsO[2] § 131 mn. 49 (each with further references). The purpose of this book does not require a closer investigation of this particular norm.

[19] BGH 25.9.1972, BGHZ 59, 230 = NJW 1972, 2084.

[20] Cf. *Reinhard Bork* (fn. 3), ch. 1 para. 1 (especially fn. 2).

[21] Indeed, *Klaus Kamlah*, Die Anfechtung in der Insolvenz von Unternehmen (1995) employs this German typology for his discussion of English law (at p. 121 ff.).

[22] In case of a floating charge created in favour of a connected person (below E), s. 245 IA applies irrespective of the company's solvency at the time of the transaction.

3. *Insolvency tests and twilight periods*

For present purposes, this book is only concerned with those components of s. 123 IA which refer expressly to the company's factual insolvency, viz.

- that the company is unable to pay its debts as they fall due (s. 123 (1) (e) IA, also known as 'cash flow insolvency'), or
- that the value of the company's assets is less than the amount of its liabilities, taking into account its contingent and prospective liabilities (s. 123 (2) IA, also known as 'balance sheet insolvency').

By and large

- the cash flow test in s. 123 (1) (e) IA corresponds to the German '*Zahlungsunfähigkeit*' (literally 'inability to pay debts') in § 17 InsO, whereas
- the balance sheet test in s. 123 (2) IA corresponds to the German '*Überschuldung*' (literally 'over-indebtedness') in § 19 InsO.[23]

Unfortunately, the language sets up a dangerous trap.[24] Whereas the English term '**inability to pay debts**' translates literally as '***Zahlungsunfähigkeit***', the manner in which the term is employed in s. 122 (1) (f) IA and in the heading of s. 123 IA covers both cash flow insolvency and balance sheet insolvency, and it is thus generally synonymous with factual insolvency (German: *materielle Insolvenz, Insolvenzreife*). The German definition of '*Zahlungsunfähigkeit*' in § 17 (2) InsO makes it clear that it means 'inability to pay debts as they fall due', hence '*Zahlungsunfähigkeit*' is the equivalent only of cash flow insolvency, not of 'inability to pay debts'. In order to avoid conceptual confusion, I shall therefore translate '*Zahlungsunfähigkeit*' as 'illiquidity'.

The primary function of these grounds of insolvency is to determine the point in time after which creditors can force the company into a winding up procedure under the supervision of the court and with the

[23] Existing differences between the English and the German concepts do not invalidate the argument put forward in this book and may therefore be left to future research; the same goes for s. 123 (1) (a) to (d) IA, which do not have a counterpart in the German Insolvency Code.

[24] At least two comparative studies have actually fallen into this trap: *Volker Beissenhirtz* (fn. 10), 69–71; *Alexander Schall*, 'The UK Limited Company Abroad – How Foreign Creditors are Protected after Inspire Art (Including a Comparison of UK and German Creditor Protection Rules)' [2005] EBLR 1534, at 1543.

office-holder taking the reins from the controllers of the company. This puts an end to possible misappropriations by the controllers because any disposition of the company's property after the commencement of insolvency proceedings will be void as against the creditors, protecting their entitlement to the assets of the insolvent debtor. A second characteristic feature of insolvency is the principle of equal treatment of creditors – known, oddly enough, by different Latin maxims to English lawyers as ***pari passu*** and to German lawyers as ***par conditio creditorum***. In England the principle is laid down in s. 107 IA. Interestingly, the German statute only speaks of 'collective satisfaction' (*gemeinschaftliche Befriedigung*, § 1 InsO), but nowhere does it say expressly that in case of insufficient assets to satisfy all claims in full, debts ranking equally shall 'abate in equal proportions between themselves' (as does rule 4.181 of the Insolvency Rules for English law), although this might be taken as implicit in the notion of 'collective satisfaction'.[25]

Avoidance remedies extend these entitlements of the creditors into the past, in that they allow for the reversing of dispositions made at a time when the material conditions for creditors to trigger insolvency proceedings were already present, but formal proceedings had not yet been initiated. This is the logic behind the German notion of 'special avoidance in insolvency', which as an idea also underlies English transaction avoidance law,[26] though English lawyers have not found it necessary to coin a phrase for it. Under English law, s. 240 (2) IA defines the 'relevant time' for a transaction to be potentially caught by either s. 238 IA (transaction at an undervalue) or s. 239 (preference), and it requires the company to be at that time unable to pay its debts within the meaning of s. 123 IA, or to become unable to pay its debts in consequence of the transaction or preference. Similarly, s. 245 (4) IA provides in effect that a floating charge – unless created in favour of a person connected with the company[27] – will become void under s. 245 IA if at the time at which the charge is created the company is unable to pay its debts within the meaning of s. 123 IA, or becomes unable to pay its debts in consequence of the creation of the charge. In each case, the reference to s. 123 IA covers both the cash flow test of insolvency laid

[25] Moreover, the principle finds an expression in § 226 InsO on the equal treatment within each group of persons involved in an insolvency plan.

[26] See, for instance, *Rizwaan Mokal*, Corporate Insolvency Law (2005), 306 ff.

[27] Above, fn. 22.

down in s. 123 (1) (e) IA and the balance sheet test of insolvency laid down in s. 123 (2) IA. No distinction is made between these two tests in relation to transaction avoidance.

In contrast, the German provisions on 'special avoidance in insolvency' in §§ 130, 131 and 132 InsO refer only to *Zahlungsunfähigkeit* (illiquidity, § 17 InsO) at the time of the act to be avoided, not to *Überschuldung* (over-indebtedness, § 19 InsO). The policy argument in support of this narrow rule is that commercial transactions would otherwise suffer from too much legal uncertainty,[28] as business partners will often be unable to ascertain, at the time of the transaction, whether the debtor is over-indebted.[29] The effect, compared to English law, is that the mechanisms for 'special avoidance in insolvency' do not extend to events that occurred at a time when the debtor was balance sheet insolvent, but not yet cash flow insolvent.

However, the German avoidance provisions in §§ 130, 131 and 132 InsO have very short twilight periods anyway, extending to a maximum of three months prior to the request for the opening of insolvency proceedings. This is in stark contrast to English law, where all three avoidance provisions operating on the basis of the debtor's inability to pay debts – ss. 238, 239 and 245 IA – can catch transactions entered into in the last two years prior to the onset of formal insolvency, provided the transaction is one with a 'connected person', a concept whose role and importance will be dealt with in detail in section E. In most practical cases, therefore, the confinement, under German law, of 'special avoidance in insolvency' to cash flow insolvency makes less of a difference than it would with longer periods. The corollary of these very short twilight periods in §§ 130, 131 and 132 InsO is that any legally relevant act which occurred more than three months prior to the request for the opening of insolvency proceedings can only be avoided under either § 133 or § 134 InsO. Hence a functional comparison must look at § 133 InsO, in particular, as a counterpart to ss. 238, 239 IA.

[28] See the preparatory report for the German insolvency reform project leading to the new Insolvency Code of 1994: Erster Bericht der Kommission für Insolvenzrecht (1985) 404; *Kirchhof* (fn. 18), § 130 mn. 28a; *Heribert Hirte* in *Uhlenbruck*, InsO[12] § 130 mn. 34; the argument goes back to the nineteenth century, see RG 28.1.1890, RGZ 25, 34 at 38–39.

[29] As to the relevance of this knowledge see below D.2.

C. Detriment to creditors

1. *The English approach*

As a point of departure for this section, let us return to the relevant provisions in the EU Insolvency Regulation. The term employed to define the characteristic nature of transactions susceptible to avoidance is that of 'legal acts', in Article 4 (2) (m), or simply 'acts', in Article 13, which are 'detrimental to all the creditors'. To English eyes this may seem little more than a collective term of a descriptive sort, whose boundaries do not even merit closer examination, as when Len Sealy and David Milman are content to say that it 'would include provisions relating to preferences, transactions at an undervalue, etc'.[30] Sealy and Milman thereby 'translate' Article 13 into a terminology with which their target readership is infinitely more accustomed to than with the abstract language of 'detrimental acts'.

English law, and perhaps common law systems in general,[31] distinguish between two fundamental categories of pre-insolvency acts that may be vulnerable in a subsequent insolvency, viz. preferences and **transactions at an undervalue**. The latter is a descendant of what was formerly known as '**fraudulent conveyance**',[32] although under current English law a transaction at an undervalue is not as such characterised by an element of fraud.

The two categories have the following as their quintessential elements. According to s. 238 (4) IA, a company enters into a transaction with a person at an undervalue if:

- (a) the company makes a gift to that person or otherwise enters into a transaction with that person on terms that provide for the company to receive no consideration, *or*
- (b) the company enters into a transaction with that person for a consideration the value of which, in money or money's worth, is

[30] *Sealy / Milman*, Insolvency Legislation (10th edn 2007), vol. I, 647.

[31] Australian Corporations Law, s. 588FA (unfair preferences) and s. 588FB (uncommercial transactions); US Bankruptcy Code, § 547 (preferences) and § 548 (fraudulent transfers and obligations).

[32] See the historical account by *John Armour* in *Armour / Bennett* (fn. 2), para. 2.7 ff. The terms '**fraudulent conveyance**' and '**fraudulent transfer**' are still used in relation to the law in the United States, e.g. *Douglas G. Baird*, 'Legal Approaches to Restricting Distributions to Shareholders: The Role of Fraudulent Transfer Law' [2006] EBOR 199.

significantly less than the value, in money or money's worth, of the consideration provided by the company.

It is the same test as in s. 423 IA (insofar as this section relates to companies). But because s. 238 IA operates without any subjective requirement of a purpose to harm creditors, s. 423 IA loses most of its relevance for transactions entered into in the last two years prior to the instigation of formal insolvency proceedings. It remains relevant only to transactions entered into at a time when the company was not (yet) factually insolvent on either a balance sheet or a cash flow basis.[33]

The core of the concept of a **preference** is defined in s. 239 (4) IA, according to which a company gives a preference to a person if:

- (a) that person is one of the company's creditors or a surety or guarantor for any of the company's debts or other liabilities, *and*
- (b) the company does anything or suffers anything to be done which has the effect of putting that person into a position which, in the event of the company going into insolvent liquidation, will be better than the position he would have been in if that thing had not been done.

This provision is complemented by s. 245 IA on the invalidation of certain floating charges, which would otherwise provide their holders with a security right that ensures their priority over the unsecured creditors of the company. The gist of the section is that every floating charge created within the particular twilight period defined by the section is automatically invalidated[34] upon the opening of the subsequent insolvency proceedings, unless the charge was granted in consideration of certain types of new value, such as money paid or goods and services supplied to the company, at the same time as, or after, the creation of the charge. In other words, the provision seeks to prevent companies from creating floating charges to secure past debts.[35] As every floating charge created to secure a pre-existing debt would equally come within the test for a preference under s. 239 IA, i.e. 'anything done . . . by the company which has the effect of putting one of the company's creditors . . . into a [better] position' in the event of a liquidation, the practical effect of the section is to define a special case of a preference which operates without

[33] And note the presumption of factual insolvency in relation to transactions with connected persons (below, fn. 163 and accompanying text).
[34] See the text accompanying fn. 10.
[35] *Re Orleans Motor Co Ltd* [1911] 2 Ch. 41, at 45.

the highly subjective test of a 'desire' to prefer one creditor over the others required by s. 239 (5) IA (more on this below).[36]

The categorical distinction between a transaction at an undervalue (ss. 238, 423 IA) and a preference (s. 239 IA, and implicit in s. 245 IA) echoes through the entire English discourse on transaction avoidance.[37] Rebecca Parry discusses the rationale underlying transaction avoidance and identifies two roles performed by the respective provisions, viz.

- maximising the pool of assets available for distribution to creditors, and
- maintaining the order of priorities.

Parry argues that the first type of provision (which includes s. 238 and s. 423 IA) can be said to protect the interests of creditors collectively by ensuring that assets which should rightly form part of the debtor's estate in insolvency in fact do so, whereas the second type of provision (comprising s. 239 and s. 245 IA) is concerned with adjusting the rights of creditors inter se.[38]

In a similar vein, John Armour stresses the differences between the two concepts. His enquiry into the purpose of s. 238 IA on transactions at an undervalue leads him to reject the view that the section supports the *pari passu* principle of equal treatment of creditors. In his succinct words the section 'is concerned with the size of the pie, rather than how it is divided up'.[39] In support of this distinction he points to judicial authority on the law of personal bankruptcy stretching back to the eighteenth century, where a sharp distinction was drawn between 'fraudulent conveyances' and preferences, and he points out that there is no indication that the Insolvency Act intended to alter this aspect of the relationship between preferences and the other avoidance provisions.[40]

The strong sense of two distinct categories is underlined by the important case of *Re MC Bacon*, one of the earliest reported decisions on the law of transaction avoidance after the Insolvency Act 1986. On the facts of this case, a charge, i.e. a security interest, granted to a creditor,

[36] *Gerard McCormack*, 'Swelling Corporate Assets: Changing What Is on the Menu' [2006] JCLS 39, at 53; *Thomas Bachner*, Creditor protection through insolvency law in England, in: *Marcus Lutter* (ed.), Legal Capital in Europe (2006) 427, at 439; *Felix Steffek*, 'Das englische Recht der Insolvenzanfechtung', KTS 2007, 451 at 474.

[37] Already in the Cork Report ('Insolvency Law and Practice: Report of the Review Committee'), Cmnd. 8558 (1982), para. 1208.

[38] *Parry* (fn. 1), para. 2.28–2.39; with reference to an American scholar, *Thomas H. Jackson*, 'Avoiding Powers in Bankruptcy', 36 Stanford Law Review 725, at 726 (1984).

[39] *Armour* (fn. 32), para. 2.24. [40] Ibid., para. 2.26.

which might as such have come within s. 239 IA, did not constitute a voidable preference because the requisite subjective element that the company be actuated by a desire to prefer the creditor[41] had not been present. But the judge, Mr Justice Millett (later Lord Millett), rejected an alternative argument that the security might constitute a transaction at an undervalue within s. 238 IA. He held that the latter section was concerned with the depletion of the company's assets, and given that the mere creation of a security right over a company's assets did not deplete them or diminish their value, it could not be a transaction at an undervalue.[42] John Armour approves of the decision because 'to hold that a grant of security could be an undervalue transaction would wash away the distinction between preferences and undervalues'.[43] He points out that the policy of the legislator has been to require a mental element in relation to s. 239 IA, which is absent in s. 238 IA; to allow a factual preference such as the grant of a charge to fall within s. 238 IA would undermine this requirement.[44]

The reasoning of Millett J received the badge of approval by the Court of Appeal in *Menzies v National Bank of Kuwait SAK*, where Lord Justice Balcombe cited it at length.[45] That case was brought by a creditor under s. 423 IA. The definition of a transaction at an undervalue in s. 423 (1) IA was said to be in all relevant aspects the same as that in s. 238 (4) IA. Both judges who gave reasoned opinions stressed that the 'real complaint' of the creditor was that the impugned act constituted a preference, but that a preference as such could only be pursued by the office-holder under s. 239 IA, not by the claimant under the pretext of a transaction at an undervalue.[46] However, in the most recent Court of Appeal decision on s. 423 IA, Lady Justice Arden expressed strong doubts about the reasoning in *Re MC Bacon*. She observed that the section did not refer to a diminution in assets and that there was no reason why the value of the right to have recourse to the security and to take priority over other creditors, which the debtor creates by granting the security, should be left out of account.[47] The doctrinal foundation for this re-evaluation is supplied by the decision of the House of Lords

[41] More on this below D.1. [42] [1990] BCC 78, at 91–92.

[43] *Armour* (fn. 32), para. 2.25; but contrast the critical comment on the case by *Michael Bridge* in *Armour / Bennett* (fn. 2), para. 1.29.

[44] *Armour* (fn. 32), para. 2.92. [45] [1994] BCC 119, at 129.

[46] Ibid. 127, 128 (Sir Christopher Slade), 129 (Balcombe LJ).

[47] *Hill v Spread Trustee Co Ltd, Re Nurkowski* [2006] EWCA Civ 542 = [2007] 1 WLR 2404, para. 138.

in *Buchler v Talbot*, where Lord Hoffmann and Lord Millett stressed the proprietary interest of the charge holder in the assets subject to the charge, which consequently fall outside the scope of the debtor's winding up.[48] Initial comment from the practitioners' side reveals an expectation that it is now only a matter of time before the Court of Appeal will reconsider *Re MC Bacon*.[49]

There is force in the argument that the granting of a charge for the chargor's own indebtedness towards the chargee constitutes a transaction that is capable of valuation, thus bringing it within the conceptual frame of s. 238 IA. John Armour considers that security rights have value to the chargee, as they put him in a better position on the company's liquidation; but he denies that there is a transfer of value from the company's point of view.[50] On the latter point, Roy Goode offers an analysis to the same effect.[51] There is a counter-argument to the effect that a company which grants security over its assets to one of its creditors can no longer utilise the same assets to obtain secured credit elsewhere, thus reducing its credit rating and increasing its cost of borrowing in the future.[52] However, in the final analysis, John Armour has a point in that the distinction between a transaction at an undervalue and a preference needs to be upheld because of the differences in the subjective requirements that set the two provisions apart.[53] Yet if this is the argument that carries the day, it limits the scope for the courts to reconsider *Re MC Bacon*, lest they come into conflict with a clear policy decision taken by the legislator – a highly controversial decision, one should add (see below), but a decision which only the legislator can reverse.

Beyond the question of whether the granting of security rights may be characterised as a transaction at an undervalue, the relationship between what constitutes a transaction at an undervalue and what constitutes a preference is a thorny issue awaiting further clarification. For instance, Roy Goode assumes that a transaction entered into with a creditor at an undervalue may constitute a preference within the meaning of s. 239 IA,

[48] [2004] UKHL 9 = [2004] 2 AC 298, para. 29 and 51; more on this case in chapter 5.

[49] *Chris Brougham*, 'Limitation periods and section 423 explained: MC Bacon questioned' [2006] Insolvency Intelligence 135, at 137.

[50] *Armour* (fn. 32), para. 2.91.

[51] *Roy Goode*, Corporate Insolvency Law (3rd edn 2005), paras. 11–37.

[52] *David Milman / Rebecca Parry*, A Study of the Operation of Transactional Avoidance Mechanisms in Corporate Insolvency Practice (1998), 12 and 36; in an elaborate German article on English transaction avoidance law *Felix Steffek* agrees with this analysis: 'Das englische Recht der Insolvenzanfechtung', KTS 2007, 451 at 460.

[53] Above, fn. 4.

and he leaves it to the liquidator to choose whether to bring an action under s. 238 or s. 239 IA.[54] Presumably, the example given by Adrian Walters of a company transferring an asset worth £10,000 to an unsecured creditor in satisfaction of an indebtedness of £5,000 would be a case in point. However, Walters concludes that 'it is arguable that proceedings in relation to the overvalue element would need to be brought under section 238',[55] seemingly denying a choice for the liquidator and thereby contradicting Goode's position.

At a fundamental level, a system of avoidance remedies built around the dichotomy of transactions at an undervalue and preferences, appealing though it may be because of the sense of functional differentiation it conveys, cannot avoid difficulties resulting from overlaps and, even more precariously, from gaps between the two concepts. Accordingly, the English discourse cannot help but develop arguments on how to resolve these difficulties. Yet German observers appear to be puzzled by a case such as *Re MC Bacon*,[56] because it raises problems that seem unnecessary if one looks at avoidance remedies with the conceptual map of German law in one's mind. At this point, it is pertinent to introduce the basic structure of German avoidance law, which reveals a profoundly different systematic approach.

2. *The German approach*

Returning to Article 4 (2) (m) of the Insolvency Regulation and looking at it from a German perspective, the words in the Regulation display a remarkable similarity to § 129 InsO, although there is nothing in the explanatory report on the Insolvency Convention (later to become the Insolvency Regulation)[57] to suggest that German law has had a particular influence in this respect. § 129 InsO introduces the part of the statute containing the provisions on '*Insolvenzanfechtung*' (avoidance in insolvency) by a statement of principle, which conveys the idea of a comprehensive notion of 'detriment to creditors' as a unifying concept that lies behind the whole law on avoidance. It reads:

[54] *Goode* (fn. 51), para. 11–76 at fn. 71 ('in practice, s. 238 would usually be relied on').

[55] *Adrian Walters* in *Armour / Bennett* (fn. 2), para. 4.104.

[56] *Kamlah* (fn. 21), 208–209; *Beissenhirtz* (fn. 10), 139–140 and 148. The lack of conceptual coherence in English avoidance law is the recurrent theme in the book by *Beissenhirtz.*

[57] The 'Virgos-Schmit Report on the Convention on Insolvency Proceedings', reprinted as Appendix 2 in *Gabriel Moss / Ian Fletcher / Stuart Isaacs* (eds.), The EC Regulation on Insolvency Proceedings (2002).

> **§ 129. Principle.** (1) Legal acts which have been committed prior to the opening of insolvency proceedings and are detrimental to the insolvency creditors may be avoided by the insolvency administrator as provided in §§ 130 to 146. (2) An omission is equal to a legal act.

The provision presents an excellent illustration of how the German legislator, aided by scholarly analysis of the law, is concerned to identify one overarching principle underpinning (in this instance) the various separate grounds for avoidance. The Insolvency Act does no more than spell out the grounds for avoidance and does not bother about statements of principle, although the arrangement of sections surrounding s. 238 IA (transactions at an undervalue) and s. 239 IA (preferences) makes it clear that these two heads of transaction avoidance share common elements in relation to the 'relevant time' (s. 240 IA) and remedial issues (s. 241 IA). In Germany, a statement of principle such as § 129 InsO is regarded as a useful aid for the scholarly and judicial interpretation of the manifold detailed provisions that follow. All the same, the reference to the subsequent provisions in §§ 130 to 146 InsO, which determine the conditions for avoidance and remedial issues, makes it clear that avoidance is only available in the circumstances defined in the statute. The 'principle' in § 129 InsO is no licence for inventing heads of avoidance on an ad hoc basis. The key element in § 129 InsO is that of 'legal acts' being 'detrimental to the creditors'. This is the core of avoidance law in Germany, and it forms the point of departure for the doctrinal analysis of the whole field.

German law does contain traces of the twofold rationale for transaction avoidance that appears to matter so much to English lawyers. § 130 and § 131 InsO, two provisions within the subgroup of avoidance grounds that has been identified as *besondere Insolvenzanfechtung* (special avoidance in insolvency), are based on the recurring term 'satisfaction or security'. German lawyers acknowledge these provisions by the name '***Deckungsanfechtung***' (literally 'avoidance of cover'). The 'cover' refers to the effect that the creditor covers his credit risk either by receiving satisfaction from the debtor, so that the creditor would no longer be caught up in the insolvency at all (to the extent of the satisfaction, if it is only partial),[58] or by receiving some kind of security from the debtor, which puts the creditor ahead of the others once insolvency strikes. The common idea underpinning the German provisions relating

[58] The law speaks of satisfaction in order to include not only payment, but other 'surrogate' forms of satisfaction, as for instance set-off: cf. *Hirte* (fn. 28), § 130 mn. 10 ff.

to 'satisfaction or security' in §§ 130, 131 InsO and the English concept of a preference in s. 239 IA is to shore up the principle of *pari passu* or *par conditio creditorum* distribution of assets in the event of an insolvent liquidation. But the wide concept of 'detriment' in § 133 InsO can cover preferences as well. Were it otherwise, preferences given more than three months before a request to the court for the opening of insolvency proceedings would not be voidable at all under German law. If a debtor has validly incurred a debt, but then makes a payment to the creditor at a time when his assets are not sufficient to satisfy all his creditors in full, this will make the remaining creditors worse off.[59] However, § 133 InsO requires an intent on the part of the debtor to prejudice those creditors who do not get paid.[60]

3. *Casting the net wide enough: 'legal act' versus 'transaction'*

The German word, which I have just translated as 'legal act', is '***Rechtshandlung***'. The alternative translation of '*Rechtshandlung*' as 'transaction' offered by Peter de Bra[61] would rather seem unhelpful, as the following analysis will demonstrate. 'Transaction' is the generic term employed by English lawyers when they discuss the subject matter of this chapter,[62] notwithstanding that the Insolvency Act consistently distinguishes between transactions (in relation to s. 238) and preferences (in relation to s. 239) where both types of 'transaction' are in issue (notably in ss. 240 and 241). At first sight, both the German and the English expression appear to involve the use of unspecific terms of broad meaning so as to cover the widest possible range of actions of debtors. But the terminology invites a closer investigation.

Indeed, in Germany, the term '*Rechtshandlung*' is understood in the widest possible terms as any act of will that produces legal consequences.[63] Moreover, § 129 InsO does not limit avoidance to legal acts committed by the debtor. The range of potentially voidable legal acts includes acts suffered by the debtor without his voluntary participation.

[59] Note that we shall encounter the same idea again in the context of directors' liability for breach of their fiduciary duty to take account of creditors' interests in chapter 5.

[60] Below D.1. [61] See fn. 11.

[62] Cf. the book titles by *Rebecca Parry*, Transaction Avoidance in Insolvencies (2001) and *John Armour / Howard Bennett* (eds.), Vulnerable Transactions in Corporate Insolvency (2003).

[63] *Hirte* (fn. 28), § 129 mn. 62; *Kirchhof* (fn. 18), § 129 mn. 7; *Ulrich Ehricke* in Handbuch des Insolvenzanfechtungsrechts (2006), ch. 3 para. 2.

This is of particular relevance in relation to the provision on *Deckungsanfechtung* (avoidance of cover) in § 130 InsO, where the concept of 'legal act' permits the avoidance of measures taken by an officer of the court to enforce a judgment against the debtor if this would allow one creditor to sail ahead of the others. Beyond the provisions on 'special avoidance in insolvency', which cover the short twilight period of three months before the request for the opening of insolvency proceedings, § 133 InsO also relies on the concept of 'legal act', but here the additional mental requirement that the debtor must act with intent to prejudice its creditors prevents the forced execution of a judgment against the debtor from being included. Two recent decisions from the Bundesgerichtshof reveal where the line is to be drawn. If the debtor pays the sum due to the order of the court officer after the latter has informed the debtor of the request by the creditor to commence enforcement proceedings, this constitutes a voluntary act capable of avoidance under § 133 InsO.[64] However, if the payment is only made after the court officer has already arrived at the premises of the debtor, so that non-payment would result in immediate enforcement action being taken, the payment can no longer be treated as an autonomous act of the debtor guided by his intent to prefer one creditor,[65] but it may still come within § 130 InsO.

As regards the use of the term '**transaction**' in the Insolvency Act 1986, it is listed among the definitions in s. 436 IA, but the section merely says that the term 'includes a gift, agreement or arrangement', which is not a true definition. The term was chosen in order to overcome a narrow interpretation given to the previous language in s. 42 of the Bankruptcy Act 1914.[66] But the new language has strong connotations of 'mutual dealing'.[67] Already the Cork Report of 1982 started with the premise that the entire body of avoidance law is 'concerned with transactions voluntarily initiated by the debtor himself'.[68] Incidentally, the Insolvency Act, in s. 128, has a specific section dealing with the 'avoidance' of 'any attachment, sequestration, distress or execution put in force against the estate or effects of the company', but this provision attracts almost no attention in the standard literature on 'transaction avoidance'.[69]

64 BGH 27.5.2003, BGHZ 155, 75 = NJW 2003, 3347.
65 BGH 10.2.2005, BGHZ 162, 143 = NJW 2005, 1121.
66 *Armour* (fn. 32), para. 2.52.
67 Cf. *Armour* (fn. 32), para. 2.53 ff.
68 Cmnd. 8558, para. 1208.
69 Cf. the works cited in fn. 62.

A case that highlights the limitations inherent in the term 'transaction' is *Knights (Liquidator of Taylor Sinclair (Capital) Limited) v Seymour Pierce Ellis Ltd*, also known as *Re Taylor Sinclair (Capital) Ltd.*[70] The defendant was owed money by the director of another company, Taylor Sinclair (Capital) Ltd, which subsequently went into liquidation. There had been no prior contact between the two companies. The director caused his company to make a payment to the defendant company, which received the money in settlement of the debt owed to it by the director and in the erroneous belief that the money was loaned by the other company to its director. Even on the limited factual information contained in the judgment as to how the money actually left the company, it seems certain that German law would characterise this payment as a 'legal act' (*Rechtshandlung*). However, to the question whether the mere transmission of the money by the company to the recipient constituted a 'transaction' between them for the purpose of s. 238 IA, the English judge gave the following answer, which captures well the connotations surrounding the word 'transaction':

> It is right to say that the word 'transaction' as a matter of ordinary language embraces a potentially wide range of possibilities. . . . Doubtless, one should be wary of circumscribing the width of the statutory language of section 238 lest the evident policy of the section be undermined. Nevertheless, as I read the section it does envisage that, apart perhaps from the case of a mere gift which is expressly included within sections 238 and 436, a transaction will be something which involves at least some element of dealing between the parties to the transaction. Not only is this implicit in the word 'transaction' itself, but it is reinforced by the references in section 238 to (a) the 'entry into' a transaction (b) 'with a person' and (c) 'on terms that provide'. Whilst plainly an actual contract is not required in order for there to be a transaction, the language of the section is redolent of contract and mutual dealing.[71]

On the face of it, the argument turns on a purely linguistic analysis, but it may have a hidden agenda whereby the notion of 'transaction', as the foundation for the concept of 'transaction at an undervalue', is enlisted, if not to say manipulated, so as to shelter one company from the effect of the insolvency of another company. The reasoning in its entirety makes it clear that the judge's real concern was the protection of the defendant company, which was uninformed and perfectly innocent

[70] [2001] 2 BCLC 176. [71] [2001] 2 BCLC 176, para. 20.

about the illicit manner in which the director had caused his company to send the money on its way. Under German law, the need to protect the counterparty in this kind of situation is fully recognised, but it is achieved in a more purposeful way by virtue of subjective elements built into the various grounds of avoidance, to which the analysis will turn later.[72] Under English law, the absence, in large measure, of subjective elements in s. 238 IA precludes a like approach.

In another case the term 'transaction' led to litigation culminating in the decision of the House of Lords in *Phillips (Liquidator of AJ Bekhor & Co) v Brewin Dolphin Bell Lawrie Ltd.*[73] A company, which later became insolvent, sold its business to another company, the first defendant in the action. The difficulty with the aspect of 'mutual dealing' resulted from the fact that the consideration for the sale was provided not by the acquiring company, but by its parent company. The High Court and the Court of Appeal had held that the arrangements could not be seen as a single transaction, hence the payments to the vendor from the parent company for the assets acquired by its subsidiary could not constitute 'consideration' for the purpose of s. 238 IA, and the transaction was accordingly struck down. The House of Lords rejected that view and held that the whole arrangement constituted a single transaction within the meaning of s. 238 IA (but it upheld the result of avoiding the transaction on grounds of valuation).

In terms of the nature of the act susceptible to avoidance, the closest German analogy with s. 238 IA can be found in § 132 InsO, whose sub-paragraph (1), insofar as it is material for present purposes, reads:

> Voidability attaches to a debtor's legal transaction (*Rechtsgeschäft*) which is directly detrimental to the insolvency creditors.[74]

Note at the outset that the concept of 'legal transaction' ('***Rechtsgeschäft***'), which appears in § 132 InsO, but not in any of the other grounds for avoidance, is different from, and narrower than, the concept of 'legal act' ('*Rechtshandlung*').[75] The question to be asked under

[72] Below D.2. [73] [2001] UKHL 2 = [2001] 1 WLR 143.

[74] For the purpose of this particular point of analysis, one may disregard the enormous difference in the applicable 'twilight period' (three months in the case of § 132 InsO – two years in the case of s. 238 IA; above B.3).

[75] The terminology here is consistent with *Basil Markesinis / Hannes Unberath / Angus Johnston*, German Law of Contract (2006), who also translate '*Rechtsgeschäft*' as 'legal transaction'. By contrast, *Tony Weir* translates '*Rechtsgeschäft*' as 'legal act': *Zweigert / Kötz*, Comparative Law (3rd edn 1998). The difficulty with the latter approach is that it precludes the use of 'legal act' for translating the wider concept of '*Rechtshandlung*'.

German law would be whether the arrangements in *Brewin Dolphin* constitute a 'legal transaction' within the meaning of § 132 (1) InsO. Strangely, though, the literature on § 132 InsO appears to be silent on such three-party arrangements, where the debtor transfers assets to A, but receives the consideration (whether adequate or not) for these assets from B. The solution lies with the concept of '*Rechtsgeschäft*', but it is to be found elsewhere, not in the Insolvency Code. Although the term '*Rechtsgeschäft*' is not defined in the Insolvency Code, its meaning for German lawyers is settled beyond any doubt, because '*Rechtsgeschäft*' is a term defined in, and is indeed a central pillar of, the German Civil Code. This is a further example for the different techniques of statutory drafting. The minimum an English lawyer would probably expect is a cross-reference to the definition of *Rechtsgeschäft* in the Civil Code; for German lawyers that connection goes without saying.

Briefly, what is the outcome of applying the concept of 'legal transaction' ('*Rechtsgeschäft*') in § 132 InsO to a situation as in *Brewin Dolphin*? For a start, German law has never had any difficulty in accepting three-party arrangements as a single *Rechtsgeschäft*.[76] The overriding principle is the mutual agreement of the parties. As it was established on the facts that all parties had consented to the payments from the acquirer's parent being regarded as the consideration for the acquisition by the subsidiary, German law would accept this as the substance of their *Rechtsgeschäft*. That the payments were dressed up as leasing payments only served the dual purpose of allowing one party to reap tax advantages and to avoid the need for explanations to regulators. German lawyers would characterise such 'labelling' as *falsa demonstratio*, which has no impact on the rights and obligations as between the parties.[77] As a consequence of this settled understanding of *Rechtsgeschäft* and its application in § 132 InsO, any German court would have reached the same conclusion as the House of Lords ultimately did, but it would have needed a lot less argument.

Yet the limitation in § 132 (1) InsO that an act must qualify as a *Rechtsgeschäft* is itself exceptional within the German framework for avoidance in insolvency. § 132 (2) InsO goes on to say that any other

[76] Note that by virtue of § 328 BGB it has always been possible to confer a benefit on a third party not privy to a contract, whereas English law has only recently abolished the doctrine of privity of contract in that respect: Contracts (Rights of Third Parties) Act 1999.

[77] *Ernst Kramer* in Münchener Kommentar BGB[5] § 117 mn. 18.

'legal act' (*Rechtshandlung*) of the debtor whereby he loses a right, or can no longer enforce it, or whereby a pecuniary claim against him is upheld or enforceable shall be treated in the same manner. It is this term that the Insolvency Code employs in laying down the 'principle' in § 129, where sub-paragraph (2) even extends it to include omissions,[78] and throughout the avoidance provisions in §§ 130 to 146 InsO. This virtually boundless concept corresponds to the equally all-encompassing concept of detriment to creditors (*Benachteiligung der Gläubiger*), whose effect should not be hampered by too narrow a rule about what constitutes a voidable 'act' or 'transaction' in the first place.

4. Direct detriment, unequal bargains and 'pure detriment' to creditors

In the next step of their analysis German lawyers introduce a distinction between a 'direct' and an 'indirect' detriment (*unmittelbarer* versus *mittelbarer Nachteil*). One German ground for avoidance, viz. § 132 InsO, is expressly limited to cases of a direct detriment, and the concept also appears in § 133 (2) InsO (to which the analysis will return later). A detriment to creditors is direct if it flows from the legal act as the immediate result.[79] Thus, where the company transfers assets to a counterparty for a consideration less than the fair value of the assets, the creditors suffer a direct detriment because, in the case of a hypothetical liquidation, the assets available for their satisfaction would be diminished. English readers will immediately recognise this as similar to a transaction at an undervalue. But the concepts of 'direct detriment' and 'transaction at an undervalue' are not identical, because what is required under §§ 132 and 133 (2) InsO is a direct detriment to the creditors. While the focus of ss. 238 and 423 IA is on the exchange between the debtor (company) and the counterparty, German law does not look to the position of the debtor, but always looks to the position of the creditors.[80]

[78] Provided the omission was conscious and deliberate: BGH 24.10.1996, ZIP 1996, 2080; BGH 10.2.2005, BGHZ 162, 143 = NJW 2005, 1121; BGH 22.12.2005, BGHZ 165, 343 = NJW 2006, 908.

[79] *Kirchhof* (fn. 18), § 129 mn. 112–120; *Hirte* (fn. 28), § 129 mn. 124–126; *Ehricke* (fn. 63), ch. 4 para. 28–29.

[80] This principle was recognised by the Reichsgericht in one of its earliest decisions on transaction avoidance: RG 17.3.1885, RGZ 13, 298 at 300–301.

As it happens, English law and Austrian law (which follows German law in this respect) offer a series of cases decided on very similar facts, which are ideally suited for contrasting the two different approaches. The English case law starts with *Agricultural Mortgage Corporation Plc v Woodward*.[81] A farmer had created an agricultural tenancy over his land in favour of his wife. The rent was stipulated at the full market value, but the tenancy reduced the market value of the land for the bank, which sought to have it sold under the terms of its mortgage. The Austrian case[82] arose out of the rather dubious 'business model' of a group of self-styled 'rescue experts'. They persuaded debtors who ran their businesses from land which they owned to enter into a contractual agreement with a shell company under which the company acquired a long-term right – terminable, for the first time, after 100 years – to operate the business. The overall effect was the same as in *Woodward*, in that the creditors found the value of the land severely diminished.[83]

In both jurisdictions, the courts eventually found a way to rid the creditor(s) of the encumbrance on the land. However, the courts in England could not achieve this result by simply comparing the value of the land from the creditor's point of view before and after the completion of the tenancy agreement. Rather, they had to wrestle with the argument that the tenancy agreement was not a transaction at an undervalue, because the debtor (the farmer) had received full consideration, as the rent payable under the tenancy agreement was the market rent obtainable at the time. The Court of Appeal, in *Woodward*, held that s. 423 IA required viewing 'the transaction as a whole', and it took this as the starting point for detecting various non-pecuniary elements to be factored into the valuation of 'money or money's worth' (the words in ss. 238 and 423 IA). The wife, it was said, had obtained enhanced benefits from her tenancy in that the family home and business were safeguarded,

[81] [1994] BCC 688. [82] OGH 9.3.1989, ÖBA 1989, 1018.

[83] At first sight, it is easy to see why the market will not pay the full value for the tarnished property, but in each jurisdiction the question arises how the subsequent right can have this detrimental effect. Under English law, a tenancy or lease is a proprietary right, and the later right of the spouse defeated the earlier right of the mortgagee because of the intricacies of s. 99 of the Law of Property Act 1925 (concerning leasing powers of mortgagor and mortgagee in possession), read in conjunction with paragraph 12 of Schedule 14 to the Agricultural Holdings Act 1986 (rendering the powers contained in s. 99 immune to any derogation by virtue of the mortgage deed). In Austria, the right created was merely a contractual right under a *Pachtvertrag*, which is not of a proprietary nature in general, but it can obtain quasi-proprietary status if entered in the land register and thereby made binding upon subsequent purchasers of the land: § 1095 ABGB.

a surrender value acquired and that she had the power of 'ransom', i.e. she could stipulate a high price of compensation before permitting the bank to take possession. These additional personal benefits were not covered by the market rent, and the wife thus received a benefit greater than the consideration provided by her. The outcome was thought to be dictated by 'common sense',[84] but only the peculiar approach to the valuation of 'money or money's worth' made it possible to describe the transaction as one 'at an undervalue'. Although this ingenious argument may have won the day in that particular case, the underlying problem with the limitations imposed by the concept of 'transaction at an undervalue' remained acute. As between husband and wife, nothing prevents them from agreeing almost any rent they wish over and above the market rent with the premium reflecting the 'surrender' or 'ransom value' – the money, after all, stays in the family. Predictably, that argument was put forward in a subsequent case, *National Westminster Bank v Jones*, where the transaction was only struck down on a point of valuation, the court holding that the premium over the market rent was significantly less than the true value of the additional benefits accruing to the wife.[85] But then creating a tenancy that is safe against avoidance is only a matter of pitching the rent high enough, or so it would seem. The truth, and the fundamental logical difficulty with this approach to transactions at an undervalue, is that it is virtually impossible to calculate objectively a figure for the ransom value, for which only the sky is the limit. At the same time, this opens the backdoor through which the courts should normally be able to set aside any such transaction, although the explanation remains somewhat unsatisfactory.

Incidentally, the reaction of the English legislator to the problem under consideration may aptly be called a tribute to the phenomenon of path dependence in the law. The legislator could have climbed down the evolutionary tree to the point from where the concept of 'transaction at an undervalue' started to grow, and remedied its fundamental flaw. This would have required extensive statutory amendments, and quite possibly overcoming resistance from practitioners. Instead, the legislator opted for clipping a little twig on the old branch, by scrapping paragraph 12 of Schedule 14 to the Agricultural Holdings Act 1986,[86] thereby making every grant of an agricultural tenancy (like any other

[84] [1994] BCC 688, at 697 (Sir Christopher Slade).
[85] [2001] 1 BCLC 98 (ChD); affirmed [2001] EWCA Civ 1541 = [2002] 1 BCLC 55 (CA).
[86] See fn. 83.

tenancy) subject to the mortgagee's consent.[87] That may have solved the problem for mortgage lenders (who, one is inclined to assume, lobbied the government to this effect[88]). But it does not solve the problem for other creditors. Little imagination is needed to envisage analogous situations, as where a creditor seeking to enforce a judgment debt by way of a charging order finds itself confronted with a lease created on the day that judgment was handed down, or where a company grants a lease over its unencumbered land in favour of its controlling shareholder shortly before going into liquidation.

In Germany (as in Austria) there is no need to resort to artificial arguments about the valuation of personal benefits in money's worth, because the higher cost, or even the delay as such, for the office-holder in obtaining vacant possession as the prerequisite for realising the full market value of the land in a sale are enough to find a 'detriment to creditors',[89] and arguably even a 'direct detriment' as is required under §§ 132[90] and 133 (2) InsO, because it is the impugned act itself which creates the obstacle, not any subsequent event. The key passage from the judgment of the Austrian Supreme Court can be translated as follows:

> Even if it were true that the rent was realistic with regard to the situation of the business at the time of the [agreement], this would not argue against the detrimental character of the legal transaction. If a higher rent could not be obtained, then the whole [agreement] could not be seen as a reasonable rescue measure. Where the debtor disposes of his business for a consideration that is not even remotely sufficient to cover the business debts, that cannot be considered as an appropriate way of running the business in the interest of the creditors.[91]

[87] Agricultural Tenancies Act 1995, s. 31.

[88] The new law came into force on 1 September 1995, a mere 15 months after *Agricultural Mortgage Corporation Plc v Woodward* had been decided. *National Westminster Bank v Jones* was decided under the old law because the mortgage had been created before that date.

[89] See *Kirchhof* (fn. 18), § 129 mn. 101; *Ehricke* (fn. 63), ch. 4, para. 18.

[90] Cf. *Hirte* (fn. 28), § 132 mn. 2 ('langfristiger Miet- oder Pachtvertrag').

[91] OGH 9.3.1989, ÖBA 1989, 1018 at 1020: 'Selbst wenn es richtig wäre, dass dieser Pachtzins im Hinblick auf den Betrieb und dessen Zustand zum Zeitpunkt der Verpachtung realistisch gewesen wäre, würde dies nicht gegen die Nachteiligkeit des Rechtsgeschäftes sprechen. Wäre nämlich ein höherer Pachtzins nicht zu erzielen gewesen, dann könnte die Verpachtung als solche nicht als eine vernünftige Sanierungsmaßnahme angesehen werden. Verzichtet nämlich der Gemeinschuldner auf eine Verfügungsmöglichkeit über seinen Betrieb gegen ein Entgelt, das keinesfalls ausreichen kann, auch nur annähernd die Betriebsschulden zu decken, so ist das nicht als eine im Interesse der Gläubiger zweckmäßige Wirtschaftsführung anzusehen.'

The point here is that finding a detriment to the creditors hinges not on whether or not the rent stipulated is the market rent, but whether the entire transaction improves the net position of the creditors in the event of a subsequent insolvent liquidation. It is also pertinent to note the reference to rescue efforts (in response to an argument advanced on behalf of the self-styled 'rescue experts'). This opens the way for an argument that a serious rescue effort with a realistic prospect of making the creditors better off is to be taken into account in determining whether or not, from an ex ante perspective, a particular transaction was detrimental to the creditors.[92] Similarly, English law makes allowance for rescue efforts by virtue of s. 238 (5) IA, but tellingly, it does so against the yardstick of the interests of the company. The subsection provides a defence where a transaction at an undervalue was entered into in good faith and for the purpose of carrying on business, if at that time there were reasonable grounds for believing that the transaction would benefit the company (again, not the creditors).

From the foregoing analysis it seems clear that every transaction at an undervalue within the meaning of ss. 238 and 423 IA will constitute a detriment to creditors within the meaning of § 129 InsO. But the converse is not true. There may be a kind of 'pure detriment' to the creditors over and above a harm suffered by the debtor company as a result of a bad bargain. For the same reason the Bundesgerichtshof has made it clear that the reversal of a detriment to creditors in Germany is not based on, or limited by, any notion of enrichment on the part of the defendant.[93] On the other hand, German law does apply rules on unjust enrichment where the insolvency estate would otherwise be enriched at the expense of the defendant as a result of reversing the antecedent legal act.[94]

In discussing possible lessons from *Agricultural Mortgage Corporation Plc v Woodward*, Rebecca Parry contemplates whether it would be better if the requirement that a transaction should have been entered into at an undervalue were removed from s. 423 IA. She realises, though, that one

[92] BGH 18.7.2002, NJW 2002, 3252.

[93] BGH 3.12.1954, BGHZ 15, 333 = NJW 1955, 259; BGH 29.1.1964, BGHZ 41, 98 = NJW 1964, 1319. The principle is qualified by a statutory exception in § 143 (2) InsO that the bona fide recipient of a gratuitous disposition (§ 134 InsO) is only liable to restore or replace it to the extent of his or her enrichment. An analysis of English law to the contrary effect is provided by *Simone Degeling*, 'Restitution for Vulnerable Transactions', in *Armour/Bennett* (fn. 2), para. 9.11 ff. (with a discussion of *Agricultural Mortgage Corporation Plc v Woodward* at para. 9.23 f.).

[94] See, in particular, § 143 (1) second sentence and § 144 (2) InsO; compare *Degeling* (fn. 93.) para. 9.63 ff.

of the reasons for its existence is commercial certainty, because the requirement ensures that the counterparty is likely to be aware of the transaction's potential detriment to creditors' interests. But Parry goes on to argue that the section does not concern normal transactions in the ordinary course of business, because it always requires the debtor's purpose to prejudice his creditors. Thus, she concludes, even if the issue of consideration were disregarded, commercial certainty should be less of an issue.[95] There remains, however, a difficulty with commercial certainty if the counterparty does not know of the debtor's malicious purpose or, in the case of s. 238 IA, the debtor's factual insolvency. This is the reason why German law insists on a subjective requirement of knowledge (to be discussed in the next section) in order to ensure that only the non-deserving are caught by the unravelling of their dealings with the debtor, but with the burden of proof firmly on the counterparty, where it is a person connected to the debtor. This arguably allows for a more targeted selection of defendants.

5. *Indirect detriment*

The German distinction between direct and indirect detriment implies that there must be some kind of legally relevant detriment that goes even beyond the 'pure detriment' caused by frustrating activities as in *Woodward*. This indirect detriment can be any detriment to the creditors in the sense of any reduction in their dividend, which arises after the impugned legal act because of circumstances beyond the act itself.[96] Classic textbook examples[97] are that the debtor sells assets for their full and fair value, but uses the cash to flee the country or dissipates it beyond the reach of the creditors; or that assets are originally sold for their full and fair value, but their value later increases so that it would have been better for the creditors had they been kept (as where the market value of a plot of land has increased[98]); or conversely, where the debtor acquires assets which later fall in value. The endpoint in relation to which the detriment accruing from the legal act is to be assessed is the time of the trial against the defendant.[99]

95 *Parry* (fn. 1), para. 10.26.

96 A recent case which recalls this principle is BGH 9.12.1999, BGHZ 143, 246 = NJW 2000, 1259.

97 E.g. *Bork* (fn. 17), 113.

98 Cf. BGH 24.9.1996, NJW 1996, 3341.

99 BGH 9.12.1999, BGHZ 143, 246 = NJW 2000, 1259; *Kirchhof* (fn. 18), § 129 mn. 125; *Hirte* (fn. 28), § 129 mn. 128.

No English provision takes the idea of detriment to creditors to these lengths.[100] The obvious objection to such far-flung grounds for ex post avoidance is the resulting uncertainty for commercial transactions. German law realises this, and for this reason it insists on a subjective, or mental, element on the part of the defendant. This subjective element supplies the moral turpitude which justifies drawing the defendant into the maelstrom of insolvency proceedings.

D. Subjective elements in avoidance grounds

1. *The debtor's bad faith as justification for avoidance*

Subjective elements play an important role in both systems of avoidance law, but they do so in profoundly different ways. As noted at the beginning of this chapter, there is a common point of reference in that English law and German law each provide for a remedy to set aside transactions or legal acts whereby a debtor voluntarily inflicts prejudice on his creditors by frustrating their (contingent) right to satisfy their claims out of his assets. However, given that the two laws operate in different languages, one cannot take it for granted that the terms employed to define the requisite mental element cover exactly the same ground. This leads to yet another linguistic enquiry where language and law are closely intertwined.

As for English law, s. 423 IA requires that the transaction be entered into by the debtor 'for the purpose' of putting assets beyond the reach or otherwise prejudicing the interests of creditors. That has given rise to some uncertainty as to whether the statute should be read as requiring a 'dominant purpose' to prejudice creditors, a test inspired by the case law on the provision in the previous statute, s. 172 of the Law of Property Act 1925. The argument turns on whether an action under s. 423 IA is bound to fail unless the defendant can convince the court that another purpose was equally important to him at the time of the transaction. The latest judicial interpretation from the Court of Appeal in *Inland Revenue Commissioners v Hashmi* is to the effect that no 'dominant purpose' needed to be present in the mind of the debtor, but merely a

[100] Although the 'subsequent events' approach to valuation in the *Brewin Dolphin* decision may have created uncertainty in this respect: see *Rizwaan Jameel Mokal / Look Chan Ho*, 'Consideration, Characterisation, Evaluation: Transactions at an Undervalue after *Phillips v Brewin Dolphin*', [2001] JCLS 359, at 367–369; *Rebecca Parry*, 'Case Commentary' [2001] Insolvency Lawyer 58, at 62.

'substantial purpose' to prejudice creditors, which could co-exist with another purpose.[101] This has made it easier for the claimant to prove the mental element.[102] But doubts have been expressed as to whether the statute actually requires a 'substantial purpose' or why it does not suffice that the debtor acted with a purpose to prejudice creditors, without the need to show any particular kind of purpose.[103]

In Germany, § 3 AnfG and its twin provision in § 133 InsO speak of '***Vorsatz***' ('intent'). This notion seems to go some way beyond that of 'purpose' in s. 423 IA, even in its more liberal construction as 'substantial purpose'. The requisite 'intent' under German law includes what is known as '*bedingter Vorsatz*',[104] the Latin term for which is '*dolus eventualis*'.[105] One introductory book on the German legal system translates '*bedingter Vorsatz*' literally as 'conditional intent',[106] although that may give rise to a misunderstanding that it has the same technical meaning as the term 'conditional intention' in English criminal law 'where a person intends to bring about the element of a crime conditionally upon the occurrence of some event'.[107] This is not what '***bedingter Vorsatz***' or '***dolus eventualis***' means. Rather, it means something akin to 'recklessness',[108] although this is a concept which, in turn, is difficult to translate into German legal terminology. A German lawyer would perhaps explain *dolus eventualis* by comparing it to conscious or advertent negligence. In both situations the perpetrator foresees the harm likely to flow from his act. The crucial difference to advertent negligence lies in the mental attitude towards this risk. A person guilty of *dolus eventualis* not only foresees the risk, but positively accepts the likely consequence of hurting another.[109]

101 [2002] EWCA Civ 981 = [2002] BCC 943 para. 23 (Arden LJ, who gave the leading judgment).

102 *Armour* (fn. 32), para. 3.51.

103 *Andrew Keay*, 'Transactions Defrauding Creditors: the Problem of Purpose under Section 423 of the Insolvency Act' [2003] Conveyancer 272.

104 BGH 27.5.2003, BGHZ 155, 75 = NJW 2003, 3347.

105 *Hirte* (fn. 28), § 133 mn. 12; *Peter de Bra* in *Braun*, InsO[3] § 133 mn. 9.

106 *Heribert Schumann*, 'Criminal Law', in: *Mathias Reimann / Joachim Zekoll* (eds.), Introduction to German Law (2nd edn 2005) 387, at 392.

107 Halsbury's Laws of England, 4th edn, vol. 11, para. 12.

108 For a recent authoritative exploration of 'recklessness' in criminal law, see *R v G* [2003] UKHL 50 = [2004] 1 AC 1034.

109 Cf. *Gerhard Wagner*, 'Distributions to Shareholders and Fraudulent Transfer Law' [2006] EBOR 217, at 220 ('the debtor somehow approved of the detrimental effect'); for brief systematic expositions in English, see *Basil Markesinis / Hannes Unberath*, German

One must, however, bear in mind that these are subtle nuances which should not be overstated so as to create the impression of hard and fast legal rules. The vagueness of the concepts involved means that reliable information about their content can only be gathered from judicial pronouncements. In Germany, the ninth civil senate of the Bundesgerichtshof, which is competent in matters of insolvency law, has recently developed a noticeable tendency to push the limits of *dolus eventualis* in cases brought under § 133 InsO. This case law provides a welcome opportunity to pull together some of the major strings of the foregoing analysis so that readers may get a better picture of the complex doctrinal web of German avoidance law.

Recall the preference-type avoidance grounds in §§ 130, 131 InsO acknowledged by the name of '*Deckungsanfechtung*' ('avoidance of cover') and grouped together with § 132 InsO under the concept of 'special avoidance in insolvency'. The rationale for this class of avoidance grounds is that the *pari passu* or *par conditio creditorum* principle of equal treatment of creditors should kick in as a result of the debtor's illiquidity, i.e. cash flow insolvency, during the short twilight period of up to three months prior to the request for the opening of insolvency proceedings. § 133 InsO, which operates in respect of legal acts committed by a debtor within ten years prior to the onset of formal insolvency proceedings, may cover acts in the nature of a preference as well, but it is based on a different policy consideration. The moral turpitude that renders a payment by a debtor to its creditor vulnerable under § 133 InsO is the intent on the part of the debtor to prejudice those creditors who do not get paid, coupled with the creditor's knowledge of this intent on the part of the debtor. We shall deal with the latter aspect below, whereas the focus here is on the debtor's intent.

At first blush, any such intent would seem to presuppose that the debtor acts with some sort of mala fides. There could be no such intent as long as the debtor genuinely believes that he will be able to pay all creditors in full.[110] However, the ninth civil senate of the Bundesgerichtshof, applying the doctrine of *bedingter Vorsatz* or *dolus eventualis*, takes an increasingly tough line where the debtor is objectively cash flow insolvent at the time of the payment. In one recent decision the court was prepared to 'assume as a rule' that the debtor makes the payment

Law of Torts (4th edn 2002), 83–84 and – from a criminal law perspective, with a glimpse of the difficulties surrounding the concept – *Schumann* (fn. 106.).

110 E.g. BGH 4.12.1997, NJW 1998, 1561.

with the requisite intent to prejudice its creditors if, at the relevant time, he was unable to pay his debts as they fell due (illiquid, *zahlungsunfähig*, as defined in § 17 InsO).[111] Once the debtor was aware of his cash flow insolvency, the requisite intent in the form of *dolus eventualis* could only be negated if there was a 'realistic' prospect, for instance, that a customer order would generate enough cash to pay off all creditors.[112] In a subsequent decision the court held that a debtor who is cash flow insolvent at the time of the payment can only be said not to act with the requisite intent to prejudice the creditors if concrete facts, such as the certain expectation to obtain credit or receive payment at short notice, allow him to reckon with the early overcoming of the cash crisis.[113]

Although the Bundesgerichtshof declares its considerations to be mere '*Beweiszeichen*', that is guidance for the lower courts as to how they should deal with the necessarily subjective evidence in such cases, the effect may be to render the intent-based avoidance ground in § 133 InsO more and more 'objective' on the basis of an argument that the debtor's knowledge of his cash flow insolvency implies his *dolus eventualis* to prejudice all those creditors who do not receive payment. There is a danger that by tinkering with the notion of 'intent' the courts may end up undermining the boundary between § 130 and § 133 InsO,[114] a distinction that reflects fundamental conceptual classifications within German avoidance law and whose practical relevance is evident from a look at the length of the respective twilight periods: three months versus ten years.

On the other hand, an English judge may be persuaded to find the requisite 'purpose' of putting assets beyond the reach or otherwise prejudicing the interests of creditors notwithstanding that the debtor only acted with a view to shielding assets from possible future risks. Thus, in *Re Nurkowski*, Lady Justice Arden contemplates that a solvent person may have the necessary purpose of prejudicing his creditors where he enters into a transaction just in case he becomes unable to pay his debts later, for instance where a person is about to begin a new and

[111] BGH 8.12.2005, NJW 2006, 1348 para. 25: 'Der Bundesgerichtshof geht in der Regel davon aus, dass der Schuldner die angefochtene Rechtshandlung mit Benachteiligungsvorsatz vorgenommen hat, wenn er . . . zahlungsunfähig war.'

[112] Ibid., para. 26.

[113] BGH 24.5.2007, ZIP 2007, 1511 para. 8: 'Ist der Schuldner im Zeitpunkt der Vornahme der Rechtshandlung bereits zahlungsunfähig, handelt er folglich nur dann nicht mit dem Vorsatz, die Gesamtheit der Gläubiger zu benachteiligen, wenn er aufgrund konkreter Umstände – etwa der sicheren Aussicht, demnächst Kredit zu erhalten oder Forderungen realisieren zu können – mit einer baldigen Überwindung der Krise rechnen kann.'

[114] Thus the critique by *Bork* (fn. 3), ch. 5 para. 46 and 48.

risky business venture,[115] although 'there is a line to be drawn between mere hopes and settled aims'.[116]

The difference between English and German law may well be one of how a case is pleaded rather than how a court would decide on a given set of facts, not least because of the considerable latitude that any trial judge necessarily has in evaluating evidence on a person's state of mind. On the facts of the *Hashmi* case, any claimant in a German court would be well advised to plead his case as one of *dolus eventualis*, just to be on the safe side. But eventually the English judge did arrive at a finding of the requisite purpose that was left undisturbed by the Court of Appeal. It is only with this caveat that one should conclude that German law may hold the balance slightly more in favour of creditors than English law.

Additional grounds for transaction avoidance in insolvency under English law

In English law, reliance on a particular state of mind of the debtor goes far beyond s. 423 IA, where a mental element is arguably indispensable in view of its function to redress wrongdoing by a debtor irrespective of insolvency, and extends into the area of 'special avoidance in insolvency' of acts committed at a time when the company was already factually insolvent.

As regards transactions at an undervalue, the basic test of 'no consideration, or . . . a consideration the value of which, in money or money's worth, is significantly less than the value, in money or money's worth, of the consideration provided by the company' in s. 238 (4) IA is purely objective. But the section goes on to provide for a defence in s. 238 (5), which combines objective and subjective criteria. The defence rules out a transaction at an undervalue if

- the company which entered into the transaction did so in good faith and for the purpose of carrying on its business (thus involving a subjective element and an objective element),
- and at the time it did so there were reasonable grounds for believing that the transaction would benefit the company (an entirely objective test).

[115] *Hill v Spread Trustee Co Ltd, Re Nurkowski* [2006] EWCA Civ 542 = [2007] 1 WLR 2404 para. 111 and 125.

[116] Ibid., para. 132.

The provision has been criticised on the systematic ground that a subjective defence based on the good faith of the debtor company rather than the counterparty to the transaction runs counter to the general principle of English law that it is the party seeking relief who must show good faith, and it may also seem objectionable that a company, acting through the office-holder, should be able to invoke its own bad faith to undo the effects of a transaction with another party who acted in good faith.[117]

The courts have had little opportunity so far to shed light on how they intend to deal with this defence. In *Re Barton Manufacturing Co Ltd* the facts were so clear-cut as to leave virtually no doubt about the outcome.[118] The case of *Lord (Liquidator of Rosshill Properties Ltd) v Sinai Securities Ltd*, albeit merely a preliminary ruling on a strike-out application, does provide some guidance, however. There, the judge appears to have stressed the objective requirements of the defence. If the defendant has succeeded in establishing the good faith of those who acted on behalf of the debtor company, the liquidator may still rely on either of two objective tests, i.e. that the transaction was not necessary for the purpose of carrying on the company's business and/or that there were not objectively reasonable grounds for believing that it would benefit the company. Given that in, a case under s. 238 IA, the price paid by the company must ex hypothesi exceed the value to it of what it is to receive, such a course of action could only be justified under subsection (5) if the company had no cheaper means of obtaining the benefit necessary for the purpose of carrying on its business.[119] This ruling certainly reinforces the objective character of the avoidance ground in s. 238 IA.

Arguably the much greater difficulty with subjectivity arises in relation to preferences, where s. 239 (5) IA requires that the company which gave the preference was influenced by a 'desire' to produce the effect of putting the creditor in a better position in the event of a subsequent insolvency. The most authoritative judicial exposition of this provision is still to be found in the first case that came to the courts under the new legislation, *Re MC Bacon Ltd*.[120] Mr Justice Millett (later Lord Millett) found that the wording of the new statute was, if anything, even more subjective than the test of 'dominant intention' hitherto applied by the courts.[121] As the judge put it:

117 Thus the critique by *Goode* (fn. 51), para. 11–40. 118 [1998] BCC 827.
119 [2004] EWHC 1764 (Ch) = [2004] BCC 986 para. 21–22. 120 [1990] BCC 78.
121 See *Walters* (fn. 55), para. 4.12 with further references.

> A man is taken to intend the necessary consequences of his action, so that an intention to grant a security to a creditor necessarily involves an intention to prefer that creditor in the event of insolvency . . . Intention is objective, desire is subjective. A man can choose the lesser of two evils without desiring either.[122]

With regard to the multiplicity of consequences that often flow from a particular act, the judge held:

> A man is not to be taken as *desiring* all the necessary consequences of his action. Some consequences may be of advantage to him and be desired by him; others may not affect him and be matters of indifference to him; while still others may be positively disadvantageous to him and not be desired by him, but be regarded by him as the unavoidable price of obtaining the desired advantages. . . . Under the new regime a transaction will not be set aside as a voidable preference unless the company positively wished to improve the creditor's position in the event of its own insolvent liquidation.[123]

Even allowing, as the judge did, for indirect evidence by which the requisite desire could be inferred from the circumstance of the case, the consensus among commentators is that this saddles the liquidator with a significant evidential burden.[124] Accordingly, s. 239 IA has been heavily criticised as failing to shore up the *pari passu* principle of equal treatment of creditors with sufficient rigour.[125] Rebecca Parry, in particular, has argued that many conventional analyses of preference laws for jurisdictions other than England cannot explain the rationale of s. 239 IA, which limits itself to dealing with favouritism by the debtor.[126] Andrew Keay has gone further and argued for a radical amendment of the law by moving to 'an objective approach, whereby a liquidator is not required to prove any subjective element whatsoever'.[127]

As so often, English lawyers find their points of reference in other common law jurisdictions. With regard to these, notably the laws of

[122] [1990] BCC 78, at 87; critical comment by *Ian Fletcher*, [1991] JBL 71, calling it an 'unconvincing judicial foray into the realm of semantics' (at p. 73).

[123] [1990] BCC 78, at 87–88 (emphasis in the original).

[124] *Parry* (fn. 1), para. 5.99; *Walters* (fn. 55), para. 4.73; *Vanessa Finch*, Corporate Insolvency Law (2002), 393. As for the reversal of the burden of proof where the preference has been given to a connected person see below, text accompanying fn. 160. and 161.

[125] *Goode* (fn. 51), para. 11–69. [126] *Parry* (fn. 7), para. 2.39–2.48.

[127] *Andrew Keay*, 'Preferences in Liquidation Law: A Time for a Change' [1998] CFILR 198.

Australia and the United States, Roy Goode delivers his general critique of English transaction avoidance law:

> The rules as to transactions at an undervalue and preferences are predicated on the assumption that the purpose of the legislation is not to preserve the *pari passu* principle as such but to avoid voluntary transfers which are not made in good faith. Hence the legislation looks not to the fact of the preference or loss of value but to the state of mind of those acting on behalf of the company in entering into the transaction under attack. . . . If there is to be any real prospect of improving the position of unsecured creditors it is necessary to substitute an objective test for a subjective test.[128]

English law and German law compared

Does German law do any better? In particular, does it follow an 'objective' approach, as advocated by Keay and Goode? In Germany, § 3 AnfG and its twin provision for insolvency situations in § 133 InsO are the only grounds of avoidance to contain such an element. And on the basis of the analysis that 'desire' in s. 239 (5) IA is at least as subjective as 'dominant intention', if not more, the wider reach of the German '*Vorsatz*' ('intent'), which includes *dolus eventualis*, should produce a more marked difference here than in relation to 'purpose' in s. 423 IA. Recall, however, that in terms of the relevant twilight periods, § 133 InsO also extends over much of the ground covered by s. 238 IA, which does not require the liquidator to show an element of bad faith on the part of the debtor, although it allows for a defence that builds on the absence of bad faith with the debtor. At this point, further complexity is added to the comparison by § 133 (2) InsO, which – arguably[129] – envisages a similar reversal of the procedural roles between the office-holder and the defendant in relation to the debtor's bad faith for certain types of transaction entered into by the debtor in the last two years prior to the request for the opening of insolvency proceedings, but only where the counterparty to the transaction is a person connected with the debtor. A closer look at this provision will follow in section E, in the context of 'connected persons'. Suffice it to say here that, in relation to connected persons, § 133 (2) InsO operates quite close to an 'objective' avoidance regime.

128 *Goode* (fn. 51), para. 11–142; and already in *Goode*, 'The Secured Creditor and Insolvency Under English Law', RabelsZ 44 (1980), 674 at 709.

129 The issue is a matter of dispute, see fn. 159. and accompanying text.

In addition, legal acts that have occurred in the last three months prior to the request for the opening of insolvency proceedings may be dealt with under §§ 130 to 132 InsO, the provisions on 'special avoidance in insolvency', which step in once the debtor has reached the stage of illiquidity (*Zahlungsunfähigkeit*),[130] but which have no recourse to any element of bad faith on the part of the debtor. The difference is most visible in comparing s. 239 IA with the provisions for the avoidance of cover (*Deckungsanfechtung*) in §§ 130, 131 InsO. As has been mentioned before, the latter two paragraphs are concerned with creditors who have obtained satisfaction or security for their claims against the debtor within the twilight period. Of course, both measures are not per se unlawful or reprehensible, as creditors are always well advised to look to the best possible protection. But German law regards with disfavour any competition between creditors in the immediate run-up to the opening of insolvency proceedings, where the quickest, or the most ruthless, gain a last-ditch advantage over the others. A comparative analysis following the approach advocated by Zweigert and Kötz, notably their 'presumption of similarity' (*praesumptio similitudinis*) according to which nations answer the needs of legal business in the same or a very similar way unless a topic is heavily impressed by moral views or values,[131] would probably explain this as a situation where German law differs from English law on account of an underlying divergence in what is considered to be acceptable behaviour in terms of 'commercial morality'. The obvious difficulty with this kind of 'cultural' approach is whether there really is a consensus within a certain community of people about such moral values. The Cork Committee on the review of insolvency law was divided on this issue, but the majority recommended that genuine pressure by the creditor should continue to afford a defence against avoidance.[132] In view of the many critics of this state of the law,[133] it seems doubtful whether this position can still be seen as representative for any wider sense of moral values in society.

In large measure, therefore, German law follows the line advocated by Andrew Keay and Roy Goode, at least where a transaction takes place between the debtor and a connected person and § 133 (2) InsO applies.

[130] As regards the somewhat abnormal position of § 131 (1) n. 1 and n. 3 InsO see fn. 18 and the references cited there.

[131] *Zweigert/Kötz*, Comparative Law (3rd edn 1998), 40.

[132] Cork Report (fn. 37), para. 1252 and 1256.

[133] In addition to those cited above, fn. 125 to 127: *Finch* (fn. 124), 400; *Mokal*, (fn. 26), 336–337.

Moreover, this 'objective' approach is a general feature of German avoidance law for the most critical period, viz. in relation to events that occur within three months prior to the request for the opening of insolvency proceedings and after the debtor has already become insolvent on a cash flow basis (illiquid, *zahlungsunfähig*). At this last stage, the debtor's bad faith ceases to be of any relevance for the retrospective avoidance of legal acts in the subsequent insolvency proceedings. But this is only one side of the coin with regard to the role of good faith in German avoidance law.

2. *The counterparty's awareness and alternative ways to protect commercial certainty*

The other side is a feature unknown to present-day English avoidance law, where the good faith, or generally the state of mind, of the counterparty is thought to be irrelevant as to the operation of any of the avoidance provisions.[134] In stark contrast, the German statute is replete with mental elements on the part of the counterparty. Crucially, this mental element never takes the form of volition (as with the 'intent' or 'purpose' or 'desire' of the debtor), but is always an element of knowledge. This is relied on in two different ways, which once more draw on the distinction between avoidance of intentionally detrimental acts (§ 133 InsO and § 3 AnfG) and 'special avoidance in insolvency' (§§ 130 to 132 InsO). In the former instance, what is required is the counterparty's knowledge of the intent on the part of the debtor to prejudice his creditors. In cases of 'special avoidance in insolvency' it is knowledge of the debtor's illiquidity (*Zahlungsunfähigkeit*), or alternatively knowledge of a request for the opening of insolvency proceedings already filed against the debtor, or knowledge that the act is detrimental to the insolvency creditors. Either way it is obvious that any mental element on

[134] See *Goode* (fn. 51), para. 11–40 (s. 238), para. 11–96 (s. 239); *Parry* (fn. 1), para. 2.31 (s. 423), para. 4.135 (s. 238), para. 5.116 (s. 239); *Walters* (fn. 55), para. 4.65 (s. 239); *Ian Fletcher*, Voidable Transactions in Bankruptcy, in: *Jacob S. Ziegel* (ed.), Current Developments in International and Corporate Insolvency Law (1992), 297 at 305 (s. 238) and 308 (s. 239); *Gerard McCormack*, 'Swelling Corporate Assets: Changing What Is on the Menu' [2006] JCLS 39, at 46 (s. 239). To avoid confusion, it should be noted that the defence of good faith in s. 241 (2) IA does not extend to a person who acquired property or received a benefit directly from the debtor, i.e. the counterparty in the original transaction. Moreover, note that prior to the Bankruptcy Act 1883 English preference law did rely on the knowledge of the creditor: Cork Report (fn. 37), para. 1243.

the part of the defendant renders it more difficult to bring a successful action than it would be without that element, especially as a particular state of mind is notoriously hard to prove. Returning to Roy Goode's point that more protection of (unsecured) creditors is only to be had for less subjectivity in defining grounds for avoidance, it might appear that German law, through its requirement of a subjective element for the counterparty, takes with one hand what it gives with the other by largely dispensing with subjective elements on the part of the debtor.

Are German commentators therefore equally critical of their law's approach? It would appear that, on the whole, they not only accept it, but see the subjective element as indispensable in order to solve the fundamental dilemma for avoidance law. It must find a balance between the creditors caught up in the insolvency, whose legal entitlements are curtailed by the insufficiency of the debtor's funds and who stand to gain from unravelling earlier transactions of the debtor, and those other parties who, prior to the commencement of insolvency proceedings, had dealings with the debtor from which they have acquired legal entitlements which would be safe from insolvency, were it not for the fact that these transactions fall within the ambit of avoidance.

English lawyers are also aware of the problem. Thus, Rebecca Parry observes that some forms of transaction avoidance 'have the potential to undermine certainty in contractual dealings ... Where a party has acted in innocent reliance on the validity of the transaction, and will struggle to comply with an order made in respect of the transaction, the undesirable consequence of hardship will be caused.'[135]

German lawyers would, it is submitted, go further than that and see it not only as a problem of hardship in particular cases, but as a problem of fairness in all cases where the party has acted in justified reliance on the validity of the legal act. Behind this noble sounding cause stands a strong sense of policy, namely that '***Verkehrsschutz***' (the German term conveying the idea of 'commercial certainty') should be upheld in as many cases as possible, by ensuring that a party who has relied on the validity of the legal act cannot be subject to its avoidance unless specific circumstances in its own sphere make the outcome objectionable. This explains the frequent recourse to the knowledge of the counterparty, which appears in §§ 130, 131 (1) n. 3, 132 and 133 InsO.

[135] *Parry* (fn. 1), para. 2.19.

Manifest detriment: significant undervalue and gratuitous disposition

Yet there are other grounds for avoidance, viz. § 131 (1) n. 1 and n. 2 and § 134 InsO, which do not rely on such a subjective element, thus suggesting that they are based on an alternative principle to balance the interests of creditors against those of counterparties to antecedent legal acts of the debtor. This alternative principle looks to the nature of the act and allows for it to be challenged where, on the face of it, there was a suspicious transaction, the counterparty to which deserves no protection. Mimicking English lawyers' parlance, one might call this a 'constructive awareness' approach, as opposed to actual awareness or knowledge. As regards English law, Rebecca Parry suggests that the limitation in s. 423 to transactions at a significant undervalue serves this purpose.[136] The same idea had earlier been expressed by Dan Prentice in relation to s. 238 IA.[137] German law, however, takes a stricter line. Not every transaction at an undervalue, in the sense of a significant imbalance in a bargain, will suffice to justify upsetting the transaction, but only a gratuitous disposition, where the recipient gives nothing in exchange and cannot reasonably expect to prevail over the donor's creditors in a possible future insolvency. This is the rationale behind § 134 InsO (and behind the parallel provision in § 4 AnfG).

Manifest detriment: congruent versus incongruent cover

The only other class of legal act which is so manifestly suspicious as to justify an objective approach is that of a preference termed 'incongruent cover' (*inkongruente Deckung*) in § 131 InsO, through which German law targets a creditor receiving security or satisfaction to which he is not entitled or not entitled in the manner or at the time, and which is therefore not a strictly commercial way of dealing.

We have already encountered § 131 InsO together with its twin provision in § 130 InsO as the two heads of avoidance that German lawyers call '*Deckungsanfechtung*' ('avoidance of cover').[138] The point here is to explore the difference between the two paragraphs, entitled somewhat obscurely 'congruent cover' (***kongruente Deckung***) in § 130 and 'incongruent cover' (***inkongruente Deckung***) in § 131 InsO. The

[136] Ibid., para. 2.32.

[137] *D. D. Prentice*, 'The Effect of Insolvency on Pre-Liquidation Transactions', in: *B. G. Pettet* (ed.), Company Law in Change (1987), 69 at 78.

[138] Above C.2 and D.1.

substance of the distinction is easy to grasp by looking at the opening words in of each of the provisions. In § 130 (1) these words read:

> Voidability attaches to a legal act which has accorded to, or made possible for, an insolvency creditor any security or satisfaction . . .

Crucially, § 131 (1) adds the following words marked in italics:

> Voidability attaches to a legal act which has accorded to, or made possible for, an insolvency creditor any security or satisfaction *to which he was not entitled or not entitled in the manner or at the time* . . .

The two provisions operate alongside each other and are not mutually exclusive.[139] § 130 InsO is the more general provision. It includes the situation where the creditor gets no more than is actually due to him at the time – and that may become subject to ex post avoidance, if (but only if) the creditor knew, at the time when he obtained the security or the satisfaction, that the debtor was already factually insolvent on a cash flow basis (illiquid, *zahlungsunfähig*). That knowledge makes it objectionable for him to retain the security or to remain a satisfied ex-creditor and watch the game from the sidelines. Instead, the law requires him to deliver up the security or the money, respectively, to the office-holder and to rejoin the queue of creditors in the same position which he had occupied prior to receiving the voidable security or satisfaction.[140]

In § 131 InsO the law captures a course of action by the creditor which appears suspicious on its face, because the creditor receives security or satisfaction over and above his original deal with the debtor. If that happens in the last month prior to the request for the opening of insolvency proceedings, the law considers the creditor not worthy of any protection at all – just like the recipient of a gift.[141] His security or satisfaction will be taken away from him even where, at the time of the act, the debtor was still solvent. This is the harsh rule laid down in

[139] *Hirte* (fn. 28), § 130 mn. 5; *Hans-Kirchhof* (fn. 18), § 131 mn. 4; *Schoppmeyer* (fn. 18), ch. 8 para. 9.

[140] Remember the general requirement for all avoidance grounds that detriment to other creditors has been caused (§ 129 InsO, see above). No such detriment will be caused, and hence no avoidance is possible, where, at the time of the satisfaction, the creditor holds a valid security right which would give him priority in the case of an insolvent liquidation and whose value covers his claim (or so much of it as he receives in satisfaction of it): *Hirte* (fn. 28), § 130 mn. 28. For the like result under English law see *Parry* (fn. 1), para. 5.45 to 5.47.

[141] Cf. *Wolfram Henckel*, 'Die Gläubigeranfechtung – ein taugliches Mittel zur Beseitigung von Verkürzungen der Konkursmasse?', ZIP 1982, 391 at 396.

§ 131 (1) n. 1 InsO. It is a risk which creditors cannot escape under German law: to accept earlier repayment or additional security without advancing fresh credit and lose it again within a month because the debtor unexpectedly becomes caught up in insolvency proceedings. § 131 (1) n. 2 InsO extends this rule to a period of up to three months prior to a request for the opening of insolvency proceedings where the debtor was, at the time of the act, insolvent on a cash flow basis (illiquid, *zahlungsunfähig*); but unlike in § 130 InsO the avoidance takes place irrespective of any knowledge on the part of the creditor. It is the incongruence of the security or satisfaction as such that makes it objectionable if, with hindsight, the debtor was at the time unable to satisfy all his creditors in full.[142]

A German take on English law

Would the standard analysis of German avoidance law be able to explain the English provisions, too? Arguably, it would for three out of four provisions, which conform to the 'constructive awareness' approach that the transaction can be set aside without a mental element for the counterparty on the basis that it was manifestly harmful to the interests of the debtor's creditors. In the case of a transaction at an undervalue, in s. 238 IA as in s. 423 IA, the nature of the act susceptible to avoidance is defined in such terms as to make it possible for the counterparty to discern objectively that the debtor parts with more than he receives. The same can be said of s. 245 IA, where the debtor company creates a security right in favour of an existing creditor without receiving adequate new value. In some ways, the section mirrors the German concept of incongruent cover, but without achieving the comprehensive coverage of the latter.

However, the one remaining ground for the avoidance of a preference under s. 239 IA would appear to be problematic in the light of the German model.[143] There, the nature of the act is defined in extremely wide terms and may include wholly innocent steps by a creditor, such as receiving payment when it is due as a result of which the creditor is in a better position than if the company had delayed the payment and

[142] For the sake of completeness mention must be made of § 131 (1) n. 3 InsO, which is based on the defendant's knowledge that the impugned act was detrimental to the other creditors; see fn. 18.

[143] See the harsh critique by *Kamlah* (fn. 21), 161–162, who refers to s. 239 IA as a 'legislative blunder' ('*legislativer Fehlgriff*').

subsequently gone into insolvent liquidation. True, s. 239 IA requires a highly subjective element on the part of the debtor company ('desire'). But that, German lawyers would argue, does not solve the problem because the reproachable conduct of the debtor cannot be a criterion by which to judge whether a creditor who merely took what was due to him should be exposed to an avoidance action. To this, English lawyers would probably give the pragmatic reply that in most practical cases where the debtor has such a desire, the creditor will hardly be unaware of it, because the desire will have a motive, usually a special relationship between the debtor and the creditor. But then, the German argument would continue, why not make this involvement a formal legal test, possibly with the burden of proof incumbent on the creditor that it was not in any way privy to the preferential treatment? We have it on the authority of Helmut Koziol and Franz Bydlinski, two Austrian law professors, that a (hypothetical) avoidance rule which does not require a subjective element on the part of the counterparty – like the actual rule in s. 239 IA – must, in their view, be rejected as unsatisfactory on grounds of principle.[144] But English lawyers do not need to venture out to the Continent for this insight because it has been voiced in very similar terms by Dan Prentice:

> The difficulty with [s. 239 IA] is that although the wrong-doing is attributed to the debtor company, recovery of the preference is made against the preferred creditor. . . . If the rationale for preference law is to preclude debtor favouritism, some protection needs to be afforded to the innocent creditor, that is, a creditor who receives payment but is ignorant of the company's pending insolvency.[145]

His conclusion is a call for a reform of the law:

> One solution would be to abandon any requirement of debtor intent to prefer and make the act of payment at least *prima facie* improper. Creditors who are ignorant of the fact that the company was unable to pay its debts at the time payment was made should have a defence to any action seeking recovery of the preference. Such a rule would be more in keeping with the collective nature of insolvency law.[146]

It would also bring English law somewhat closer to the thoroughly principled German approach to avoidance, which adds a further layer of

[144] *Helmut Koziol*, Grundlagen und Streitfragen der Gläubigeranfechtung (1991), 23–24; *Franz Bydlinski*, System und Prinzipien des Privatrechts (1996), 309–311.

[145] *Prentice* (fn. 137), 83–84. [146] Ibid., 85 (italics in the original).

sophistication by virtue of its distinction between congruent and incongruent cover.

From principle to pragmatism

Notwithstanding the fundamental importance of the principle that only an element of awareness justifies taking pre-insolvency entitlements from a defendant, the principle allows for a certain leeway in its implementation. As part of the work programme for what would eventually become the Insolvency Code 1994, avoidance remedies were designated for a thorough overhaul, because it was felt that the then-existing law placed too many obstacles in the way of office-holders pursuing claims.[147] As a result mechanisms were built into the law which mitigate the effects of its subjectivity, while leaving intact the principled approach that there needs to be some element of awareness to supply the moral turpitude tainting the counterparty to the vulnerable act.

One way in which the reform has aided the office-holder is by slightly broadening the relevant knowledge on the part of the defendant. In § 133 (1) InsO, the subjective avoidance ground which requires that the counterparty had knowledge of the debtor's intent to prejudice his creditors, this knowledge is presumed if the counterparty knew that the debtor's illiquidity was threatening and that the act was detrimental to the creditors.[148] Under the regime of 'special avoidance in insolvency', knowledge of the debtor's illiquidity or of the detriment of a certain act to the other creditors is deemed to be established by 'knowledge of circumstances which compellingly bespeak' the illiquidity or the detriment, respectively (*Kenntnis von Umständen, die zwingend darauf schließen lassen*): § 130 (2), § 131 (2) first sentence, § 132 (3) InsO. The point here is that a creditor will often lack a complete picture of the debtor's financial situation, especially a supplier, who will hardly be informed about the debtor's current lines of credit or ongoing negotiations with banks. But even where the creditor is only aware of the debtor's conduct in dealing with him, this may hold sufficient clues so as to leave little doubt that a state of illiquidity exists.

[147] *Wolfram Henckel*, (fn. 141), 391; Erster Bericht der Kommission für Insolvenzrecht (1985) 399–443; *Christoph G. Paulus / Wolfgang Schröder*, 'Über die Verschärfungen des Rechts der Insolvenzanfechtung', WM 1999, 253.

[148] On a recent application of this presumption and its rebuttal see BGH 24.5.2007, ZIP 2007, 1511.

One colourful illustration is provided by a case where the creditor had demanded payment of a substantial sum (over DM 900,000, roughly €450,000) due to him. When payment was not forthcoming, the creditor accompanied the debtor to visit one of the debtor's main customers in order to collect money there and, after this had failed to produce sufficient funds, the creditor took security in the form of an assignment of receivables against 31 customers of the debtor.[149] Certainly a more common type of situation is that of a newly incorporated company failing to pay over to the tax office moneys deducted from employees' pay more or less from the first day of its business life. Tax officials were fully aware of the mounting arrears, and within a few months they commenced legal action to enforce payments. The court found their knowledge sufficient to warrant an inference of illiquidity.[150] Finally, another not uncommon situation is that of a creditor receiving payment as a result of his filing a request for the opening of insolvency proceedings, a request which is usually withdrawn after the payment. In such a case the creditor, who is convinced of the debtor's state of insolvency at the time of his request,[151] cannot rely on his belief that he took the payment made to him as a sign that the debtor's solvency had been comprehensively restored, without adducing proof of facts which objectively warranted such an inference.[152]

A second mechanism which may help the office-holder to overcome the difficulties resulting from the requirement of a mental element on the part of the counterparty leads straight to a discussion of the concept of 'connected persons'.

E. Connected persons

In both jurisdictions the concept of 'connected persons' has received a statutory definition. In England it consists of two interlocking provisions, ss. 249 and 435 IA. The German statute gives a definition to the term '*nahestehende Personen*' (which translates as 'connected persons') in § 138 InsO. These provisions are very technical, and although they

[149] BGH 25.9.1997, NJW 1998, 607. [150] BGH 9.1.2003, ZIP 2003, 410.

[151] English readers should note that, in the absence of provisions akin to s. 123 (1) (a) and (b) IA, a request for the opening of insolvency proceedings presented in a German court must necessarily contain an allegation that the debtor is factually insolvent at the time of the request.

[152] BGH 25.10.2001, BGHZ 149, 100 = NJW 2002, 512; BGH 20.11.2001, BGHZ 149, 178 = NJW 2002, 515.

differ on several points of substance, little would be gained for the purpose of this book from an in-depth analysis of them. Suffice it to remind readers that companies within a group will often be (legal) persons connected with each other according to the relevant definition. Much more rewarding is a look at the different roles that these concepts play in the two jurisdictions, which mirror the different approaches to avoidance set out in this chapter.

1. Germany

The widespread use of subjective elements on the part of the counterparty under German law raises the issue of proof. As a rule, if the subjective element constitutes a substantive element of the cause of action, the burden of proof lies with the claimant.[153] However, if the defendant is connected to the debtor within the statutory definition of 'connected persons' in § 138 InsO, the burden of proof shifts to the defendant, who must show that he did not know of the debtor's particular intent or of the debtor's illiquidity (*Zahlungsunfähigkeit*) or the detriment to the creditors, whichever is relevant: § 130 (3), § 131 (2) second sentence, § 132 (3) InsO. This does not render the liability of the defendant strict. But certainly in the case of an unusual transaction, e.g. a sale of a major asset which would not normally occur in the ordinary course of business, it will be difficult for the defendant to come up with a convincing explanation for entering into the transaction with the debtor while allegedly being ignorant of the latter's intent and/or financial precariousness. This reversal of the burden of proof is one of two uses to which German law puts the concept of connected persons.

The other use relates to the subjective element on the part of the debtor under § 133 InsO. At this point the analysis allows us to pull together many strings of German avoidance law that we have encountered so far. Sub-paragraph (1) of § 133 InsO contains the far-reaching avoidance ground for legal acts committed by the debtor in the last ten years prior to the request for the opening of insolvency proceedings with intent to prejudice its creditors, which has been discussed at several points before (B.1, D.1 and D.2). Sub-paragraph (2) builds on this and should be understood as a modification of sub-paragraph (1) in respect of a certain class of legal act, not as a separate head of avoidance. In order to qualify for § 133 (2) InsO, a legal act must satisfy all of the following:

[153] Cf. BGH 14.12.1983, BGHZ 89, 189 = NJW 1984, 1557; BGH 20.6.2002, ZIP 2002, 1408.

- a contract for a valuable consideration (*entgeltlicher Vertrag*),
- concluded between the debtor and a connected person,
- in the last two years prior to the request for the opening of insolvency proceedings and
- causing a direct detriment (*unmittelbarer Nachteil*) to the creditors.

To begin with, the notion of a 'contract for valuable consideration' (*entgeltlicher Vertrag*) requires a brief explanation, as lawyers from a common law system might assume that it is part of the very nature of a contract to be supported by consideration. This is not so under German law, where the essence of ***Vertrag*** is the meeting of minds, or to be precise: a legal transaction (*Rechtsgeschäft*) that consists of two corresponding declarations of intention (*übereinstimmende Willenserklärungen*).[154] A gratuitous performance such as a gift may be the subject matter of a *Vertrag*.[155] However, if there is a total lack of consideration, the office-holder does not need to rely on § 133 (2) InsO, but can bring an action under the purely objective avoidance ground for gratuitous dispositions in § 134 InsO.

§ 133 (2) InsO covers the situation where there is some consideration, but the value of the consideration received by the debtor is less than the value of the consideration provided by the debtor so that the exchange results in a direct detriment to the creditors (C.4.). The analogy with s. 238 IA is obvious. Earlier, § 132 InsO has been discussed as the closest German equivalent to s. 238 IA (C.3). But this holds true only where the legal transaction occurs within the short twilight period of no more than three months prior to the request for the opening of insolvency proceedings that applies to § 132 InsO as one of the grounds for 'special avoidance in insolvency' (B.2, B.3). § 133 (2) InsO assumes the role of the equivalent to s. 238 IA for a much more extended twilight period of two years, provided the contract is entered into between the debtor and a connected person.

As seen, the concept of direct detriment will always cover what English lawyers know as a transaction at an undervalue, but it may just as well cover a preference (C.2). The trickier question is whether every form of a preference comes within the notion of *Vertrag*, because the mere fulfilment of an obligation would not normally be considered a contract

[154] *Basil Markesinis/Hannes Unberath/Angus Johnston*, German Law of Contract (2006) 25.

[155] Ibid., 148–149.

under the Civil Code.[156] However, there is case law that § 133 (2) InsO should be given a wide purposive interpretation in this respect so that even the payment of a debt is considered an *entgeltlicher Vertrag.*[157] The direct detriment then results from the violation of the principle of *pari passu* or *par conditio creditorum*, which puts all those creditors whose claims against the debtor remain unsatisfied at a disadvantage. That leaves the debtor's intent to prejudice the creditors (D.1) as the only remaining element that needs to be satisfied for § 133 InsO to operate.

Given that the conditions for avoidance under § 133 (2) InsO are narrower than under § 133 (1) InsO, there must be some advantage to be gained by the office-holder in relying on the second sub-paragraph. This advantage finds a subtle expression in the last sentence of § 133 (2) InsO:

> The avoidance is precluded if . . . at the time of concluding the contract, the other party did not know of the debtor's intent to prejudice the creditors.

By necessary inference this presupposes that such intent exists on the part of the debtor – at this point it becomes clear why § 133 (2) InsO is merely a modification of § 133 (1) InsO, and not a separate ground for avoidance.[158] § 133 (2) InsO only reverses the burden of proof as regards the subjective element. But given the notorious difficulties of proving a state of mind, that is anything but trivial in practice. There is, however, a dispute in the literature as to how far that reversal extends. The better view is that the onus of proof is distributed as follows:

- The office-holder must prove no more than the existence of a contract for valuable consideration, the direct detriment caused to the creditors, and the participation of the defendant as the counterparty.
- It is then upon the defendant to exonerate himself, and he can do this in one of three ways: (i) by showing that the contract was not entered into in the last two years prior to the request for the opening of insolvency proceedings; (ii) that no intent of the debtor to prejudice

[156] The issue is not free from doubt, and various theories have been advanced seeking to answer the question whether the fulfilment of an obligation constitutes a legal transaction; see *Joachim Wenzel* in Münchener Kommentar BGB[5] § 362 mn. 5 ff.

[157] RG 11.3.1902, RGZ 51, 76; BGH 15.2.1990, NJW 1990, 2687; *Kirchhof* (fn. 18), § 133 mn. 40; *Hirte* (fn. 28), § 133 mn. 37.

[158] *Hirte* (fn. 28), § 133 mn. 33; *Bork* (fn. 3), ch. 5, para. 57.

its creditors existed; or (iii) accepting its existence, that the defendant, or the connected person who was the counterparty to the contract, did not know of the debtor's intent.[159]

2. *England*

Under English law, a similar effect is achieved by s. 239 (6) IA, which reads:

> A company which has given a preference to a person connected with the company (otherwise than by reason only of being its employee) at the time the preference was given is presumed, unless the contrary is shown, to have been influenced in deciding to give it by such a desire as is mentioned in subsection (5).

Although this presumption does not by any means guarantee success for the office-holder, and has been successfully rebutted in some cases,[160] in the vast majority of reported cases against connected persons defendants have been unable to rebut it successfully.[161]

Apart from this sole instance of reversing the onus with regard to a mental element on the part of the debtor company, English law relies on its concept of 'connected persons' for two entirely different purposes. Both are linked to the time frame for the operation of the avoidance provisions in ss. 238, 239 and 245 IA, but are implemented throughout these provisions in a somewhat inconsistent manner.

[159] This view is supported by case law: RG 11.3.1902, RGZ 51, 76; BGH 22.12.1971, BGHZ 58, 20 = NJW 1972, 495; BGH 18.5.2000, ZIP 2000, 1550; it is also supported by the majority of writers: *Kirchhof* (fn. 18), § 133 mn. 45; *Bork* (fn. 3), ch. 5, para. 57–59; *Johann Killinger*, Insolvenzanfechtung gegen Insider (1991), 38–41; *Kristof Biehl*, Insider im Insolvenzverfahren (2000), para. 254; but contrast *Hirte* (fn. 28), § 133 mn. 41 and *Christoph Paulus*, EWiR 2000, 947 at 948 (case comment), who argue that § 133 (2) InsO requires positive evidence, to be provided by the office-holder, that the debtor actually had the intent to prejudice the creditors.

[160] *Re Beacon Leisure Ltd* [1991] BCC 213; *Re Fairway Magazines Ltd* [1992] BCC 924.

[161] *Re DKG Contractors* [1990] BCC 903; *Weisgard v Pilkington* [1995] BCC 1108; *Wills v Corfe Joinery Ltd* [1997] BCC 511; *Re Exchange Travel (Holdings) Ltd (No. 4), Katz v McNally* [1999] BCC 291 (CA), affirming *Re Exchange Travel (Holdings) Ltd (No. 3)* [1996] BCC 933 on the substantive point; *Re Brian D. Pierson (Contractors) Ltd* [1999] BCC 26; *Re Shapland Inc, Mills v Edict Ltd* [2000] BCC 106; *Re Conegrade Ltd, Saxton v Clarke* [2002] EWHC 2411 (Ch) = [2003] BPIR 358; *Re Cityspan Ltd, Brown v Clark* [2007] EWHC 751 (Ch) = [2008] BCC 60; in *Re MDA Investment Management Ltd, Whalley v Doney* [2003] EWHC 2277 (Ch) = [2005] BCC 783 the defendant director was able to rebut the presumption for some, though not all of the impugned payments.

First, s. 240 (1) IA extends the absolute twilight period for the application of s. 239 IA from six months for the preferential treatment of an unconnected person to two years for a person connected with the company (otherwise than by reason only of being its employee). In contrast, the absolute twilight period for transactions at an undervalue under s. 238 IA is always two years, irrespective of whether the transaction is with a connected person or not.

Under s. 240 (2) IA, both grounds for transaction avoidance require, in addition, that the company is unable to pay its debts at the time of the transaction, or become so as a consequence of it.[162] By virtue of a rider towards the end of s. 240 (2) IA, the requisite state of factual insolvency is presumed in relation to any transaction at an undervalue which is entered into by a company with a person who is connected with the company (otherwise than by reason only of being its employee). As the act susceptible to avoidance under s. 238 IA is defined in the same terms as under s. 423 IA, the latter section no longer has any role to play as regards transactions with connected persons, save for the case where the defendant can successfully rebut the presumption of inability to pay debts.[163] German law only applies a presumption against connected persons that they knew of the debtor's illiquidity (where this is relevant; D.2), but proof of the existence of that factual insolvency always rests with the office-holder. In English law, the importance of this presumption should be seen in the light of the long twilight period of two years, which may cause difficulties when it comes to assessing the debtor's financial situation at the time of the transaction years after the event. The rule may produce the salutary side effect that, where the history of the company's demise is difficult to chart due to a lack of proper documentation, the presumption may well work against those who could have ensured that better records were kept. Interestingly, however, no such presumption aids the office-holder in pursuing a preference claim against a connected person under s. 239 IA.[164]

Finally, the treatment of connected persons in s. 245 IA combines both aspects. Its subsection (3) determines the time at which a floating charge must have been created in order to come within the ambit of the section as (a) within two years prior to formal insolvency in the case of a charge created in favour of a person connected with the company, and (b) within twelve months in the case of a charge created in favour

[162] As for the meaning of this term see above, B.3.

[163] See already fn. 33 and accompanying text.

[164] But see *Walters* (fn. 55), para. 4.90.

of any other person. Subsection (4) goes on to say that if the person in favour of whom the charge is created is not connected with the company, that time is not a relevant time unless the company was unable to pay its debts or became unable to do so in consequence of the transaction under which the charge is created. *E contrario*, no requirement of factual insolvency applies if a floating charge is created in favour of a connected person, which operates just as if the inability to pay debts were irrebuttably presumed (whereas this is rebuttably presumed for transactions at an undervalue).

F. Summary and outlook

Notwithstanding the different uses to which German and English law put the concept of 'connected persons', the analysis has made it clear that both jurisdictions recognise the need to have stricter rules for transactions or legal acts between a debtor company and persons connected to it. Returning to the functional problems identified in the introductory chapter as the starting point for the analysis in this book,[165] one may see this as a recognition, in both legal systems, that the company's controllers do not deal with the company at arm's length and are likely to exercise their influence over the company to their own advantage,[166] and that the law can combat this abuse of limited liability through avoidance remedies.

In a functional perspective it is tempting to conceptualise avoidance remedies in the binary logic of transactions at an undervalue and preferences as two categories that mirror two specific risks to creditors. Transactions at an undervalue shift value from the debtor company to third parties, notably to persons exercising a controlling influence over the company, thus reducing the pool of assets for all creditors alike. Preferences, on the other hand, come into play if the same persons, in their capacity as creditors of the company, cause the debtor company to put them in a more favourable position than other creditors before insolvency strikes. The distinction is deeply engrained in the minds of English lawyers. Moreover, it is possible to identify traces of these two functions or aims of avoidance remedies in German law as well,[167] which is precisely the result one would expect to find in accordance with the *praesumptio similitudinis* postulated by Zweigert and Kötz.[168] But

[165] Chapter 1 B.2. [166] Cork Report (fn. 37), para. 1258.
[167] *Kamlah* (fn. 21), 229. [168] Chapter 1 B.3.

function is not all that matters in the legal discourse. Many of the current issues arise from the manner in which the law is laid out in the statute, and here the two laws differ widely. Whereas the distinction between transactions at an undervalue and preferences weighs heavily on the structure of English avoidance law, German law attaches much less importance to it and instead relies on the all-encompassing notion of 'detriment to creditors' as the central structural element.

One potential problem that follows on the heels of the categorical distinction between transactions at an undervalue and preferences is the possibility that creditors suffer harm from a transaction that cannot be placed easily within either of the two categories. This has come to light in the cases on agricultural tenancies,[169] and the solutions found in these particular circumstances have failed to get to the root of the problem, which, incidentally, is exacerbated by the narrow understanding of the term 'transaction'.[170]

The reverse problem is that of a potential overlap between the two categories, which has been exposed mainly in relation to the question of whether the granting of a security right may be a transaction at an undervalue.[171] That this is a problem is not, however, the inevitable consequence of the binary structure of transactions at an undervalue and preferences. Instead, it follows from the divergence in the subjective requirements of s. 238 and s. 239 IA. The use of these subjective, or mental, elements appears more as the result of discrete policy choices by the legislator than as part of a larger plan. On the one hand, a preference (s. 239 IA) is only susceptible to avoidance if there has been a 'desire' of the debtor company to prefer one creditor over the other creditors, which makes it difficult for the office-holder to pursue a claim under the section unless he can invoke the presumption that the company has been influenced by such a desire in giving a preference to a person connected to the company. On the other hand, avoidance of a transaction at an undervalue (s. 238 IA) does not require the office-holder to provide evidence regarding any mental element on the part either of the debtor company or the counterparty to the transaction. The empirical study by David Milman and Rebecca Parry concludes that, after initial

169 *Agricultural Mortgage Corporation Plc v Woodward* [1994] BCC 688; *National Westminster Bank v Jones* [2001] 1 BCLC 98 (ChD), affirmed [2001] EWCA Civ 1541 = [2002] 1 BCLC 55 (CA).

170 *Knights (Liquidator of Taylor Sinclair (Capital) Limited) v Seymour Pierce Ellis Ltd, Re Taylor Sinclair (Capital) Ltd* [2001] 2 BCLC 176.

171 *Re MC Bacon* [1990] BCC 78.

'teething difficulties', the provision appears to have worked relatively well in practice.[172]

In comparison it is, I think, fair to say that German law presents the more principled and coherent approach to the avoidance of pre-insolvency acts that are detrimental to creditors. English law conveys the image of simply a compilation of discrete rules, whose correlation is defined more by how they differ than by what they share. The multitude of grounds for avoidance in German law is built on the strong foundation of a unitary idea. It balances the interests of creditors and the need for commercial certainty through the combination of a wide and seamless concept of detriment to creditors and the recourse to adverse knowledge of the counterparty, with clearly defined exceptions where the act is suspicious on its face as being either gratuitous or an incongruent cover. The manifold differentiations are all recognisable as variations of this common theme, and their raison d'être is 'the legislative tribute to a more balanced justice'.[173] Incidentally, the consistent structure of §§ 130 to 134 InsO is in part due to the continuing influence of legal scholarship on German legislation. The law was moulded into its present form through over a century of judicial application and academic comment, from previous provisions going back to 1877,[174] which were less neatly set out than the new ones. Not all lights have gone out in the German legal discourse.[175]

Neither the academic input nor the strong sense of principle prevents German law from adopting pragmatic solutions, all the more so when it comes to transactions between the debtor and connected persons, as is evident from § 133 (2) InsO, in particular. Moreover, the concurrent application of several grounds of avoidance also has a very practical

[172] *Milman / Parry* (fn. 52), 12. The analysis so far has disregarded what has turned out to be the single biggest obstacle to bringing successful office-holder actions in court. It is a problem of litigation funding that is peculiar to English law, but is not linked to the different systematic approaches to transaction avoidance studied in this chapter. For a concise account of the latest developments from the point of view of transaction avoidance, see *Gerard McCormack*, 'Swelling Corporate Assets: Changing What Is on the Menu' [2006] JCLS 39, at 55–65. The issue will be explored in detail in the context of wrongful trading: chapter 5 C.2.

[173] *Fritz Baur / Rolf Stürner*, Zwangsvollstreckungs-, Konkurs- und Vergleichsrecht (12th edn 1990), para. 4.32 ('ausgewogenere Gerechtigkeit [verlangt] ihren legislatorischen Tribut').

[174] Chapter 1 A.3 (at fn. 47).

[175] See *Stefan Vogenauer*, 'An Empire of Light? Learning and Lawmaking in the History of German Law' [2005] CLJ 481, at 500.

effect. The office-holder can bring proceedings on the basis of more than one ground, and then concentrate his claim on whichever turns out to be easier to prove. Where the office-holder finds it more difficult to prove the requirements of §§ 130 to 132 InsO, it will always be open to him to pursue an action under § 133 InsO, notwithstanding that the act complained of occurred during the last three months prior to the request for the opening of insolvency proceedings.

But then, if German lawyers have this elegantly designed edifice of avoidance law at their disposal, why is it that they seem not to place full reliance on it to remedy abuses of limited liability? The reason may well lie in the residual subjective aspects of their system. Could German law go further, and yet remain faithful to its principled approach, by broadening the idea inherent in § 131 InsO (incongruent cover) and § 134 InsO (gratuitous dispositions), where no mental element is required at all, because the act is potentially detrimental on its face, so that the counterparty cannot rely on its validity in any future insolvency irrespective of its knowledge? Might not German law develop this into a rule that catches not just gratuitous dispositions, but also unequal bargains between the debtor company and connected persons? Arguably it could, but the reason why German lawyers seem to have felt no particular urge to develop such a rule within the field of avoidance law is that they have always had an alternative instrument at their disposal which produces precisely this effect. This is where capital maintenance enters the stage.

3

Capital maintenance and unlawful distributions

A. Introduction

Capital maintenance and the wider concept of legal capital, of which capital maintenance is part, have been among the most controversial topics in European company law in recent years. From its epicentre in the United Kingdom, the policy debate developed simultaneously on two fronts. While the UK Company Law Review raised questions about a number of technical points in the existing law,[1] a series of academic contributions doubted the relevance of legal capital rules for the protection of creditors at a fundamental level.[2] The White Paper from the DTI on 'Company Law Reform' stated with confidence: 'Capital maintenance is largely irrelevant to the vast majority of private companies and their creditors.'[3] Following the recommendations by the Company Law Review,[4] the Companies Act 2006 introduced a significant relaxation for private companies as regards the reduction of its share capital (below, B.3) and virtually abolished the prohibition on granting financial assistance for the acquisition of a private company's own shares, a field of regulation adjacent to capital maintenance. However, a more radical departure from the existing law was thwarted by the wish to preserve coherence within the Companies Act, because the law for public

[1] 'The Strategic Framework' (February 1999) ch. 5.4. (p. 81–91); 'Company Formation & Capital Maintenance' (October 1999) ch. 3; 'Capital Maintenance: Other Issues' (June 2000).

[2] *Brian Cheffins*, Company Law (1997), 531–537; *John Armour*, 'Share Capital and Creditor Protection: Efficient Rules for a Modern Company Law' (2000) 63 MLR 355; *Luca Enriques / Jonathan R. Macey*, 'Creditors Versus Capital Formation: The Case Against the European Legal Capital Rules', 86 Cornell Law Review 1165 (2001). In Germany, a critical examination of the interrelationship between legal capital and corporate finance took place at a symposium organised by *Friedrich Kübler* in Frankfurt in July 1997; the contributions by *Paul Davies* (UK), *Peter Nobel* (Switzerland), *Angel Rojo* (Spain), *Marco Saverio Spolidoro* (Italy), *Marcus Lutter* (Germany) and others are published in AG 1998, issue 8, p. 345–395.

[3] Cm. 6456 (March 2005), p. 41.

[4] 'Completing the Structure' (November 2000), ch. 7; Final Report (June 2001), ch. 10.

companies remains wedded to the concept of legal capital by virtue of the Second Company Law Directive.[5]

Against this backdrop it was natural that the UK – along with a few other Member States – would push for fundamental change at EU level. The Government's official position to this effect[6] was supported by an impressive study that came to be known after its lead author as the 'Rickford Report'.[7] Initially, these efforts, accompanied by an increasing amount of scholarly criticism of legal capital rules flowing from the pens of British writers,[8] met with some success in Brussels. In May 2003 the European Commission published an action plan for 'Modernising Company Law and Enhancing Corporate Governance in the European Union',[9] which announced a simplification of the Second Directive as a short term priority and a study into the feasibility of an alternative to the capital maintenance regime in the medium term. Subsequently, a minor review of the Second Directive with a modest amount of deregulation was enacted in 2006.[10] But the advances against the Second Directive prompted resistance, notably from the German side, where it was masterminded by Marcus Lutter.[11] Finally, in February 2008, the European Commission published the long-awaited feasibility study on alternatives to the capital maintenance regime, carried out by KPMG Germany,[12]

[5] Second Council Directive of 13 December 1976 on coordination of safeguards which, for the protection of the interests of members and others, are required by Member States of companies within the meaning of the second paragraph of Article 58 of the Treaty, in respect of the formation of public limited liability companies and the maintenance and alteration of their capital, with a view to making such safeguards equivalent (77/91/EEC), OJ L 26 of 31.1.1977, p. 1.

[6] Expressed, inter alia, in the White Paper 'Company Law Reform' (fn. 3), p. 43.

[7] *Jonathan Rickford* (ed.), 'Reforming Capital – Report of the Interdisciplinary Group on Capital Maintenance' [2004] EBLR 919.

[8] *John Armour*, 'Legal Capital: An Outdated Concept?' [2006] EBOR 5 ('a form of primitive regulatory technology . . . likely to generate more costs than benefits', at 27); *Eilís Ferran*, 'The Place for Creditor Protection on the Agenda for Modernisation of Company Law in the European Union' [2006] ECFR 178.

[9] COM (2003) 284 final, CELEX number 52003DC0284.

[10] Directive 2006/68/EC of 6 September 2006 amending Council Directive 77/91/EEC as regards the formation of public limited liability companies and the maintenance and alteration of their capital, OJ L 264 of 25.9.2006, p. 32.

[11] *Marcus Lutter* (ed.), Legal Capital in Europe (2006) = Das Kapital der Aktiengesellschaft in Europa (2006), though it is worth noting that the contributions to this collective work display a wide variety of opinion on legal capital.

[12] 'Feasibility study on an alternative to the capital maintenance regime established by the Second Company Law Directive 77/91/EEC of 13 December 1976 and an examination of the impact on profit distribution of the new EU-accounting regime', available (in 3 parts) at http://ec.europa.eu/internal_market/company/capital/index_en.htm.

together with its own conclusions from the study, according to which 'no follow-up measures or changes to the Second Company Law Directive are foreseen in the immediate future'.[13] There can be no doubt that, for the time being, those advocating the abandonment of the legal capital regime have suffered a severe set-back.

Although the Second Company Law Directive does not apply to private companies, to which this book is confined, the discussion may serve as a reference point to investigate the relationship between company law rules on capital maintenance and insolvency rules on the avoidance of pre-insolvency acts that are detrimental to the interests of creditors, insofar as they catch what English law defines as transactions at an undervalue. Other writers have already pointed out the functional similarity between these two regimes, in that they both seek to prevent value transfers from the company to a shareholder, or a person connected to a shareholder, leaving fewer assets with the company to satisfy its creditors' claims.[14] The different views on the Second Directive reveal something about the unequal importance attached to capital maintenance and avoidance remedies, respectively, in Germany and England.

This chapter does not present a complete analysis of the entire legal capital regime. Instead, its focus is on one particular aspect which has the closest connection with the functional problems set out in the introductory chapter,[15] namely its potential to counteract the abuse of limited liability by means of transfers of assets from the company into the hands of its controllers during a period of financial instability, defined in this case by an absence of equity capital available to support lawful distributions. The chapter consists of two main parts. Section B will clarify the notion of 'capital maintenance' in two ways: first because the meanings ascribed to the term by lawyers in England and Germany deviate, and secondly as a way to focus attention on the role of capital maintenance in regulating transfers of assets from the company into the hands of the company's shareholders.

[13] On p. 2 of the informal document published at http://ec.europa.eu/internal_market/company/docs/capital/feasbility/markt-position_en.pdf.

[14] E.g. *Brian Cheffins* (fn. 2), 526–527, 536; *Rebecca Parry*, Transaction Avoidance (2001), para. 2.13; *Marcel Kahan*, 'Legal Capital Rules and the Structure of Corporate Law: Some Observations on the Differences Between European and U.S. Approaches', in: *Klaus Hopt/Eddy Wymeersch* (eds.), Capital Markets and Company Law (2003), 145; *Gerhard Wagner*, 'Distributions to Shareholders and Fraudulent Transfer Law' [2006] EBOR 217.

[15] Chapter 1 B.2.

Section C forms the heart of this chapter and will be devoted to the remedies that are available to a company in order to claw back assets given away in an unlawful distribution. This will include an analysis of concealed distributions, i.e. exchanges between a company and one of its shareholders which look like commercial transactions, but are capable of bringing about a transfer of value from the company to the shareholder without compliance with the procedures for lawful distributions or a reduction of the share capital. In the context of concealed distributions, the section will take us back to the concept of connected persons already encountered in the previous chapter. There is no need for long explanations to see that any law against controllers of the company siphoning off assets into their own hands would be easy to evade if only shareholders were targeted, because they would no doubt find other persons closely connected to them, or other corporate entities controlled by them and maybe even set up for this purpose, to which assets could be transferred. Avoidance law has always been alert to this problem and has developed tighter rules in relation to connected persons.[16] In contrast, capital maintenance is, from its point of departure, a concept applicable only to shareholders. If, as is the case with Germany, capital maintenance rather than avoidance law is meant to operate as the backbone to combat the abuse of limited liability by the controllers of the company, the law must find a way to extend the concept to persons connected with shareholders.

B. Capital maintenance and the boundaries of lawful distributions

1. *Capital maintenance defined*

Before embarking on a substantive analysis of capital maintenance, it seems pertinent to deal with a potential terminological pitfall. The English term '***capital maintenance***' is the literal correspondence of the German word '***Kapitalerhaltung***'. Accordingly, the Commission's Action Plan on 'Modernising Company Law and Enhancing Corporate Governance in the European Union',[17] in chapter 3.2, speaks of 'capital maintenance' in the English version and of '*Kapitalerhaltung*' in the German version. Moreover, virtually all the articles in the two language versions of the collective work edited by Marcus Lutter on 'Legal Capital

[16] Chapter 2 E. [17] Fn. 9.

share capital. Thus, Knight has rightly concluded that 'the rule in *Trevor v Whitworth* is not a prohibition against the company acquiring its own shares but a prohibition on the payment of money or money's worth to shareholders. . . . What is prohibited is clearly a gratuitous transfer of funds.'[47]

Moreover, the effect of a value transfer from the company to one of its shareholders may be brought about in a wholly different manner through what looks on the face of things like a commercial transaction between the shareholder and the company. In principle, the separate legal personality of the company allows for such transactions, and this was confirmed in the seminal case of *Salomon v Salomon & Co Ltd*,[48] where the House of Lords upheld a transaction in which Mr Salomon gave a loan to his company and took security over its assets. Such transactions are innocent as long as they are carried out 'at arm's length', i.e. both sides act as if they were independent of each other and agree on terms that are no different from any market transaction.

It is only when the company accords more favourable conditions to its shareholder than it would accord to an independent counterparty that a value transfer takes place, which may be called a 'disguised' or '**concealed distribution**'. This is the case whenever the company acquires from its shareholder goods or services, including services as a director or manager,[49] at a price above their market value, or supplies such goods or services to its shareholders at a price below their market value or even gratuitously.[50] There are other, more indirect ways in which such a value transfer may be brought about. In *Aveling Barford Ltd v Perion Ltd*,[51] a company sold a piece of land to another company, with both companies being beneficially controlled by the same person, at a value far below its market value, thereby ultimately enriching its controlling shareholder to the detriment of the company's creditors.

In the widest sense, every distribution can be characterised as a transfer of value from the company to a shareholder without full and adequate consideration moving from the shareholder to the company. Yet English lawyers seem reluctant to contemplate such a wide concept

[47] *Knight* (fn. 20), 53–54. [48] [1897] AC 22.

[49] As in *Re Halt Garage* and in BGH 15.6.1992, NJW 1992, 2894.

[50] As in BGH 14.12.1959, BGHZ 31, 258 at 275–276 = NJW 1960, 285: shareholder using corporate aircraft for private purposes without any consideration received by the company (the *Lufttaxi* case).

[51] [1989] BCC 677.

of distribution. Palmer's Company Law, for instance, gives the following definition:

> A 'distribution' is the transfer of funds (or assets) without consideration.[52]

From a German perspective this definition would appear too narrow. But it dovetails with the Rickford Report, which, in Part IV of Chapter 2, considers as mechanisms for the return of capital to shareholders: dividends, purchases and redemptions of own shares, and reductions of capital.[53] The self-contained character of this section of their paper suggests that the authors of the Report regard it as an exhaustive list of techniques for returning capital to shareholders. Although the Report is presented as a full review of the law on capital maintenance,[54] its failure to address the law's reaction to such concealed distributions leaves a gap, which may be a significant pointer to the way English lawyers apply capital maintenance differently from their German colleagues. This chapter, in section C, will demonstrate that the difference between the English and German approaches to the definition of a distribution is not a remote point of detail. The practical importance of capital maintenance to German lawyers lies to a large degree in its ability to counteract concealed distributions, whereas English law would rather employ avoidance remedies, notably s. 238 IA on transactions at an undervalue, to achieve a functionally equivalent result.[55]

3. *Components of equity capital and restrictions on distributions*

Thus far the nature of a distribution has been identified as a transfer of value from the company to a shareholder without full and adequate

[52] Palmer's Company Law, para. 9.705, with reference to *Clydebank Football Club Ltd v Steedman* [2002] SLT 109.

[53] *Rickford* (fn. 44), 937–943, see also the definitional paragraph on 'distributions' at 922–923.

[54] Ibid. 921.

[55] The reader wishing to consult German-language sources should be aware of a somewhat confusing terminology. In German parlance 'concealed distributions' are often referred to as '***verdeckte Gewinnausschüttungen***', which translates as 'concealed distributions of profits' (or 'concealed distribution of dividends': *Frank Wooldridge*, 'Aspects of German Law Governing Private Limited Liability Companies', in: *David Feldman / Frank Meisel* (eds.), Corporate and Commercial Law: Modern Developments – Published in Honour of Professor R.R. Pennington (1996), 33 at 42). This is a misnomer, derived from tax law, and is not to be taken literally; see *Welf Müller* in *Ulmer / Habersack / Winter*, GmbHG § 29 mn. 157 ff.; *Pentz* (fn. 42), § 29 mn. 158 ff. The company law doctrine applies precisely when there are no profits (or reserves) available for distribution.

consideration received by the company. Returning to the 'capital' aspect of capital maintenance, the lawfulness of a distribution depends on how the value transfer is mapped onto the liabilities side of the balance sheet. A look at any balance sheet of a company reveals that equity capital is not recorded there as a single item but consists of several components. One of the reasons for this, and probably the main reason, is that these components differ as to their availability to support a distribution to shareholders. One can discern three categories.

First, there may be a layer of the most robust sort of equity capital, which must never be returned to shareholders apart from a total liquidation at the end of the company's life and after all creditors have been paid off in full, although it may be used to offset losses incurred while the company is a going-concern. Secondly, a type of equity capital may be capable of supporting a distribution to shareholders, but only after certain procedural steps have been taken, which are meant to safeguard the interests of the creditors. Thirdly, as the logical conclusion, some parts of a company's equity capital may already be earmarked for immediate distribution and can be used for this purpose without further formalities. English readers may think of the latter category in terms of 'distributable profits', but for the purpose of comparison a wider term is called for, such as 'equity capital available for immediate distribution', because, under German law, distributions may be made out of equity components that can not be called 'profit' by any description.

Share capital and its reduction

Oddly enough, given today's vigorous criticism among UK scholars of the concept of legal capital as an instrument of creditor protection, the original position of the English courts with regard to the company's share capital was especially tough. The Companies Act 1862 provided that the memorandum of association of a company could only be amended as explicitly provided in the Act; the Act provided for the possibility of an increase, but not a reduction of the nominal capital stated in the memorandum.[56] From this the judges inferred that the entire share capital was excluded from any reduction and subsequent return to the shareholders, bringing it within the most robust layer of equity capital described above.[57]

[56] *Droitwich Patent Salt Company Ltd v Curzon* (1867) LR 3 Exch. 35.

[57] *Guinness v Land Corporation of Ireland* (1882) 22 ChD 349.

In modern company law, this type of equity capital only exists in the form of a statutory minimum capital. Although, in general, the share capital may be reduced so as to allow for distributions to the shareholders, such reduction cannot go below the statutory minimum. Under English law this is the effect of the provisions on the minimum share capital requirement for public companies enacted to give effect to Article 6 of the Second Company Law Directive,[58] but there are no present instances of such a 'life-long' capital for private companies. In Germany the statutory minimum share capital for a GmbH[59] represents precisely this type of equity capital.

To the extent that it exceeds the statutory minimum (if any), the company's share capital may be reduced in order to make distributions to shareholders, or as the Companies Act puts it, 'to repay any paid-up share capital in excess of the company's wants'.[60] The key issue here is procedure which must be followed and the costs associated with it. Prior to the Companies Act 2006, in England, the only route available to private and public companies required an application to the court for an order confirming the reduction.[61] The process includes a full hearing of the case in open court, which adds to the expenses of the process. A DTI document singles this out as an especially onerous cost factor for businesses:

> The main cost to the company in effecting a capital reduction using the court approved route is incurred in dealing with the company's creditors (i.e. settling a list of creditors who are entitled to object and putting arrangements in place with those creditors which are sufficient to satisfy the court that the interests of creditors will not be jeopardised by the proposed reduction of capital).
>
> There are also court costs and associated legal and professional costs. It is difficult to come up with an average cost for a court approved capital reduction, but informal discussions with stakeholders indicate that costs associated with a court approved reduction of capital are **frequently in the region of £100k, but in extreme cases concerning lots of overseas creditors these costs could be as high as £1m.**[62]

[58] CA 2006, Part 20, Chapter 2, ss. 761 to 766; previously CA 1985, ss. 117, 118; *Re Allied Domecq Plc* [2000] BCC 582.
[59] See Chapter 1 A.4 for the legal situation after the MoMiG.
[60] CA 2006, s. 641 (4) (b) (ii). [61] CA 1985, ss. 136 to 138.
[62] Regulatory Impact Assessment for the Companies Act 2006 (January 2007), www.berr.gov.uk/files/file29937.pdf, at p. 29 (emphasis in the original).

Under the Companies Act 2006, this procedure is still available,[63] and for public companies it remains the only permissible route. However, for private companies, the Act introduced an alternative route, viz. a reduction of the share capital supported by a solvency statement from the directors and without the need for court approval.[64] The Company Law Review had favoured a bolder approach, whereby the need to seek court approval for a reduction in the share capital would have been replaced by a declaration of solvency from the directors for private and public companies alike, except that in the case of a public company, in order to comply with Article 32 of the Second Company Law Directive, creditors would be given the opportunity, at their initiative, to challenge the reduction in court.[65]

In Germany, the relevant provision in § 58 GmbHG must be read in conjunction with the procedure for companies registration, which is itself a court procedure, but on the basis of written submissions and without a hearing in open court. In the case of a reduction of the share capital the company, after publishing the notice to its creditors prescribed in § 58 GmbHG and providing them, upon demand, with the security to which they are entitled, submits the relevant documentation for registration in the companies register, which the court scrutinises ex officio, but without the creditors being parties to the court proceedings. For private companies the process does involve a significant delay, because the application to court may not be made before the expiry of one year since publication of the notice to the creditors. For public companies the court element of the procedure[66] is of the same type as for private companies, although the overall procedure is actually less onerous for public companies, because the period for the notice to creditors is only six months[67] and the application to court need not wait until after the end of the notice period. Still, these proceedings are fully compliant with the Second Company Law Directive. Moreover, the proceedings obviously involve costs, especially for the necessary certifications by a public notary, but in normal circumstances these costs would seem nowhere near the figures given by the DTI. Perhaps the

[63] CA 2006, ss. 645 to 649.

[64] CA 2006, ss. 642 to 644. For the sake of completeness it should be mentioned that either route also requires a shareholder resolution: s. 641 (1) CA 2006.

[65] 'Company Formation & Capital Maintenance' (October 1999) para. 3.27–3.35; Final Report (June 2001) para. 10.6.

[66] §§ 223, 224, 227 AktG. [67] § 225 AktG.

more onerous nature of the court proceedings in the UK, though not actually required under the Second Directive, provides some explanation why a reform of the Directive is seen as such an urgent priority in the UK, but not in Germany.

Distributions from the share premium account

Remarkable differences between English and German law also exist in relation to the treatment of share premiums, i.e. amounts paid by shareholders upon subscription of newly issued shares over and above the par-value of the shares. In England, the courts had originally held that any premium was not part of the company's capital and not subject to the restrictions on the return of capital to the shareholders.[68] In response, the legislature introduced restrictions on the application of share premiums.[69] Thus, if a company issues shares at a premium, whether for cash or otherwise, a sum equal to the aggregate amount or value of the premiums on those shares must be transferred to an account called 'the share premium account', and this share premium account may only be used by the company to write off the expenses incurred in the issue of those shares or any commission paid on the issue of those shares, or for allotting bonus shares to members. Otherwise, the provisions of the Companies Act relating to the reduction of a company's share capital apply as if the share premium account were part of its paid up share capital. What is clearly not permitted is an application of the share premium account towards a distribution of assets to shareholders without going through the process of a formal reduction. Hence, in terms of the Second Directive, the share premium account constitutes a non-distributable reserve pursuant to Article 15 (1) (c), which limits the amount of a distribution to shareholders by reference to the 'amount of the profits at the end of the last financial year plus any profits brought forward and sums drawn from reserves available for this purpose'. Yet nothing in the Second Directive forces any Member State to define the share premium account as a non-distributable reserve. Moreover, the provision in the Companies Act applies irrespective of whether the company is a public or a private company.

[68] *Drown v Gaumont-British Picture Corporation Ltd* [1937] Ch. 402.

[69] CA 2006, s. 610, in force from 1 October 2008; re-enacting with modifications CA 1985, s. 130 (on the differences see, for instance, *Hannigan & Prentice*, Companies Act 2006 para. 7.9); a similar provision was first enacted in CA 1947, s. 72.

In contrast, under German law, restrictions on the permissible use of share premiums only apply to public companies.[70] The German logic behind the allocation of the share premium to a special capital reserve account is somewhat different from that in the UK. The share premium account of a German public company is mainly designed as a reserve that may be used to compensate an annual deficit, which would otherwise translate into a balance sheet loss. Only if the share premium account and certain other non-distributable reserves together stand at more than 10 per cent of the company's share capital, may the excess amount be converted into share capital in an issue of bonus shares. The share capital thus increased could subsequently be reduced in accordance with the regular procedure. Otherwise, the German rules do not allow, as the UK Companies Act does, for the share premium account to be converted into distributable funds by applying the provisions on the reduction of a company's share capital. However, for private companies German law does not contain any restrictions on the application of share premiums at all. In other words, funds provided by the shareholders of a private company over and above the par-value of their shares constitute equity capital that is available for distribution to the shareholders at any time without going through any formalities of capital reduction.

4. *Equity capital available for immediate distribution*

A distribution to shareholders made against equity capital within the third layer, i.e. capital already earmarked for immediate distribution without further formalities is, by definition, a lawful one. This part of a company's equity capital is the first to be eroded by any transfer of value from the company to one of its shareholders, but there is no prohibition on such a transfer. In other words, this layer of equity represents capital that is provided by the shareholders at will. Although it will be shown on the balance sheet, the creditors cannot rely on its continued existence at any given time after the balance sheet date.

The distinction between the second and the third layer of equity capital lies in the requirement, or the absence thereof, respectively, to observe certain formalities before a lawful distribution to shareholders can be made. This distinction remains unaffected by the new procedure in the Companies Act 2006 for the reduction of the share capital of a

[70] The relevant provision is § 150 AktG.

private company supported by a solvency statement.[71] The procedure dispenses with court formalities, but it comprises two significant formal steps, viz. the solvency statement from the directors and the shareholder resolution. Compliance with these formal requirements will not create a particular obstacle where a distribution is made openly. However, a concealed distribution, viz. a transaction entered into by the company without openly revealing the effect of a value transfer to a shareholder, will fall foul of these formal requirements almost by default, as it is difficult to envisage such a transaction being accompanied by a solvency statement from the directors or a shareholder resolution. Under the Companies Act 2006, as before, concealed distributions can only be lawful distributions to the extent that the transfer of value to the shareholder is supported by equity capital available for immediate distribution.

As regards the definition of what counts as equity capital available for immediate distribution at any given time, there is a crucial difference between the approaches taken by English and German law, respectively. In the UK Companies Act a complex set of provisions defines in positive terms the pool of equity out of which distributions may be made.[72] The basic rule is to be found in s. 830 (1):

> A company may only make a distribution out of profits available for the purpose.[73]

This rule is complemented by s. 830 (2), which defines the pivotal concept of 'profits available for distribution' as:

> accumulated, realised profits, so far as not previously utilised by distribution or capitalisation, less its accumulated, realised losses, so far as not previously written off in a reduction or reorganisation of capital duly made.[74]

By virtue of s. 836[75] the notion of 'profits available for distribution' is then linked to the profits and losses shown in the company's accounts

[71] CA 2006, ss. 642 to 644; above, fn. 64.

[72] CA 2006 Part 23, ss. 829 to 853; previously CA 1985, Part VIII, ss. 263 to 281; CA 1980, Part III, ss. 39 to 45.

[73] Previously CA 1985, s. 263 (1), which expressed the same idea by means of a double negation: 'A company shall not make a distribution except out of profits available for the purpose.'

[74] This definition is taken verbatim from CA 1985, s. 263 (3).

[75] Previously, CA 1985, s. 270.

(usually its latest annual accounts) as prepared under the relevant statutory framework.[76] It follows that a distribution will be unlawful if it does not comply with the legal requirements that define positively what comes within 'profits available for distribution' as the layer of equity capital earmarked for immediate distribution. In *Precision Dippings Ltd v Precision Dippings Marketing Ltd*,[77] the unlawful character of the dividend resulted from a procedural irregularity in connection with the audit of the company's financial statements.[78] Moreover, a dividend payment constitutes an unlawful distribution if it is made on the basis of incorrect accounts which overstate the profits,[79] or if a parent company does not have sufficient profits itself, but relies on profits in its subsidiary companies.[80]

The logic of the German statute is different. At first glance, § 29 (1) GmbHG looks pertinent. The provision reads:

> The shareholders have a right to the annual profit (*Jahresüberschuss*) plus any profit carried over and less any loss carried over, as far as the resulting amount is not excluded from distribution among the shareholders by law, by the company's constitution [or] by a resolution under sub-paragraph (2) . . .

§ 29 (1) GmbHG defines the extent to which the shareholders have a right to receive a dividend from the company's annual profit, subject to profits being retained as a source of internal finance in accordance with certain rules on the internal governance of the company. § 29 (1) does not say that distributions beyond that amount are unlawful. What is missing is an equivalent to the rule in s. 830 (1) CA 2006 that a company shall make a distribution *only* out of profits available for that purpose. In fact the German law on private companies does not contain any

[76] CA 2006, ss. 394 to 397; Small Companies and Groups (Accounts and Directors' Report) Regulations 2008, SI 2008/409; Large and Medium-sized Companies and Groups (Accounts and Reports) Regulations 2008, SI 2008/410; pursuant to CA 2006, s. 395, a company may opt to prepare individual accounts in accordance with international accounting standards (IAS), which will then serve as the basis for distributions in accordance with Part 23. As the book is only concerned with private companies, the additional requirements for public companies in CA 2006, s. 831 need not be taken into account.

[77] [1986] Ch. 447. [78] See below, text accompanying fn. 92.

[79] As *Inland Revenue Commissioners v Richmond, Re Loquitur Ltd* [2003] EWHC 999 (Ch) = [2003] 2 BCLC 442 (failure to make proper provision for tax charges in the accounts).

[80] As in *Bairstow v Queens Moat Houses plc* [2001] EWCA Civ 712 = [2002] BCC 91.

positive definition of what may lawfully be distributed to shareholders.[81] It only contains a negative rule in § 30 (1) GmbHG:

> The assets of the company necessary to maintain the share capital must not be paid over to the shareholders.[82]

One can infer from this by an *argumentum e contrario* that assets may be distributed to the shareholders as long as the company's net assets exceed the amount of the share capital.[83] This wider basis for distributions includes any amounts retained from distributable profits and shown in the balance sheet as 'profit reserves'. In addition, as has been demonstrated, it includes any amounts paid in by shareholders as share premiums. In this respect, the German law on private companies appears more flexible than English law. It allows for the return of capital contributions made in a form other than by taking up shares. This is compensated to a certain extent by the need to maintain, at all times throughout the company's existence, a minimum share capital.[84] Under English law, a company can be incorporated with a share capital of no more than £1. But whenever that is not sufficient in terms of working capital, any additional contribution made by the shareholders to the company in the form of equity capital will be barred from distribution, because it does not come within the notion of profit as defined in s. 830 CA. In Germany, shareholders may in principle structure their equity investment above the minimum share capital in a way which allows them to withdraw it again from the company without a formal reduction of capital by way of a simple distribution. In reality, however, this flexibility is often a moot point because many shareholders prefer to supply the necessary resources to keep the company going by way of loans or other forms of borrowed capital (e.g. premises or equipment leased to the company). This widespread practice, encouraged by tax law, forms the background to the importance which German law has traditionally accorded to the doctrine of equity-substituting shareholder credit and the restrictions it imposes on the withdrawal of such funds by the shareholder.[85]

[81] As for public companies, § 57 (3) and § 158 AktG together contain a rule akin to s. 830 (1) and (2) CA 2006, so as to give effect to Article 15 (1) (c) of the Second Directive.

[82] The MoMiG inserted two further sentences in § 30 (1); the first of these two sentences lies beyond the scope of this study; the other sentence relates to the repeal of the existing law on equity-substituting shareholder credit, see the text accompanying fn. 197.

[83] E.g. *Pentz* (fn. 42), § 30 mn. 1.

[84] But see chapter 1 A.4 regarding the legal situation after the MoMiG.

[85] See the excursus at D below.

5. *The potential usefulness for creditors*

As noted in the introduction to this chapter, this book does not undertake to assess the real impact which capital maintenance has on creditor protection. But in order to do justice to capital maintenance, it is important to understand how it is meant to work.

For a start, one must assume that creditors of a limited liability company feel the need to obtain information about the likelihood of the company being able to serve its debts and that they find the company's financial statements a potentially useful source of such information. As a minimum, a rational (unsecured) creditor would demand that the company's assets are at all times sufficient to cover the total of all outstanding creditors' claims. Yet the figures present the creditor with a problem of timeliness, because they relate to a past accounting reference period, and that period may have ended as long as a year before the publication of the data, assuming that the company bothers to comply with the statutory time-frame for publication.[86] All that the creditors see from the financial statements is that at a given point in the past there were indeed sufficient assets to cover all outstanding liabilities, and possibly a certain amount of equity acting as a 'cushion' to ensure that potential future losses would not immediately cut into those assets needed to pay off the creditors. Unless creditors are in a position to bargain for more information, they will not receive an update on this information until the publication of the next set of financial accounts. In the meantime, all they can do is to make intelligent guesses as to how the company's financial situation may have developed since the end of the last accounting reference period, always bearing in mind the creditors' primary concern that there be sufficient assets to cover all liabilities.

At this point the information about the equity 'cushion' can – again, potentially – be useful in the following way: creditors with an understanding of the industry in which the company operates may infer from the size of the company, its turnover and its cost structure, how long it would take for all the equity existing at a given date in the past to be 'consumed' if the company's profit margin deteriorates by a certain extent, or conversely, how bad a deterioration in its profit margin a company could sustain for a given time since the last accounting

[86] The maximum period allowed to a private company or GmbH for filing its annual accounts with the registrar of companies, or with the court keeping the commercial register, respectively, is 9 months in England, s. 442 (2) (a) CA 2006, and 12 months in Germany, § 325 (1) HGB.

reference date until it suffers a balance sheet deficit indicative of impending insolvency. Apart from any unforeseeable cataclysmic events in the company's trading, this could provide creditors with a fairly reliable picture of the company's present financial situation. But such an assessment hinges on a critical point: it will not work to the extent that shareholders are permitted to withdraw assets from the company, because the creditors, as company outsiders, will not be in a position to establish the amount of such transfers. Once the financial position of the company starts to deteriorate, the creditors would probably expect such transfers to become more prevalent, as shareholders might try to preserve as much as they can from their personal wealth stuck in the doomed company. Creditors must therefore discount all the equity capital that comes within the third layer, as described above. But the creditors can rely on equity capital within the second layer because this type of equity may only be used to support a transfer of assets to shareholders after the completion of a formal procedure of capital reduction designed to safeguard the interests of existing creditors. Finally, equity capital that comes within the first layer is always off limits for supporting lawful value transfers to shareholders. This is the intrinsic logic of capital maintenance. Whether creditors actually find this information useful and take it into account in their decision-making is, of course, a matter for further debate and empirical research, which lies beyond the scope of this study.

C. Remedies to reverse unlawful distributions

1. The statutory basis

We now turn from the preliminary question of what may lawfully be distributed to shareholders to the sanctions in case of a contravention. This goes to the heart of the programme set out in the introductory chapter. The remedies that the law accords to the company, and through it to the office-holder in the company's insolvency, for restoring to the pool of company assets the value of any unlawful distributions have a direct impact on the chances that persons exercising a controlling influence over a company can get away with abusing limited liability by way of value transfers from the company into their own hands. In this respect the remedies to reverse unlawful distributions work towards the same goal as the avoidance remedies targeting transactions at an undervalue discussed in chapter 2. The parallelism of the two institutions might give rise to a premature conclusion that capital maintenance could easily be dispensed with. For an English lawyer this may look like an intuitively sensible solution. However, as indicated at the end of chapter 2, from a German perspective, remedies based on capital maintenance have some definitive advantages over avoidance remedies. This is the point to explore them in detail.

In both jurisdictions the statutory limitations on lawful distributions are backed up by a statutory cause of action for the company to recoup any unlawful distributions. In England the relevant provision was first enacted as s. 44 (1) of the Companies Act 1980 to give effect to Article 16 of the Second Company Law Directive.[87] The provision was subsequently re-enacted without material change in the Companies Act 1985, s. 277 (1) and in the Companies Act 2006, s. 847 (1) and (2). The current provision reads:

(1) This section applies where a distribution, or part of one, made by a company to one of its members is made in contravention of this Part.
(2) If at the time of the distribution, the member knows or has reasonable grounds for believing that it is so made, he is liable –
  (a) to repay it (or that part of it, as the case may be) to the company, or
  (b) in the case of a distribution made otherwise than in cash, to pay the company a sum equal to the value of the distribution (or part) at that time.

Notwithstanding that the provision was created as part of thc implementation of the Second Directive, its scope of application has always included public and private companies alike.

In Germany § 31 GmbHG provides:

(1) Payments which have been made in contravention of § 30 must be restored to the company.
(2) If the recipient has acted in good faith, restoration can only be demanded as far as it is necessary for the satisfaction of the company's creditors.

The third sub-paragraph in § 31 GmbHG makes all the other shareholders liable for the restoration of unlawful distributions if

[87] *Vanessa Edwards*, EC Company Law (1999), 70.

the claim against the recipient fails, e.g. on account of the latter's insolvency.[88]

(3) If restoration cannot be obtained from the recipient, the other shareholders are liable for the amount to be restored, insofar as it is required for the satisfaction of the company's creditors, in proportion to their shares. Contributions which cannot be obtained from particular shareholders will be divided among the others in the designated proportion.

A simple textual comparison of the provisions yields some immediate insights. Both formulate a special rule targeted at shareholders, or members in the terminology of the Companies Act (because the Act applies equally to companies that are not companies limited by shares). This limitation raises the important question of how the law copes with attempts at evasion, where the company makes an unlawful distribution not to a shareholder but to a 'connected person', a problem which will be dealt with in some detail at the end of this chapter (C.3). Further, in both jurisdictions, the law seeks to accommodate the situation where shareholders have unwittingly received unsuspicious dividend payments, and any such defence must necessarily rely on subjective elements. This aspect accounts for the major difference between the rules in England and Germany, and these will be investigated presently.

In Germany the provisions in §§ 30, 31 GmbHG have been in place since the original legislation was enacted in 1892, and they have been hailed as a core element in the legal framework for companies of the GmbH-type.[89] The courts have always felt confident in dealing with them and have extended their scope of application in relation to concealed distributions and distributions to third parties.[90]

The situation in England presents somewhat of a contrast. For the better part of the time during which it was in force s. 277 (1) CA 1985 led a shadowy life. There was a single reported case, *Precision Dippings*

[88] *Harm Peter Westermann* in *Scholz*, GmbHG[10] § 31 mn. 27; *Pentz* (fn. 42), § 31 mn. 40 (both giving further applications of the rule).

[89] RG 15.12.1941, RGZ 168, 292 at 297–298; BGH 30.6.1958, BGHZ 28, 77 at 78 = NJW 1958, 1351; *Westermann* (fn. 88), § 30 mn. 1; *Pentz* (fn. 42) § 30 mn. 1; *Peter Ulmer*, 'Gesellschafterhaftung gegenüber der GmbH bei Vorteilsgewährung unter Verstoß gegen § 30 Abs. 1 GmbHG', in: Festschrift 100 Jahre GmbH-Gesetz (1992), 363.

[90] Equally, §§ 30, 31 GmbHG provided the fertile ground on which the BGH developed the doctrine of equity-substituting shareholder credit (see D below).

Ltd v Precision Dippings Marketing Ltd,[91] decided under s. 44 (1) CA 1980, which was notable less for what it contributed to the interpretation of the section than for the readiness of the judges to abandon it in favour of the pre-existing common law or equitable rules. In that case the Court of Appeal found it difficult to construe the wording in the statute that the recipient is only liable to repay a distribution 'made in contravention of [the relevant statutory provisions]' if, at the time of the distribution, 'he knows or has reasonable grounds for believing that it is so made'. The contravention of the statute concerned a rather fine point of detail. The claimant company had sufficient distributable profits for making the distribution. But the company's auditors had delivered a qualified report on the annual accounts, and the company had failed to obtain a written statement from the auditors as to the materiality of their qualification for the proposed distribution, as was required by the statute.[92] The claimant company was a wholly owned subsidiary of the defendant company. Both companies had the same directors hence their knowledge could be imputed to either of the companies. The directors knew everything about the accounts and about the qualification in the report, which was not material for the distribution. But the directors did not know the terms of the statutory provision contravened by the distribution, viz. the procedural requirement that the company's auditors needed to deliver a separate statement that the distribution would not be in contravention of the statute. Counsel for the defendant contended that 'the belief referred to is the belief that the distribution was made in contravention of a section, and that must depend on some knowledge of the section'.[93] But the Court of Appeal effectively sidestepped the question, and with it the statutory remedy in s. 277 (1) CA 1985, by refusing to decide the point, since the defendant was anyway liable on another ground, and it was therefore unnecessary to express an opinion on the proper construction of the statute.[94]

In holding the parent company liable to repay the unlawful distribution, the Court of Appeal relied on s. 44 (2) CA 1980 (subsequently s. 277 (2) CA 1985, now s. 847 (3) CA 2006), which retains any obligation imposed apart from this section on a shareholder to repay a distribution unlawfully made to him. An unlawful distribution amounts to a breach of fiduciary duty on the part of the directors and triggers the

[91] [1986] Ch. 447.

[92] CA 1980, s. 43 (3) (c); CA 1985, s. 271 (4); CA 2006, s. 837 (4).

[93] [1986] Ch. 447, at 453. [94] Ibid., 457–458.

liability of the shareholder under the equitable rules on 'knowing receipt'. This liability will be analysed in more detail in chapter 4, after a discussion of directors' duties generally. At this point it suffices to say that liability for knowing receipt, as the name suggests, requires 'knowledge' on the part of the recipient, which, incidentally, presents the most difficult and contentious aspect of knowing receipt. But this seemed the lesser evil because liability for knowing receipt only required knowledge in relation to the factual circumstances amounting to the breach of fiduciary duty, not in relation to the law which had been contravened.[95] The continuing uncertainty about the requisite knowledge under s. 277 (1) CA 1985 meant that knowing receipt appears to have been the preferred route to claim the return of unlawful distributions from shareholders,[96] and for a long time no case decided under s. 277 (1) CA 1985 was reported.[97]

It took almost two decades until the Court of Appeal was presented with a fresh opportunity to look at s. 277 (1) CA 1985. In *It's a Wrap (UK) Ltd v Gula*,[98] Lady Justice Arden, who gave the leading judgment, approached the interpretation of s. 277 (1) on the basis that the provision is designed to implement Article 16 of the Second Company Law Directive, and because she found there to be nothing in the wording or purpose of Article 16 to oust the general principle that a person is deemed to know the law, she concluded that s. 277 (1) CA 1985 must, as far as possible, be interpreted in the same way.[99] Similarly, Lord Justice Chadwick held that for liability under s. 277 (1) CA 1985 to arise, it is enough that the shareholder 'has the relevant knowledge of facts which, if they exist, lead to the conclusion that the distribution does contravene the statutory provisions; it is not necessary that the member has the relevant knowledge of the legal rules'.[100] The third judge on the panel, Lord Justice Sedley, put it succinctly when he said that 'the decisive principle here, both in domestic and in European jurisprudence, is that people are taken to know the law'.[101]

[95] In a contemporary statement to this effect *Eilís Ferran*, Company Law and Corporate Finance (1999), 424.
[96] E.g. in *Allied Carpets Group plc v Nethercott* [2001] BCC 81.
[97] In *Liquidator of Marini Ltd v Dickenson* [2003] EWHC 334 (Ch) = [2004] BCC 172 the judge repeatedly referred to s. 277 CA 1985, although the section was not actually in point because the liquidator sued the defendants only in their capacity as directors; see the judgment at para. 35. The same situation arose in the Scottish case of *Clydebank Football Club Ltd v Steedman* [2002] SLT 109; see that judgment at para. 57.
[98] [2006] EWCA Civ 544 = [2006] BCC 626. [99] Ibid., at para. 26.
[100] Ibid., at para. 50. [101] Ibid., at para. 39.

It's a Wrap clearly revived the fortunes of s. 277 (1) CA 1985 and, by extension, of s. 847 (2) CA 2006. As a result of this decision, a shareholder will be liable to repay an unlawful dividend under s. 847 (2) CA 2006 if he was aware of or had reasonable grounds for believing in the existence of the facts which amount to a contravention, whether or not he was conscious of the contravention itself.[102] However, the onus of proof remains with the company to show that, in terms of Article 16 of the Directive, the shareholder had knowledge of the irregularity of the distribution or alternatively that the shareholders could not in view of the circumstances have been unaware of that irregularity.[103] Presumably, this translates into s. 847 (2) CA 2006 that the company must prove that the shareholder 'knows or has reasonable grounds for believing' the facts that make the distribution unlawful.

Turning now to German law, it is obvious from the wording of § 31 GmbHG that subjectivity has a much more limited role to play in the restoration of unlawful distributions to the company. To begin with, the provision only gives the recipient a defence, which puts the burden on him to show that he acted in good faith when receiving the distribution.[104] Yet even this defence is not available to the recipient where the claim against him is needed to satisfy the company's creditors. In other words, whenever the company becomes insolvent with an excess of liabilities over assets, the defence does not apply and the company's claim against the shareholder under §§ 30, 31 GmbHG is in effect a claim of strict liability, subject only to the limitation period of ten years, running from the day of the distribution.[105] Even the liability of the co-shareholders under § 31 (3) GmbHG, which cannot be explained as a reversal of any receipt on their part, does not depend on fault either. It is a strictly objective liability to make good the shortfall for the creditors insofar as it results from an unlawful distribution.[106] There can be no doubt that this is a harsh rule – but it is also a vivid testimony of the importance German law attaches to capital maintenance for the protection of creditors.

Just how robustly German law applies capital maintenance rules for the purpose of asset swelling in insolvency is demonstrated by a recent

[102] *Stephen Robins*, 'Knowledge, ignorance, and unlawful dividends' [2007] Insolvency Intelligence 33, at 36; see also *Jennifer Payne*, 'Recipient Liability for Unlawful Dividends' [2007] LMCLQ 7.

[103] *It's a Wrap* (fn. 98), para. 21 (Arden LJ).

[104] *Westermann* (fn. 88), § 31 mn. 21; *Pentz* (fn. 42), § 31 mn. 30.

[105] § 31 (5) GmbHG. [106] *Pentz* (fn. 42), § 31 mn. 32; *Ulmer* (fn. 89), 370.

development in the case law of the Bundesgerichtshof. In 1987 the court had decided a case which is all the more interesting as it resembles the facts of *MacPherson v European Strategic Bureau Ltd*,[107] an English case on which there will be more to say later. In the German case one of the shareholder-directors in a partnership-style company resigned, yet the other shareholder was unable to purchase his share for its full value. The share was transferred for a much lower price, and the two parties agreed that certain sums due from customers of the company would be paid directly to the resigning shareholder in proportion to his previous share in the company. Assuming the material conditions for a claim under § 31 (1) GmbHG to be satisfied, the court accepted an argument advanced on behalf of the defendant that the company could not recover unlawful distributions to the extent that the company's net assets had subsequently been restored to the level of the share capital through trading profits or in some other way, as the shareholder could then lawfully receive what he had earlier received as an unlawful distribution.[108] Despite a favourable comment from Karsten Schmidt[109] the overwhelming reaction from scholarly writers was negative.[110] When the issue came before it again, the second civil senate of the Bundesgerichtshof accepted their arguments as convincing and explicitly overruled its earlier decision. The court held that there was no legal basis for such a defence, hence the only requirement for a company to succeed with a claim under § 31 (1) GmbHG was to demonstrate that there had been a contravention of § 30 (1) GmbHG at the time when the distribution was made.[111]

Unlike the UK Companies Act, the German Limited Liability Companies Act does not expressly retain other causes of action, but it does not exclude their applicability either. In particular, a claim arising out of the law on unjust enrichment may be pursued in parallel with a claim

[107] [2002] BCC 39. [108] BGH 11.5.1987, NJW 1988, 139.

[109] In the third edition of his textbook 'Gesellschaftsrecht' at § 37 III (p. 1136–1137).

[110] Two articles dedicated to an explicit analysis and critique of the court's reasoning are *Hans Erich Brandner*, 'Wegfall oder Beständigkeit des Erstattungsanspruchs aus § 31 GmbHG bei anderweitiger Wiederherstellung des Stammkapitals?', in: Festschrift für Hans-Joachim Fleck (1988), 23 and *Peter Hommelhoff*, 'Zum Wegfall des Erstattungsanspruchs aus § 31 GmbHG', in: Festschrift für Alfred Kellermann (1991), 165; other critics included: *Ulmer* (fn. 89), 385–387; *Westermann* (fn. 88), § 31 mn. 7; *Heinz Rowedder* in *Rowedder*, GmbHG^3 § 31 mn. 10; *Marcus Lutter / Peter Hommelhoff* in *Lutter / Hommelhoff*, GmbHG^{16} § 31 mn. 11.

[111] BGH 29.5.2000, BGHZ 144, 336 at 341–342 = NJW 2002, 2577 (*Balsam / Procedo*), with references to all writers cited in fn. 110.

under § 31 GmbHG.[112] The interest in such alternative remedies appears to be more academic than practical because in most cases the company law remedy for reversing unlawful distributions will provide the easier route for the claimant. The Bundesgerichtshof has made it clear that the claim under § 31 GmbHG is itself not based on any notion of enrichment on the part of the recipient.[113] It follows that the defendant cannot invoke a defence in the nature of change of position.[114] Moreover, the Bundesgerichtshof has declared the company's claim under § 31 GmbHG to be immune against an otherwise permissible set-off with a claim held by the defendant against the company. The argument in support of this judge-made rule is an extension by analogy of a statutory provision on the payment of capital contributions due from a shareholder to the company, where the law expressly excludes a set-off.[115] The Bundesgerichtshof finds a 'close functional correlation between the raising of capital and the maintenance of capital' and no reason why the legislator should have intended to prohibit set-off where the company initially calls in the subscribed capital from its shareholders, but not where it does so once again after capital has been unlawfully returned to a shareholder.[116] In the process the Bundesgerichtshof once more saw no difficulty in resting its decision on arguments put forward by scholarly writers[117] and expressly distancing itself from its own precedent.[118]

2. *Treating concealed distributions as unlawful distributions*

The German approach

At this point readers will no doubt begin to understand why German lawyers appear to value capital maintenance so much more than their English colleagues. The picture becomes even clearer once we look into how concealed distributions by way of ostensibly commercial transactions between a company and a shareholder fit into this concept. After all, § 31 (1) GmbHG only speaks of 'payments'. How can this cover, for instance, the case already mentioned of a shareholder using a corporate aircraft for private purposes without any consideration received by the

[112] As in BGH 27.11.2000, BGHZ 146, 105 = NJW 2001, 830.
[113] BGH 14.12.1959, BGHZ 31, 258 at 265 = NJW 1960, 285 (*Lufttaxi*).
[114] *Pentz* (fn. 42), § 31 mn. 32. [115] The provision is part of § 19 (2) GmbHG.
[116] BGH 27.11.2000, BGHZ 146, 105 at 107–108 = NJW 2001, 830 at 831.
[117] *Hommelhoff* (fn. 110), 175–176; *Ulmer* (fn. 89), 382–383.
[118] BGH 29.9.1977, BGHZ 69, 274 = NJW 1978, 160.

company?[119] The answer lies in a straightforward exercise in German-style 'purposive' or 'teleological' interpretation. The Reichsgericht (the predecessor of the Bundesgerichtshof) had already emphasised that it was the outcome in economic terms that counted, i.e. whether the remaining assets of the company were sufficient to cover the amount of the share capital.[120] Ever since then it has been firmly established that the purpose of the provision is to catch not just cash payments made to shareholders, but any transfer of value that has the effect of diminishing the company's net value. This purpose alone, which is recognised by scholarly writers[121] and by the courts,[122] suffices to develop the simple word 'payment' into a comprehensive doctrine on concealed distributions.

The core element of this doctrine is the distinction between a concealed distribution, which is prohibited, and an unobjectionable arm's length transaction, where the position of the shareholder vis-à-vis the company is no different from that of an outsider entering into a regular business contact with the company, and for which German lawyers have coined the term '*Drittgeschäft*' (literally 'third-party transaction', with the 'third party' existing only as a hypothesis to determine the character of the transaction).

At one point in the past the legal discourse in Germany came under the spell of an idea which also plays a somewhat problematic role in the English discourse. In one early decision the Bundesgerichtshof held that it was 'a necessary condition for the application of § 30 GmbHG that a shareholder, *in his capacity as such*, has received value from the company at the expense of the share capital'.[123] The Latin phrase often used in this context is that the transfer of value from the company to the shareholder

[119] BGH 14.12.1959, BGHZ 31, 258 = NJW 1960, 285 (*Lufttaxi*, above, fn. 50).

[120] RG 20.12.1935, RGZ 150, 28 at 36. As early as RG 4.10.1912, RGZ 80, 148 it was recognised that 'payments' included the conveyance of property and receivables (in yet another case whose facts are remarkably similar to *MacPherson v European Strategic Bureau Ltd* [2002] BCC 39).

[121] See, for instance, *Westermann* (fn. 88), § 30 mn. 1; *Lutter/Hommelhoff* (fn. 110), § 30 mn. 8.

[122] BGH 14.12.1959, BGHZ 31, 258 = NJW 1960, 285 (*Luftttaxi*); BGH 1.12.1986, NJW 1987, 1194.

[123] BGH 24.3.1954, BGHZ 13, 49 at 54 = NJW 1954, 1157: 'Eine notwendige Voraussetzung für die Anwendung des § 30 GmbHG besteht darin, daß ein Gesellschafter *in seiner Eigenschaft als solcher* Vermögenswerte von der Gesellschaft auf Kosten des Stammkapitals empfangen hat' (emphasis added here and in the English text).

must have occurred *causa societatis*. Interestingly, the Bundesgerichtshof never returned to this formula, and a later decision seemed to require nothing more than the objective incongruity between the value moving from the company to the shareholder and the consideration received by the company.[124] The lack of clear guidance from the judiciary led to a slightly confused debate in the literature as to the meaning and relevance of *causa societatis*. Several writers stressed that the incongruity of the value given and received by the company was not decisive on its own and that there was a separate, additional requirement of the transaction being 'rooted' in the membership of the shareholder.[125] Such a requirement would almost inevitably lead to an inquiry into the motives of the parties.[126] Other writers maintained that there was a requirement of *causa societatis*, while seemingly content to derive this element from the objective imbalance in the exchange and disputing that the motives of the parties had any role to play.[127] Ultimately, the prevailing opinion among scholars settled on a formula borrowed from tax law,[128] which was soon taken over by the Bundesgerichtshof. The standard test now applied by the courts is whether a diligent company director, acting upon commercial considerations, would have concluded the transaction with an unconnected counterparty on the same terms.[129] The test is understood to move the appraisal of concealed distributions firmly onto an objective track.[130] It certainly is irrelevant whether a recipient's capacity as shareholder was the motive for the transaction.[131] Although the notion of *causa societatis* keeps

[124] BGH 29.3.1973, BGHZ 60, 324 at 328, 330–331 = NJW 1973, 1036 at 1037–1038; cf. the reading of this case by *Harm Peter Westermann in Scholz*, GmbHG[6] (1983) § 30 mn. 18 and by *Martin Winter*, 'Verdeckte Gewinnausschüttungen im GmbH-Recht', ZHR 148 (1984), 579 at 586.

[125] *Jan Wilhelm*, 'Die Vermögensbindung bei der Aktiengesellschaft und der GmbH und das Problem der Unterkapitalisierung', in: Festschrift für Werner Flume (1978) vol. II, 337 at 378 ff.; *Werner Flume*, 'Der Gesellschafter und das Vermögen der Kapitalgesellschaft und die Problematik der verdeckten Gewinnausschüttung', ZHR 144 (1980), 18 at 20.

[126] *Reinhard Goerdeler / Welf Müller* in *Hachenburg*, GmbHG[7] § 30 mn. 36; *Ernst Geßler*, 'Zur handelsrechtlichen verdeckten Gewinnausschüttung', in: Festschrift für Robert Fischer (1979) 131 at 136.

[127] *Westermann* (fn. 124), § 30 mn. 17; *Winter* (fn. 124) 584–585.

[128] See in particular *Goerdeler / Müller* (fn. 126), § 30 mn. 38–39.

[129] BGH 1.12.1986, NJW 1987, 1194; BGH 13.11.1995, NJW 1996, 589.

[130] *Flume* (fn. 125) 22; *Hermann-Josef Tries*, Verdeckte Gewinnausschüttungen im GmbH-Recht (1991), 53; *Hans-Joachim Fleck*, ZHR 156 (1992), 81 at 82 (book review on *Tries*); *Andreas Cahn*, Kapitalerhaltung im Konzern (1998), 54–61.

[131] *Westermann* (fn. 88), § 30 mn. 20; *Lutter / Hommelhoff* (fn. 110), § 29 mn. 52.

wandering through the literature,[132] the better view is that it adds nothing to this test and should accordingly be dispensed with altogether.[133]

The remaining task is essentially one of valuation. Ideally, in an arm's length transaction equal value is given and received by either side. But in the real world goods and services do not necessarily have a single correct price that can be determined with certainty. The issue, then, is how far the courts will accept a valuation by parties who were not acting at arm's length as conclusive or, conversely, how much the courts are prepared to intervene and override an exchange agreed by the parties with what the judge considers the 'true' valuation. The Bundesgerichtshof accepts that an objectively diligent company director[134] may have a 'margin of appreciation' that cannot be reviewed[135] and which, depending on the type of transaction, may be 'considerable'.[136] But the court applied a strictly objective approach in a case where the directors, allegedly by oversight, failed to realise that the price agreed with the shareholder was below cost. It does not help the shareholder if he can show that the directors genuinely believed in the price being appropriate so that the same diminution of the company's assets could have resulted from a similar loss contract entered into with an independent counterparty, because a diligent director would not conclude such a contract.[137]

The English approach

English company lawyers start their analysis more or less from the opposite polar end. We have noted above the definition of a distribution in *Clydebank Football Club Ltd v Steedman*, which seemed too narrow from a German point of view.[138] John Armour's summary of the present position of English law builds on this definition and conveys a sense of a noticeably different approach:

> Generally, a distribution will mean a transfer to a shareholder in his capacity as such without consideration given by the recipient.[139] Where a

[132] E.g. *Pentz* (fn. 42), § 30 mn. 31 (published in 2002).

[133] *Tries* (fn. 130), 49–53; *Hans-Joachim Fleck*, 'Der Grundsatz der Kapitalerhaltung – seine Ausweitung und seine Grenzen', in: Festschrift 100 Jahre GmbH-Gesetz (1992), 391 at 400.

[134] As to the centrality of this standard of diligence in German company law see chapter 4 B.2.

[135] BGH 13.11.1995, NJW 1996, 589.

[136] BGH 15.6.1992, NJW 1992, 2894 (a case concerning a director's remuneration).

[137] BGH 1.12.1986, NJW 1987, 1194. [138] Above, fn. 52.

[139] Reference to *Clydebank Football Club Ltd v Steedman* [2002] SLT 109, at 124.

> transaction between a company and shareholder is explicitly intended to be a dividend or other gratuitous payment to a shareholder, then it will clearly be a 'distribution'. More difficult is the position where the company enters into a transaction with a shareholder that is not ex facie gratuitous – for example, a sale or a contract for services. Provided that the transaction is not a sham, then in most cases it will not be characterised as a 'distribution' because it is not with the member in his capacity as such. A solvent company is permitted to exercise its powers in any way the shareholders think fit, and this may include business transactions with persons who are amongst their number, even if the transaction is at an undervalue. Yet in cases of extreme undervalue, courts may recharacterise transactions between companies and their shareholders as unlawful distributions.[140]

The English cases carefully collated at the end of the passage do indeed support this proposition. The earliest of them, *Re Halt Garage (1964) Ltd*,[141] concerned a married couple who were the sole shareholders and directors of a small owner-managed company. They had paid themselves a weekly remuneration as a means of earning their living from the business, even though one of them had become seriously ill and was unable to render any services to the company apart from responsibilities for the mere holding of office. The reasoning of Mr Justice Oliver does not express a clear statement of law, but gives the impression of a long-winded wrestling with the peculiar facts, in the course of which the judge refers to a variety of standards or yardsticks. A notion that comes up repeatedly is that of a 'genuine' exercise of the company's power to pay remuneration to its directors, having regard to the size and profitability of the company and the amount of work put in by the director; this is then contrasted with payments that are 'patently excessive or unreasonable' and which would allow the court to intervene and substitute a remuneration at a different rate which appears to be more appropriate.[142] Only in relation to the director who had fallen ill did the

140 *John Armour* in *Armour/Bennett*, Vulnerable Transactions (2003) para. 7.38, with reference, inter alia, to: *Re Halt Garage (1964) Ltd* [1982] 3 All ER 1016, at 1039–44; *Aveling Barford Ltd v Perion Ltd* [1989] BCC 677, at 683; *Redweaver Investments Ltd v Lawrence Field Ltd* (1991) 9 ACLC 1032, at 1036–37; *MacPherson v European Strategic Bureau Ltd* [2000] 2 BCLC 683, at 701–4; *Sasea Finance Ltd v KPMG* [2002] BCC 574, at 584–585; *Clydebank Football Club Ltd v Steedman* [2002] SLT 109, at 124–25; and with further reference to: *Richard Calnan*, 'Corporate Gifts and Creditors' Rights' (1990) 11 CoLaw 91; *Nigel Doran*, 'Transactions at an Undervalue and the Maintenance of Capital Principle' (1991) 12 CoLaw 169.

141 [1982] 3 All ER 1016. 142 Ibid., 1040.

judge find that the payments were not genuinely directors' remuneration, but were gratuitous distributions to a shareholder conveniently labelled, or dressed up, as remuneration.[143] He then went on:

> The difficulty must necessarily be to draw the line between what could reasonably be described as a genuine reward for service and what could not. Remuneration does not cease to be remuneration because it is generous or even, perhaps, unwisely generous, but there is an obvious difficulty about fixing any point at which it can be said that a purported exercise of the power to pay ceases to be genuine. In the absence of any evidence of actual motive, the court must, I think, look at the matter objectively and apply the standard of reasonableness.[144]

So in a sense, there is an objective standard of reasonableness that sounds similar to the test applied by the German courts, but it only comes into play as a default standard if the parties have been so unwise as to provide no indication of any rational attempt to quantify the consideration with reference to some commercial yardstick. In the subsequent discourse, it is the test of 'genuineness' that has turned out to be the crucial element.

At the heart of the test of 'genuineness' lies a subjective approach. In *Re Halt Garage* the judge was explicit that 'the motive is more important than the label',[145] and this was cited with approval by Mr Justice Hoffmann in *Aveling Barford Ltd v Perion Ltd.*[146] In that case the claimant and defendant companies were both beneficially controlled by the same person, at whose instigation the claimant company had sold to the defendant company a piece of land valued at £650,000 for a price of £350,000. The judge held this to be an unlawful distribution. In concluding his judgment he returned to the subjective side of the transaction and said:

> I accept that [the transaction] was in law a sale. The false dressing it wore was that of a sale at arm's length or at market value. It was the fact that it was known and intended to be a sale at an undervalue which made it an unlawful distribution.[147]

But Hoffmann J also referred to a passage in *Re Halt Garage* where Oliver J had given pre-eminence to an objective approach because:

[143] Ibid., 1041–1042. [144] Ibid., 1043. [145] Ibid., 1039.
[146] *Aveling Barford Ltd v Perion Ltd* [1989] BCC 677, at 682. [147] Ibid., 683.

> the sums paid to [the director] were so out of proportion to any possible value attributable to her holding of office that the court is entitled to treat them as not being genuine payments of remuneration at all but dressed-up dividends out of capital.[148]

The continuing uncertainty about the respective roles of a subjective intention of the parties and an objective difference in value carries through to the latest (Scottish) case on 'concealed distributions', viz. *Clydebank Football Club Ltd v Steedman*, where, based on the ratio of *Aveling Barford*, the defendants accepted that:

> an unlawful distribution may be constituted not only by a wholly gratuitous transfer but also by a sale (and presumably by any other form of transfer or exchange) which was known and intended to be at an undervalue, at least in circumstances where the undervalue was gross.[149]

In the same case, the judge speaks of a 'margin of appreciation', but his words make it patently clear that this margin is of a different magnitude than the margin of appreciation tolerated by the Bundesgerichtshof:

> If the transaction is genuinely conceived of and effected as an exchange for value and the difference ultimately found does not reflect a payment 'manifestly beyond any possible justifiable reward for that in respect of which allegedly it is paid', does not give rise to an exchange 'at a gross undervalue' and is not otherwise unreasonably large, there will not to any extent be a 'dressed up return of capital'. In assessing the adequacy of the consideration, a margin of appreciation may properly be allowed.[150]

The test of 'genuineness' has been described as 'more interventionist than a test based solely on honesty', but at the same time one where only 'patently excessive or unreasonable terms' would trigger an intervention of the court.[151] Another analysis could be that the test of 'genuineness' in fact consists of three alternative limbs. One is overtly subjective, in that an intention of the parties to make a distribution rather than enter into a commercial transaction will produce the legal effect of a distribution (which may or may not be an unlawful distribution, depending on available profits). The second limb 'treats' (in the words of Oliver J) a transaction as if the parties had intended it to be a distribution, because

148 *Re Halt Garage (1964) Ltd* [1982] 3 All ER 1016, at 1042, as cited in *Aveling Barford Ltd v Perion Ltd* [1989] BCC 677, at 682.

149 *Clydebank Football Club Ltd v Steedman* [2002] SLT 109, at 119–120.

150 Ibid., at 125.

151 *Eilís Ferran*, Corporate Finance Law (2008), 186.

its terms are 'manifestly beyond any possible justifiable reward for that in respect of which allegedly it is paid' and constitute a 'gross undervalue', without the need for the claimant to lead evidence as to the intentions of the parties. The third limb would deal with the point raised by Oliver J in *Re Halt Garage* that an objective valuation was called for where the parties had failed to quantify the consideration with reference to some commercial yardstick. If that analysis is correct, it would confine an objective valuation to a standard of (ordinary) reasonableness to a mere gap-filling function, while the motives of the parties remain centre-stage. Under German law, as we have seen, the motives of the parties are quite simply irrelevant, and accordingly there is no need for the claimant to lead evidence of either the motives or a gross undervalue from which to infer the motives or absence of any relevant motives in the parties.

The recent English case of *MacPherson v European Strategic Bureau Ltd*,[152] albeit broadly in line with the authorities cited above, casts a slight doubt on the law. In that case the three shareholders of a company, who were also its directors, had agreed to conduct business on the basis that they would not be reimbursed for their services to the company, but would only receive a share in its profits. When their partnership broke down, they entered into a written agreement to the effect that the gross proceeds of one outstanding transaction would be paid to them directly after paying some, but not all of the company's liabilities, to the exclusion of other creditors. The majority (Lord Justices Chadwick and Peter Gibson), affirming the view of the first-instance judge on this point, held that the payments in question, labelled as payments for consultancy services, but representing in fact a profit-sharing agreement, did not fall within the prohibition in s. 263 (1) CA 1985[153] because those payments were not to be made to the recipients in their capacity as members of the company, but as individuals who had previously worked for the company, notwithstanding that the payments were to be made to individuals who happened to be shareholders (sic!) and were to be in proportion to the amount of their shareholdings.[154] However, Lord Justice Buxton, who agreed with the majority over the outcome of the case, added some separate observations because he thought that the agreement between the company and its shareholders on its true construction did provide for a distribution of assets, contrary to s. 263 (1) CA 1985. Even where the

[152] [2002] BCC 39. [153] Now s. 830 (1) CA 2006, see fn. 73.
[154] At para. 51–52 (Chadwick LJ).

parties genuinely thought that they were rewarding each other for services, the method of reward can be in danger of being characterised as distribution of assets unless the basis on which it was explained and justified was capable of some other construction in law.[155] Yet if 'genuineness' is not the test, the question arises as to what other criterion might take its place, or whether English law might in the future go down the path of an objective approach similar to that of German law. The latter conclusion, if tempting for a German observer, has not found any resonance in the English discourse so far. It would seem premature to conclude that *MacPherson v European Strategic Bureau Ltd* has changed this.

The marked difference between, on the one hand, the strong subjective overtones as well as the continuing uncertainty surrounding the test of genuineness in English law and, on the other hand, the straightforwardly objective approach in German law may provide a double explanation. It may explain why German lawyers are so much more enthusiastic about capital maintenance to counteract value transfers through concealed distributions from a company to its shareholders, while, at the same time, it may also explain why English lawyers seem to have a preference for reversing such value transfers through the avoidance of transactions at an undervalue pursuant to s. 238 IA. Len Sealy and David Milman make the latter argument explicit in considering the subjectivity imported into s. 238 IA through its subsection (5): 'There may be problems, too, with regard to the "genuineness" of directors' remuneration [reference to *Re Halt Garage*], but it is very likely that the present section will make it easier to impeach such transactions.'[156]

This conclusion brings us back to an observation made in the introductory chapter about the adverse impact of EU developments destabilising long-established balances within national laws.[157] As long as English and German law were able to prescribe a single coherent framework to any company operating within the respective jurisdiction, it did not matter much whether capital maintenance or avoidance remedies offered the more effective route for office-holders to bring shareholders to book for siphoning off value from the company. This has changed dramatically with the new European framework for the

[155] At para. 59.

[156] *Sealy/Milman*, Insolvency Legislation (10th edn 2007), vol. I, 265; chapter 2 D.1 (text on pages 72–73).

[157] Chapter 1 A.2.

conflict of laws in relation to company law and insolvency law. For the classic *Centros*-type company incorporated under English law and operating in Germany, the German insolvency administrator will be denied the benefit of applying German company law rules on capital maintenance (his preferred choice), while at the same time, he will be unable to rely on English transaction avoidance laws (presumably the preferred route for an English liquidator).

3. Distributions by way of value transfers to related third-party recipients

The statutory remedy under the Companies Act, s. 847 (1) and (2), according to its wording, does not extend to defendants other than shareholders. However, the aim behind the principle of capital maintenance, viz. to ensure in the interests of creditors that shareholders' claims to the company's assets remain strictly subordinate to those of the creditors, requires a somewhat broader view of potential defendants. The case of *Aveling Barford Ltd v Perion Ltd* [158] provides a good illustration of the potentially unlimited ingenuity of shareholders seeking to get away with value transfers. In that case the controlling shareholder of the claimant company was a certain Dr Lee, and the property was sold at an undervalue to a company the shares in which were held by a Jersey trustee company for the benefit of Dr Lee's family. A more straightforward variant of the problem is presented by *Inn Spirit Ltd v Burns*,[159] where the company made a distribution not to its sole shareholder, another company, but to the sole shareholder of the parent company and to his wife.

Against the background of *Aveling Barford*, John Armour suggests an analogy with the statutory definition of 'connected persons' in the Insolvency Act,[160] so that transactions in favour of spouses or children of individual shareholders would also be viewed as distributions.[161] Assuming the English courts were to adopt this position in principle, it is worth noting that their approach to this 'analogy' is nevertheless likely to differ from the concept of 'analogy' in German law. In the German legal discourse, reasoning by analogy is an accepted technique of judicial lawmaking (*richterliche Rechtsfortbildung*), whereby the judge applies a given rule or provision beyond the meaning of its words in order to fill a

[158] [1989] BCC 677. [159] [2002] EWHC 1731 (Ch) = [2002] 2 BCLC 780.
[160] Chapter 2 E. [161] *Armour* (fn. 140), para. 7.44.

'lacuna' (*Lücke*) in the statute that is recognised as inconsistent with the 'telos' or 'purpose' (*Zweck*) of that statute.[162] But in every other respect the judge would be bound by the meaning of the rule thus extended by analogy. In contrast, the courts in England might well prefer not to limit their room for manoeuvre by importing the strict limitations laid down in the statutory definition of 'connected persons' into their common law concept of capital maintenance. Thus, if a situation arises where the relationship between a company and the recipient of value happens to fall outside the statutory definition in the Insolvency Act, an English court might still consider it apt to extend the common law rule in *Aveling Barford* so as to cover the situation. Such a form of reasoning from case to case is also a form of reasoning by analogy, albeit of a different kind to the application of statutes by analogy practised in Germany.[163] When considering the respective roles of analogy in German and English law it is important to bear in mind that English courts can partly compensate their less flexible approach to statutory interpretation by shifting the analysis into the sphere of the common law, something which is obviously not open to German courts.

Returning to the problem of value transfers to a recipient related to a shareholder, German law is obviously faced with a parallel problem, in that § 31 GmbHG refers to 'payments made in contravention of § 30', whereas § 30 GmbHG only speaks of shareholders as recipients of payments. German law has nevertheless shown itself remarkably capable of overcoming the seeming limitation built into this wording of the statute and accommodating recipients other than shareholders within the doctrine of capital maintenance in order to reap its full advantages over avoidance remedies or the general law of restitution. The way in which German law approaches the matter is highlighted by an important early case from the Bundesgerichtshof, which is known as the *Lufttaxi* case. The defendant had previously run a company providing air transport services, but had been banned from this activity by the authorities. He set up a new company through two persons who held the shares on his behalf and for his account, thus acting as his 'straw men'. The defendant then proceeded with various machinations,

[162] *Karl Larenz*, Methodenlehre der Rechtswissenschaft (6th edn 1991), 370–404. The book continues to be perhaps the most authoritative text in the field of '*Methodenlehre*' ('methodology'), by which German lawyers understand roughly that part of jurisprudence which covers the cognition and application of the positive law.

[163] See generally *Katja Langenbucher*, 'Argument by Analogy in European Law' [1998] CLJ 481.

including the personal use of the company's aircraft without giving any consideration for it to the company and a sale of assets from the old company, in which the defendant was by then the sole shareholder, to the new company for a price that was alleged to be more than twice their actual value. The Bundesgerichtshof held that, for the purpose of applying §§ 30, 31 GmbHG, the defendant was to be treated as a shareholder of the new company. The key passage can be translated as follows:

> These provisions [viz. §§ 30, 31 GmbHG] do not literally apply to [a person] for whose account an incorporator has acted, because it is not he that becomes a member, but the agent (trustee, straw man), and he attains the position of a member only by acquiring a share. It would not, however, do justice to the purpose of §§ 30, 31 GmbHG to safeguard the maintenance of the share capital if these two provisions, which are crucial to the law of private companies, were not applied to the case where the share capital is touched in order to make payments to someone on whose behalf and for whose account an incorporator has acted.[164]

Note the explicit reference to the 'purpose' (*Zweck*) of the statutory provisions. It is the same concept that we have just encountered in relation to reasoning by analogy, where the court relies on the 'purpose' of the statute in order to determine whether there is a 'lacuna'. But here, the Bundesgerichtshof does not actually apply §§ 30, 31 GmbHG by way of analogy. Instead, the court engages in yet another exercise of German-style 'purposive' or 'teleological' interpretation similar to the one extending the word 'payments' in § 31 GmbHG to cover also concealed distributions.[165] The recognised freedom of the German courts to interpret a statute goes much further than the 'purposive approach' that English readers may have in mind at this point, thinking of the seminal case of *Pepper v Hart*, where the House of Lords permitted reference to parliamentary materials in the form of statements by a

[164] BGH 14.12.1959, BGHZ 31, 258 at 266 = NJW 1960, 285 (*Lufttaxi*): 'Diese Bestimmungen treffen auf denjenigen, für dessen Rechnung ein Gründer gehandelt hat, wörtlich nicht zu, da nicht er, sondern der Beauftragte (Treuhänder, Strohmann) Gesellschafter wird und er die Stellung eines Gesellschafters nur dadurch erlangt, daß er einen Gesellschaftsanteil erwirbt. Man würde jedoch dem Zweck der §§ 30, 31 GmbHG, die Erhaltung des Stammkapitals zu sichern, nicht gerecht, wollte man diese beiden spezifisch GmbH-rechtlichen Bestimmungen nicht auf den Fall anwenden, daß das Stammkapital zu Zahlungen an jemanden angegriffen wird, in dessen Auftrag und für dessen Rechnung ein Gründer gehandelt hat.'

[165] Above, text accompanying fn. 119 to 122.

Minister or other parliamentary materials in order to give effect to the true intentions of the legislature where legislation is ambiguous or obscure.[166] German lawyers, in turn, would not refer to this kind of interpretation as 'teleological', but rather as 'historic' interpretation, which may be a preliminary stage to 'teleological interpretation' properly speaking.[167] The point of the German idea of 'teleological interpretation' is that the judge, or any other person interpreting a statute, should enquire into the purpose that the legislature must have sought to achieve, but without being restricted to historic evidence of this purpose; indeed, it is not necessary that anyone involved in the legislative process had a particular consequence in mind, if only the intrinsic reason of the statute leads to the conclusion that this consequence best accords with the purpose of the statute.[168] The boundary between the teleological interpretation of a statute and reasoning by analogy is drawn with regard to whether or not the solution may still rest on an extensive interpretation of the words of the statute. In the *Lufttaxi* case, to take the example at hand, the word 'shareholder' was given an extensive meaning so as to include a person on whose behalf another person acts as shareholder in the technical sense; on this basis, there is no 'lacuna' in the statute, hence no analogy is needed.

English lawyers may harbour some reservations against such a method of interpreting statutes, given the amount of controversy generated even by the much more conservative approach adopted by the House of Lords in *Pepper v Hart*.[169] As regards the German tradition, however, one must bear in mind the importance of the scholarly discourse to clarify such matters. Quite often the 'purpose' of a statute has been determined by a consensus among commentators long before any case has reached a court. But there is no denying that the method also invites scholarly disputes, and there may well be no consensus on the purpose of a particular statute for a very long time.

Following the *Lufttaxi* decision the Bundesgerichtshof applied §§ 30, 31 GmbHG to similar situations where the legal holder of the shares acts on someone else's behalf and the value moves from the company not to the shareholder, but directly to the person standing behind the shareholder. Thus, the court applied §§ 30, 31 GmbHG to the principal of a

[166] [1993] AC 593, at 640 (Lord Browne-Wilkinson). [167] *Larenz* (fn. 162), 328–331.
[168] Ibid., 332–339.
[169] For references see *Michael Zander*, The Law-Making Process (6th edn 2004), 164–179.

trust (in the German sense of *Treuhand*),[170] without excluding the liability of the shareholder acting as trustee (in the German sense of *Treuhänder*).[171] At this point, it might be tempting to refer to the recipient as the 'beneficial shareholder', were it not for the potential confusion with the settled meaning of this term in relation to the English law of trusts, because the Bundesgerichtshof extended the application of §§ 30, 31 GmbHG even further to a defendant with an indirect interest in the company through an intermediate (100 per cent) subsidiary[172] (where the term 'beneficial shareholder' would be misleading to English readers).

The reverse situation, so to speak, occurs where the legal shareholder is himself the beneficial shareholder, but a distribution is made to a third party acting as the agent, trustee (*Treuhänder*) or 'straw man' of the shareholder. The shareholder is beneficially entitled to the value received by the agent (et al.), who will be liable to account to the shareholder for the value received by him from the company. There are good arguments to assume that the remedy under § 31 GmbHG lies against the shareholder, not against the primary recipient, and this is thought to be the case even where the recipient has not yet accounted to the shareholder, with the consequence that the shareholder bears the risk of the recipient's insolvency (to the extent that his claim against the latter is not a proprietary one).[173]

Whereas the solution for these two situations appears more or less clear, this is not so for the plethora of remaining situations where the recipient is neither the principal or parent company nor the agent or trustee of the shareholder. The two archetypical cases here are a value transfer between 'sister companies' and one from the company to the spouse or a close relative of a shareholder. In this respect, a sprawling academic debate[174] has led to manifold categorisations, distinctions

[170] BGH 20.2.1989, BGHZ 107, 7 = NJW 1989, 1800.

[171] BGH 19.9.1988, BGHZ 105, 168 = NJW 1988, 3143.

[172] BGH 21.9.1981, BGHZ 81, 311 = NJW 1982, 383.

[173] *Holger Altmeppen*, '"Dritte" als Adressaten der Kapitalerhaltungs- und Kapitalersatzregeln in der GmbH', in: Festschrift für Bruno Kropff (1997), 641 at 645–646 (but see references to contrary opinions cited there).

[174] Monographic treatments include: *Andreas Cahn*, Kapitalerhaltung im Konzern (1998); *Brigitte Rust*, Verdeckte Einlagenrückgewähr durch Leistung an Dritte in der Kapitalgesellschaft (2000); specifically in relation to public limited liability companies, *Jens Riedel*, Unzulässige Vermögenszuwendungen und ihre Rechtsfolgen im Recht der Aktiengesellschaft (2004).

and analogies, whose detailed exposition would go beyond the scope of this book.

As early as 1979 Claus-Wilhelm Canaris published an article, which merits special mention as the first attempt to put the law in this area on a systematic basis.[175] Although some of his propositions no longer represent the mainstream of the argument, his contribution introduced several fundamental ideas which continue to shape the debate. Foremost of them was the realisation that different approaches were required for the two related aspects of liability arising from such transactions, viz. (i) the liability of the shareholder, notwithstanding that he had not actually received any value directly from the company, and (ii) the liability of the third-party recipient, notwithstanding that he was not expressly included in §§ 30, 31 GmbHG. As regards the liability of the shareholder, its legal basis is normally found in §§ 30, 31 GmbHG, and the debate centres on identifying his relationship with the recipient and/or the nature of his involvement in the distribution which justify a claim against the non-receiving shareholder. The latter point is of obvious relevance to the recipient's liability as well, but here the problem also lies in identifying a legal basis for liability in the first place. Behind this determination of the conditions under which the liability of the non-shareholder arises, stands the problem that the harshness of §§ 30, 31 GmbHG is difficult to reconcile with the protection of innocent counterparties. Hence this liability normally includes some sort of subjective element on the part of the counterparty.[176] Some writers deny the applicability of §§ 30, 31 GmbHG to third-party recipients altogether and are only prepared to accept liability on the basis of unjust enrichment according to the Civil Code.[177]

Unfortunately, the Bundesgerichtshof has not always been helpful in this debate. On several occasions the court has extended liability under §§ 30, 31 GmbHG to persons more or less closely connected with shareholders so as to avoid potential loopholes. In one of its earliest decisions in this field, the court extended liability to the son (a minor) of

[175] *Claus-Wilhelm Canaris*, 'Die Rückgewähr von Gesellschaftereinlagen durch Zuwendungen an Dritte', in: Festschrift für Robert Fischer (1979), 31; soon after its publication the article was cited by the Bundesgerichtshof: BGH 28.9.1981, BGHZ 81, 365 at 369 = NJW 1982, 386 at 387 (a case featuring a minor son of a shareholder).

[176] *Hans-Joachim Fleck*, 'Der Grundsatz der Kapitalerhaltung – seine Ausweitung und seine Grenzen', in: Festschrift 100 Jahre GmbH-Gesetz (1992), 391 at 412 ff.; *Westermann* (fn. 88), § 30 mn. 33, § 31 mn. 12; *Pentz* (fn. 42), § 31 mn. 10.

[177] *Canaris* (fn. 175), 37–38 and 56; *Altmeppen* (fn. 173), 646–648.

the company's sole shareholder.[178] The case was remanded back to the lower court, which found that the father had no longer been a shareholder at the relevant date, but had continued to act as the sole director and, via a web of other entities, the person ultimately in control of the company. Upon a further appeal, the Bundesgerichtshof still held the son liable, noting, however, the son's knowledge of the company's financial crisis.[179] Further cases include the spouse of a shareholder,[180] a recipient company (almost) wholly owned by the spouse of a shareholder[181] and all companies which, together with the shareholder, are part of a group (*Konzern*).[182] The problem with these and other cases is that the grounds for the decision given by the court variously refer to objective (single economic unit) and subjective (intervention from the shareholder, knowledge of the recipient) arguments without offering a clear and consistent account of how they relate to each other.

The foregoing account of German law can do no more than provide a glimpse of a vigorous debate, where many details are still disputed. It gives the reader a flavour of the complex legal arguments revolving around the treatment of third-party recipients. The key element needed to understand these arguments is the centrality of the role of the shareholder within the concept of capital maintenance. The price for this approach is a debate about the range of sufficiently 'connected' persons. Only one firm conclusion is possible at this stage: the law remains unsettled, but the willingness of the courts to expand the reach of §§ 30, 31 GmbHG so as to include recipients connected to shareholders cannot be in doubt.

As regards English law, on traditional principles of statutory interpretation it seems questionable, at the very least, whether the provision in s. 847 (2) CA 2006, which is specifically directed at distributions 'made by a company to one of its members', i.e. shareholders, could be extended by way of analogy to cover also value transfers to non-shareholders. But this may not be necessary after all, as the flexibility of English law appears to trump even the latitude of teleological interpretation in German law. This is due to a combination of the method of legal reasoning within the common law, which allows for an even wider

178 BGH 28.9.1981, BGHZ 81, 365 at 368–369 = NJW 1982, 386 at 387.
179 BGH 10.10.1983, NJW 1984, 1036. 180 BGH 1.12.1986, NJW 1987, 1194.
181 BGH 14.10.1985, ZIP 1986, 456.
182 BGH 21.9.1981, BGHZ 81, 311 = NJW 1982, 383; BGH 20.3.1986, ZIP 1987, 1050; BGH 16.12.1991, NJW 1992, 1167.

range of 'connected persons', as is evidenced by *Aveling Barford*,[183] and a different doctrinal approach as regards the basis for liability. The latter point already leads over to the next chapter. We have seen that English law can impose liability on the recipient of an unlawful distribution without recourse to the statutory remedy in s. 847 (1) and (2) CA by virtue of the equitable liability for 'knowing receipt'.[184] In establishing this liability English law looks at the conduct of the director in making the distribution and classifies this conduct as breach of a 'fiduciary duty', a pivotal concept in English company law, which will be explained in some detail in chapter 4. Building on this breach of a fiduciary duty, English law then directs the remedy of 'knowing receipt' against the recipient of the unlawful distribution. This liability hinges critically on the recipient's knowledge of the breach of duty, but it is not a priori restricted to certain categories of defendant.[185]

D. Excursus: Equity-substituting shareholder credit (*eigenkapitalersetzender Gesellschafterkredit*)

Each chapter so far has included at least one reference to the topic of 'equity-substituting shareholder loan' (*eigenkapitalersetzendes Gesellschafterdarlehen*) or 'equity-substituting shareholder credit' (***eigenkapitalersetzender Gesellschafterkredit***). The first expression is more widely used in Germany, although the second expression would seem more accurate, as the doctrine applies not only to loans, but to any form of borrowed capital (e.g. premises or equipment leased to the company).[186] The topic is a massive one, even by German standards. The core of the doctrine lies in the re-characterisation of debt capital as equity capital on account that it has been supplied by a shareholder at a time when the company was in a financial crisis, being either insolvent on a cash flow or balance sheet basis or otherwise unable to obtain such credit from an outside financier on arm's length terms.[187] Whilst the shareholder is free to decide whether to inject fresh funds from his own pocket into the crisis-ridden company or to liquidate it, his

[183] Fn. 158 and subsequent text. [184] Above, text accompanying fn. 94.

[185] Further details of this liability will be analysed in section C of chapter 4.

[186] BGH 16.10.1989, BGHZ 109, 55 = NJW 1990, 516.

[187] BGH 24.3.1980, BGHZ 76, 326 = NJW 1980, 1524; further details: *Ulrich Huber/ Mathias Habersack*, 'Special Rules for Shareholder Loans: Which Consequences Would Arise for Shareholder Loans if the System of Legal Capital Should be Abolished?', in: *Marcus Lutter* (ed.), Legal Capital in Europe (2006), 308 at 312–314.

'responsibility for the proper financing of the company'[188] prevents him from funding the failing business with debt rather than equity, thus shifting part of the risk onto the creditors. The main consequences of a shareholder providing equity-substituting credit to his company are a prohibition on repayment as long as the company remains in a financial crisis, sanctioned by an obligation on the part of the recipient to restore any unlawful repayment, and a mandatory subordination of his claim for repayment to regular claims of creditors in insolvency proceedings.

The doctrine of equity-substituting shareholder credit is a judicial creation. It first appeared in the *Lufttaxi* case,[189] the early leading case of the Bundesgerichtshof on many aspects of capital maintenance, which, accordingly, has been cited before in this chapter.[190] The court based its entire decision on the provisions of §§ 30, 31 GmbHG, which testifies to the creativeness that German lawyers have shown in relation to the concept of capital maintenance. The doctrine of equity-substituting shareholder credit complements the picture that emerges from the analysis in this chapter by adding a further piece to the mosaic of capital maintenance as the all-purpose instrument in German law to protect creditors against the opportunistic behaviour of those who control companies with limited liability. At the same time the common doctrinal roots proved to be of great assistance to courts and doctrinal writers because they enabled them to borrow from established principles, thereby ensuring the overall coherence of the framework in a very dynamic evolutionary process. Incidentally, it was often the law on equity-substituting shareholder credit which was at the forefront of new developments. Beside the *Lufttaxi* case, several other cases cited earlier in this chapter were also cases in this field, the reasoning of which (e.g. on persons connected to shareholders) may be applied more broadly in relation to capital maintenance.[191]

In 1980 the legislator decided to recast the hitherto entirely judge made law in a set of statutory provisions, viz. two paragraphs in the immediate context of the capital maintenance rules in the Limited Liability Companies Act (§§ 32a, 32b GmbHG) and supplementing provisions in insolvency law (which later became § 39 (1) n. 5 and § 135

188 BGH 19.9.1988, BGHZ 105, 168 at 175–176 = NJW 1988, 3143 at 3147.

189 BGH 14.12.1959, BGHZ 31, 258 at 271–274 = NJW 1960, 285 at 288.

190 In fn. 50, 113, 119, 122, 164.

191 BGH 21.9.1981, BGHZ 81, 311 = NJW 1982, 383 (fn. 172, 182); BGH 28.9.1981, BGHZ 81, 365 = NJW 1982, 386 (fn. 178); BGH 19.9.1988, BGHZ 105, 168 = NJW 1988, 3143 (fn. 171); BGH 16.12.1991, NJW 1992, 1167 (fn. 182).

InsO); these are the so-called 'amendment rules' ('*Novellenregeln*').[192] But the Bundesgerichtshof plainly refused to give up its previous case law because of the perceived gaps in the new statutory provisions.[193] From then on, Germany had two sets of rules on equity-substituting shareholder credit, which were blended together in a way whereby the 'case law rules' ('*Rechtsprechungsregeln*') continued to play the bigger part.[194] And given that the subject is notoriously prone to litigation, the courts found ever new opportunities to refine their already impressive jurisprudence. In the end a standard commentary on the Limited Liability Companies Act could easily devote 5 per cent of the entire work to the discussion of equity-substituting shareholder credit.[195] Clearly, the law was ripe for reform even before the *Centros* case.

That case added a whole new problem dimension. Given the complex interrelation of rules originating from capital maintenance principles with statutory rules laid down partly in the Limited Liability Companies Act and partly in the Insolvency Code, it became virtually impossible to draw a clear line whether, in the conflict of laws, the rules were governed by the *lex societatis*, the law governing the incorporation and internal affairs of the company, or the *lex concursus*, the law governing insolvency proceedings, and the question soon became mired in controversy.[196]

The MoMiG seeks to cut through this Gordian knot by replacing the entire body of existing law with a simple, yet harsh rule in the Insolvency Code providing for the general subordination of all shareholder loans (or equivalent provision of credit) in the insolvency of the company, irrespective of whether the company was in financial difficulties at the time when the loan was given. The core of this new concept is to be found in the amended § 39 (1) n. 5 InsO and the newly inserted § 39 (4) and (5) InsO, whereas §§ 32a, 32b GmbHG are repealed, and a new sentence is inserted in § 30 (1) GmbHG so as to prevent any future interpretation along the lines of the 'case law rules'.[197] The explanatory notes leave no

192 *Huber/Habersack* (fn. 187) 309.

193 BGH 26.3.1984, BGHZ 90, 370 = NJW 1984, 1891.

194 *Karsten Schmidt* in *Scholz*, GmbHG[10] §§ 32a, 32b mn. 15.

195 Take the example of the current 16th edition of *Lutter/Hommelhoff*, GmbHG, where the subject accounts for 67 pages out of a total of 1279 pages.

196 Contrast the diverging opinions by *Ulrich Forsthoff/Martin Schulz*, 'Gläubigerschutz bei EU-Auslandsgesellschaften', in: *Heribert Hirte/Thomas Bücker* (eds.), Grenzüberschreitende Gesellschaften (2nd edn 2006) § 16 mn. 41–53 and by *Sebastian Mock/Charlotte Schildt*, 'Insolvenz ausländischer Kapitalgesellschaften mit Sitz in Deutschland' in the same volume at § 17 mn. 111–115 (each with further references).

197 Bundestags-Drucksache 16/6140, p. 42.

doubt that one of the aims of this reform is to ensure the application of the new law to foreign-registered companies subject to insolvency proceedings in Germany under the COMI principle.[198]

E. Summary and outlook

As this chapter draws to a conclusion, readers will understand why German lawyers are so keen on capital maintenance. It provides companies and office-holders with a sharp and swift remedy to bring to book shareholders who have siphoned off company assets into their own hands. Interestingly, and perhaps contrary to what English readers might expect, the salient feature of capital maintenance in relation to German Limited Liability Companies lies not in a particularly restrictive approach in defining the amounts of lawful distributions to shareholders. At first sight, German law seems very relaxed about returning capital contributions made by the shareholders beyond the stated share capital,[199] although, in practice, it is the law on equity-substituting shareholder credit which creates the real hurdles in this respect.[200]

The primary advantage of capital maintenance lies in the enforcement of claims. Subjective defences on the part of the shareholder are largely non-existent in case of insolvency,[201] which presents a marked contrast with the principles identified for the German law on the avoidance of pre-insolvency legal acts in chapter 2. The lack of subjective defences, together with the absence of a requirement of factual insolvency at the time of the distribution, make the pursuit of a capital maintenance remedy, rather than an avoidance remedy or any remedy for unjust enrichment under the Civil Code, a natural choice for office-holders. Interestingly, in the controversial debate about the subjective or objective nature of concealed distributions the analogy with the law on avoidance of acts that are detrimental to creditors hardly ever came to the fore.[202] This reinforces the point made in the introductory chapter about the traditional separation of company law and insolvency law scholarship in Germany.[203] It seems to have been easier for German company lawyers to derive inspiration from tax law[204] than from insolvency law. Apparently there is only one writer

198 Bundestags-Drucksache 16/6140, p. 56–57. 199 Above, B.3 and B.4. 200 Above, D.

201 Above, C.1.

202 Possibly the only exception is *Flume* (fn. 125), 18 at 25 (but on the different question of whether the transaction was void or merely voidable).

203 Chapter 1 A.3 (text accompanying fn. 44). 204 Above, fn. 128.

who argues that a shareholder should be allowed to keep the benefit of an advantageous bargain with the company unless he has a controlling influence over the company.[205] This is probably as close as the German company law discourse on capital maintenance comes in apprehending the functional parallel in respect of the need for the protection of the counterparty that is so prominent in avoidance law. Most writers appear to be content that a shareholder of a company with limited liability is in a special position with regard to the maintenance of the company's share capital, which trumps any protection that commercial certainty might otherwise accord to him.[206] Even in relation to connected third-party recipients, the analogy is more readily drawn with the law on unjust enrichment[207] than with avoidance law,[208] although the latter is not based on unjust enrichment and may go beyond it.[209]

The doubtless advantage of capital maintenance remedies from the perspective of the office-holder already goes a long way towards explaining why German lawyers value the doctrine so much. But the centrality of the concept can only be fully appreciated in the light of its doctrinal offspring. Capital maintenance became the licence for the German courts to extend the rather terse rules in §§ 30, 31 GmbHG so as to develop rules about concealed distributions,[210] value transfers made to persons connected to shareholders for no equivalent consideration[211] and equity-substituting shareholder credit. Having all these instruments derived analytically from the same conceptual source greatly facilitated teleological interpretation and reasoning by analogy. At the same time, the flourishing doctrine of capital maintenance, which seemed to provide everything that was needed to protect creditors of companies with limited liability, provoked a tendency among company law scholars to insulate their discourse from neighbouring fields of law. On its own, the law was both functional and aesthetic.

But then the ECJ moved the goalposts – or so it seemed. In the ensuing debate some writers favoured extensive structural reforms that would transfer essential creditor protection functions from the realm of

205 *Wilhelm* (fn. 125), vol. II, 337 at 382.

206 Cf. *Martin Winter*, 'Verdeckte Gewinnausschüttungen im GmbH-Recht', ZHR 148 (1984), 579 at 585–586; *Tries* (fn. 130), 51 and 76.

207 See the references in fn. 176 and fn. 177.

208 But note the reference to avoidance law in some decisions form the BGH: 28.9.1981, BGHZ 81, 365 at 369 = NJW 1982, 386 at 387; 14.10.1985, ZIP 1986, 456 at 458.

209 Chapter 2 C.4 (text accompanying fn. 93).

210 Above, C.2.

211 Above, C.3.

company law to insolvency law,[212] whereas others emphasised the insolvency elements in their analysis of the existing law.[213] However, as the dust begins to settle, capital maintenance emerges virtually unscathed in its role as the core element of creditor protection in German company law. As noted in the introductory chapter,[214] the resolutions at the 66th Juristentag in September 2006 demonstrated a fairly conservative attitude. With the MoMiG the legislature has taken the strategic decision to abandon the minimum share capital requirement in a bid to end the drain of incorporations abroad, whereas, apart from the abolition of the rules on equity-substituting shareholder credit, the framework of capital maintenance has been left largely intact.[215] Less than a decade after the *Centros* case, German company law looks almost as if it had never been disturbed in its stable trajectory.

What then about the evolutionary potential of capital maintenance in English law? There is clear authority that concealed distributions can be accommodated within the concept of unlawful distributions,[216] even where the recipient of the value transfer is not a shareholder, but a person connected to a shareholder.[217] However, a company seeking to rely on this authority to recover the value of such transfers will need to overcome the hurdle raised by the subjective test of 'genuineness'. A subjective element is also present in the statutory remedy under s. 847 (2) CA 2006, where the company must show that the shareholder knew or had reasonable grounds for believing that a distribution was made unlawfully.[218] At this point of the analysis, it seems that the doctrine of capital maintenance cannot provide the office-holder with any real advantage in dealing with concealed distributions by way of ostensible exchange transactions, compared with the essentially objective avoidance remedy in s. 238 IA, which is purpose-built to catch transactions at an undervalue.[219]

[212] E.g. *Michael Fischer*, 'Die Verlagerung des Gläubigerschutzes vom Gesellschafts- in das Insolvenzrecht nach "Inspire Art"', ZIP 2004, 1477; *Gerhard Wagner*, 'Distributions to Shareholders and Fraudulent Transfer Law' [2006] EBOR 217.

[213] E.g. *Volker Röhricht*, 'Insolvenzrechtliche Aspekte im Gesellschaftsrecht', ZIP 2005, 505.

[214] Chapter 1 A.4 (text accompanying fn. 64).

[215] Although some have already warned of lasting structural damage that may result from seemingly innocent amendments to the law, e.g *Karsten Schmidt*, 'Reform der Kapitalsicherung und Haftung in der Krise nach dem Regierungsentwurf des MoMiG', GmbHR 2007, 1072.

[216] *Re Halt Garage* [1982] 3 All ER 1016; above C.2.

[217] *Aveling Barford Ltd v Perion Ltd* [1989] BCC 677; above C.3.

[218] *It's a Wrap (UK) Ltd v Gula* [2006] EWCA Civ 544 = [2006] BCC 626.

[219] Above, text accompanying fn. 156, and chapter 2 D.1.

In a recent article, John Vella takes the analysis of capital maintenance further.[220] He suggests that the test of 'genuineness' applied by the courts lacks clarity and that cases like *Re Halt Garage*[221] and *Aveling Barford*,[222] along with other cases, could be better explained and justified as expressions of a purposive approach to interpretation. The crucial effect of this re-evaluation of the case law is that a concealed distribution would have to be looked at from a purely objective perspective. Notwithstanding that the legal substance of the transaction in question is a sale, its characterisation as an unlawful distribution would depend solely on whether an exchange had taken place 'in a realistic and economic sense', whereas the intentions of the parties should be immaterial.[223] On this analysis one might expect the English doctrine of capital maintenance to become an instrument of creditor protection no less versatile than its German counterpart. But there remains the intriguing fact that the courts have failed to pick up on it. The entire judicial authority on capital maintenance principles being applied to concealed distributions consists of a handful of cases, none of which is above High Court level. Moreover, it is pertinent to note that the leading case, *Re Halt Garage*, was decided before the avoidance ground for transactions at an undervalue became available in consequence of the insolvency law reform of 1985/86. If the same set of facts were to occur today, there is every reason to assume that the office-holder would go for a straightforward application under s. 238 IA, rather than explore the uncertain territory of purposive interpretation of capital maintenance rules. In the final analysis, the existence of this objective avoidance ground means that even the purposive interpretation put forward by John Vella does not stimulate the doctrine of capital maintenance to the point of giving it a competitive advantage over transaction avoidance, apart from cases where a shareholder is able to rebut the presumption of the company's inability to pay debts raised against him by virtue of s. 240 (2) IA or where, exceptionally, a third-party recipient falls outside the statutory range of connected persons in ss. 249 and 435 IA, yet is caught by way of an extensive interpretation of *Aveling Barford*. Given this lack of incentives to pursue capital maintenance remedies, from an evolutionary perspective one might expect this area of law to remain in a fairly underdeveloped state, certainly if compared with the situation in Germany.

[220] *John Vella*, 'Departing from the Legal Substance of Transactions in the Corporate Field: the Ramsay Approach beyond the Tax Sphere' [2007] JCLS 243.

[221] See fn. 216. [222] See fn. 217. [223] See *Vella* (fn. 220), 251, 253–254, 265–268.

4

Directors' liability for contraventions of capital maintenance rules

A. Introduction

Directors' duties have received more attention from comparative lawyers than other topics covered in this book, not least because their relevance extends into the fashionable theme of corporate governance. More than the previous chapters, therefore, this chapter can build on an existing comparative scholarly literature.

The present chapter follows in the wake of the chapter on capital maintenance by focusing on the personal liability of directors for committing acts amounting to unlawful distributions. However, in the course of the argument, salient features of the general law on directors' duties in England and Germany will be explored so as to ensure that the analysis is rooted in a solid understanding of the relevant doctrinal structures, which, in this area, differ considerably as between England and Germany. It will be shown that the different doctrinal approaches in the two systems lead to practical differences for directors' liability. Again, the substantive analysis will be closely interwoven with terminological clarifications on key concepts such as 'duties of care' and 'fiduciary duties', on the one hand, and '*Sorgfaltspflichten*' and '*Treuepflichten*', on the other. These are further examples to demonstrate the perils of terminology in comparative law where there is a failure to appreciate the contents of what may appear to be little more than convenient labels. Several of the insights gained from this wider analysis will be put to use again in chapter 5, dealing with the personal responsibility of directors for trading in the vicinity of insolvency.

Subsequently, section C will demonstrate how the breach by a director of a fiduciary duty incumbent on him may give rise to remedies against a third party, viz. the beneficiary of the breach committed by the director. From an English perspective, characterising a duty as 'fiduciary' opens the way for this far-reaching third-party liability. This explains why English lawyers need to exercise a certain restraint when they characterise a duty as fiduciary duty, whereas in a comparative context the term fiduciary duty is often used in a rather general sense and without regard to the precise concept and its legal consequences within English law.

B. Directors' duties and contraventions of capital maintenance rules

1. Comparative classifications and the need for conceptual clarity

The popularity of directors' duties as a subject of comparative research has not only produced an ever growing body of literature. It has also created the need for a new phraseology and classifications which – abiding by the demands of the functional method – should be 'cut loose from their conceptual context and stripped of their national doctrinal overtones'.[1] The aim is to:

> develop a framework that is independent of the jurisprudential idiosyncrasies of any particular jurisdiction, and is therefore generally applicable. This framework provides common categories and a common language ('*gemeinsame Problemsprache*') within which most divergent perspectives on corporate law can be framed as competing empirical claims.[2]

The obvious danger here is that of conceptual confusion. As the possibilities for coining an entirely new language are limited, no comparative analysis can avoid using the same words as the national legal system(s) in whose language the comparative study happens to be written, but it may well attach deviant meanings to them. Add to this an international audience, many of whom read the language of the study only as a second language and will not be experts in the foreign law so as to recognise where the functional terminology ends and the national terminology – perhaps unwittingly – starts to creep in.

An especially influential comparative classification of directors' duties is based on the duality of '**duties of care or diligence**' and '**duties of loyalty**'.[3] Occasionally, this typology has started to appear in relation to

[1] *Zweigert / Kötz*, Comparative Law (3rd edn 1998), 44.

[2] *Kraakman et al.*, Anatomy of Corporate Law (2004), 216.

[3] *Klaus Hopt*, 'Directors' Duties to Shareholders, Employees, and Other Creditors: A view from the Continent', in: *Ewan McKendrick* (ed.), Commercial Aspects of Trusts and Fiduciary Obligations (1992), 115 at 121, 127, whose categories in this work are 'The Duty of Diligence' and 'The Duty of Loyalty and Secrecy'; more recently *Holger Fleischer*, 'The Responsibility of the Management and Its Enforcement', in: *Guido Ferrarini / Klaus*

domestic English company law.[4] Some years ago, a DTI publication stated that company directors' general duties to their companies 'are commonly divided into duties of loyalty and duties of care'.[5] One German professor even asserts that 'the differentiation between the duty of care and the duty of loyalty has its origin' in the case law of the English courts.[6]

However, the truth is that this typology has not been common at all in England. While the Company Law Review made some use of the term,[7] the Companies Act 2006 contains not a single reference to a 'duty of loyalty'. Where it appears in the English discourse, the term represents a novelty which may have been prompted by recent comparative scholarship. Yet even Paul Davies, one of the most prominent English academics on the comparative law scene and co-author of 'The Anatomy of Corporate Law',[8] hardly mentions a duty of loyalty as such in his two most recent books.[9] Instead, a glance at any traditional textbook shows English lawyers finding their primary reference grid in a distinction between what they call 'duties of care and skill' (or similarly), on the one hand, and '**fiduciary duties**', on the other.[10] This, in turn, is linked to the dualism of common law and equity which will be explained further below in this chapter. The Companies Act 2006 remains squarely within this reference grid. Thus, s. 178, which supplements the enumeration of specific duties laid down in ss. 171 to 177, provides:

(1) The consequences of breach ... of sections 171 to 177 are the same as would apply if the corresponding common law rule or equitable principle applied.

Hopt / Jaap Winter / Eddy Wymeersch (eds.), Reforming Company and Takeover Law in Europe (2004), 373 at 374.

4 Most prominently in *Brenda Hannigan*, Company Law (2003) ch. 9 to 11; see also *Item Software (UK) Ltd v Fassihi* [2004] EWCA Civ 1244 = [2004] BCC 994.

5 Consultative document on 'Director and Auditor Liability' (December 2003), p. 8.

6 *Tim Drygala*, 'Directors Liability in the Member States of the European Union', in: *Marcus Lutter* (ed.), Legal Capital in Europe (2006), 232 at 248.

7 'Developing the Framework' (March 2000) para. 3.49 ff.; 'Completing the Structure' (November 2000) para. 3.15 ff.

8 Above, fn. 2.

9 Neither his 'Introduction to Company Law' (2002) nor his latest edition of *Gower & Davies*' Company Law (8th edn 2008) carries the term in the subject index, although the latter book contains two brief references to 'duties of loyalty' (on p. 488 and p. 495).

10 *Gower & Davies*' Company Law (8th edn 2008), ch. 16; *Robert Pennington*, Company Law (8th edn 2001), 709; *John H. Farrar / Brenda M. Hannigan*, Farrar's Company Law (4th edn 1998), 378.

(2) The duties in those sections (with the exception of section 174 (duty to exercise reasonable care, skill and diligence)) are, accordingly, enforceable in the same way as any other fiduciary duty owed to a company by its directors.

This raises two issues where terminology matters not for its own sake, but in order to understand legal concepts in their context. First, the question arises whether the functional category 'duty of diligence' deployed in the comparative literature covers the same ground as the English category 'duty of care'. Klaus Hopt explains the scope of his functional category in these words:

> The duty of diligence is just a general formula for more specific duties which have been concretized by case law and legal literature. One of these is the duty to act within the limits of the law.[11]

The capital maintenance regime, with its prohibition on asset transfers from the company to the shareholders, provides for a legal limitation on the directors' powers to act on behalf of the company. However, as will be demonstrated presently, lawyers in England and Germany approach the matter via different routes, with their minds firmly anchored in their respective general frame of reference for directors' duties. For German lawyers, the statement about the 'duty to act within the limits of the law' as one aspect of the 'duty of diligence' makes perfect sense. But when English lawyers think of directors transgressing the legal boundaries of the company's powers, they are more likely to see this act as a breach of a fiduciary duty rather than a breach of a duty of care or diligence.

Next, we need a terminological clarification in relation to 'fiduciary duties'. In a recent comparative study, the co-authors of 'The Anatomy of Corporate Law' undertake a functional assessment of company law across several major industrialised countries, including Germany and the United Kingdom.[12] In their chapter on creditor protection, they adopt the notion of 'fiduciary duties' as the synonym for what they call the 'standards strategy', as opposed to the 'rules strategy' of legal capital rules. Under the umbrella notion of 'fiduciary duties' they then discuss, inter alia, wrongful trading, directors' personal liability resulting from 'the board's gross negligence or narrow pursuit of shareholder interests when the company is insolvent or nearly so'[13] and shareholder liability under such doctrines as shadow directorship, equitable subordination or

[11] *Hopt* (fn. 3), at 121. [12] *Kraakman et al.*, Anatomy of Corporate Law (2004).
[13] Ibid. 89.

piercing the corporate veil. The thread that binds these diverse doctrines together seems to be the idea of 'holding influential corporate insiders – directors, auditors, "inside" creditors, or controlling shareholders – liable for participating in corporate opportunism in the vicinity of insolvency'.[14] Yet it seems that in giving such a wide meaning to 'fiduciary duties' the authors have borrowed, without much reflection, from the standard terminology in the United States, which uses the term as a synonym for 'directors' duties' generally, a superordinate concept comprising duties of care and duties of loyalty.[15] This is by no means a terminology adopted universally even within the common law world. In England 'fiduciary duties' are understood in a narrower sense as a subset of 'directors' duties', not a synonym, and the duty of care is invariably treated as distinct from fiduciary duties.

The terminological complications are further compounded by the perils of translation.[16] It has become widespread practice among German writers to translate 'fiduciary duties' as '*Treuepflichten*'. Indeed, these terms could pass as literal translations of each other. But it is a use of language which is bound to create confusion given that '***Treuepflicht***' is a term of art in German company law. Its use is highly problematic where 'fiduciary duty' refers to the broad sense of the term, as is understood in the United States.[17] Yet difficulties also arise if '*Treuepflichten*' is used to express the narrower meaning of 'fiduciary duties'

[14] Ibid. 95.

[15] Cf. *William T. Allen*, 'The Corporate Director's Fiduciary Duty of Care and the Business Judgment Rule under U.S. Corporate Law', in: *Klaus Hopt et al.* (eds.), Comparative Corporate Governance (1998), 307. *Robert Clark*, Corporate Law (1986) has a revealing entry in the subject index (p. 833): 'Fiduciary duty – *See* Duty of care, Duty of loyalty'; a similar entry exists in the subject index of the 'Anatomy' (p. 229). In fact, the situation in the United States may be more complex as there appears the be a third category, viz. a 'fiduciary duty of good faith': *Melvin Eisenberg*, 'The Duty of Good Faith in American Corporate Law' [2006] ECFR 1, who submits that 'the duty of good faith rationalizes and explains a variety of specific obligations that . . . do not fit comfortably or at all within the duties of care and loyalty' (at 43–44).

[16] *Holger Fleischer* has already wrestled somewhat inconclusively with the issue; compare his two articles 'Legal Transplants in European Company Law – The Case of Fiduciary Duties' [2005] ECFR 378 and 'Zur organschaftlichen Treuepflicht der Geschäftsleiter im Aktien- und GmbH-Recht', WM 2003, 1045, where the terms 'fiduciary duties', 'duties of loyalty' and '*Treuepflichten*' are deployed without a clear sense of the various shades of meaning.

[17] As in *Marcus Roth*, Unternehmerisches Ermessen und Haftung des Vorstands (2001), 173–177; *Oliver Rieckers*, 'Treuepflichten versus Vertragsfreiheit – Neues zur Wirksamkeit von Deal-Protection-Klauseln in der Rechtsprechung Delawares', RIW 2003, 668.

employed in England,[18] because the overlap between the two concepts is only partial.

For a start, it is pertinent to note that English lawyers are currently debating the scope of their concept. In *Bristol & West Building Society v Mothew*, Lord Justice Millett (later Lord Millett) expressed concern about the unjustifiably wide use of the term. In his view the expression 'fiduciary duty' should be confined to those duties which are peculiar to fiduciaries and the breach of which attracts legal consequences differing from those consequent upon the breach of other duties. His Lordship identified the obligation of loyalty as the core duty of a fiduciary: acting in good faith; not making a profit out of his trust; not placing himself in a position where his duty and his interest may conflict; not acting for his own benefit or the benefit of a third person without the informed consent of his principal.[19] In the same vein, Sarah Worthington writes: 'The only real "fiduciary" obligation is the obligation of loyalty.'[20] If the term 'fiduciary duty' is understood in this limited sense, it comes close to what German lawyers mean when they speak of the *Treuepflicht* to the company owed by a director. In many English cases, however, the term 'fiduciary duty' has a wider meaning, as will become clear from the discussion below. Moreover, the Companies Act 2006, in s. 178 (2), clearly applies the term 'fiduciary duty' in the sense of 'every duty apart from the duty to exercise reasonable care, skill and diligence', which amounts to an implicit rejection of the terminological specification proposed by Sarah Worthington and Lord Millett.

Let us now turn to *Treuepflichten* in German company law. The area had long received scant attention, but has seen a significant development over the last few decades, not least through cross-fertilisation achieved by comparative scholarship.[21] The concept of *Treuepflichten*

[18] As in *Peter Behrens* (ed.), Die Gesellschaft mit beschränkter Haftung im internationalen und europäischen Recht (2nd edn 1997), 866; *Gebhard Rehm*, 'Die *Private Company Limited by Shares* (Ltd.) nach englischem Recht', in: *Horst Eidenmüller* (ed.), Ausländische Kapitalgesellschaften im deutschen Recht (2004) § 10 mn. 60; *Boris Kasolowsky / Alexander Schall*, 'Die Private Limited Company – England und Wales', in: *Heribert Hirte / Thomas Bücker* (eds.), Grenzüberschreitende Gesellschaften (2nd edn 2006) § 4 mn. 34.

[19] *Bristol & West Building Society v Mothew* [1998] Ch. 1, at 18; cf. also *Robert Flannigan*, 'The Adulteration of Fiduciary Doctrine in Corporate Law' (2006) 122 LQR 449.

[20] *Sarah Worthington*, Equity (2nd edn 2006) 130; see already her articles 'Fiduciaries: When is Self-Denial Obligatory?' [1999] CLJ 500 and 'Corporate Governance: Remedying and Ratifying Directors' Breaches' (2000) 116 LQR 638.

[21] Below, fn. 39 and subsequent text.

offers new routes to deal with conflicts of interest as between a director and the company. But it goes a lot further than that. German law understands *Treuepflichten* as mutual duties of loyalty between a director and the company, akin to those existing between employee and employer.[22] Moreover, and this is a point of the greatest importance, German law accepts that shareholders, and even shareholders of a listed company, owe *Treuepflichten* to each other and to their company, a proposition confirmed by the Bundesgerichtshof in the well-known *Girmes* case.[23] This is the background one needs to know in order to put things into perspective when a German scholar writes that 'there seems to be a clear trend towards generally accepting that shareholders do owe fiduciary duties'.[24] Such a statement may be equally appropriate to describe the legal situation in the United States,[25] which brings to light a further issue where the American legal discourse and the English legal discourse have gone separate ways. Certainly, the same proposition put forward in relation to English law, namely that shareholders owe fiduciary duties – as the term is understood by English lawyers – to each other or to their company, would have to be considered heretical.[26]

Two immediate conclusions follow: first, given the incongruities between the two terms, translating 'fiduciary duties' as '*Treuepflichten*' should be avoided. If there has to be a translation, it is perhaps best to speak of '*fiduziarische Pflichten*',[27] which is close to the English original in terms of resonance and avoids false connotations. Conversely, it makes sense to translate '*Treuepflicht*' as 'duty of loyalty' provided there is an understanding that such duties may be owed also by persons who are not in a fiduciary position.

[22] BGH 18.12.1954, BGHZ 16, 50 = NJW 1955, 501 (where, under exceptional circumstances linked to the war and the collapse of the Third Reich in 1945, *Treuepflicht* formed the basis for awarding the director a pension from the company in the absence of a contractual agreement).

[23] BGH 20.3.1995, BGHZ 129, 136 = NJW 1995, 1739.

[24] *Heinz-Dieter Assmann*, 'The Impact of Insider Trading Rules on Company Law', in: *Klaus Hopt / Eddy Wymeersch* (eds.), Capital Markets and Company Law (2003), 529 at 544.

[25] The analysis of 'shareholder fiduciary duties' offered by *David C. Donald*, 'Shareholder Voice and its Opponents' [2005] JCLS 305, at 320–326, is explicitly restricted to US law.

[26] Cf. *Robert Flannigan*, 'Fiduciary Duties of Shareholders and Directors' [2004] JBL 277, at 285–287 with references to judicial authority from England, Canada, Australia and New Zealand.

[27] Already *Carsten Bödecker*, Die Kapitalerhaltung im englischen Gesellschaftsrecht (1994); similarly *Holger Fleischer*, 'Zur organschaftlichen Treuepflicht der Geschäftsleiter im Aktien- und GmbH-Recht', WM 2003, 1045 at 1047: 'fiduziarische Pflichtenbindung'.

Second, as regards the use of the term 'fiduciary duty' by English lawyers, foreign observers must bear in mind that this category has traditionally been understood as something broader than a mere 'duty of loyalty', but is always considered as distinct from and mutually exclusive with a 'duty of care'. It follows logically that fiduciary duties cover some ground which cannot be ascribed to either of the two latter categories. Crucially, this is the area where English lawyers find their solution to the problem of directors' liability for an infringement of capital maintenance rules.

These are not harmless linguistic discrepancies. A failure to understand concepts in their historic and doctrinal context will make it much harder to grasp certain important consequences for the personal liability of directors and also for the liability of the recipients of funds paid out in contravention of capital maintenance rules.

2. *The German approach to directors' duties and capital maintenance*

Turning to Germany, with its codified system of private law, English lawyers might expect to find a comprehensive statement of directors' duties in the relevant statute, the Limited Liability Companies Act (GmbH-Gesetz), akin to what the Companies Act 2006 introduced in the UK. They will be disappointed. A senior German judge has drawn attention to the lack of a statutory 'profile' of how company directors are required to act and concluded that 'scholarship, legal practice and to a certain extent also the courts' – note the order of appearance – were called upon to develop norms for a prudent and conscientious director.[28]

The closest approximation to such a statement would seem to be § 43 GmbHG. Like the provisions in §§ 30, 31 GmbHG discussed in the previous chapter, § 43 GmbHG belongs to the original core of the statute; apart from a trivial modification in sub-paragraph (3), the entire paragraph has been in the statute in its present form since the original

[28] *Wulf Goette* (then an ordinary member and since 2005 president of the second civil senate of the Bundesgerichtshof, which deals with matters of company law), writing extra-judicially: 'Leitung, Aufsicht, Haftung – zur Rolle der Rechtsprechung bei der Sicherung einer modernen Unternehmensführung', in: Festschrift 50 Jahre Bundesgerichtshof (2000), 123 at 125.

enactment in 1892. The provision starts off with two statements of principle, each in one sub-paragraph:

(1) The directors, in attending to the affairs of the company, must apply the diligence of a prudent businessman (*Sorgfalt eines ordentlichen Geschäftsmannes*).
(2) Directors who offend against their duties are jointly and severally liable to the company for the resulting damage.

Sub-paragraph (3) contains a non-exhaustive list of specific prohibitions, the contravention of which renders a director personally liable in application of the principles set forth in sub-paragraphs (1) and (2). Among these exemplary prohibitions are 'payments [that] have been made out of the assets of the company' in contravention of § 30 GmbHG, the main plank of the capital maintenance regime.

For the purpose of a purely functional analysis, this would seem all that is needed in terms of information about German law. The problem is clear, as is the solution. That German law places its solution in the context of the director's duty of diligence would seem to have little significance beyond classification. But the focus of this book, on fostering mutual understanding between lawyers of different jurisdictions, makes it apposite to convey more of the context and flavour of this classification, with a view to providing background information as to why German law does not do what English readers may think of as the most natural thing, viz. to regard a director's infringement of capital maintenance rules as breach of a fiduciary duty.

German lawyers view § 43 GmbHG as 'the central statutory provision' in respect of directors' duties and liability towards the company,[29] and commentaries accordingly devote considerable space to its interpretation. Yet if this 'central statutory provision' on directors' duties and their liability for breach of duty were to be judged by English standards of legislative drafting, it would have to be called imprecise, to put it mildly.[30] By German standards it is not so unusual given that every statute can be expected to gain its contours from scholarly writing which precedes and accompanies each act of the legislator, so that lawyers familiar with the current discourse will have a good idea of what

[29] *Rüdiger Volhard / Jürgen Taschke*, 'Managing Directors and Authorized Representatives', in: *Rüdiger Volhard / Arndt Stengel* (eds.), German Limited Liability Company (1997), 137 at 161; *Uwe Schneider* in *Scholz*, GmbHG[10] § 43 mn. 14.

[30] Recall the observation about different styles of legislative drafting in chapter 1 A.4.

is meant. German lawyers realise that § 43 GmbHG presupposes or implies some legal rules rather than actually laying them down.[31] Thus, sub-paragraph (2) speaks of 'duties' without naming any of them, but it clearly implies that there is a whole array of duties to which directors are subject and whose breach renders them liable to compensate the company for any loss, and of which sub-paragraph (3) then offers a non-exhaustive list. Sub-paragraph (1) defines a standard of diligence without explicitly saying that the directors owe a duty to apply proper diligence in the management of the company. But it is implicit that such a duty exists as one of the duties to which sub-paragraph (2) refers, although an academic (in the sense of: not very practical) debate exists as to where the legal basis for the duty should be located within the statute, whether it is to be derived from § 43 sub-paragraph (1) GmbHG[32] or from the status of the directors as the competent managerial organ of the company.[33]

Throughout this chapter, the term '**(duty of) diligence**' will be used in relation to German law so as to avoid speaking of '**(duty of) care**'. The latter is a common law term of art and does not exactly mirror the German notion of '***Sorgfaltspflicht***', although the two could pass as literal translations. German law draws a distinction between the unlawfulness (***Rechtswidrigkeit***) of an act and the culpability or fault (***Verschulden***) of the person committing the act.[34] Both need to be satisfied for a claim for compensation to arise. Strictly speaking the breach of a duty of diligence (*Sorgfaltspflicht*) relates to the unlawfulness of the act,[35] but the separate requirement of culpability is greatly diminished in importance where the law imposes an objective standard of diligence (*Sorgfaltsmaßstab*), as is the case for company directors by virtue of the standard of the 'prudent businessman' in § 43 (1) GmbHG. English lawyers would perhaps not find it necessary to distinguish between the two in the first place. Yet it is this conceptual distinction which English readers need to know in order to understand a German writer when he says that 'it is hard to tell whether courts are referring to the general duty of the director to act diligently or are focusing on his or

[31] See, for instance, *Ulrich Haas* in *Michalski*, GmbHG § 43 mn. 39–40 and *Walter Paefgen* in *Ulmer / Habersack / Winter*, GmbHG § 43 mn. 3.

[32] *Hans-Joachim Mertens* in *Hachenburg*, GmbHG^8 § 43 mn. 15.

[33] *Hans Georg Koppensteiner* in *Rowedder / Schmidt-Leithoff*, GmbHG^4 § 43 mn. 8; *Haas* (fn. 31), § 43 mn. 39.

[34] *Basil Markesinis / Hannes Unberath*, German Law of Torts (4th edn 2002), 79–85.

[35] Ibid., 85–86 (speaking of 'duties of care').

her negligence as the relevant standard of care (fault)'.[36] The distinction does have practical consequences. A person, e.g. a company director, whose conduct is objectively incompatible with the requisite standard of diligence and therefore unlawful, does not act culpably and will therefore escape liability if he relies bona fide on advice obtained from an independent, suitably qualified professional expert with comprehensive information on the company's situation and access to all relevant documents.[37] Similarly, it has been held that a director does not act culpably as long as he relies bona fide on an interpretation of the statute supported by commentators and several decisions by appeal courts, even though the Bundesgerichtshof later declares the interpretation to be erroneous.[38]

Returning to classification, where does § 43 GmbHG leave any duty of loyalty or fiduciary duty of a company director under German law? The statute neither creates nor precludes such a duty. When the smaller corporate form of the Limited Liability Company (GmbH) was created by the German legislature at the end of the nineteenth century (and this holds true also for the gradual emergence of the modern Joint Stock Company, the Aktiengesellschaft, during that century), not only did German law lack the concept of the trust, on which English law modelled company directorships, it did not have a coherent concept of what is today called *Treuepflicht* (duty of loyalty) either. To this day, no paragraph in the Limited Liability Companies Act or in the Joint Stock Companies Act speaks of a director's *Treuepflicht*. Rather, the concept is a fairly recent innovation of doctrinal writing, with considerable input from comparative observations about Anglo-American company law,[39]

[36] *Erich Schanze*, 'Directors' duties in Germany' [1999] CFILR 286, at 289–290.

[37] BGH 14.5.2007, NJW 2007, 2118 (certified auditors called in to examine whether the excess of liabilities over assets in the company's annual accounts constitutes over-indebtedness for the purpose of § 19 InsO).

[38] BGH 5.2.2007, BGHZ 171, 46.

[39] *Friedrich Kübler*, 'Erwerbschancen und Organpflichten – Überlegungen zur Entwicklung der Lehre von den "corporate opportunities"', in: Festschrift für Winfried Werner (1984), 437 (with references to US law); *Klaus Hopt*, 'Self-Dealing and Use of Corporate Opportunity and Information: Regulating Directors' Conflict of Interest', in: *Klaus Hopt / Gunther Teubner* (eds.), Corporate Governance and Directors' Liabilities (1985), 285 at 295, writing before the 1985 case from the BGH (below, fn. 42) became known and admitting that the corporate opportunity doctrine was less developed in Germany than in the United States and Great Britain; extensive monographic treatment by *Thomas Abeltshauser*, Leitungshaftung im Kapitalgesellschaftsrecht – Zu den Sorgfalts- und Loyalitätspflichten von Unternehmensleitern im deutschen und im US-amerikanischen Kapitalgesellschaftsrecht (1998).

and with the wording of § 43 GmbHG proving flexible enough for the subsequent judicial recognition of such a duty of loyalty.

In 1985 the Bundesgerichtshof was confronted with a classic situation of a director abstracting a corporate opportunity (*Geschäftschance*), very much reminiscent of the facts of a well-known English case on the subject.[40] The defendant had learned of a new technological development affecting the company's product range, but instead of seeking to exploit it for the benefit of the company, he quit as a director and later set up a rival business. The second civil senate of the Bundesgerichtshof had previously held that directors were under a duty not to compete with the company,[41] but found it impossible to extend this argument to the case before it, as the competition had taken place after the director's termination of office. Instead, the judges found a more general duty owed by the director to the company requiring him to protect the company's interests over and above his own personal interests. On the facts of the case, the Bundesgerichtshof held that the director, while still in office, had failed to comply with this duty of loyalty in that he did not, with due diligence, procure the acquisition of the new technology on behalf of the company.[42] The reference to due diligence (*gebotene Sorgfalt*) is significant. Throughout the text of the judgment, insofar as it is reported, the notion of '*Sorgfalt*' (diligence) appears four times, whereas '*Treuepflicht*' appears only once, and this is in combination with diligence as '*Sorgfalts- und Treuepflicht*' (duty of diligence and loyalty). Moreover, the Bundesgerichtshof cites § 43 (1) GmbHG as the legal basis for its decision. The duty of loyalty is thus conceptualised as an aspect of the wider duty of diligence.

In this respect company law simply reflects a general approach taken by German law. Notwithstanding a few isolated pockets of strict liability, the German Civil Code is firmly rooted in a civilian tradition[43] that all compensation for loss (*Schadensersatz*) is based on fault. That applies not only to liability in delict (§ 823 BGB), but – more surprising to English lawyers – it extends to liability for breach of contract, at least in

[40] *Industrial Development Consultants Ltd v Cooley* [1972] 1 WLR 443; the leading English case on the exploitation of corporate opportunities by directors is *Regal (Hastings) Ltd v Gulliver* [1967] 2 AC 134n, although this decision by the House of Lords is surrounded by doubt: *Sealy/Worthington*, Cases and Materials in Company Law (2007), 316–317.

[41] BGH 9.11.1967, BGHZ 49, 30 = NJW 1968, 396.

[42] BGH 23.9.1985, NJW 1986, 585.

[43] *Reinhard Zimmermann*, Law of Obligations (1996), 1032–1035.

principle (§ 276 BGB).[44] Against this background, the key issue addressed by § 43 GmbHG is not whether a director owes a specific duty of care to the company, but whether a director, in breaching whatever duty is incumbent on him, has fallen below the requisite standard of diligence. This explains the structure of the provision, which serves a limited purpose. Far from being a comprehensive statement of directors' duties, it merely defines the benchmark for the conduct of the directors as an objective standard of diligence; that needs to be said, because elsewhere, for instance among the partners in a partnership (§ 708 BGB), the standard of diligence is subjective. § 43 GmbHG does not define a specific duty owed by the director to the company to conduct or monitor management activities with appropriate care or diligence; that is taken for granted.

Once this is understood, the looseness of § 43 GmbHG reveals itself as an ingenious device for fitting in any number of specific duties recognised by scholars and courts as pertaining to the status and functions of company directors. Paradoxically, German law on directors' duties today relies more heavily on 'unwritten' norms than English law after the Companies Act 2006. Typically for German law, much of it is shaped by scholarly writing. Virtually all current editions of commentaries on § 43 GmbHG present the directors' duty of loyalty (*Treuepflicht*), which has only recently been carved out from the provision, on an equal footing with their duty to apply due diligence to the management of the company. This forms the domestic background against which German scholars, in particular, have embraced the comparative classification of directors' duties as based on the duality of 'duties of care or diligence' and 'duties of loyalty'.[45]

But there remains a significant conceptual difference between English and German law. English lawyers understand the directors' duty to exercise reasonable care, skill and diligence as one duty out of an array of duties, which can be contrasted with fiduciary duties, that do not rely on a standard of due care or diligence; the Companies Act 2006, in s. 178 (2), makes this explicit. German lawyers, on the other hand, view the directors' duty to act with due diligence as a general principle underpinning the exercise of all those specific duties to which directors are submitted, including their duty of loyalty. That does not mean German

[44] See *Reinhard Zimmermann*, The New German Law of Obligations (2005), 50–51.
[45] Above, fn. 3; the same terminology is also applied by *Schanze* (fn. 36).

directors will escape liability easily. It is generally agreed that where a breach of duty has caused loss to the company, a lack of diligence is presumed against the director and the burden is upon him to disprove his culpability.[46] From a functional perspective one may argue, with some justification, that this brings German law on directors' liability, although notionally based on fault, quite close to a system of strict liability. However, there are exceptions, as we have seen,[47] where a director may exculpate himself on the ground that he obtained independent professional advice or that he relied on a prevailing interpretation of the law. These grounds for exculpation seem to apply to the duty of loyalty just as they apply to other duties. In any case, drawing attention to the difference is pertinent in order to help English lawyers understand why their German colleagues refer to 'diligence' where English lawyers would instinctively see a breach of a fiduciary duty. Against this background it should no longer surprise English readers that German lawyers can and do accommodate a 'duty to act within the limits of the law' within their concept of *Sorgfaltspflicht* (their general duty to carry out all duties with due diligence). For them there is no need to look for a solution elsewhere, and in particular, they do not resort to any notion of a fiduciary duty for this purpose.

3. *The English approach to directors' duties and capital maintenance*

English lawyers operate in a very different conceptual environment, which derives from a complex body of judge-made law developed since the beginnings of modern company law in the mid-nineteenth century. This conceptual environment remains intact notwithstanding that, for the first time in the history of English company law, the Companies Act 2006 introduced a codification of the general duties of directors.[48] This

[46] Again, the Limited Liability Companies Act does not actually say this, but an express provision to this effect exists for Joint Stock Companies in § 93 (2) AktG, and it applies to Limited Liability Companies by analogy: *Koppensteiner* (fn. 33), § 43 mn. 36; for a more detailed analysis of the difficulties with this analogy see *Haas* (fn. 31), § 43 mn. 248 ff. and *Uwe Schneider* in *Scholz*, GmbHG[9] § 43 mn. 167 ff.

[47] Above, text accompanying fn. 37 and 38.

[48] Part 10, Chapter 2 (ss. 170 to 181); Company Law Review, Final Report (2001) para. 3.5–3.11 (with references to earlier documents) and vol. II, Schedule 2; in this respect, the Company Law Review was able to build on work previously undertaken by the Law Commission: 'Company Directors: Regulating Conflicts of Interests' (Law Comm. No. 261, Scottish Law Comm. No. 173, Cm. 4436) (1999).

statutory 'code of conduct'[49] was designed with a view to providing 'greater clarity on what is expected of directors and make the law more accessible'.[50] A fortiori, not only company directors should find the law more accessible, but also foreign lawyers seeking to understand English law.[51]

But the codification exercise comes with several important caveats that have found their legislative expression in s. 170 (3) and (4) of the Companies Act 2006:

(3) The general duties are based on certain common law rules and equitable principles as they apply in relation to directors and have effect in place of those rules and principles as regards the duties owed to a company by a director.
(4) The general duties shall be interpreted and applied in the same way as common law rules or equitable principles, and regard shall be had to the corresponding common law rules and equitable principles in interpreting and applying the general duties.

The codification is neither comprehensive, nor is it a break with the past. The wording in s. 170 (3), whereby the statutory duties are based on 'certain' common law rules and equitable principles, leaves open the possibility that common law rules and equitable principles not covered by the statutory restatement of directors' duties are still applicable and that the courts are free to develop such rules.[52] The analysis in chapter 5 will encounter one particular instance of a duty that remains uncodified, viz. the duty to consider the interests of creditors in times of threatened insolvency.[53] Moreover, if the statutory duties 'have effect in place of' the common law rules and equitable principles on which they are based, the previous case law will continue to be of relevance, if not as authority for the existence of a rule, then as authoritative guidance on what the drafters of the statute had in mind.[54]

49 Thus the explanatory notes to the Companies Act 2006 para. 298.
50 Ibid. para. 301; Company Law Review, Final Report (2001), para. 3.7.
51 For a first analysis of the new law in German, see *Felix Steffek*, Geschäftsleiterpflichten im englischen Kapitalgesellschaftsrecht – Kodifizierung der directors' duties im Companies Act 2006, GmbHR 2007, 810.
52 *Hannigan & Prentice*, Companies Act 2006 para. 3.11.
53 Explanatory notes to the Companies Act 2006 para. 306.
54 See the explicit statement to this effect in Company Law Review, Completing the Structure (November 2000) para. 3.12: 'existing authorities will be capable of being invoked to explain the nature of the duties which they codify'.

Certainly the most difficult aspect for lawyers from a civilian background is the distinction between 'common law rules' and 'equitable principles'. There is nothing comparable, for instance, in German law. The dualism of **common law** and **equity** as two distinct bodies of rules within the English legal system is deeply rooted in the history of English law, yet its significance for modern company law is anything but trivial, let alone merely historical. The Companies Act 2006 expressly preserves the distinction in two respects, viz. in s. 170 (4), which prescribes that the statutory duties 'shall be interpreted and applied in the same way as common law rules or equitable principles', and in s. 178 (1), which provides that the 'consequences of breach ... are the same as would apply if the corresponding common law rule or equitable principle applied'. It may seem a bit eccentric that the most recent codification of company law in Europe does not reveal its secrets to the (foreign) reader who fails to understand just what this age-old classification means. But it provides a prime example of the genius of legal language, which can convey plenty of meaning in just a few words.

Trust origins and the central role of fiduciary duties in English company law

English company law developed straight out of the great institution of the trust, which was a creation of the courts of equity and not recognised at common law. The intellectual commitment to the distinction between common law and equity continued after the court reforms of 1873 and 1875 had amalgamated the different courts of common law and equitable jurisdiction, as the Chancery Division of the new High Court, though not a separate court, was entrusted with the specialised task of administering, inter alia, trusts and company law.[55] Barristers maintained their segregation into common law and equity (or 'chancery') practices,[56] and legal education tended to focus on the differences rather than the commonalities between the two sets of rules.[57] Against this background, it was natural

[55] Supreme Court of Judicature Act 1873, s. 16 (transferring the jurisdiction of the High Court of Chancery to the new High Court of Justice), s. 31 (establishing the Chancery Division, along with four other divisions, 'for the more convenient despatch of business in the said High Court of Justice'), and s. 34 (matters assigned to the Chancery Division).

[56] Down to the present day, it appears: 'Barristers who specialise in equity generally practise in Lincoln's Inn and it is from their ranks that judges are normally chosen for the Chancery Division of the High Court where cases primarily concerned with equity are heard.' – *D. J. Hayton*, Law of Trusts (4th edn 2003), 36.

[57] *Worthington* (fn. 20), 13.

for chancery judges to treat the new institution of the company director as analogous to that of the trustee. This led to a flourishing development of fiduciary duties on the part of company directors,[58] but left the development of duties of care and skill lagging behind.[59]

The conceptualisation of company directors as trustees, or at least as analogous to trustees, happened not because chancery lawyers lacked imagination. In the true spirit of an evolutionary development of the law, the analogy provided them with the means to answer a number of legal questions which arose in practical cases. One example of a recurring problem in many company law cases of that period concerned the limitation of actions against delinquent directors. Before the Trustee Act 1888, the Statute of Limitations[60] did not apply to actions against trustees for breach of trust. The trustee analogy allowed the judges to extend this rule to company directors.[61] After the Trustee Act 1888 the question presented itself in the reverse: was the new Act also applicable to company directors? This gave rise to an oft-cited passage by Lord Justice Lindley concerning the role of directors as trustees:

> Although directors are not properly speaking trustees, yet they have always been considered and treated as trustees of money which comes to their hands or which is actually under their control; and ever since joint stock companies were invented directors have been held liable to make good moneys which they have misapplied upon the same footing as if they were trustees, and it has always been held that they are not entitled to the benefit of the old *Statute of Limitations* because they have committed breaches of trust, and are in respect of such moneys to be treated as trustees. Then, when the Legislature passed an Act of Parliament – the *Trustee Act*, 1888 (. . .) – protecting trustees against actions for breaches of trust, how can it be with any reason said that directors are not to have the benefit of this statute? I cannot go that length. I am satisfied that the statute does apply.[62]

58 A profound enquiry is offered in two articles by *Len Sealy*, 'Fiduciary Relationships' [1962] CLJ 69, and 'Some Principles of Fiduciary Obligation' [1963] CLJ 199; a critical assessment of the case law is provided by *Robert Flannigan*, 'The Adulteration of Fiduciary Doctrine in Corporate Law' (2006) 122 LQR 449.

59 Duties of care and skill will be dealt with in more detail in chapter 5 C.3.

60 Limitation Act 1623.

61 *Re Exchange Banking Co (Flitcroft's case)* (1882) 21 ChD 519, at 535 (Brett LJ), 537 (Cotton LJ); *Re Sharpe, Re Bennett, Masonic & General Life Assurance Co v Sharpe* [1892] 1 Ch. 154, at 167.

62 *Re Lands Allotment Co* [1894] 1 Ch. 616, at 631; similarly, Kay LJ states (at 639) that although 'as directors they are not trustees at all', by virtue of the property which is put into their hands or under their control, they must be conceived as 'trustees by

In a later case, we find the following exposition of the relationship between company directors and trustees, which demonstrates how much the trustee analogy still informs the thinking of English company lawyers:

> However much the company's purposes and the directors' duties, powers and functions may differ from the purposes of a strict settlement and the duties, powers and functions of its trustees, the directors and such trustees have this indisputably in common – that the property in their hands or under their control must be applied for the specified purposes of the company or the settlement; and to apply it otherwise is to mis-apply it in breach of the obligation to apply it to those purposes for the company or the settlement beneficiaries. So, even though the scope and operation of such obligation differs in the case of directors and strict settlement trustees, the nature of the obligation with regard to property in their hands or under their control is identical, namely, to apply it to specified purposes for others beneficially. This is to hold it on trust for the company or the settlement beneficiaries as the case may be. That is what holding it on trust means. That is why a misapplication of it is equally in each case a breach of trust.[63]

The notion of a 'misapplication of company property' also links directors' fiduciary duties to early forerunners of what is now s. 212 of the Insolvency Act 1986. Although the section is of a procedural nature only and does not create any new rights and obligations,[64] it has long been of great practical value and frequent use. It empowers the court to order any director to repay, restore or account for the money or property of the company, or to compensate the company for the loss resulting from any misfeasance or breach of duty. Its aim is to provide the liquidator with a speedy tool for the recovery of money or property due to the company where, on the basis of the written submissions to the court, the facts are sufficiently clear so as to allow for summary judgment.[65]

implication of law'. Examples of earlier cases in the same vein are *Russell v Wakefield Waterworks Co* (1875) LR 20 Eq. 474; *Re Forest of Dean Coal Mining Company* (1878) 10 ChD 450; *Re Exchange Banking Co (Flitcroft's case)* (1882) 21 ChD 519.

63 *Selangor United Rubber Estates Ltd v Cradock (No 3)* [1968] 1 WLR 1555, at 1575C-E (Ungoed-Thomas J); for subsequent references to this trustee analogy see, for instance, *Belmont Finance Corporation Ltd v Williams Furniture Ltd (No 2)* [1980] 1 All ER 393, at 405 (Buckley LJ); *Rolled Steel Products (Holdings) Ltd v British Steel Corporation* [1986] Ch. 246, at 298 (Slade LJ); *Re Duckwari Plc* [1999] Ch. 253, at 262 (Nourse LJ); *Allied Carpets Group plc v Nethercott* [2001] BCC 81, at 86–87.

64 *Cohen v Selby* [2002] BCC 82; *Wightman v Bennett* [2005] BPIR 470.

65 For a full account of the procedural advantages to be gained by invoking s. 212 IA, see *Fidelis Oditah*, 'Misfeasance proceedings against company directors' [1992] LMCLQ 207, at 210.

In the Companies Act 1862, s. 165, the first ancestor of the modern provision, was framed in the following words:

> Where, in the course of the Winding-up of any Company under this Act, it appears that any past or present Director, Manager, Official or other Liquidator, or any Officer of such Company, has misapplied or retained in his own Hands or become liable or accountable for any Monies of the Company, or been guilty of any Misfeasance or Breach of Trust in relation to the Company, the Court may . . . compel him to repay any Monies so misapplied or retained, or for which he has become liable or accountable, . . . or to contribute such Sums of Money to the Assets of the Company by way of Compensation in respect of such Misapplication, Retainer, Misfeasance, or Breach of Trust, as the Court thinks just.[66]

Terms such as 'misapplied any moneys or property of the company'[67] and 'breach of trust' had obvious connotations with the position of trustees. Although the courts never reached a definitive conclusion as to the meaning of '**misfeasance**', there was a thinking that it too needed to bear some relation to a misapplication of company assets or a breach of trust[68] and that mere negligence was not included.[69] Bringing a claim under the heading of breach of trust or breach of a fiduciary duty, therefore, had the added advantage of opening the procedural route via this so-called 'misfeasance remedy'. Not until the Insolvency Act 1986 was the section extended in scope so as to cover 'any misfeasance or breach of any fiduciary or other duty in relation to the company', and this is now thought of as including mere negligence.[70] Whereas this amendment has somewhat diminished the importance of the distinction

[66] Since re-enacted as Companies (Winding up) Act 1890, s. 10; Companies (Consolidation) Act 1908, s. 215; Companies Act 1929, s. 276; Companies Act 1948, s. 333; Companies Act 1985, s. 631; Insolvency Act 1986, s. 212.

[67] The wording in the Companies (Winding up) Act 1890, s. 10, which differed on minor editorial points.

[68] *Re Canadian Land Reclaiming and Colonizing Co (Coventry and Dixon's case)* (1880) 14 ChD 660, at 670 (James LJ); *Re London & General Bank* [1895] 2 Ch. 166, at 171 (Lindley LJ), 172 (Lopes LJ); *Re Kingston Cotton Mill Co (No 2)* [1896] 2 Ch. 279 at 283 (Lindley LJ), 288 (Lopes LJ). See also the Cork Report ('Insolvency Law and Practice: Report of the Review Committee'), Cmnd. 8558 (1982), para. 1753–1757.

[69] *Re Kingston Cotton Mill Co (No 2)* (fn. 68); *Re B Johnson & Co (Builders) Ltd* [1955] Ch. 634, at 648.

[70] *Re D'Jan of London Ltd* [1993] BCC 646; *Sally Wheeler*, 'Swelling the Assets for Distribution in Corporate Insolvency' [1993] JBL 256, at 258; *Sealy/Milman*, Insolvency Legislation (10th edn), vol. I, 228–229 (with further references).

between fiduciary and other duties, it does not make the distinction redundant.

The fiduciary duty not to misapply company property and capital maintenance

What do English lawyers actually mean when they speak of a '**misapplication of company property**'? One obvious case of a director misapplying company property is that of embezzling company funds for the personal benefit of the director or some other person close to him.[71] But the concept of 'misapplication of company property' goes much further. For well over a century English cases have framed conduct of directors in contravention of capital maintenance rules as breaches of their fiduciary duty not to misapply company property. Again, the origins of this categorisation lie in the law of trusts. Where a trustee receives property on trust, the instrument creating the trust invariably lays down instructions on how to invest the property, and how to distribute the property, including the fruits of the investment, among the beneficiaries of the trust. In discharging his functions, the trustee is under a strict fiduciary duty to comply with the terms of the trust instrument. Failure to do so constitutes a breach of trust.[72] It is easy to see how nineteenth-century chancery lawyers extended this idea from trusts to companies by substituting for the trust deed the company's constitution, i.e. its memorandum and articles of association in the old terminology.[73]

It has been said that this duty is now less relevant because few corporate constitutions impose explicit limits on the capacity of companies or their directors.[74] But from the early days of company law the same fiduciary duty has been relied on by the courts to supply sanctions where directors have acted in contravention of certain prohibitions in the Companies Act.[75] This has been viewed as one aspect of the wider

[71] As in *International Sales & Agencies Ltd v Marcus* [1982] 3 All ER 551: director using company funds to repay a personal debt of a close friend and former co-director.

[72] *Robert Pearce / John Stevens*, Trusts and Equitable Obligations (4th edn 2006), 736, and the cases there cited (stretching back to the eighteenth century).

[73] The CA 2006 abolished the distinction between the memorandum and the articles, so that in the future, the company's constitution will be contained in a single document, see *Hannigan & Prentice*, Companies Act 2006 para. 2.3.

[74] *Sarah Worthington*, 'Corporate Governance: Remedying and Ratifying Directors' Breaches' (2000) 116 LQR 638, at 656.

[75] Cf. *Gower & Davies*' Company Law (8th edn 2008), 498–499; *Worthington* (fn. 74) 658–659.

principle that directors must not misapply company property. Two cases from the late nineteenth century, which were decided within just a few years of each other, are instructive because they show the developing logic of imposing liability for breach of trust in cases where the directors had acted contrary to statutory prohibitions in relation to the company's share capital. The first case, *Re Faure Electric Accumulator Co*,[76] concerned the unlawful payment of a commission to a broker for placing shares issued by the company. The analogy with the prohibition of issuing shares below their par value already played a certain role in the argument. But the legal analysis of the judge still relied on the doctrine of ultra vires, which used to treat acts outside the company's memorandum of association as incapable of being sanctioned even by a unanimous consent of the shareholders.[77] To commit such an act would automatically render the directors liable as for a breach of trust:

> If directors apply money of the company for purposes so outside its powers that the company could not sanction such application, they may be made personally liable as for a breach of trust. On the other hand, if they apply the money of the company or exercise any of its powers in a manner which is not *ultra vires*, then a strong and clear case of misfeasance must be made out to render them liable.[78]

In the event, the judge held the payment to be ultra vires on the ground that the memorandum of the company could not be construed as permitting it.

In the second case, *Re Sharpe, Re Bennett, Masonic & General Life Assurance Co v Sharpe*,[79] the impugned conduct consisted in the payment of interest on shares in accordance with an express provision in the articles of association, but at a time when there were no distributable profits to pay a dividend. The Court of Appeal repeated the principle that:

> [a]s soon as the conclusion is arrived at that the company's money has been applied by the directors for purposes which the company cannot sanction, it follows that the directors are liable to replace the money, however honestly they may have acted.[80]

This time, however, the impossibility for the company to sanction the action was no longer explained by the court as a matter of construing

[76] (1888) 40 ChD 141.
[77] *Ashbury Railway Carriage & Iron Co Ltd v Riche* (1875) LR 7 HL 653.
[78] *Re Faure Electric Accumulator Co* (1888) 40 ChD 141, at 152. [79] [1892] 1 Ch. 154.
[80] Ibid., at 165–166.

the memorandum. Instead, the nature of the act as being incapable of sanction was derived directly from the law as found by the House of Lords in *Trevor v Whitworth*,[81] namely the general prohibition of any return of capital to the shareholders.[82]

The case law has since provided ample authority that actions against directors based on their infringement of statutory prohibitions may be brought under the head of 'misapplication' or 'misappropriation' of company property (the two seem to be used interchangeably), and the courts have consistently referred to this as a breach of trust or a breach of a fiduciary duty.[83] In particular, the payment of dividends out of capital was held to be a breach of trust,[84] and the rule was carried over to distributions made in contravention of Part VIII of the Companies Act 1985.[85] In view of ss. 170 (4) and 178 of the Companies Act 2006, there is every reason to assume that the concept of 'misapplication' or 'misappropriation' of company property will continue to apply in all situations where new provisions replace existing statutory prohibitions without a change in the nature of the prohibition. Thus, presumably, a breach of a director's fiduciary duty will arise upon his making a distribution in contravention of Part 23 of the Companies Act 2006, which replaces Part VIII of the Companies Act 1985.

In addition it is pertinent to note a statutory prohibition in a related field, the breach of which has equally been treated by the courts as a director's breach of fiduciary duty, viz. the application of company funds in contravention of the prohibition on financial assistance for the acquisition of the company's own shares.[86] The prohibition survives in

[81] (1887) 12 App.Cas. 409.

[82] *Re Sharpe, Re Bennett, Masonic & General Life Assurance Co v Sharpe* [1892] 1 Ch. 154, at 165 (Lindley LJ), 170 (Bowen LJ), 172 (Fry LJ).

[83] See the compilation in *Boyle & Birds'* Company Law (5th edn 2004), 500, which includes further cases relating to other statutory prohibitions outside the field of capital maintenance.

[84] *Re National Funds Assurance Co* (1878) 10 ChD 118; *Re Exchange Banking Co (Flitcroft's case)* (1882) 21 ChD 519.

[85] *Precision Dippings Ltd v Precision Dippings Marketing Ltd* [1986] Ch. 447 (citing *Flitcroft's case*); *Bairstow v Queens Moat Houses plc* [2001] EWCA Civ 712 = [2002] BCC 91 para. 37–48 (holding that the principle in *Flitcroft's case* applies equally to a company which is not insolvent).

[86] *Steen v Law* [1964] AC 287; *Selangor United Rubber Estates Ltd v Cradock (No 3)* [1968] 1 WLR 1555; *Wallersteiner v Moir* [1974] 1 WLR 991 and *Wallersteiner v Moir (No 2)* [1975] QB 373 (where the equitable nature of the claim was crucial for the interest payable on the sum awarded against the director); *Belmont Finance Corporation Ltd v*

the Companies Act 2006 with a much reduced scope,[87] applying only in relation to public companies as required by the Second Company Law Directive. But the cases decided under the old law will remain of wider interest as authority for the legal consequences attaching to a director's breach of fiduciary duty generally.

If a director has been involved in a misapplication of company assets, he becomes accountable and liable to make good any loss upon the same footing as if he were a trustee.[88] Yet – and here comes the surprise for German readers – the claim is one of strict liability.[89] It is not based on fault, hence, as a rule, no argument about having acted with due care provides the director with a defence.[90] This may have important practical consequences where the director (acting in good faith) relied on professional advice as to the lawfulness of his course of action. In one particular case, the directors were aware of a possible infraction of the rules prohibiting financial assistance for the acquisition of the company's shares,[91] but had obtained legal advice that their project would fall outside the statutory prohibition. This did not prevent the directors from becoming liable for breach of fiduciary duty in principle.[92] The court may, however, take such circumstances into account in deciding whether to exercise its discretion to relieve a director from liability under s. 1157 CA (see below). Contrast this with Germany, where § 43 GmbHG clearly establishes that liability for the contravention of capital maintenance rules as specified in sub-paragraph (3) only arises if the director did not act in accordance with the objective standard of diligence of a prudent businessman as required by sub-paragraph (1). It follows that a director may escape liability as of right by pleading that he complied with the objective standard of diligence incumbent upon him

Williams Furniture Ltd [1979] Ch. 250. Apart from *Steen v Law* (an Australian case), these cases were decided under the Companies Act 1948, s. 54.

[87] Part 18, Chapter 2 (ss. 677 to 683).

[88] *Re Lands Allotment Co* [1894] 1 Ch. 616 (above, fn. 62).

[89] *Lord Wedderburn*, 'The Legal Development of Corporate Responsibility – For Whom Will Corporate Managers Be Trustees?', in: *Klaus Hopt / Gunther Teubner* (eds.), Corporate Governance and Directors' Liabilities (1985) 3, at 24; *John Armour* in *Armour/ Bennett*, Vulnerable Transactions (2003), para. 7.59.

[90] *Sarah Worthington*, 'The Duty to Monitor: A Modern View of the Director's Duty of Care', in: *Fiona Patfield* (ed.), Perspectives on Company Law 2 (1997) 181, at 183.

[91] See above n. 86.

[92] *Belmont Finance Corporation Ltd v Williams Furniture Ltd (No 2)* [1980] 1 All ER 393, at 404–405; cf. *Steen v Law* [1964] AC 287, at 300.

where he acted in good faith upon the advice of a suitably qualified lawyer,[93] notwithstanding that the court may subsequently find his action unlawful.

There is, however, one exception to the rule of strict liability for a breach of a fiduciary duty. As it happens, the exception concerns cases where the directors have made an unlawful distribution, though apparently not other infringements of capital maintenance rules. In *Bairstow v Queens Moat Houses plc*, Mr Justice Nelson concluded on the authorities that no repayment of an improperly paid dividend will be ordered where the payment was made without fault on the part of the directors.[94] While previous authority on the specific point of unlawful dividends would only support the liability of the director in fairly narrow circumstances, viz. if he knew that the dividends were unlawful, or if he knew the facts that established the impropriety of the payments, even though he was unaware that such impropriety rendered the payment unlawful, or if in all the circumstances he must be taken to have known all the facts which render the payments unlawful,[95] Nelson J broadened the relevant circumstances by reference to more recent authority on the directors' general duty of care and skill so as to render the director liable also if he ought to have known, as a reasonably competent and diligent director, that the payments were unlawful.[96] The issue was not in argument in the Court of Appeal,[97] which partly reversed the decision of the first instance judge on other grounds and criticised the presentational format which the judge had adopted in order to ensure that he had covered all relevant issues.[98] But the authority cited by the judge does indeed support his conclusion as to the fault element. On the face of it, this looks like an anomaly, because it blurs the line so strictly drawn – not least by the Companies Act 2006 – between fiduciary duties and the duty to exercise due care, skill and diligence.

[93] BGH 14.5.2007, NJW 2007, 2118. See *Stefan Grundmann* in Münchener Kommentar BGB[5] § 276 mn. 73 and the cases there cited.

[94] [2000] BCC 1025 at 1031.

[95] Ibid. at 1031–1033 with reference to *Re Kingston Cotton Mill Co (No 2)* [1896] 1 Ch. 331, at 347 (reversed on other grounds [1896] 2 Ch. 279); *Dovey v Cory* [1901] AC 477, at 490; *Precision Dippings Ltd v Precision Dippings Marketing Ltd* [1986] Ch. 447, at 457.

[96] Ibid., at 1033, with reference to *Norman v Theodore Goddard* [1992] BCC 14 and *Re D'Jan of London Ltd* [1993] BCC 646; more on these two cases in chapter 5 C.3.

[97] [2001] EWCA Civ 712 = [2002] BCC 91.

[98] At paras. 55–56.

The court's discretion to relieve a director from liability

At this point a peculiar statutory provision comes into sight. The Companies Act 2006 re-enacts it as s. 1157 without substantive amendment from its predecessor, s. 727 of the Companies Act 1985, but the history of the section goes back much further.[99] On the evidence of the reported cases, the section seems to be pleaded by directors as a matter of routine, although it has been referred to as 'expensive to invoke',[100] and the courts' willingness to actually apply it in favour of directors appears to be limited.[101] The gist of the provision is summed up quickly.[102] Where a company director has become guilty of a breach of duty, the court has the power, as a matter of discretion, to relieve the director from his liability (wholly or partly), provided that the director 'acted honestly and reasonably', and that having regard to all the circumstances of the case he 'ought fairly to be excused'. From a German perspective, the manner in which the provision operates looks decidedly strange. It clearly contemplates that a director can act 'reasonably' while committing a breach of duty, although 'reasonably' would seem to define a normative standard similar to the 'prudent businessman' (*ordentlicher Geschäftsmann*) in § 43 (1) GmbHG. Yet the normative figure of the prudent businessman, by definition, acts in accordance with the law.[103] His behaviour is necessarily *pflichtgemäß* (duty-bound). Doing the opposite, i.e. acting *pflichtwidrig*, is essentially the same as acting in breach of duty. A German lawyer would find it impossible to argue that a prudent businessman would, or even could, commit a breach of duty. Moreover, the section provides a good example of how, to this day, the thinking of common lawyers is coloured much more by the concept of a remedy in court than by the concept of a substantive right (*Anspruch, materielles Recht im subjektiven Sinn*), which plays such a pivotal role in the thinking of German lawyers.

[99] Companies Act 1907, s. 32; subsequently re-enacted with various modifications as Companies (Consolidation) Act 1908, s. 279; Companies Act 1929, s. 372; Companies Act 1948, s. 448.

[100] Company Law Review, 'Completing the Structure' (November 2000), para. 3.27.

[101] Company Law Review, 'Developing the Framework' (March 2000), para. 3.77: 'This provision is little used but still, we believe, of value.'

[102] Note in passing that the section applies not only to directors but generally to 'officers' of the company (which includes the company secretary) and to auditors. The procedural contents of subsections (2) and (3) are immaterial for present purposes.

[103] *Koppensteiner* (fn. 33), § 43 mn. 10; *Haas* (fn. 31), § 43 mn. 44 ff.

The double requirement that the director who seeks relief from liability has acted 'honestly' and 'reasonably' is the absolutely necessary precondition so that the court will be in a position to exercise its discretion.[104] Whereas 'honestly' would appear to be a subjective test,[105] 'reasonably' has been held to be an objective test.[106] But how does the requirement that a director acted 'reasonably' relate to the duty to exercise 'reasonable care, skill and diligence' now codified in s. 174 CA 2006? The matter is complicated by the fact that from the earliest days the forerunners of s. 1157[107] have always included 'negligence', being defined as a lack of reasonable care.[108] In *Re D'Jan of London Ltd*, the very case considered as the milestone on the way towards the modern duty of care, Lord Justice Hoffmann (later Lord Hoffmann) decided that relief under s. 727 CA 1985 was available in a case of negligence, although he wrestled with the difficulty whether:

> a person found to have been guilty of negligence, which involves failing to take reasonable care, can ever satisfy a court that he had acted reasonably. Nevertheless, the section clearly contemplates that he may do so and it follows that conduct may be reasonable for the purposes of s. 727 despite amounting to lack of reasonable care at common law.[109]

The availability of relief in a case of negligence was confirmed in *Equitable Life Assurance Society v Bowley*.[110] But it creates a serious logical contradiction, and Lord Hoffmann's analysis has been criticised in this respect.[111] The Company Law Review also felt that it was 'hard in logic to regard a director as having acted reasonably if he is liable in negligence', and it therefore suggested deleting the requirement that the director must have acted reasonably, while retaining the other conditions.[112]

[104] *Bairstow v Queens Moat Houses plc* [2001] EWCA Civ 712 = [2002] BCC 91, para. 63.

[105] Although doubts have been expressed about this: ibid. at para. 58 with reference to *Royal Brunei Airlines Sdn Bhd v Tan* [1995] 2 AC 378, at 389, where Lord Nicholls said: 'The standard of what constitutes honest conduct is not subjective. Honesty is not an optional scale, with higher or lower values according to the moral standards of each individual.'

[106] *Coleman Taymar Ltd v Oakes* [2001] 2 BCLC 749; *Re MDA Investment Management Ltd, Whalley v Doney (No 2)* [2004] EWHC 42 (Ch) = [2005] BCC 783.

[107] Above, fn. 99.

[108] *Re Brazilian Rubber Plantations and Estates Ltd* [1911] 1 Ch. 425; *Re City Equitable Fire Insurance Co Ltd* [1925] Ch. 407; chapter 5 C.3.

[109] [1993] BCC 646, at 649. [110] [2003] EWHC 2263 (Comm) = [2003] BCC 829.

[111] *Stephen Griffin*, Personal Liability and Disqualification of Company Directors (1999), 32–33.

[112] 'Developing the Framework' (March 2000), para. 3.77.

However, the legislator did not follow this advice. The explanatory notes to the Companies Act 2006 make it explicit that s. 1157 restates s. 727 of the Companies Act 1985 without substantive amendment.[113] Thus, all cases on the previous enactments continue to be of relevance.

To illustrate positively what English courts understand by 'reasonable', consider the case of *Coleman Taymar Ltd v Oakes.*[114] The defendant was a director in a company which had been taken over and whose operations were subsequently shut down by the new owners. He set up a competing business after his contract of employment had been terminated but while he was still technically a director. It was for acts committed during this period of time, which lasted for three months, that the director was relieved from his liability. The judge gave the following reasons for granting relief:

> In all the circumstances it would be reasonable to grant him relief from any liability in respect of the purely technical breach of his duty as a director in respect of his competition with Taymar after the termination of his employment. He was, so far as the evidence goes, given no information about the progress (such as it was) of the company, nor was he paid anything, nor was he asked to do anything. Neither Taymar nor anyone in any part of the Coleman Group treated him as a director after the end of March.[115]

On the facts of this case, German lawyers might conceivably argue an implicit waiver (*konkludenter Verzicht*) of its rights on the part of the company. However, the catchword for the English lawyer is the notion of a 'purely technical breach', which keeps recurring in the cases and can be applied to a variety of fact situations.

One further example can be found in *Re Duomatic Ltd,*[116] a case decided under s. 448 CA 1948. The articles of the company provided that the remuneration of the directors was to be determined by the company in general meeting, but no shareholder resolution to this effect had ever been passed, given the directors were the only shareholders with voting rights. Subsequent changes in the company meant that the sole remaining director was no longer the only shareholder with voting rights, although he retained a majority shareholding sufficient to pass a resolution for his remuneration with his own votes. It was conceded on behalf of the director that the payment of the remuneration to himself amounted to a breach of duty, but upon application the court granted

[113] At para. 1481. [114] [2001] 2 BCLC 749. [115] At para. 100. [116] [1969] 2 Ch. 365.

relief. The crucial argument was the fact that the director remained in control of the majority vote:

> He could have passed, in general meeting, any resolution he chose. It was an oversight that no resolution was ever passed authorising him to retain the amount of these drawings. He has not held the company to ransom in any way by what he did. As I see the position he has not put the company in an embarrassing position by drawing sums to which he might or might not become entitled in the future. Here the error was one of substance, but still of a *technical nature*. It was just that he did not appreciate that, in order to retain what he had in all honesty drawn as his remuneration from the company, he ought to procure the passing of a resolution.[117]

In *Re Duomatic* the power of the director to authorise his remuneration by way of a shareholder resolution was indeed critical. In another case concerning a director's remuneration paid in contravention of the company's articles, the House of Lords made it very clear that relief cannot be invoked by a director if that would lead to him retaining the money unlawfully paid to him and thus perpetuating the harm to the shareholders who are meant to be protected by the articles.[118] German lawyers would perhaps analyse the situation with reference to one of their favourite tools, the protective ambit (*Schutzbereich*) or protective purpose (*Schutzzweck*) of a norm. The House of Lords does not use the same language, but it employs a similar idea. The articles limiting directors' remuneration or making payment dependent on a certain procedure (board approval, shareholder approval) serve the purpose of protecting shareholder interests. Relief under s. 1157 CA must not be allowed to subvert this purpose. Hence the court, in exercising its discretion, will be concerned whether shareholder interests have or have not effectively been harmed.

From a German perspective s. 1157 CA could be viewed as serving a double function. It imports an element of fault through the possibility for exculpation in cases of honest and reasonable behaviour. This is of particular relevance for breaches of strict fiduciary duties,[119] whereas its application to breaches of the duty of care creates certain anomalies.[120] By this route the court may also allow for the director's reasonable reliance on professional advice. In *Bairstow v Queens Moat Houses plc*

[117] Ibid. 376B-C (italics supplied by the author).
[118] *Guinness Plc v Saunders* [1990] 2 AC 663, at 695H.
[119] As in *Coleman Taymar Ltd v Oakes* (fn. 106) and *Re Duomatic* (fn. 116).
[120] *Re D'Jan of London* (fn. 109); *Bairstow* (fn. 121).

the judge at first instance granted relief, in part, on the basis that, although the directors were in breach of their duty in failing to be aware of their obligations under the Companies Act in relation to the payment of dividends, and in failing to see that on the face of the accounts there were insufficient reserves in the company to pay the dividends, an honest and reasonable director may in fact overlook these obligations by placing too much reliance upon his auditors.[121] By contrast, in *Inland Revenue Commissioners v Richmond* the judge refused to grant relief as he thought that the directors had not followed through the advice they had received and had failed to refer back to confirmatory advice.[122]

Still, it must be borne in mind that even in a case of honest and reasonable behaviour, a director guilty of a breach of duty cannot rely on s. 1157 CA as of right to obtain exculpation. It remains the discretion of the court to determine whether the director, in fairness and with regard to all circumstances of the case, ought to be excused. In applying this loosely worded test of fairness, the courts appear to take into account whether the interests of other parties have been adversely affected by the breach. In some cases, the courts have used their discretion in a way which German lawyers would not characterise as belonging to the fault element of liability (*Verschulden*), but as belonging to unlawfulness (*Rechtswidrigkeit*), by tailoring the breach of duty to take account of matters of protective purpose (*Schutzzweck*). In the final analysis, however, there may well be situations where a German director could expect to plead a defence as of right, while an English director in similar circumstances may not be granted relief from his liability. A perfect illustration of this outcome can be found in *Liquidator of Marini Ltd v Dickenson*, where the court was persuaded that the directors did seek professional advice in relation to a dividend payment and acted honestly and reasonably upon that advice in making the distribution. But the court declined to exercise the discretion in favour of the directors if the consequence of doing so would be to leave the guilty director in enjoyment of the benefits of his breach, at the expense of the company's creditors.[123]

[121] [2000] BCC 1025, at 1044; the judge's grant of relief was partly reversed in the Court of Appeal, but not on this point: [2001] EWCA Civ 712 = [2002] BCC 91, para. 64–67.

[122] *Inland Revenue Commissioners v Richmond, Re Loquitur Ltd* [2003] EWHC 999 (Ch) = [2003] 2 BCLC 442.

[123] [2003] EWHC 334 (Ch) = [2004] BCC 172, para. 57.

C. Recipient liability based on a director's breach of fiduciary duty

An important feature and a further peculiarity of English law is that it relies on the director's breach of fiduciary duty to not only hold the director personally liable, but to impose liability on the third party who received the property disposed of by the director in breach of his duty. This liability has already been mentioned in chapter 3, in the course of the analysis concerning remedies to reverse unlawful distributions, as an alternative to the statutory remedy against shareholders preserved by virtue of s. 847 (3) CA 2006[124] and as the chief remedy against recipients irrespective of their qualification as shareholders.[125] The remedy is commonly called '**knowing receipt**',[126] although following the Court of Appeal decision in *Bank of Credit and Commerce International (Overseas) Ltd v Akindele*,[127] some prefer to speak of 'unconscientious' or 'unconscionable receipt',[128] or perhaps even 'dishonest receipt'.[129] As so often, the terminological variety is an indicator of the substantive uncertainty surrounding the concept.

Liability for knowing receipt depends on the following three requirements being met cumulatively: (i) a disposal of the claimant's assets in breach of a fiduciary duty – hence the classification of making an unlawful distribution as a breach of fiduciary duty assumes great importance; (ii) the beneficial receipt by the defendant of assets which are traceable as representing the assets of the claimant; and (iii) knowledge on the part of the defendant that the assets received are traceable to a breach of fiduciary duty.[130]

The most problematic of these requirements is the subjective test of 'knowledge' on the part of the recipient. For many years, legal uncertainty in this area resulted from two conflicting lines of authority. Some

[124] Chapter 3 C.1. [125] Chapter 3 C.3.

[126] *City Index Ltd v Gawler* [2007] EWCA Civ 1382 = [2008] Ch. 313.

[127] [2001] Ch. 437.

[128] *Susan Barkehall-Thomas*, '"Goodbye" Knowing Receipt. "Hello" Unconscientious Receipt' (2001) 21 OJLS 239; *Graham Virgo*, Law of Restitution (2nd edn 2006) 647–654.

[129] Lord Millett in *Dubai Aluminium Co Ltd v Salaam* [2002] UKHL 48 = [2003] 2 AC 366, para. 87; cf. the analysis by *Robert Pearce / John Stevens*, Trusts and Equitable Obligations (4th edn 2006) 843–850, who conclude that 'dishonesty' is the relevant test.

[130] *El Ajou v Dollar Land Holdings plc* [1994] 2 All ER 685, at 700 (Hoffmann LJ). For the purpose of this study the second requirement will not be dealt with; an inquiry into the law of tracing and the equivalent rules in German law (insofar as there are any at all) is beyond the scope of this work.

cases followed a narrow line under which the requisite level of knowledge was set at actual knowledge, including 'wilfully shutting one's eyes to the obvious' and 'wilfully and recklessly failing to make such inquiries as an honest and reasonable man would make'.[131] Other cases extended liability to include 'knowledge of circumstances which would indicate the facts to an honest and reasonable man' and 'knowledge which would put an honest and reasonable man on inquiry'.[132] The debate took a new turn with the Court of Appeal decision in *Bank of Credit and Commerce International (Overseas) Ltd v Akindele*, where Lord Justice Nourse rejected not only the fivefold classification of the *Baden* case, but the distinction between actual and constructive knowledge as a whole. Instead, there should be a single test of whether 'the recipient's state of knowledge [is] such as to make it unconscionable for him to retain the benefit of the receipt'.[133] His Lordship thought the test helpful as it would 'better enable the courts to give commonsense decisions'.[134] But there is a palpable sense of disquiet among commentators about the lack of determination inherent in this test.[135]

Liability for knowing receipt has frequently been linked to the notion of 'constructive trust',[136] but this terminology is now discredited.[137] At the heart of a trust in its true sense lies a dualistic conception of property. The trust property is vested in the trustee as the legal

[131] *Eagle Trust Plc v SBC Securities Ltd* [1993] 1 WLR 484; *Eagle Trust Plc v SBC Securities Ltd (No 2)* [1995] BCC 231. The taxonomy is derived from *Baden, Delvaux and Lecuit v Société Générale pour Favoriser le Développement du Commerce et de l'Industrie en France SA* [1993] 1 WLR 509, at 575–576; a test to this effect had earlier been applied in *Belmont Finance Corporation Ltd v Williams Furniture Ltd* [1979] Ch. 250, at 267.

[132] Again, the categories are those of *Baden v Société Générale* (fn. 131), which applied all of them; other cases in this line include *Selangor United Rubber Estates Ltd v Cradock (No 3)* [1968] 1 WLR 1555 and *Karak Rubber Co Ltd v Burden (No 2)* [1972] 1 WLR 602. In *Agip (Africa) Ltd v Jackson* Millett J at first instance strongly endorsed the narrower view ([1990] Ch. 265, at 292–293), but in the Court of Appeal Fox LJ accepted both *Selangor United Rubber Estates Ltd v Cradock (No 3)* and *Baden v Société Générale* ([1991] Ch. 547, at 567).

[133] [2001] Ch. 437, at 455E-F. [134] Ibid., at 455F-G.

[135] *Richard Nolan*, 'How Knowing Is Knowing Receipt?', [2000] CLJ 447, at 448; *Gower & Davies*' Company Law (8th edn 2008) 600; *Pearce / Stevens* (fn. 129), 849–850.

[136] As in *Precision Dippings Ltd v Precision Dippings Marketing Ltd* [1986] Ch. 447, at 458.

[137] *Peter Birks*, 'Trusts in the Recovery of Misapplied Assets: Tracing, Trusts, and Restitution', in: *Ewan McKendrick* (ed.), Commercial Aspects of Trusts and Fiduciary Obligations (1992) 149, at 153–156; Lord Millett in *Dubai Aluminium Co Ltd v Salaam* [2002] UKHL 48 = [2003] 2 AC 366, para. 142: 'a trap'; *Virgo* (fn. 128), 606: 'completely inappropriate'; but contrast *Pearce / Stevens* (fn. 129), 841–842.

owner,[138] while the beneficiary of the trust has an equitable proprietary interest in it. Liability for knowing receipt does not depend on such a proprietary interest. Instead, knowing receipt is a personal remedy. It imposes upon the defendant the personal obligation of a trustee to account for the trust property or its value, which subsists even when the recipient no longer holds the property in his hands:[139]

> In such a case the expressions 'constructive trust' and 'constructive trustee' are misleading, for there is no trust and usually no possibility of a proprietary remedy; they are 'nothing more than a formula for equitable relief'.[140]

Why should German lawyers be concerned with such detail? In the first place, there is a real danger that those who wish to investigate English law do not grasp its contents adequately because they fail to come to terms with its doctrinal complexity. One does find evidence of this in the German literature. The author of a doctoral thesis on capital maintenance in English company law mentions briefly the liability of the directors for breach of their fiduciary duty, but with regard to recipient liability the only claim which receives mention is the statutory remedy under s. 277 (1) CA 1985, whereas liability for knowing receipt is ignored.[141] Another problem with the German analysis of English law is even more to the point of this book, which calls for an investigation of the foreign law that penetrates deep enough so as to reveal the issues at the cutting edge of the national discourse. Two German writers analyse recipient liability on the mistaken assumption that the 'constructive trust' is a proprietary remedy.[142] Clearly, it is hard to blame them if even Lord Millett refers to this as a 'trap'.[143]

138 But see the elucidating critique of this – commonly used – phrase 'legal owner' by *F. H. Lawson / Bernard Rudden*, The Law of Property (3rd edn 2002), 86.

139 *Re Montagu's Settlement Trusts* [1987] Ch. 264 is the leading case on the distinction between personal and proprietary remedies; for a detailed exposition see *Pearce / Stevens* (fn. 129), 837–852.

140 *Paragon Finance plc v DB Thakerar & Co (a firm)* [1999] 1 All ER 400, at 408 (Millett LJ), citing *Selangor United Rubber Estates Ltd v Cradock (No 3)* [1968] 1 WLR 1555, at 1582 (Ungoed-Thomas J); cf. above, fn. 63.

141 *Carsten Bödecker*, Die Kapitalerhaltung im englischen Gesellschaftsrecht (1994), 50–51.

142 *Henning Bloß*, Die Unternehmensgruppe im englischen und deutschen Recht der Kapitalgesellschaften (1999), 95–96; *Alexander Schall*, 'The UK Limited Company Abroad – How Foreign Creditors are Protected after Inspire Art (Including a Comparison of UK and German Creditor Protection Rules)' [2005] EBLR 1534, at 1551 ('a right in rem').

143 Above, fn. 137.

Still more important is the fundamental debate which lies behind the difficulty about the requisite standard of knowledge in cases of knowing receipt. Increasingly English lawyers recognise that the nature of the liability for knowing receipt is restitutionary. This raises the question why a claim based on unjustified receipt should, in addition, be based on a fault-element on the part of the defendant. The latter is all the more problematic because the common law imposes a strict liability for unjust enrichment, subject to a defence of change of position.[144] This has led to an argument that the receipt-based claim in equity should also be a claim of strict liability.[145] There is some tenuous support for this position in the case law.[146] But the House of Lords decision in *Westdeutsche Landesbank Girozentrale v Islington London Borough Council* stands firmly on the traditional ground,[147] and the Court of Appeal in *Bank of Credit and Commerce International (Overseas) Ltd v Akindele* expressed doubts on policy grounds as to a strict liability approach in equity.[148] As the law stands, the better view appears to be that a subjective requirement on the part of the defendant continues to apply in cases of receipt of property misapplied in breach of a fiduciary duty by making an unlawful distribution to a shareholder.

This takes our analysis back to the earlier observation about Lord Millett and Sarah Worthington arguing in favour of limiting the notion of 'fiduciary duty' to conflicts of interest, which would exclude, among other things, the present fiduciary duty not to misapply company property in breach of statutory limitations.[149] Defining the core 'fiduciary duty' as a narrow duty of loyalty allows them to argue that other duties hitherto considered as 'fiduciary', albeit historically derived from equitable principles on trusts, should better be seen as analogous to existing common law rules. It would then be imperative that the legal system as a whole, in order to maintain its coherence, should impose parallel legal

[144] *Lipkin Gorman v Karpnale Ltd* [1991] 2 AC 548.

[145] *Birks* (fn. 137), 159–161; *Lord Nicholls*, 'Knowing Receipt: The Need for a New Landmark', in: *William R. Cornish / Richard Nolan / Janet O'Sullivan / Graham Virgo* (eds.), Restitution – Past, Present and Future (1998) 231, at 238; in depth discussion (though reaching the opposite conclusion) by *Pearce / Stevens* (fn. 129), 852–862.

[146] *El Ajou v Dollar Land Holdings plc* [1993] 3 All ER 717, at 738a-b, 739j; *Twinsectra Ltd v Yardley* [2002] 2 AC 164, para. 105 (both dicta are by Peter Millett, who was the first-instance judge in *El Ajou* and delivered a dissenting opinion in the House of Lords in *Twinsectra*).

[147] [1996] AC 669, at 705 (Lord Browne-Wilkinson).

[148] [2001] Ch. 437, at 455–456 (Nourse LJ).

[149] Above, B.1.

consequences.[150] Taking this line of argument further, recipient liability for unlawful dividends might even be explained as entirely based on the law of unjust enrichment,[151] although this view is contested.[152] All this is part of an ongoing intellectually challenging debate. If we are serious about the idea of *Europäische Rechtswissenschaft*, a European legal discourse, there is every reason for scholars from a civilian background, if not to get involved, then at the very least to know what is happening.

D. Summary and outlook

Much of this chapter has revolved around the tricky term 'fiduciary duty', which has been revealed as a source of confusion in the comparative legal discourse. The reasons for this confusion are twofold. First, there is a noticeable divergence in the use of the English-language term between the United States, where 'fiduciary' has become little more than an epithet for all duties of company directors, and the United Kingdom, where the Companies Act confirms the status of fiduciary duties as a subset of directors' duties, with certain characteristic features that set them apart from the directors' duty to exercise reasonable care, skill and diligence. Second, the problems of terminology are compounded by problems of translation because the German term '*Treuepflicht*' is often falsely equated with 'fiduciary duty'. To resolve the latter problem, '*Treuepflicht*' should always be translated as 'duty of loyalty', whereas 'fiduciary duty' has no real equivalent in German company law and is best rendered by means of a neologism such as '*fiduziarische Pflicht*'.

The immediate relevance of this point for the subject of creditor protection results from the different approaches deployed by English law and German law, respectively, to answer the question how a violation of capital maintenance rules is conceptualised as an instance of directors' breach of duty. Under German law, a distribution in contravention of § 30 GmbHG is treated as a transgression of the principle enunciated in § 43 (1) GmbHG, according to which the directors, in attending to the affairs of the company, must apply the diligence of a prudent businessman. Under

150 This is the gist of *Sarah Worthington's* book on 'Equity' (fn. 20); more specifically in relation to directors' duties *Sarah Worthington*, 'Corporate Governance: Remedying and Ratifying Directors' Breaches' (2000) 116 LQR 638.

151 *Jennifer Payne*, 'Unjust Enrichment, Trusts and Recipient Liability for Unlawful Dividends' (2003) 119 LQR 583.

152 *Chee Ho Tham*, 'Unjust Enrichment and Unlawful Distributions: A Step too Far?' [2005] CLJ 177.

English law, a distribution in contravention of Part 23 of the Companies Act 2006 constitutes a breach of the directors' fiduciary duty not to misapply company property, which characterisation matters not only for the personal liability of the directors, but also for the liability of the recipients of unlawful distributions under the equitable head of 'knowing receipt'. The difference casts doubt on the functional logic of directors' duties being categorised in the binary logic of 'duties of care or diligence' and 'duties of loyalty', as it appears that the fiduciary duty not to misapply company property in contravention of capital maintenance rules does not fit easily within either of the two categories. Prima facie, English lawyers understand fiduciary duties as strict duties that do not depend on whether the director acted with reasonable care, skill and diligence, although the director must at least have acted reasonably (and honestly) so as to come within reach of the court exercising its discretion to relieve him from liability under s. 1157 CA. Curiously, though, the characterisation of fiduciary duties as strict duties does not seem to be carried through to the last consequence, as there is authority that the liability of directors to compensate the company for distributions made unlawfully (but apparently not for other infringements of capital maintenance rules) requires fault on the part of the directors.

At this point, the wisdom of the new provision in s. 178 (2) of the Companies Act 2006, according to which 'fiduciary duty' is taken to mean 'every duty apart from the duty to exercise reasonable care, skill and diligence', may be called into question. The conservatism of the position adopted by the legislature produces something of a set-back for efforts to develop the law on directors' duties further. This concerns, in particular, the view according to which the concept of 'fiduciary duty' should be applied more restrictively so as to include only the obligation of loyalty as the core duty of a fiduciary.[153] Among other things, this proposition has potential for resolving the anomaly that directors' liability for the repayment of distributions made in breach of the fiduciary duty not to misapply company property apparently does depend on the same fault criteria as the duty to exercise reasonable care, skill and diligence. It would be a pity if the new Companies Act had the effect of cutting this debate short. We shall have occasion to revisit this point in chapter 5.

[153] Above, text accompanying fn. 19 and 20.

5

Directors' liability for conduct in the vicinity of insolvency

A. Introduction

The previous chapter dealt with the general duties of directors and their application to capital maintenance restrictions, notably the prohibition of unlawful distributions. Like the entire concept of capital maintenance, this aspect of creditor protection is not linked to a state of factual insolvency.[1] However, many legal systems – with England and Germany among them – impose further and more specific creditor-regarding responsibilities on company directors where the company approaches, or has already reached, a situation of insolvency or financial distress.[2] The rationale underpinning these additional responsibilities towards creditors is that, once the shareholders' investment has been wiped out, the creditors replace the shareholders as the residual risk-takers.[3] At this point directors should instigate some kind of organised response designed to protect the interests of the creditors. That may take various forms and aim at either rescuing the business or liquidation, in a formal procedure or by way of informal arrangements with creditors. If the company, and more specifically the directors, fail to take appropriate steps, the creditors, often unaware of the company's precarious state of affairs, are likely to suffer harm from the continued trading of the company, while the chances that the company will ever regain solid

[1] Chapter 3 B.2.

[2] An overview is provided by *Susanne Kalss / Nikolaus Adensamer / Janine Oelkers*, 'Director's Duties in the Vicinity of Insolvency – a comparative analysis with reports from Germany, Austria, Belgium, Denmark, England, Finland, France, Italy, the Netherlands, Norway, Spain and Sweden', in: *Marcus Lutter* (ed.), Legal Capital in Europe (2006), 112; further comparative observations are included in the contribution by *Karsten Schmidt*, 'Grounds for Insolvency and Liability for Delays in Filing for Insolvency Proceedings – Necessary Supplement to Capital Protection', in the same volume at 144.

[3] In-depth economic analysis by *Rizwaan Mokal* in, 'An Agency Cost Analysis of the Wrongful Trading Provisions: Redistribution, Perverse Incentives and the Creditors' Bargain' [2000] CLJ 335.

financial ground will usually dwindle rapidly. In this respect, German liability for delayed filing for insolvency and English liability for wrongful trading or for the breach of a fiduciary duty to consider creditors' interests can be seen as functional equivalents aiming at an identical double goal, namely the deterrence of directors in order to admonish them to comply with the standards of creditor protection defined by the law and the compensation of those creditors who suffer loss as a result of non-compliance.

Notwithstanding these similarities, one must not lose sight of the complex doctrinal frameworks deployed to solve the functional problem in order to appreciate more fully the different consequences flowing from them. Due to this complexity and the significant differences prevailing between English law and German law, this chapter is split into two sections akin to country reports (although, on the whole, this is a structure that I have sought to avoid in this book). Section B discusses the German concept of '***Insolvenzverschleppungshaftung***' (or '*Konkursverschleppungshaftung*', the word used prior to the new terminology introduced by the Insolvency Code 1994; both terms convey the same meaning, viz. 'liability for delayed filing for insolvency'). This type of liability has strong connections with the general law of delict. The resulting tensions with insolvency law will be revealed as an important driving factor in the recent evolution of German law. Section C deals with English law. The tension here is between wrongful trading, which is conceived as a specific instrument of insolvency law at the hands of the office-holder rather than an instance of directors' duties generally, and those aspects of directors' duties (properly speaking) that overlap with wrongful trading in the run-up to the company's financial collapse. Parallel developments in both fields have created the need to reconcile insolvency law and company law in order to avoid inconsistent results, although this has not yet been achieved to a satisfactory level, and the Companies Act 2006 effectively sidestepped the issue. The exposition aims to emphasise the complexity of German and English law and their striking dynamism which lend support to the proposition that the study of foreign law must not fall back on a static presentation, but should aim for a dynamic observation as developments unfold within the respective national discourse.

The space devoted to these problems and the depth of analysis serve no idle purpose. In its May 2003 action plan on 'Modernising Company Law and Enhancing Corporate Governance in the European

Union'[4] the European Commission envisaged a new directive on 'wrongful trading' designed to hold company directors 'personally accountable for the consequences of the company's failure, if it is foreseeable that the company cannot continue to pay its debts and they do not decide either to rescue the company and ensure payment or to put it into liquidation'.[5] However, following the Commission's consultation on the future of the action plan carried out in 2006,[6] this project is unlikely to be carried further at present.

The Commission's initiative for a harmonisation of 'wrongful trading' had been preceded by extensive scholarly analysis.[7] However, this comparative work seems to have been beset by a number of problems. On a point of terminology it is interesting to note that the English language version of the action plan spoke of 'wrongful trading' while the German version used the term '*Konkursverschleppungshaftung*', as if the two were synonymous. The truth is that the two concepts differ fundamentally, and in more than one respect.[8] Divergences range from doctrinal considerations to policy implications and include certain premises about the availability of collective insolvency proceedings. Moreover, for a thorough debate with a view to possible European legislation, it is essential to grasp that neither English law nor German law are open and shut in terms of legal certainty. Both have loose ends where the law is in a state of continuing debate and development. Yet these areas are path-dependent in that they grow out of the peculiar approaches taken by the two systems. At the end of this chapter readers will be aware of just how much scope there is for ongoing legal evolution, but also that these evolutionary developments are highly idiosyncratic for each legal system. These findings raise serious doubts as to the suitability of this area of law for European legislation, which will be further explored at the end of this chapter and in the final conclusions.

4 COM (2003) 284 final, CELEX number 52003DC0284; see already chapter 3 at fn. 9.

5 Action plan (fn. 4) p. 16.

6 A summary report is available at http://ec.europa.eu/internal_market/company/docs/consultation/final_report_en.pdf.

7 *Forum Europaeum Konzernrecht*, 'Konzernrecht für Europa', ZGR 1998, 672; *Forum Europaeum Corporate Group Law*, 'Corporate Group Law for Europe' [2000] EBOR 165; Final Report of the High Level Group of Company Law Experts on a Modern Regulatory Framework for Company Law in Europe (November 2002), available at http://ec.europa.eu/internal_market/company/docs/modern/report_en.pdf (the 'Winter report').

8 For some additional aspects not covered in this book see *Thomas Bachner*, 'Wrongful Trading – A New European Model for Creditor Protection?' [2004] EBOR 293.

B. Directors' duties towards creditors in Germany: a victory of delict over insolvency law

1. Directors' personal liability in delict – internal versus external liability

When German lawyers discuss directors' special responsibilities towards creditors in the vicinity of insolvency, they do so under the heading of '*Insolvenzverschleppung*' (delayed filing for insolvency). In order to guide English readers towards understanding this concept, it is of the utmost importance to grasp how deeply it is rooted in the general law of delict, rather than being primarily a concept of company law or insolvency law. It is helpful to start from a common vantage point. German law and English law both recognise that a director may, in principle, become personally liable for committing a tort or delict, even though the delictual conduct is related to his directorial office. The point is well illustrated by two English cases from the House of Lords, which have also been noted in Germany,[9] namely *Williams v Natural Life Health Foods Ltd*[10] and *Standard Chartered Bank v Pakistan National Shipping Corporation.*[11] The two cases are all the more interesting as they fall on either side of the line.

In *Williams v Natural Life Health Foods Ltd* the tort in question was 'negligence' in its particular variety of the 'extended *Hedley Byrne* principle'. This head of liability provides a remedy for the recovery of damages in respect of economic loss caused by providing inaccurate information ('negligent misstatement')[12] or negligence in the performance of services.[13] The constitutive elements for this type of liability are that the defendant assumed personal responsibility towards the claimant and that the claimant could reasonably rely on this assumption of personal responsibility. In such circumstances, a duty of care arises on the part of the defendant, and breach of that duty renders the defendant

9 *Holger Fleischer*, 'Deliktische Geschäftsführerhaftung gegenüber außenstehenden Dritten im englischen Gesellschaftsrecht – Vergleichende Betrachtungen zu einer aktuellen Grundsatzentscheidung des House of Lords', ZGR 2000, 152; *idem*, 'Erweiterte Außenhaftung der Organmitglieder im Europäischen Gesellschafts- und Kapitalmarktrecht – Insolvenzverschleppung, fehlerhafte Kapitalmarktinformation, Tätigkeitsverbote', ZGR 2004, 437 at 441–442.

10 [1998] 1 WLR 830. 11 [2002] UKHL 43 = [2003] 1 AC 959.

12 *Hedley Byrne & Co Ltd v Heller & Partners Ltd* [1964] AC 465.

13 *Henderson v Merrett Syndicates Ltd* [1995] 2 AC 145.

liable to compensate the claimant for harm caused by the breach, notwithstanding that this harm may be pure economic loss.

In the *Williams* case, the claimants had been induced to enter into a franchise agreement with a company on the basis of information supplied by the company which turned out to be unreliable, leaving the claimants with a financial loss. Initially, the claimants sued the company, but after the company had been wound up and dissolved the claimants sought to hold the director personally liable in negligence. The House of Lords rejected the claim on the ground that the director had only acted on behalf of the company. Only the company, not the director, had assumed responsibility towards the claimants for the information supplied. The claim against the director failed because no tortious conduct was made out on his part.

In contrast, in *Standard Chartered Bank v Pakistan National Shipping Corporation* the director was held liable because all the elements of the tort were fulfilled in his person. The court distinguished *Williams* on the basis that the tort in question was a different one. In the *Pakistan Shipping* case, the director had personally prepared and submitted forged documents and had thus become guilty of deceit. In such a case, no director could hide behind the veil of incorporation by arguing that his deceit was committed by him on behalf of the company. The crucial difference lies in the nature of the relevant tort. A director will only be personally liable if all the ingredients of the tort are present in his person.

The same problem has also plagued German lawyers. English law and German law have in common that the directors' personal liability in tort or delict hinges critically on the structural elements of the wrong involved. One cornerstone of delict in German law is a broadly framed provision of the most general application, viz. § 823 (1) BGB, which contains a list of absolutely protected interests comprising life, bodily integrity, health, freedom and property. Any person who interferes with any of these interests of another in an unlawful and culpable manner[14] is liable to compensate the victim for any harm thus caused. Company directors will not often take an active role in interfering with such interests on the company's behalf. But their responsibility may be an indirect one, based on the concept of *Organisationspflichten* (organisational duties). By this German lawyers mean duties to provide for adequate procedures and controls within the company's organisation to ensure its smooth

[14] As to the distinction between unlawfulness and culpability see chapter 4 B.2 (text accompanying fn. 34).

operation.[15] Normally such duties are owed to the company, and a director failing in his organisational duties will only be liable to make good any loss suffered by the company. But there are exceptions.

The catalyst for the debate was a decision by the Bundesgerichtshof in 1989, which is known as the *Baustoff* (building materials) case.[16] A company had purchased building materials under a contract which provided for the retention of title until payment of the purchase price was complete. However, as the building materials were used in the construction process, they lost their character as separately identifiable property (English lawyers would say: it was no longer possible for the supplier to trace his goods), hence the retention of title ceased to be legally effective. The supplier lost his ownership and security, and the contractual claim against the purchasing company became worthless in the latter's financial collapse. The supplier then sued the director of the company, who had not even been aware of the particular transaction. The Bundesgerichtshof – more precisely the sixth civil senate of the Bundesgerichtshof, which is competent in delict cases, as opposed to the second civil senate, which decides company law matters – held the director liable in delict under § 823 (1) BGB for the unlawful and culpable, i.e. negligent, infringement of the claimant's property right. Although the sixth civil senate was at pains to stress that directors could not be made liable for each and every unlawful act committed by the company, it found the risk to the supplier's property right such as to require the director's personal attention in taking adequate organisational steps, e.g. instructions to employees, to prevent the property right from being extinguished, failing which the director rendered himself liable in delict.[17] The decision took many German company lawyers by surprise and caused considerable consternation. Some writers agreed with the Bundesgerichtshof,[18] whereas others advocated caution.[19] The

[15] See, for instance, *Walter Paefgen* in *Ulmer / Habersack / Winter*, GmbHG § 43 mn. 67; *Hans Georg Koppensteiner* in *Rowedder / Schmidt-Leithoff*, GmbHG[4] § 43 mn. 16–17.

[16] BGH 5.12.1989, BGHZ 109, 297 = NJW 1990, 976.

[17] Ibid., 304–305 and 977–978, respectively.

[18] E.g. *Gert Brüggemeier*, 'Organisationshaftung – Deliktsrechtliche Aspekte innerorganisatorischer Funktionsdifferenzierung', AcP 191 (1991) 33; *Barbara Grunewald*, 'Die Haftung von Organmitgliedern nach Deliktsrecht', ZHR 157 (1993) 451; *Holger Altmeppen*, 'Haftung der Geschäftsleiter einer Kapitalgesellschaft für die Verletzung von Verkehrssicherungspflichten', ZIP 1995, 881.

[19] E.g. *Dieter Medicus*, 'Zur deliktischen Eigenhaftung von Organpersonen', in: Festschrift für Werner Lorenz (1991), 155; *Marcus Lutter*, 'Zur persönlichen Haftung des Geschäftsführers aus deliktischen Schäden im Unternehmen', ZHR 157 (1993) 464; a

debate turns on how to draw the line between the two types of liability to which a director's failure to comply with his organisational duties may give rise: mere internal liability (*Innenhaftung*) towards the company, requiring the director to compensate the company for any loss resulting from the company's exposure to third-party claims, or as the *Baustoff* case would have it, external liability (*Außenhaftung*) vis-à-vis third parties who have suffered harm from an organisational failure within the company. Various theories have been advanced to determine the boundary between internal and external liability, but no consensus has yet been reached. It is not necessary, for the purpose of this book, to trace the doctrinal intricacies of the German discourse in any greater detail. But it is important to appreciate just how much ink has been spilt on the matter. Apart from numerous articles, at least five books have been published on the issue.[20] In the face of the authority from the Bundesgerichtshof, it required a considerable effort by German writers to limit the external liability of company directors to an acceptable level.

In this extensive debate the notions of '*Innenhaftung*' and '*Außenhaftung*' occupy a central role. ***Innenhaftung*** (internal liability) means that the director is liable only towards the company. In an insolvent liquidation, the office-holder is entitled to sue the director for the benefit of the estate. As the claim is undoubtedly an asset of the company, it is possible that an individual creditor seizes this asset in order to satisfy his claim against the company by way of execution, after having obtained judgment against the company.[21] However, in order to uphold the *pari passu* principle, no such execution by an individual creditor is permitted during insolvency proceedings.[22]

In contrast, ***Außenhaftung*** (external liability) gives rise to a claim which is not in any way owned or held by the company. Instead, if it is a claim in delict, the victim whose protected interests have been violated

critical comment in English on this and a subsequent case is provided by *Thomas Krecek / Daniela Weber-Rey*, 'Germany: Company Law – Liability of Managing Directors' [1996] ICCLR C192.

20 *Jens-Uwe Nölle*, Die Eigenhaftung des GmbH-Geschäftsführers für Organisationspflichtverletzungen (1995); *Ulrich Haas*, Geschäftsführerhaftung und Gläubigerschutz – Unternehmerische Verhaltenspflichten des GmbH-Geschäftsführers zum Schutz Dritter (1997); *Detlef Kleindiek*, Deliktshaftung und juristische Person (1997); *Andreas Sandberger*, Die Außenhaftung des GmbH-Geschäftsführers (1998); Gerald Spindler, Unternehmensorganisationspflichten – Zivilrechtliche und öffentlich-rechtliche Regelungskonzepte (2001).

21 The relevant procedural rules are to be found in §§ 828 ff. ZPO.

22 Stay of execution (*Vollstreckungsverbot*) under § 89 InsO.

will hold the claim against the director, and it follows that the company's insolvency will not bar the claimant from pursuing this claim. The obvious dangers here are a multiplicity of proceedings and a race against the clock if the director is indebted to the company and to third parties, although such a situation will frequently lead to the director's personal bankruptcy.

In the *Baustoff* case, the director's delictual liability was based on § 823 (1) BGB. But directors may just as well commit a delict under any other head, notably by contravening a ***Schutzgesetz*** (protective norm) in the sense of § 823 (2) BGB.[23] The gist of the concept of *Schutzgesetz* is that the infraction of a legal norm designed to protect specific interests will as such give rise to a claim for damages on the part of the protected party. Depending on the protective ambit (*Schutzbereich*) of the enactment, that may even include pure economic loss, a type of harm deliberately omitted from the list in § 823 (1) BGB. The Civil Code thereby creates a cause of action without having to enumerate all protective norms, which would be a virtually impossible task. Instead, whether an enactment comes within the concept of protective norm in § 823 (2) BGB turns on the interpretation of that particular enactment. The concept resembles the English tort category of 'breach of statutory duty', although this must not lead to the conclusion that the two concepts, and in particular the methods by which the courts establish the protective character of any given enactment, are the same. Whereas 'breach of statutory duty' appears to be a tort of rather limited application in English law,[24] delictual claims based on the violation of a *Schutzgesetz* play a vital role in Germany. As early as 1904 – within five years from the BGB coming into force – the Reichsgericht spoke out against an overly narrow approach to identifying protective norms.[25]

It follows that a company director may incur personal liability by personally committing a violation of a protective norm. The remainder of this section will focus on one peculiar delict which exists in Germany – a delict which is based on a protective norm that relates specifically to directors' responsibility towards creditors in the vicinity of insolvency.

[23] For an introduction to the concept of 'protective norm' see *Basil Markesinis / Hannes Unberath*, German Law of Torts (4th edn 2002), 885–888 or *Walter van Gerven et al.* (eds.), Tort Law (2000), 227–228.

[24] *Simon Deakin / Angus Johnston / Basil Markesinis*, Markesinis and Deakin's Tort Law (6th edn 2007) 377; *K.M. Stanton*, Breach of Statutory Duty in Tort (1986).

[25] RG 1.12.1904, RGZ 59, 236.

2. *Delictual liability for Insolvenzverschleppung* (delayed filing for insolvency)

The relevant statutory provisions before and after the MoMiG

Since the original enactment of the Limited Liability Companies Act in 1892, the statutory provision in point has been § 64 GmbHG.[26] As the provision stood immediately before the MoMiG was adopted in 2008, it consisted of two sub-paragraphs. The structure of the provision had rightly been criticised, because the interrelationship between the two sub-paragraphs was anything but free from doubt.[27] The MoMiG did not address these structural concerns. It did, however, bring a significant change, in that the contents of what used to be § 64 sub-paragraph (1) GmbHG were transferred to a new paragraph in the Insolvency Code, viz. § 15a InsO.

The previous first sub-paragraph in § 64 GmbH – now § 15a InsO – contains the explicit duty of company directors to present a petition to the court requesting the opening of insolvency proceedings by the court.[28] This duty is based on the two tests of insolvency, viz. *Zahlungsunfähigkeit* (illiquidity, § 17 InsO) and *Überschuldung* (over-indebtedness, § 19 InsO), which we have already encountered in relation to the avoidance of pre-insolvency acts and which broadly correspond to what English lawyers know as 'inability to pay debts as they fall due'[29] (cash flow insolvency) and 'excess of liabilities over assets' (balance sheet insolvency). The directors' duty to request the opening of insolvency proceedings is triggered once either of the two tests is satisfied, subject to a short period of no more than three weeks during which the directors may take steps to avoid the opening of insolvency proceedings, provided there is a reasonable expectation that

[26] The paragraph has undergone various amendments over the years, but these are not material for present purposes.

[27] See, for instance, *Karsten Schmidt*, 'Konkursantragspflichten bei der GmbH und bürgerliches Deliktsrecht', JZ 1978, 661, whose elaborate analysis of § 64 GmbHG – since repeated and refined, most recently in his contribution to *Karsten Schmidt / Wilhelm Uhlenbruck* (eds.), Die GmbH in Krise, Sanierung und Insolvenz (3rd edn 2003), 889–904 – is, however, not shared by the majority of writers, nor by the Bundesgerichtshof; see below, text accompanying fn. 50 and 51.

[28] German law does not provide for a formal out-of-court insolvency procedure akin to creditors' voluntary winding up under the UK Insolvency Act.

[29] Recall the important terminological clarification in chapter 2 B.3 (text accompanying fn. 24).

the state of factual insolvency will be brought to an end within these three weeks.[30]

The wording of the provision goes no further than stipulating the duty on the part of the directors. In particular, the Limited Liability Companies Act does not specify a civil sanction against the directors in case of non-compliance with the duty to request the opening of insolvency proceedings.[31] But the courts in Germany have long recognised this provision as a protective norm (*Schutzgesetz*) within the meaning of § 823 (2) BGB.[32] Directors who culpably (intentionally or negligently) fail in their duty to request the opening of insolvency proceedings commit a delict and will be personally liable for any damage caused, even though this damage will usually be in the nature of pure economic loss.

The previous second sub-paragraph in § 64 GmbH – now the only remaining sub-paragraph in § 64 GmbHG – is built around the same two tests of illiquidity (*Zahlungsunfähigkeit*) and over-indebtedness (*Überschuldung*). The sub-paragraph specifies a sanction, but without clearly spelling out the underlying duty. It makes directors liable to 'compensate the company for any payments made' after the occurrence of the company's cash flow insolvency or after the ascertainment[33] of its balance sheet insolvency, unless the payment was compatible with the diligence of a prudent businessman even after this time.[34] The duty

30 For a comparison with wrongful trading in this respect see *Thomas Bachner* (fn. 8), at 306–309; for a critique of the mandatory invocation of a formal insolvency procedure see *Paul Davies*, 'Directors' Creditor-Regarding Duties in Respect of Trading Decisions Taken in the Vicinity of Insolvency' [2006] EBOR 301, at 314–315.

31 By virtue of § 84 GmbHG a director who does not comply with his duty to request the opening of insolvency proceedings in accordance with § 64 (1) GmbHG was guilty of a criminal offence. The MoMiG has moved this criminal sanction to § 15a InsO (see below).

32 Going back to RG 5.6.1935, JW 1935, 3301, an important case, though not reported in the RGZ official reports; a summary of the court's reasoning is given by *Christoph Poertzgen*, Organhaftung wegen Insolvenzverschleppung (2006), 251 f.

33 In consequence of an oversight by the legislator on the occasion of an amendment in 1986, the word 'ascertainment' in the text of the statute must no longer be construed literally; what is meant is 'ascertainability' by the director, which is presumed against him/her: BGH 29.11.1999, BGHZ 143, 184 = NJW 2000, 668.

34 After some wrangling between different senates of the Bundesgerichtshof, the second civil senate recently conceded that payments of employee social security deductions and pay-as-you-earn income tax to the respective collecting agencies are compatible with the diligence of a prudent businessman (BGH 14.5.2007, NJW 2007, 2118; overruling BGH 8.1.2001, BGHZ 146, 264 = NJW 2001, 1280 and BGH 18.4.2005, NJW 2005, 2546 on this point), because the fifth criminal senate insisted that directors who withheld such payments rendered themselves liable to criminal prosecution (BGH 9.8.2005, NJW 2005, 3650 [with references to earlier cases]).

implicit in this sub-paragraph is not to make such payments in the first place, so as to safeguard the assets available for ratable distribution to the creditors in accordance with the principle of *pari passu* or *par conditio creditorum* underlying insolvency law.[35] It is a separate duty, which cannot be understood as a sanction for non-compliance with the directors' duty to request the opening of insolvency proceedings, because it does not presuppose that the directors have breached that duty. In particular, the duty to refrain from payments is not suspended for three weeks pending rescue efforts, as is the duty to request the opening of insolvency proceedings. Accordingly, during these three weeks, directors must assess on a case-by-case basis whether a particular payment is compatible with the diligence of a prudent businessman, bearing in mind that a blanket cessation of payment may well undermine any rescue effort.[36]

One of the most contentious issues about the directors' obligation to make good payments is the nature of the claim. The statute says clearly that the directors are 'liable to compensate the company'. But it does not follow that the quantum of the claim is determined by reference to any loss suffered by the company. If a loss-making business is continued beyond the point where it should have been stopped, the resulting additional loss constitutes damage to the company. At the same time it can be seen as an indirect harm to the creditors because the intervening loss will diminish the pay-out to them. English lawyers might be sympathetic to such an approach because it corresponds to the method adopted for determining the compensation payable in cases of wrongful trading under s. 214 IA. In *Re Continental Assurance Company of London plc* the calculation of this compensation was a contentious point. The judge, Mr Justice Park, held that the 'starting point' was the 'increase in net deficiency' or IND, which he defined as including only the loss sustained by the company itself during the period of wrongful trading.[37]

35 Thus the purpose of the provision identified by the Bundesgerichtshof: BGH 18.3.1974, NJW 1974, 1088; BGH 29.11.1999, BGHZ 143, 184 = NJW 2000, 668; BGH 8.1.2001, BGHZ 146, 264 = NJW 2001, 1280. *Ulrich Haas*, 'Der Erstattungsanspruch nach § 64 II GmbHG', NZG 2004, 737 points to interesting parallels with avoidance law; on the interrelationship between directors' liability and avoidance remedies see below, text accompanying fn. 44 to 46.

36 *Peter Ulmer* in *Hachenburg*, GmbHG[8] § 64 mn. 33; for a recent illustration see BGH 5.11.2007, ZIP 2008, 72: non-payment of water, electricity and heating bills would lead to immediate stoppage of operations, defeating any rescue attempt.

37 [2001] BPIR 733, at para. 5 ff. of the interim judgment reported as Annex B to the final judgment; the more extensive basis ruled out by the judge is there referred to as the '10C

'Starting point' indicates that other factors may have to be taken into account,[38] but the judge made it clear that this 'starting point' is also the maximum of compensation payable under s. 214 IA.[39]

But what if, during the period of wrongful trading or delay in filing for insolvency, the directors apply company assets to pay off a creditor whose claim predates the relevant time? Every such payment extinguishes a debt owed by the company, so that the company itself is in no way worse off than before. Only the remaining creditors will suffer a reduction in the dividend payable to them, as the following example demonstrates:

> Assume that the company holds assets totalling 40 and owes debts totalling 100. Creditors would receive a pay-out of 40% on their nominal claims. If the directors apply assets worth 20 to satisfy one creditor, there remain assets of 20 and debts of 80, so that the dividend for the other creditors drops to 25%.

In the *Continental Assurance* case the judge specifically excluded from the IND-measure such harm suffered by the creditors as a result of payments made to certain creditors in preference over others. He considered the latter to be exclusively within the scope of transaction avoidance law, more specifically s. 239 IA on preferences.

This contrasts sharply with the German approach under § 64 GmbHG. For a start, any loss inflicted on the company by negligent conduct of its directors is recoverable by the company under the general provision concerning the liability of directors in § 43 GmbHG.[40] The office-holder can realise this asset by bringing a claim on behalf of the company, thereby swelling the assets available for distribution to creditors. The point of § 64 GmbHG is that it goes beyond § 43 GmbHG. The Bundesgerichtshof explains the company's claim against the director as a 'claim for compensation of a special kind' (*Ersatzanspruch eigener Art*):

basis', an unhelpful shorthand which is based on a designation of documents prepared for the trial and does not explain anything about its substance.

38 On these see the discussion below on the discretion of the judge, text accompanying fn. 218 to 225, and *Thomas Bachner* (fn. 8), at 313–316.

39 At para. 296–297 of the final judgment (fn. 37); further details below, text accompanying fn. 209 to 217 (regarding causation).

40 See already chapter 4 B.2 and the discussion below, section C.3, on the overlap between wrongful trading and the general duty of directors to exercise reasonable care, skill and diligence in English law.

> Although the claim for compensation under [§ 64 GmbHG] . . . belongs to the company alone . . ., it is in fact a liability owed to the creditors as a whole who are placed at a disadvantage by the delayed filing for insolvency and the reduction of the insolvency estate following the intervening satisfaction of particular creditors, whereas the company itself suffers no loss insofar as only its debts are being repaid.[41]

This reasoning, which has since been applied repeatedly,[42] invites reflections at various levels. At a theoretical level it is pertinent to note the willingness of German law to look through the corporate person at the situation of the creditors as the stakeholders affected by the company's insolvency. The reason for this seemingly artificial construction lies in the ingenious compromise between protecting the interests of creditors rather than the interests of the company (which allows for a wider basis to determine the quantum), yet concentrating enforcement in the hands of the office-holder acting in the name of the company (which is conducive to procedural efficiency and guarantees equal treatment of all creditors). Recall the similar observation made in the chapter on avoidance remedies, where we contrasted the German concept of 'detriment to creditors' with the English concern to identify a 'transaction at an undervalue' from the perspective of the company.[43]

The overlap between the claim against the director for making a payment prohibited by § 64 GmbHG and possible avoidance remedies, especially those under §§ 130, 131 InsO (avoidance of cover, *Deckungsanfechtung*),[44] against the recipients of such a payment requires a clarification of their order of precedence. The Bundesgerichtshof has held that the claim against the director is in no way subsidiary to avoidance remedies, nor is the recipient entitled to resist the restoration of the value received by him on account of the concurrent liability of the director. The director is not allowed to raise the prior availability of the avoidance claim as a defence if the latter has become time-barred as a consequence of the office-holder's inaction. The office-holder does not

[41] BGH 18.3.1974, NJW 1974, 1088: 'Obwohl . . . der Ersatzanspruch nach [§ 64 GmbHG] allein der Gesellschaft zusteht . . ., handelt es sich bei ihm der Sache nach um eine Haftung gegenüber der Gläubigergesamtheit, die bei verspäteter Konkursanmeldung durch eine Verminderung der Konkursmasse infolge zwischenzeitlicher Befriedigung einzelner Gläubiger benachteiligt ist, wogegen die Gesellschaft selbst keinen Schaden erleidet, soweit lediglich ihre Schulden bezahlt werden.'

[42] E.g. BGH 29.11.1999, BGHZ 143, 184 = NJW 2000, 668; BGH 8.1.2001, BGHZ 146, 264 = NJW 2001, 1280.

[43] Chapter 2 C.4. [44] Chapter 2 C.2.

owe a duty to mitigate the loss looming over the director and is free to decide which claim to pursue with a view to achieving the best result for the creditors.[45] Moreover, in a later dictum, the Bundesgerichtshof held that, in exchange for his compensation payment to the estate, the director is entitled to demand the assignment from the office-holder to him of a 'claim for recovery' against the recipient.[46] While the passage did not specifically mention avoidance claims, a subsequent decision from the OLG Oldenburg applied the dictum in this sense and allowed the office-holder to pursue a claim against the director concurrently with an avoidance claim against the recipient, provided that the office-holder would not recover the same amount twice.[47] In effect, the director is liable to compensate the company to the full amount of any payment made in contravention of § 64 GmbHG and can only seek recourse from the recipient to the extent of a valid and enforceable avoidance claim (if any).[48]

The structural parallel with avoidance law is not without its problems. As a cause of action, § 64 GmbHG relies on a specified payment made to a specified recipient at a specified time within the critical period of factual insolvency on either a cash flow or balance sheet test (or, in practice, any number of such payments). These are all the elements that the office-holder needs to show in order to succeed against the director.[49] The quantum of compensation recoverable from the director under this head of liability is not related to the aggregate loss suffered by the creditors over any particular period of time. In this respect, the calculation differs fundamentally from the quantification of the loss recoverable under the delictual heads of liability based on the directors' delay in requesting the opening of insolvency proceedings in accordance with § 15a InsO (as we shall see presently) as well as from the IND-measure for recovery under s. 214 IA. That this is a profound misinterpretation of the regime, as it was previously configured in the two sub-paragraphs of § 64 GmbHG, has been the thrust of the critique by Karsten Schmidt for many years.[50]

[45] BGH 18.12.1995, BGHZ 131, 325 = NJW 1996, 850.

[46] BGH 8.1.2001, BGHZ 146, 264 at 279 = NJW 2001, 1280 at 1283.

[47] OLG Oldenburg 10.5.2004, GmbHR 2004, 1014.

[48] This is also the conclusion reached by *Christoph Poertzgen* (fn. 32), 231.

[49] It is for the director to show that the payment was compatible with the diligence of a prudent businessman at the time when it was made: BGH 18.3.1974, NJW 1974, 1088.

[50] Starting with his article in JZ 1978, 661 (fn. 27) long before the courts 'discovered' the second sub-paragraph in § 64 GmbHG and forged it into the sharp weapon for office-holders that it is today.

By simply adding up payments without looking at the overall picture of the company's financial situation, one can quickly arrive at fantastic figures that bear no relation to the actual loss suffered by the creditors. In one of his more recent articles,[51] Schmidt pulls out all the stops in deploying his rhetorical gift, calling the current practice of the courts 'a downright liability club',[52] an 'overreaction'[53] and a miracle reminiscent of the biblical *Brotvermehrung*,[54] when Jesus fed the five thousand with five loaves and two fishes.[55]

Examining particular 'payments' in isolation may actually produce strange results in either direction. A recent decision by the Bundesgerichtshof illustrates the curious distinctions in the application of the provision. If a cheque received by the company is paid into the company's bank account at a time when the balance of the account is in debit, the director thereby makes a 'payment' within the meaning of § 64 GmbHG, because an asset of the company (the cheque) is applied towards the satisfaction of one particular creditor (by reducing the balance owed by the company to the bank). On the other hand, a remittance in satisfaction of a debt owed to any other creditor which increases the debit balance of the account is not a 'payment' within the meaning of § 64 GmbHG, because the transaction merely swaps one creditor for another, but does not involve assets that would be available for distribution to the creditors.[56] A further problem with the provision is that its scope may be too narrow, as 'payments' out of the company's assets are not the only way in which the creditors may suffer a loss. Some commentators argue that, on teleological grounds, 'payments' should be interpreted so widely as to include even a reduction in the net asset position as a consequence of the company incurring new debts without receiving equivalent value,[57] although this is really stretching the

[51] *Karsten Schmidt*, 'Verbotene Zahlungen in der Krise von Handelsgesellschaften und die daraus resultierenden Ersatzpflichten', ZHR 168 (2004), 637.

[52] Ibid., 644 ('*eine rechte Haftungskeule*'). [53] Ibid., 649 ('*Überreaktion*').

[54] Ibid., 649, and in the subtitle of the article.

[55] Matthew 14:15–21; Mark 6:35–44; Luke 9:12–17; John 6:5–13.

[56] BGH 26.3.2007, ZIP 2007, 1006.

[57] *Karsten Schmidt* in *Scholz*, GmbHG[9] § 64 mn. 23; *Christian Schmidt-Leithoff* in *Rowedder / Schmidt-Leithoff*, GmbHG[4] § 64 mn. 28; *Holger Altmeppen* in *Roth / Altmeppen*, GmbHG[5] § 64 mn. 80; contra: *Joachim Schulze-Osterloh* in *Baumbach / Hueck*, GmbHG[18] § 64 mn. 79; *Ulmer* (fn. 36), § 64 mn. 40; undecided: *Marcus Lutter / Detlef Kleindiek* in *Lutter/Hommelhoff*, GmbHG[16] § 64 mn. 59.

ordinary meaning of 'payments' beyond recognition, and it appears that the Bundesgerichtshof does not share this view either.[58]

This limitation offers an explanation why German courts have been all too willing to find additional civil sanctions outside the previous § 64 (2) GmbHG by having recourse to the directors' duty to request the opening of insolvency proceedings as a protective norm. There can be no doubt that the directors' obligation to restore 'payments' to the company will continue to be of immense practical importance, not least because it is relatively easy for the office-holder to mount a successful action under this head of liability. But the more interesting provision for the purpose of our comparative doctrinal analysis is the delictual liability resulting from non-compliance with the duty to request the opening of insolvency proceedings. Whilst the MoMiG transferred this duty from the Limited Liability Companies Act to the Insolvency Code, it did nothing to change its character; hence the debate on the scope of the civil liability arising from the previous § 64 (1) GmbHG, to which the analysis now turns, continues to be of undiminished relevance under the new § 15a InsO.

Liability in delict and the distinction between 'old' and 'new' creditors

In order to get the full picture, it is pertinent to recall some previous observations. We have seen that the Bundesgerichtshof explained the recovery of illicit payments under § 64 (2) GmbHG as a 'claim for compensation of a special kind', which is technically owned by the company, yet calculated on the basis of damage to the creditors rather than damage to the company.[59] Moreover, in this context, we have noted a correspondence with avoidance law, where German law looks directly at the situation of the creditors as the stakeholders affected by the company's insolvency.[60] Against this background, it is natural for German lawyers to recognise the creditors as the victims of a delict committed against their financial interests. But when it comes to claims under the general law of delict, the creditors are also the holders of the claims. The significance of this attribution of entitlements will become clear as the following analysis unfolds. To begin with, let us look at the determination of the quantum of such a claim in delict.

[58] BGH 30.3.1998, BGHZ 138, 211 at 216–217 = NJW 1998, 2667 at 2668.
[59] Fn. 41. [60] See the text accompanying fn. 43 and chapter 2 C.4.

One way to establish the quantum is to compare the hypothetical dividend that would have been received by the creditors at the time when the directors should have requested the opening of insolvency proceedings with the (lower) actual dividend payable to them from the remaining assets. The difference is referred to as '***Quotenschaden***' or '***Quotenverringerung***' (the two terms are used interchangeably), which literally means the damage to, or the diminution of, the 'quota', that is the dividend which the creditors receive in relation to their full claims. The diminution of the quota represents an aggregate figure calculated over the entire duration of the directors' failure to request the opening of insolvency proceedings. It does include the increase in net deficiency (IND) as defined by Park J in *Re Continental Assurance.*[61] As with the IND-measure, there is no need to separate between giving away assets and taking on further debts, because both have the same negative effect on the company's net asset position. Yet the diminution of the quota is wider than the IND-measure in that it also includes the harm suffered by creditors as a result of preferential payments (used here in a purely objective sense) made to certain other creditors, whereas the proceeds of a successful avoidance remedy brought by the office-holder will increase the actual quota, thereby reducing the damage to the creditors and the quantum of their claims against directors. But whereas the diminution of the quota is already wider than the IND-measure under s. 214 IA, it is still not exhaustive of the compensation that may be recoverable from the directors. It is at this point that the delictual conception of the directors' duty to request the opening of insolvency proceedings starts to collide with the idea that lies at the heart of insolvency law, viz. the principle of *pari passu* or *par conditio creditorum.*

It is possible that a creditor suffers a loss which is caused by the continuance of trading during a time when the business should have been closed down and/or put into liquidation, but is not reflected in a diminution of the quota. This occurs whenever a creditor extends fresh credit to the company after the point at which insolvency proceedings should have commenced. Knowing of the insolvency, the creditor would not have entered into a transaction with the company. In the German literature this class of creditor is technically known as the 'new creditors' (***Neugläubiger***), in order to distinguish them from the 'old creditors' (***Altgläubiger***), i.e. those creditors whose claims predate the point in time when the directors came under a duty to request the opening of

[61] Above, text accompanying fn. 37.

insolvency proceedings. It is clear that a new creditor can lodge a proof of his claim in the liquidation just as every other creditor can, and he will be treated on an equal footing within the *pari passu* distribution that follows the realisation of the company's assets. But it is equally clear that the loss of the new creditor attributable to the directors' previous failure to request the opening of insolvency proceedings is not linked to the diminution of the quota. His advance may even inject assets into the business with the effect of increasing the (hypothetical) quota for the old creditors (if only temporarily in most cases). Any one person can, of course, have claims as both an old and a new creditor, arising from different transactions before and after the material time, with different legal consequences attaching to each type of claim.[62] In particular, if a company had earlier been granted an overdraft facility, the bank is treated as a new creditor for the amount by which the debit balance has increased after the critical point when the directors should have requested the opening of insolvency proceedings.[63] It is self-evident that such a distinction will have to wrestle with serious practical difficulties resulting from the need to establish exactly when this point arose on the facts of each case.

Under English law, nothing in the wording of s. 214 IA suggests that such a distinction could or should be made in relation to wrongful trading, although the wide discretion given to the judge[64] might open up the possibility of introducing such a differentiation. The question has been considered, rather briefly, by one writer, who concludes that insolvency law does not have the aim of creating new rights for any creditors and that the section gives the office-holder the sole right to sue without succession to any pre-existing right in any creditor.[65] In the subsequent case of *Re Purpoint Ltd* the court explicitly rejected the liquidator's contention that creditors whose claims were founded after the time when the directors ought to have known about the insolvency should be paid in full.[66] We shall see later why this position is consistent

[62] As in the case of a regular supplier of goods to the company: BGH 12.3.2007, NJW 2007, 3130.

[63] BGH 5.2.2007, BGHZ 171, 46.

[64] Above, text accompanying fn. 37 to 39 (starting point) and below, text accompanying fn. 218 to 225.

[65] *Fidelis Oditah*, 'Wrongful trading' [1990] LMCLQ 205, at 221–222.

[66] *Re Purpoint Ltd* [1991] BCC 121, at 128–129; approving comment by *D.D. Prentice*, 'Creditor's Interests and Director's Duties' (1990) 10 OJLS 265, at 272–273. Of course, payment in full would not be the same as, and may exceed, the reliance loss; but see below, text accompanying fn. 87 and 88.

with the nature and systematic context of wrongful trading,[67] which differs strikingly from that of German liability for delayed filing for insolvency.

Under German law of delict there is a direct relationship between the protective ambit (*Schutzbereich*) or protective purpose (*Schutzzweck*) of a particular norm and the damages recoverable for breach. Hence, the treatment of the new creditors turns on the interpretation of § 15a InsO as to its protective purpose. In an early decision the Bundesgerichtshof had ruled that § 64 (1) GmbHG also protected creditors who only became creditors after the time when the company should duly have filed for insolvency. The duty of the directors to request the opening of insolvency proceedings is a permanent one, continuing as long as the company remains in a state of factual insolvency, and it therefore protects every creditor acquiring a claim against the company during this period. However, the Bundesgerichtshof saw the protective purpose of the provision as being limited to preventing the assets available for distribution, and hence the quota for old and new creditors alike, from being further diminished. The court explicitly rejected the argument that the protective purpose extended so far as to protect the new creditors in their reliance on the continued solvency of the debtor, inducing them to extend fresh credit to the company.[68] This narrow interpretation of the protective purpose in § 64 (1) GmbHG met with repeated criticism in the literature.[69] The Bundesgerichtshof, though, confirmed its position on several occasions.[70] Yet the discursive style of German judgments helped to keep the debate alive, in that the courts felt the need to engage with the contrary arguments put forward in the literature and, as a result, by counsel on behalf of their clients.

Even so the interpretation offered by the Bundesgerichtshof still made it necessary to distinguish between old and new creditors in one respect.

[67] Below C.2. [68] BGH 16.12.1958, BGHZ 29, 100 = NJW 1959, 623.

[69] *Eberhard Winkler*, 'Zum Schutzumfang des § 64 Abs. 1 GmbH-Gesetz', MDR 1960, 185; *Hans Georg Graf Lambsdorff / Peter Gilles*, 'Zur Haftung der GmbH-Geschäftsführer bei unterlassenem oder verzögertem Konkursantrag', NJW 1966, 1551; *Günter Kühn*, 'Gläubigerschutz nach § 823 Abs. 2 BGB bei Überschuldung einer GmbH', NJW 1970, 589; *Walter Lindacher*, 'Direkte Haftung der AG-Vorstandsmitglieder und GmbH-Geschäftsführer gegenüber Gesellschaftsgläubigern bei unterlassenem oder verzögertem Konkursantrag', DB 1972, 1424; *Peter Gilles / Michael Baumgart*, 'Schadensersatzpflicht des GmbH-Geschäftsführers nach § 823 II BGB i.V. mit § 64 I GmbHG (Schutzbereichsproblematik)', JuS 1974, 226.

[70] Up to BGH 3.2.1987, BGHZ 100, 19 = NJW 1987, 2433; BGH 26.6.1989, BGHZ 108, 134 = NJW 1989, 3277.

For the latter, the loss resulting from the diminution of the quota could not be calculated with reference to the earliest time, when the directors should have requested the opening of insolvency proceedings, but only with respect to the (later) time, when the claimant became a creditor, and the hypothetical quota he would have received at that time. This point in time would be different for each creditor, and the ensuing need to calculate hypothetical quotas for many different stages of the company's decline was hardly practicable.[71] It could also lead to unsatisfactory results in another respect: the further the company had descended into factual insolvency – and hence the heavier the moral blame on the directors for entering into ever new transactions – the less there was a difference between the hypothetical quota at the time when a new creditor advanced fresh money, and the actual quota that this creditor would subsequently receive. The Bundesgerichtshof was quite explicit that such a differential treatment of individual new creditors was needed,[72] and several decisions from appellate courts applied the law in this sense.[73] However, the existence of separate claims based on the circumstances of individual creditors raised the prospect of a multiplicity of actions, which was clearly undesirable. One prominent academic commentator went so far as to argue that, despite the delictual nature of the claims, on grounds of 'convenience' (*Zweckmäßigkeit*) it was 'acceptable' (*vertretbar*) that all creditors' claims were calculated on the same basis of the diminution of the quota since the time when the duty to request the opening of insolvency proceedings arose (i.e. the calculation which, in principle, was only relevant for the old creditors), and that all claims could be pursued by the office-holder on behalf of the estate, and hence for the benefit of all creditors on a *pari passu* basis.[74] It appears that this practice, known as '*Gesamtschadensliquidation*' (aggregate loss settlement), was widely treated as the current state of the law before 1994,[75] and on one occasion, at least, the Bundesgerichtshof seems to have condoned this practice.[76]

[71] *Christoph Poertzgen* (fn. 32), 32.

[72] BGH 16.12.1958, BGHZ 29, 100 at 107 = NJW 1959, 623 at 624–625.

[73] OLG Celle 1.10.1970, OLGZ 1971, 367; OLG Köln 13.7.1982, ZIP 1982, 1086; OLG Hamburg 16.12.1988, ZIP 1989, 249.

[74] *Peter Ulmer* in *Hachenburg*, GmbHG[7] § 64 mn. 50 and 55.

[75] *Dieter Medicus*, 'Die Außenhaftung des GmbH-Geschäftsführers', GmbHR 1993, 533 at 538; *Reinhard Bork*, 'Haftung des GmbH-Geschäftsführers wegen verspäteten Konkursantrags', ZGR 1995, 505 at 523.

[76] BGH 14.10.1985, ZIP 1986, 456.

Just as the debate in the literature over the protective ambit of § 64 (1) GmbHG appeared to subside, a published doctoral thesis breathed new life into it.[77] This time the judges were prepared to rethink the policy behind the law, and within four years the second civil senate of the Bundesgerichtshof overruled the earlier cases in a groundbreaking decision.[78] In preparation for this step, the senate launched a special procedure designed to ensure consistency within the Bundesgerichtshof and between the various German supreme courts, whereby it notified other senates of the Bundesgerichtshof and the Bundesarbeitsgericht (the Federal Labour Court) of its interim conclusions on the law and invited them to give their opinions. These interim conclusions were reported in law journals,[79] and they triggered an intense scholarly debate, where academics and practitioners sought to influence the outcome through their arguments.[80] The manner in which this change in the law was brought about has something of a textbook example, and English readers should not assume that case law developments in Germany always take place against the background of such a candid argument. But it shows the willingness of German judges, academics and practitioners to engage in a debate about the state of the law and how it should be developed further. And it disproves the view of some observers from the common law world who may still believe that civilian legal systems essentially operate by squeezing facts into the arid and inflexible categories of a code.

In the end, the second civil senate stuck to its original plan to shape a new legal rule. The Bundesgerichtshof now views the protective purpose of the directors' duty to request the opening of insolvency proceedings

[77] *Ait Stapelfeld*, Die Haftung des GmbH-Geschäftsführers für Fehlverhalten in der Gesellschaftskrise (1990), 166–172.

[78] BGH 6.6.1994, BGHZ 126, 181 = NJW 1994, 2220; an English translation of some essential passages of the reasoning can be found in *Walter van Gerven et al.* (eds.), Tort Law (2000), 228.

[79] BGH 1.3.1993, ZIP 1993, 763; BGH 20.9.1993, NJW 1993, 2931.

[80] Case notes by *Peter Ulmer*, ZIP 1993, 769; *Herbert Wiedemann*, EWiR 1993, 583; *Karsten Schmidt*, NJW 1993, 2934; articles: *Claus-Wilhelm Canaris*, 'Die Haftung für fahrlässige Verletzungen der Konkursantragspflicht nach § 64 GmbHG', JZ 1993, 649; *Gerd Müller*, 'Zur Haftung des Gesellschafter-Geschäftsführers aus culpa in contrahendo und aus § 64 Abs. 1 GmbHG', ZIP 1993, 1531; *Jan Wilhelm*, 'Konkursantragspflicht des GmbH-Geschäftsführers und Quotenschaden', ZIP 1993, 1833; *Marcus Lutter*, 'Gefahren persönlicher Haftung für Gesellschafter und Geschäftsführer einer GmbH', DB 1994, 129; *Matthias Schüppen*, 'Aktuelle Fragen der Konkursverschleppungshaftung durch den GmbH-Geschäftsführer', DB 1994, 197; *Werner Flume*, 'Die Haftung des GmbH-Geschäftsführers bei Geschäften nach Konkursreife der GmbH', ZIP 1994, 337.

more widely, in that the duty is meant to secure the elimination of insolvent companies. An effective civil sanction to implement this aim must go beyond mere compensation for the diminution of the quota and requires full compensation where an individual has suffered a higher loss from the unlawful continuation of the business. The new rule is that a culpable – intentional or negligent – breach of the duty to request the opening of insolvency proceedings renders the directors liable to compensate the new creditors for the loss caused by their entering into legal relationships with the insolvent company.[81]

The legal position of the old creditors remains unaffected by this decision. The damage to their financial interests caused by the delay in the opening of insolvency proceedings is nothing else but the diminution of the quota that occurred in the intervening period, defined as the difference between the hypothetical quota that the creditors would have received at the time when the directors should have requested the opening of insolvency proceedings and the (lower) actual quota payable from the remaining assets.[82] In this respect, every old creditor suffers the same diminution of the quota expressed as a percentage of his nominal claim. While technically the entitlement to damages belongs not to the company, but to each creditor individually, it is possible and indeed preferable to liquidate these damages collectively through the office-holder, who is vested with the exclusive power to do so for the duration of insolvency proceedings by virtue of § 92 InsO.[83]

Provided that the analysis of the Bundesgerichtshof as to the protective purpose of the directors' duty to request the opening of insolvency proceedings is correct, the ruling presents a convincing application of general principles of the law of delict. However, it also creates unpleasant side effects. By awarding damages, the new creditors are to be placed in the financial position as if their transactions with the company had not occurred. German lawyers refer to this quantification of loss interchangeably as *negatives Interesse* (negative interest) or *Vertrauensschaden* (reliance loss). The reliance loss has to be worked out for each creditor individually and will often depend on idiosyncratic circumstances. Therefore, the office-holder's standing to liquidate these damages, even on

[81] BGH 6.6.1994, BGHZ 126, 181 at 198 = NJW 1994, 2220 at 2224.

[82] *Christoph Poertzgen* (fn. 32), 276–282 deals with the exact formula for the calculation based on BGH 30.3.1998, BGHZ 138, 211 at 221 = NJW 1998, 2667 at 2669 f.

[83] *Harald Kroth* in *Braun*, InsO[3] § 92 mn. 8; *Helmut Brandes* in Münchener Kommentar InsO[2] § 92 mn. 11; *Poertzgen* (fn. 32), 283–289.

grounds of 'convenience', is now clearly out of the question, and the Bundesgerichtshof has confirmed that the office-holder has no mandate to bring proceedings on behalf of the new creditors.[84]

One can normally exclude from the reliance loss any profit which the creditor would have made if the transaction had proceeded as agreed. The 'negative interest', i.e. the loss resulting from a transaction which the creditor should have avoided in the first place, consists of the variable costs of manufacturing the products or rendering the services supplied to the company. In many cases, to establish a loss on the basis of variable costs will not only require an expert witness, but it will draw the creditor's calculation into open court and subject it to external scrutiny. For suppliers of goods and services this is certainly not a prospect they relish. Banks appear to be in a less awkward situation. Their variable costs are determined by the market rates at which they refinance the lending transaction;[85] this, and of course the principal sum of credit advanced to the creditor after the crucial point in time,[86] will be easier to prove.

In some situations, however, the reliance loss may go beyond the variable costs, as where the claimant, in reliance on the debtor's solvency, has failed to take up an alternative business opportunity and has suffered damage by way of loss of opportunity as a result. The point is illustrated by a case from Austria, where the claimant had hired out billiard tables to a company, which continued to use them during the period of delay in filing for insolvency. The Austrian Supreme Court held that the creditor could claim the full amount of the agreed monthly hire for the period if he could show that he turned down an alternative chance to hire out the tables to another customer at the same rate.[87] There are indications, though, that some German courts take a very liberal approach towards allowing creditors full recovery of their invoiced amounts under the pretext of damages for loss of opportunity. The statutory basis for this practice is found in § 252 BGB, a provision designed to alleviate the claimant's burden of proof with regard to counterfactual events, viz. his ability to earn the same amount of income from alternative contracts with other customers, 'in the ordinary course of events'.[88] In effect, these decisions boil down to a generalised (though

[84] BGH 30.3.1998, BGHZ 138, 211 at 214–216 = NJW 1998, 2667 at 2668.
[85] BGH 5.2.2007, BGHZ 171, 46 para. 21.
[86] Ibid., para. 13 (but see above, text accompanying fn. 63).
[87] OGH 22.10.1997, SZ 70/215 (at p. 555).
[88] OLG Koblenz 3.8.1999, GmbHR 2000, 31; OLG Celle, 5.12.2001, NZG 2002, 730.

rebuttable) presumption in favour of any self-employed person that his services will be in constant demand at full capacity – an assumption that seems hard to square with the realities in a competitive market economy.

In one respect, at least, the law remains unsettled and further clarification is needed. The problem relates to creditors who acquire claims against the company not through advancing fresh credit in reliance on the continued solvency of the debtor, but by operation of the law during the period of delay in filing for insolvency. Whether the loss incurred by such creditors should also be included in the protective ambit of the duty to request the opening of insolvency proceedings, as declared by the Bundesgerichtshof in 1994, is open to debate, and commentators' opinions on the point are divided.[89] Creditors in this category include the victims of delict and unjust enrichment. But the real policy implications will only become clear once it is understood that answering the question in the affirmative may open up new ways for public agencies to sue the directors of failed companies for unpaid social security contributions accruing from the continued employment of the company's workforce. The prospect is that these creditors may be willing to pursue their claims much more vigorously than private creditors or office-holders, who tend to be more concerned with cost-benefit considerations. The British experience with public enforcement of the disqualification regime under the Company Directors Disqualification Act (CDDA) certainly lends support to this conjecture.

So far the Bundesgerichtshof has ducked the question. In what appears to be the latest case brought by a social security agency, the court refused to deal with the point of law because the claimant had not sufficiently demonstrated its loss as one attributable to the director's breach of duty.[90] Incidentally, that loss was calculated on the basis of a counterfactual scenario similar to the argument about damages for loss of opportunity. The agency argued that, if the directors had instigated

[89] Arguing for such a broad ambit: *Peter Reiff/Arnd Arnold*, 'Unbeschränkte Konkursverschleppungshaftung des Geschäftsführers einer GmbH auch gegenüber gesetzlichen Neugläubigern?', ZIP 1998, 1893; *Lutter/Kleindiek* (fn. 57), § 64 mn. 50; *Jörg Nerlich* in *Michalski*, GmbHG § 64 mn. 76; contra: *Ulrich Haas*, Geschäftsführerhaftung und Gläubigerschutz (1997), 234–239; *Altmeppen* (fn. 57) § 64 mn. 71; *Schulze-Osterloh* (fn. 57) § 64 mn. 92.

[90] BGH 7.7.2003, ZIP 2003, 1713 (with a penetrative case note by *Karsten Schmidt*).

insolvency proceedings, this would have caused the company's employees to move to other, solvent employers who, in turn, would have paid their regular social security contributions. The Bundesgerichtshof held that this chain of events had not been shown to a degree of probability so as to justify the application of § 252 BGB. Comparing this case with those mentioned before, we can also see that the German courts, though not openly exercising discretion in the way English judges have little hesitation in doing, can achieve similar results through the fine-tuning of the burden of proof on the particular facts before them. However, that does not end the continuing legal uncertainty over the protective purpose of the duty to request the opening of insolvency proceedings in relation to involuntary creditors, and this is certainly an area where practitioners and academics are waiting for new cases to come to the courts.

3. *An interim summary and an explanation*

Reviewing the position of German law, directors' delay in filing for insolvency is sanctioned by a combination of no less than three concurrent types of civil liability: first, internal liability (*Innenhaftung*) towards the company for the depletion of its distributable assets based on § 64 GmbHG as amended by the MoMiG;[91] second, external liability (*Außenhaftung*) towards the old creditors for the loss resulting from the diminution of their quota in the distribution, a claim in delict based on § 15a InsO[92] as a protective norm within the meaning of § 823 (2) BGB, but where, during insolvency proceedings, the office-holder alone has standing to enforce the claims by virtue of § 92 InsO; and third, external liability towards the new creditors for the reliance loss caused by entering into the transaction with the company, also a claim in delict based on § 15a InsO as a protective norm within the meaning of § 823 (2) BGB, but which can only be enforced by each creditor individually.

In the final analysis, German law must be characterised as a victory of the law of delict over the law of insolvency. Yet the result blows a big hole into the *pari passu* treatment of creditors. It is as if Len Sealy's

[91] Previously sub-paragraph (2) of § 64 GmbHG.
[92] Previously sub-paragraph (1) of § 64 GmbHG.

words of warning from the mid-1980s had been written with – the yet to come – German law in mind:

> There are dangers in seeking to go further and base a new remedy on a duty owed directly by directors to creditors in tort. This would clash with established principles of company law and with the underlying policy of insolvency law.[93]

Sealy's article is testimony that, for a brief period in the 1980s, the idea of directors' liability towards creditors in delict or tort was a subject-matter worthy of debate for English lawyers, too. But it did not catch on in England, whereas it has become the dominant approach within the German discourse. The solution to this paradox may hold a surprise to English lawyers: When German lawyers discuss directors' personal liability towards creditors, they are perhaps less concerned with insolvency proceedings than with the situation where no such proceedings take place. The phenomenon is known as '***massearme Insolvenzen***' (asset-starved insolvencies), as many companies soldier on until so little is left that it does not even warrant the opening of formal insolvency proceedings. If this happens, *pari passu* ceases to be a relevant consideration, while every creditor is left to fight for whatever spoils he can get hold of. Karsten Schmidt, one of the most vociferous critics of the present law, has made his point forcefully:

> The motto of the law of insolvent liquidation is: *pari passu*! Against it, the motto of liquidation outside insolvency is: make way for the brave![94]

Asset-starved insolvencies constitute a recurring theme in the German discourse.[95] Several cases from the Bundesgerichtshof cited in this book concern asset-starved insolvencies.[96] Throughout the 1980s and 1990s roughly three-quarters of all requests for the opening of insolvency proceedings were turned down by the courts for want of assets sufficient

93 *Len Sealy*, 'Directors' "Wider" Responsibilities – Problems Conceptual, Practical and Procedural' (1987) 13 Monash Univ. Law Review 164, at 188.

94 *Karsten Schmidt*, 'Insolvenzrisiko und gesellschaftsrechtliche Haftung', JZ 1985, 301, 306: 'Das Motto des Konkursrechts heißt: par condicio creditorum! Das Motto der konkursfreien Liquidation dagegen heißt: freie Bahn dem Tüchtigen!'

95 See, for instance, *Stapelfeld* (fn. 77), 6–8; *Haas* (fn. 89), 30–35; *Holger Altmeppen*, 'Probleme der Konkursverschleppungshaftung', ZIP 1997, 1173; *Forum Europaeum Konzernrecht*, 'Konzernrecht für Europa', ZGR 1998, 672 at 752–753; translated as *Forum Europaeum Corporate Group Law*, 'Corporate Group Law for Europe' [2000] EBOR 165, at 245.

96 E.g. the notorious *Baustoff* case on the personal liability of the director in delict under § 823 (1) BGB (fn. 16).

even to cover the costs of the proceedings.[97] One of the declared aims of the extensive law reform project that resulted in the new Insolvency Code, which was enacted in 1994 and came into force on 1 January 1999, was a reduction in the number of asset-starved insolvencies.[98] Since then, figures have gone down, but in the most recent statistics, such insolvencies still account for between one-third and one-half of requests brought to the courts.[99] Interestingly, there is empirical evidence suggesting that the phenomenon is not unknown in England, too, where the number of insolvency proceedings is persistently dwarfed by the number of companies struck off the register without orderly liquidation.[100] It would appear counter-intuitive to assume that thousands of companies struck off the register do not leave unpaid debts behind. Yet the discourse among English lawyers does not even seem to have coined a specific phrase for the phenomenon, let alone identified it as an area of particular interest.[101] So why do German lawyers care so much more about these companies? Perhaps, the answer to this question lies in a profound structural difference between the two insolvency regimes.

The difference finds its expression in two diametrically opposed statutory provisions. In s. 125 (1) IA the court is accorded a wide discretion how to dispose of a winding-up petition. But the last half sentence in the subsection precludes one option for the court: it shall not refuse to make a winding-up order on the ground only that the company's assets have been mortgaged to an amount equal to or in excess of those assets, or that the company has no assets. In stark contrast, § 26 (1) InsO mandates precisely this response. A German court must dismiss a request for the opening of insolvency proceedings if the value of the debtor's assets is so low that they will presumably be insufficient to cover the costs of the proceedings, and by extension that also covers the situation where there are no assets left at all.

97 Figures are published in: Insolvenzstatistik 1998, ZIP 1999, 2181.

98 Government bill, Bundestags-Drucksache 12/2443 (April 1992), p. 80–81.

99 Monthly figures are available at www.destatis.de.

100 For the fiscal year 2007–08 (ending 31 March) Companies House reports 206,200 companies struck off the register and dissolved in England and Wales (source: www.companieshouse.gov.uk/about/pdf/companiesRegActivities2007_2008.pdf, Table C1), whereas the Insolvency Service reports less than 13,000 company liquidations for the same period (source: www.insolvency.gov.uk/otherinformation/statistics/insolv.htm).

101 A noteworthy exception is *Andrew Hicks*, 'Director Disqualification: Can it Deliver?' [2001] JBL 433, at 443–445.

It is obvious that the German rule deprives creditors of the protection of insolvency law where the controllers of a company have been ruthless or inept enough to wreck it completely. But there is a reason for this rule. The German system of dealing with insolvent companies relies exclusively on professionals in private practice acting as office-holders (*Insolvenzverwalter*, insolvency administrators). In other words, Germany has no equivalent to the institution of the official receiver, an officer of the court attached to the Insolvency Service, which in turn is an Executive Agency of the Department for Business, Enterprise and Regulatory Reform (BERR), formerly the Department of Trade and Industry (DTI).[102] The official receiver was introduced into English insolvency law at the end of the nineteenth century[103] and has ever since played an important role in policing insolvent companies and their controllers in the public interest.[104] The official receiver acts as the provisional liquidator as long as no other liquidator has been appointed (s. 136 IA) and thereby as a liquidator of last resort if no insolvency practitioner in private practice can be found to take over as office-holder. In this case the official receiver may apply to the registrar of companies for 'early dissolution', i.e. dissolution without going through a formal winding up process, if it appears to the official receiver that the realisable assets of the company are insufficient to cover the expenses of the winding up, but, significantly, this is subject to the proviso that 'the affairs of the company do not require any further investigation' (s. 202 IA).

This investigation into the causes of the failure of the company and, generally, into 'the promotion, formation, business, dealings and affairs of the company' (s. 132 IA) is one of the major functions of the official receiver, whether or not he is the liquidator (s. 236 IA). In particular, such an investigation may lead to disqualification proceedings brought against a director under the Company Directors Disqualification Act (CDDA). Finally, where a company has been struck off the register, the official receiver may still enforce any liability of a director for breach of duty or wrongful trading, which, according to s. 1003 (6) CA 2006, continues as if the company had not been dissolved. All this does not

[102] For an overview of the institutional framework see *Andrew Keay/Peter Walton*, Insolvency Law (2003), 30–33 and *Roy Goode*, Corporate Insolvency Law (3rd edn 2005), para. 1–19.

[103] Bankruptcy Act 1883; Companies (Winding up) Act 1890.

[104] The House of Lords delivered a forceful reminder of the public interest function of insolvency law in *Re Pantmaenog Timber Co Ltd* [2003] UKHL 49 = [2004] 1 AC 158.

mean that an official receiver will automatically scrutinise every company struck off the register. But the institutional framework is in place to respond to complaints about rogue directors and to take appropriate action, at least in order to maintain a certain degree of integrity or commercial morality in the eyes of the business community and the general public.[105] In England, the burden of effectuating creditor protection through the mechanism of insolvency law and through the closely related disqualification regime is thus partly shouldered by the public. In Germany, such a system would have to be created from scratch, and the political will to do so may not be forthcoming in times of governments defining deregulation and budget discipline as their main strategic goals.

Against this background, the practical advantages of the present German law empowering the new creditors to take matters into their own hands and sue the directors in delict outweigh the disadvantages as regards the coherence of insolvency law. In addition to the advantages of capital maintenance over avoidance remedies, which have been explored in chapter 3, these findings on directors' liability for delayed filing for insolvency and on asset-starved insolvencies hold a further clue as to why, in the past, insolvency law seems to have been somewhat neglected by German company lawyers seeking solutions for the protection of creditors.

C. Wrongful trading and directors' duties in English law: variety for its own sake?

1. *Problems and perspectives – switching between legal systems*

This section mirrors the preceding section on German law in that it presents relevant aspects of English law on directors' personal liability for conduct in the vicinity of insolvency that is detrimental to creditor interests. In keeping with the general theme of developing a dynamic presentation of the law, the description will focus on those aspects of English law which, from an English lawyer's perspective informed by his domestic judicial and academic discourse, have been most contentious, or where the law remains unsettled, with a strong potential for future evolution. As the section unfolds, it will become clear that these topics

[105] For a more detailed introduction to directors' disqualification see *Thomas Bachner*, 'Creditor protection through insolvency law in England', in: *Marcus Lutter* (ed.), Legal Capital in Europe (2006) 427, at 456–475; comprehensive coverage is provided, inter alia, by *Adrian Walters/Malcolm Davis-White*, Directors' Disqualification & Bankruptcy Restrictions (2005).

are entirely different from those discussed in respect of German law. But that only proves the point made in the introductory chapter that the movement of this 'frontier' in each legal system is contingent on the respective doctrinal approach, and that a full understanding of the current legal literature in any system requires a firm knowledge of the historic and structural context of these topical debates – something which a purely functional analysis does not deliver.

To begin with, let us briefly ask whether there is any role for directors' duties towards creditors in delict or tort, along the lines of the German model of external liability. Indeed, during the 1980s and 1990s, English law saw a brief flurry of a debate as to whether directors owed personal duties to creditors where the company was in the vicinity of insolvency. The discussion was fuelled by a passage in a well-known case from New Zealand[106] and a dictum by Lord Templeman in *Winkworth v Edward Baron Development Co Ltd*, where his Lordship opined: 'A duty is owed by the directors to the company *and to the creditors of the company* to ensure that the affairs of the company are properly administered and that its property is not dissipated or exploited . . . to the prejudice of the creditors.'[107]

Although the dictum was merely obiter, it drew immediate harsh criticism.[108] To English lawyers, speaking of a 'duty to creditors' opens up the prospect of a duty of care giving rise to liability for economic loss within the tort of negligence under the 'extended *Hedley Byrne* principle' explained above.[109] The idea of such a tortious duty to protect creditors of limited liability companies was rejected more or less unanimously.[110] It now appears to be the settled position of English law that company directors owe no direct duty to creditors of the company.[111] Directors may, however, be held to account for their conduct in the vicinity of insolvency by virtue of remedies in the hands of the company or the office-holder. From a German perspective, these remedies can all be

[106] *Nicholson v Permakraft (NZ) Ltd* [1985] 1 NZLR 242, at 249 and 250 (Cooke J).

[107] [1986] 1 WLR 1512, at 1516 (emphasis added).

[108] *Len Sealy*, 'Directors' Duties – An Unnecessary Gloss' [1988] CLJ 175, at 176: 'It is not an exaggeration to say that if sentiments like this had prevailed over the past century and a half, the limited liability company would never have got off the ground.'

[109] Text accompanying fn. 12 and 13.

[110] *Sealy* (fn. 93); *D.D. Prentice*, 'Creditor's Interests and Director's Duties' (1990) 10 OJLS 265; *Ross Grantham*, 'The Judicial Extension of Directors' Duties to Creditors' [1991] JBL 1.

[111] *Andrew Keay*, Company Directors' Responsibilities to Creditors (2007), ch. 15, with a comprehensive review of English and other Commonwealth authority.

classified as *Innenhaftung* (internal liability). But this is not the point of interest for English lawyers. Their debate revolves around the fact that no fewer than three different remedies against delinquent directors may be discerned, which are by no means in total harmony as regards preconditions and legal consequences.

In the text that follows, subsection 2 will analyse the most prominent among these remedies, viz. wrongful trading,[112] whereupon subsections 3 and 4 will discuss the interplay between wrongful trading, on the one hand, and, respectively, the duty to exercise reasonable care, skill and diligence and the fiduciary duty to consider the interests of the company's creditors, on the other hand. Whereas the duty of care, skill and diligence covers broadly the same ground as wrongful trading, but with diverging legal consequences, the duty to consider the interests of creditors represents an entirely different doctrinal approach, which cuts across wrongful trading in terms of scope and legal consequences. In a European perspective it merits particular attention as a complement to a debate which, in the past, was spellbound by the perceived dualism of wrongful trading and *Insolvenzverschleppungshaftung* (liability for delayed filing for insolvency).

Wrongful trading is largely the brain-child of the Cork Committee, a group of experts commissioned by the DTI in 1977 to review the law and practice relating to corporate insolvency and personal bankruptcy, and to consider reforms. When the Committee reported in 1982, it devoted a whole chapter to wrongful trading,[113] although the proposal was subsequently enacted with a number of important modifications. Once it had received the sanction of the legislature, the new concept stirred up a lot of interest, and not just in England.[114] German lawyers also took note, and since the late 1990s a number of comparative studies have looked at wrongful trading in more or less detail.[115] This body of

[112] First introduced as s. 15 of the Insolvency Act 1985, subsequently re-enacted as s. 214 of the (current) Insolvency Act 1986.

[113] Cork Report ('Insolvency Law and Practice: Report of the Review Committee'), Cmnd. 8558 (1982), ch. 44.

[114] Where it was described it as 'one of the most important developments in company law in this century': *Prentice* (fn. 110), at 277; *Len Sealy*, Disqualification and Personal Liability of Directors (5th edn 2000), 71, speaks of the legislator 'break[ing] new ground'.

[115] *Ernst-Markus Schuberth*, Konzernrelevante Regelungen im britischen Recht – Ein Beispiel für die Bewältigung konzernrechtlicher Fragestellungen durch Regeln des allgemeinen Gesellschafts-, Kapitalmarkt und Insolvenzrechts (1997), 191–199; *Henning Bloß*, Die Unternehmensgruppe im englischen und deutschen Recht der

literature provides enlightening opportunities to contrast English law with German perceptions of English law. German authors invariably analyse wrongful trading in terms of the classification of internal versus external liability, which matters so much in their domestic discourse, yet is hardly more than an historic footnote to English lawyers. It seems that, by writing about English law, German authors were preoccupied with finding answers to German questions – unaware that the really hot topics in English law are quite different ones.

A handful of German authors complement their presentation of wrongful trading with a glimpse of directors' general duties (often referred to as 'common law' duties, although it is clear from the context that this includes equitable duties),[116] but on the whole the analysis of this interrelationship does not go very far and lacks a genuine understanding of the structural framework of duties of care, skill and diligence and fiduciary duties set out in chapter 4.

Although the relationship between wrongful trading and directors' duties represents a key problem area for English lawyers and has sparked a significant discourse, German observers clearly have difficulties in finding access to this English discourse. Perhaps their domestic focus on legal writing as the interpretation of statutes makes it harder for them to grasp developments within the common law, let alone the interplay of common law and equity. At an even deeper level of legal methodology, their sense of synthesis and harmony in the legal system may make it a troubling experience to find that, in English law, it is quite possible (though not necessarily desirable) that the judges and the legislature come up with two strictly independent sets of rules, which are of equal legal force, yet produce inconsistent results. This, again, demonstrates

Kapitalgesellschaften (1999), 92–95; *Marcus Roth*, Unternehmerisches Ermessen und Haftung des Vorstands (2001), 186–197; *Barbara Höfling*, Das englische internationale Gesellschaftsrecht (2002), 224–230; *Christina Pernice*, Die Insolvenzverschleppung durch das Geschäftsführungsorgan der kleinen Kapitalgesellschaft im deutschen, französischen und englischen Recht (2002), 209–218; *Susanne Wimmer-Leonhardt*, Konzernhaftungsrecht (2004), 536–543; articles include: *Forum Europaeum Konzernrecht*, 'Konzernrecht für Europa', ZGR 1998, 672 at 752–757; *Holger Fleischer*, 'Neue Entwicklungen im englischen Konzernrecht', AG 1999, 350 at 356–358; comprehensive coverage of the subject in the article by *Mathias Habersack / Dirk Verse*, 'Wrongful Trading – Grundlage einer europäischen Insolvenzverschleppungshaftung?', ZHR 168 (2004), 174–215, and in the book by *Rouven Redeker*, Die Haftung für wrongful trading im englischen Recht (2007). The subject is also dealt with in the literature concerning UK-registered companies operating in Germany, see the references in chapter 1 fn. 49.

116 *Roth* (fn. 115) 181; *Pernice* (fn. 115) 201–202; *Habersack / Verse* (fn. 115) 199–201; *Redeker* (fn. 115) 175–184.

the need for a better mutual understanding as a prerequisite for a fruitful common discourse.

2. *The legal nature of wrongful trading*

Historic roots and contemporary classifications

Assuming the position of a foreign lawyer wishing to gain a first orientation about the place of wrongful trading in English law, it may be useful to consult a textbook. In a number of textbooks, the entry for wrongful trading in the index directs the reader not to a chapter on directors' duties, but elsewhere.[117] This should be seen as a warning sign that wrongful trading cannot be put into the doctrinal category of directors' duties in the straightforward manner German lawyers might expect. The warning signs become even brighter once the legislative history is taken into account.

The Cork Report on the review of insolvency law did not deal with directors' duties beyond a few scattered references, as the limited remit of the Cork Committee did not include general company law. Instead, when the Committee drew up its proposal on wrongful trading, it started from a provision already existing in the insolvency part of the Companies Act 1948, viz. s. 332 on fraudulent trading, which has since become s. 213 of the Insolvency Act 1986. Neither of the two provisions was or is limited to directors. Instead they apply (or applied, respectively) to 'any persons who were knowingly parties to the carrying on of the business in [a fraudulent] manner'. The Cork Committee accepted the test of 'a person who is party to the company's trading' as its starting point.[118] It had received evidence that the fraud requirement was hard to prove in court and deterred the issue of proceedings in many cases where a strong case existed for recovering assets from directors.[119] The Committee conceived wrongful trading as an expansion of s. 332 CA 1948 so as to include a director who honestly believed that he could trade the company out of its difficulties, although, objectively, there was no reasonable prospect of recovery. In its draft clause, the Committee recommended that wrongful trading should extend to 'any person party

[117] *Gower & Davies'* Company Law (8th edn 2008), ch. 9 ('Statutory Exceptions to Limited Liability'), 217–224; *Brenda Hannigan*, Company Law (2003), ch. 28 ('Directors' liabilities and vulnerable transactions on insolvency'), 844–848.

[118] Cork Report (fn. 113), para. 1787–1789. [119] Ibid., para. 1759 and 1776.

to the carrying on of the business of the company . . . if it appears that such person: (a) knew, or (b) as an officer of the company, ought, in all circumstances, to have known that the company's trading was wrongful'.[120] Looked at from this historical perspective, wrongful trading emerged not as an offspring of directors' duties, but as a concept carved out from a more widely applicable instrument to combat fraudulent behaviour by whoever is in charge of a company's affairs.

This history continues to influence the legislative approach to wrongful trading. The Final Report on the Company Law Review recommended for inclusion in the planned comprehensive statement of directors' duties a clause modelled on the defence in s. 214 (3) IA, namely a duty for the director to take every step to protect creditors' interests when it appears that the company has no reasonable prospect of avoiding insolvent liquidation, the test in s. 214 (2) (b) IA.[121] But the clause did not make it into the Companies Act 2006. The decision to reject it was already announced in the White Paper 'Modernising Company Law' in 2002.[122] The reasons given are telling:

> The inclusion of a special duty where there is no reasonable prospect of avoiding insolvency was suggested mainly for presentational reasons. It was not intended to alter the law (although arguably it might result in some improvement or clarification at the margins). It would, however, de-couple the obligations imposed by section 214 of the Insolvency Act 1986 from the remedies under that Act in the case of registered companies. Its inclusion in the statutory statement would therefore be incongruous, particularly given that the Government is proposing to provide a comprehensive code of remedies in the Bill for all of the other duties in the Schedule.
>
> It is important to emphasise that there is no question about the need for section 214; but to incorporate it in the statement would unhelpfully conflate company and insolvency law. . . . The Government does not believe it appropriate to single out one requirement from insolvency law and include it within the codification of common law duties owed by directors to companies.[123]

There is no denying that company directors are the defendants primarily targeted by s. 214 IA. But they are not the only targets, as the application of the section to shadow directors demonstrates. By contrast, the mere

[120] Ibid., para. 1806 (sub-clause 3).
[121] Final Report (2001), vol. II, Schedule 2, clause 9.
[122] Cm. 5553-II, Schedule 2, p. 112 ff.
[123] Cm. 5553-I, para. 3.12–3.13.

fact that a person falls within the statutory definition of 'shadow director'[124] is not enough to impose upon this person the same duties to the relevant company as are owed by directors.[125] German lawyers should be aware that, from an English perspective, wrongful trading and directors' duties are by no means two sides of the same coin. The reference to 'the remedies under that Act' (the Insolvency Act 1986) gives an important clue to the nature of wrongful trading and how strongly it is anchored in the framework of insolvency law. On a closer analysis, wrongful trading shows interesting parallels with transaction avoidance in terms of the office-holder's exclusive standing to commence proceedings and in terms of the destination of the proceeds of a successful application, both of which will be explored presently.

The claim against the director – is it an 'asset of the company'?

The way in which many German observers approach the liquidator's standing to make an application under s. 214 IA is by reference to the claim against the director as a 'claim held by the company' (*Anspruch der Gesellschaft*) or simply an 'asset of the company' (*Vermögensgegenstand der Gesellschaft*). The problem here is a massive loss of information in the process of translation because the original English phrase, 'asset of the company', encapsulates a complex doctrinal debate with important practical ramifications, of which an informed English reader will be fully aware, whereas the German terms sound more like expressions of a legal truism.

A good illustration of these difficulties, which are partly a matter of translation and partly a matter of prejudgment, can be found in an important article outlining possible developments for company law at the European level, including wrongful trading.[126] The paper was published by a group of European scholars who styled themselves 'Forum Europaeum Konzernrecht' ('Forum Europaeum Corporate Group Law'),

[124] Concordant definitions are given in the Insolvency Act 1986, s. 251, and in the Companies Act 2006, s. 251.

[125] *Ultraframe (UK) Ltd v Fielding* [2005] EWHC 1638 (Ch), para. 1284 ff., but see the critical note by *D.D. Prentice/Jenny Payne*, 'Directors' Fiduciary Duties' (2006) 122 LQR 558, at 562. The Companies Act 2006, in s. 170 (5), leaves open the question to what extent the general duties of directors apply also to shadow directors; the courts should be free to develop the law in this respect: *Hannigan & Prentice*, Companies Act 2006, para. 3.15, with references to the parliamentary debate.

[126] *Forum Europaeum Konzernrecht*, 'Konzernrecht für Europa', ZGR 1998, 672; translated as *Forum Europaeum Corporate Group Law*, 'Corporate Group Law for Europe' [2000] EBOR 165.

but it was mainly co-authored by three German academics. The original German version of the article states quite categorically:

> Antragsberechtigt ist allein der Liquidator, nicht der einzelne Gesellschaftsgläubiger. Anspruchsinhaberin ist die Gesellschaft; an sie muss der Geschäftsführer also den Schadenersatz leisten. Das entspricht der Haftungskonzentration nach dem deutschen Innenhaftungs-Modell.[127]

This could be translated literally (and with no regard to English style) as:

> Only the liquidator is entitled to make an application, not the individual creditor of the company. The claim is held by the company; it is to it [the company] that the director must pay the compensation. That corresponds with the bundling of liability under the German model of internal liability.

As a statement of English law based on judicial authority, a proposition that the claim against the director for compensation under s. 214 IA is 'held by the company' does not seem correct. But how can that be if, as the article states correctly in the preceding sentence, only the liquidator is entitled to make an application under s. 214 IA? After all, the office-holder's exclusive competence to bring an action against a director is the hallmark of *Innenhaftung* (internal liability), as opposed to *Außenhaftung* (external liability) – the classification, whose centrality to German law has been discussed above, together with the difficulties arising from it. But it does not follow that the claim must necessarily be one 'held by' the company. Indeed, this may have influenced the English translation of that passage. Whereas, in general, the translation follows the German text quite closely, it deviates significantly on this point:

> Only the liquidator – not the individual creditors – is entitled to apply for this relief against the director. The beneficiary of the claim is the company – the damages awarded must be paid to the company. This corresponds to the '*Haftungskonzentration*' under the German internal liability model.[128]

In legal terms, it makes a difference whether someone is the holder of a claim or the beneficiary of a claim. But even the latter phrase seems unsatisfactory. The company, after all, is in insolvent liquidation. It is not going to survive as a corporate entity but will be dissolved at the end of the process. What is the point of viewing the company as the

[127] ZGR 1998, 672 at 756 (footnote omitted).
[128] [2000] EBOR 165, at 248 (footnote omitted).

beneficiary of the wrongful trading claim? The only remaining purpose of the company is to apply its assets towards the satisfaction of its creditors. Looked at it from this angle, the above proposition fails to answer what English lawyers view as the crucial question: which creditors are to be the beneficiaries of the claim?

In a similar vein, the author of a doctoral thesis on groups of companies in English and German law wrestles inconclusively with the issue. He writes:

> Der Schadensersatz ist in vollem Umfang in das Gesellschaftsvermögen zu leisten, was die gleichmäßige Befriedigung der Gesellschaftsgläubiger sichert.[129]
>
> (The full amount of the compensation is payable towards the company's assets, which ensures the rateable satisfaction of the company's creditors.)

Yet in an accompanying footnote he refers to *Ward v Aitken*[130] and seeks to explain:

> [dass] eine wrongful trading action nur durch den 'liquidator' geltend gemacht werden darf und damit nicht Bestandteil des Gesellschaftsvermögens sei; daraus folgt, daß ein gesicherter Gläubiger die Kompensationsleistungen nicht für sich beanspruchen kann, sondern diese vom 'liquidator' treuhänderisch für alle Gläubiger gehalten werden müssen.
>
> (that a wrongful trading action may only be brought by the liquidator and therefore is not part of the company's assets; it follows that a secured creditor cannot claim the compensation for himself, but it must be held by the liquidator on trust for all creditors.)

The author's sense of unease about this paradox is palpable, not least because he goes on to cite *Re Purpoint Ltd*[131] in support of the proposition that the compensation must not go to any particular group of creditors, seemingly unaware that *Re Purpoint* did not concern the conflict between secured and unsecured creditors, but between 'old' and 'new' creditors.[132]

Another German observer retreats to a cautious position:

> Trotz des an sich eindeutigen Wortlauts von section 214 (1) Insolvency Act . . . ist ungeklärt, ob Kompensationszahlungen der directors zwingend

[129] *Bloß* (fn. 115), 93; almost identical words with *Wimmer-Leonhardt* (fn. 115), 543.

[130] The Times, 19 June 1995; the case is more commonly known as *Re Oasis Merchandising Services Ltd* [1995] BCC 911 (ChD), [1998] Ch. 170 (CA); see below, text accompanying fn. 160.

[131] [1991] BCC 121, at 128.

[132] Above, fn. 66 and accompanying text.

> in das Vermögen der Gesellschaft zu entrichten sind. Eine zumindest beachtliche Ansicht im Schrifttum will dem Gericht zumindest die Möglichkeit zubilligen, Zahlungen von directors wegen wrongful trading den ungesicherten Gläubigern zuzusprechen.'[133]
>
> (Despite the explicit wording of section 214 (1) Insolvency Act . . . it remains unclear whether compensation payments by directors must imperatively be paid into the assets of the company. There is an opinion in the literature at least worth taking note of that wants to allow the court at least the possibility to award payments from directors for wrongful trading to the unsecured creditors.)

The reference to scholarly opinion must of course be read in the light of German legal methodology – English lawyers would not treat it as authoritative in the same manner as German lawyers. On the other hand, the author does not provide references to the vast case law which had built up around this point by the time of his writing.[134] Contrary to the impression that might be derived from the above statement, the matter is not actually one of judicial discretion, but very much one of principle, except that the results reached on the basis of these principled arguments turned out to be unsatisfactory in some of their consequences, which led to a protracted debate.

Over time, as could be expected, some writers managed to capture the essence of the problem more precisely. Habersack and Verse aptly convey the relevance of the floating charge for the destination of the proceeds of a successful action,[135] but even they do not link this point with the related issue regarding the liquidator's costs, which is presented as an unconnected problem,[136] although, as will become clear presently, this is the link which has been the driving force behind the developments in English law.

Then again, the recent book by Redeker on wrongful trading struggles with the topic. The author refers to the Court of Appeal decision in *Re Oasis Merchandising Services Ltd*[137] as authority that the compensation from the directors is not an asset of the company so that it will not fall to the holder of a floating charge,[138] but a few pages later he criticises the Court of Appeal decision in *Re Floor Fourteen Ltd*[139] (which relied on

[133] *Roth* (fn. 115), 196 (references omitted).
[134] The author mentions *Re Oasis Merchandising Services Ltd* [1998] Ch. 170 (on p. 197 in fn. 196), but not in connection with the cited passage on the destination of recoveries.
[135] *Habersack / Verse* (fn. 115), 196. [136] Ibid., 181.
[137] [1998] Ch. 170; see below, text accompanying fn. 160.
[138] *Redeker* (fn. 115), 161–162. [139] [2001] 3 All ER 499.

Re Oasis Merchandising Services Ltd as binding precedent[140]) as 'unconvincing' (*vermag nicht zu überzeugen*) in its 'abstract treatment' of wrongful trading actions not being property of the company, given that s. 214 (1) IA expressly speaks of a 'contribution to the company's assets'.[141]

It must be acknowledged that Parliament has been less than helpful in its use of the word 'assets' in the present context. True, in a case of wrongful trading, s. 214 (1) IA empowers the court to declare a director liable 'to make [a] contribution to the company's assets', and this wording is very similar to s. 212 (3) (b) IA, where the court may compel a director 'to contribute [a sum of money] to the company's assets'. Foreign lawyers investigating English law may be forgiven for thinking that these two phrases involve identical legal consequences in each case – but they do not. The statute fails to draw a distinction whether the claim and the proceeds of it are assets of the company in the sense that they are realised by the liquidator in his capacity as the debtor company's representative, or whether they are realised by the liquidator in his capacity as office-holder – a distinction that is not found in the statute, but derives from a well-established line of cases. Again, history matters.

The impact of the floating charge on the destination of recoveries

We have already seen that the important statutory provision which is now s. 212 IA goes back almost one-and-a-half centuries to the Companies Act 1862.[142] This Act already used the ominous words 'to contribute such Sums of Money to the Assets of the Company', but at that time they probably had a quite natural meaning. Only the gradual emergence of the floating charge as a new security device fashioned by legal practice over the following decades[143] created difficulties that may not have been foreseen in 1862. The essence of a **floating charge** lies in the ease and simplicity with which a security right can be created to comprise all or virtually all of the assets of a company. A floating charge does not necessarily comprise every asset of a company. Its scope is entirely a matter for contractual agreement between chargor (debtor) and chargee (creditor). However, it is possible, through appropriate drafting, to include all assets of a company, even those not yet in

[140] See below, text accompanying fn. 163. [141] *Redeker* (fn. 115), 167–168.
[142] Chapter 4 B.3 (text accompanying fn. 66).
[143] See *Robert Pennington*, 'The Genesis of the Floating Charge' (1960) 23 MLR 630.

existence at the time when the charge is created. Without any need for specific acts of publicity in relation to particular assets, the simple registration of the charge under the relevant legislation[144] makes the charge valid and enforceable against the liquidator and all creditors of the company.

By the end of the nineteenth century it had become settled that a floating charge was capable of including claims which a company may subsequently acquire against a director for a breach of duty.[145] In response to this, development concerns emerged about the protection afforded to unsecured creditors. The reaction of the courts can be seen from the important case of *Re Yagerphone Ltd.*[146] According to the report of the case, the charge comprised 'the undertaking of [the company], and all its property whatsoever and wheresoever, both present and future'. In the course of the winding up the liquidator had successfully challenged payments to certain creditors as fraudulent preferences (now preferences within s. 239 IA), but then the proceeds were claimed by the secured creditor. The judge found two arguments to reject this claim. The first one was a somewhat artificial argument based on whether or not the money was property of the company at certain relevant times:

> When Yagerphone, Ld., paid to the creditor [the disputed sum], that sum, in my judgment, ceased to be the property of Yagerphone, Ld. The payment to that creditor could not have been attacked or impeached, unless within three months from the date of payment the liquidation of Yagerphone, Ld., had begun, and, in my judgment, at the date when the security contained in the debenture crystallised, [the disputed sum] was not the property of Yagerphone, Ld., nor property in respect of which it could, I think, be said that Yagerphone, Ld., had even a contingent interest.[147]

This reasoning set the scene for the doctrinal argument about what is properly called 'property of the company', which was to have lasting consequences. The subsequent argument makes clear what policy considerations lie behind the doctrinal argument:

> The right to recover a sum of money from a creditor who has been preferred is conferred for the purpose of benefiting the general body of creditors, and I think [counsel for the liquidators] was right when he said

[144] Companies Act 2006, Part 25; previously Companies Act 1985, Part XII.
[145] *Re Anglo-Austrian Printing and Publishing Union* [1895] 2 Ch. 891.
[146] [1935] Ch. 392. [147] Ibid., 396.

> that the sum of money, when recovered by the liquidators by virtue of [now s. 239 IA] did not become part of the general assets of Yagerphone, Ld., but was a sum of money received by the liquidators impressed in their hands with a trust for those creditors amongst whom they had to distribute the assets of the company.[148]

When wrongful trading was introduced as a novel instrument, there were similar doubts as to who would ultimately benefit from the moneys received by the liquidator. In the first reported case on the section the judge thought, without further reflection, that the proceeds of the successful application under s. 214 IA would ultimately go to the bank under the floating charge.[149] This analysis presupposes that the claim against the director under s. 214 IA constitutes an asset of the company, because otherwise the proceeds of the claim could not become subject to the floating charge over the company's assets. As a result of this case, banks reportedly set about altering the terms of charging documents to include the recoveries of wrongful trading remedies in order to avoid any ambiguity arising on account of construction.[150] In his comment on the decision, Dan Prentice expressed doubts about this conclusion. His starting point were the two lines of authority predating the Insolvency Act of 1986 which could have a bearing on the construction of s. 214, the first one being cases in the line of *Re Yagerphone* on avoiding transactions as fraudulent preferences, the other line being cases against directors for breach of duty, which the liquidator may pursue under s. 212. Prentice argued in favour of bringing s. 214 IA within the line of cases on avoiding preferences, with his position clearly inspired by policy considerations, namely that the fruits of an action brought under s. 214 IA should be reserved for the benefit of the unsecured creditors and should not go towards the holder of a floating charge.[151]

[148] Ibid.

[149] *Re Produce Marketing Consortium Ltd (No. 2)* [1989] BCC 569, at 598 (Knox J). The point was not made as an *obiter dictum*. The payment to the bank would absolve one of the directors from his personal guarantee for the company's indebtedness, and the judge made this finding the basis of an internal apportionment of the contribution as between the two directors; further on this aspect of the case *Bachner* (fn. 8), 313–315.

[150] *Oditah* (fn. 65), at 216; but the author himself rejects the outcome at 218–220.

[151] *Prentice*, (fn. 110), 271–272 (discussing *Re Produce Marketing*, but not *Re MC Bacon*; the article must have been finished before the latter decision became known).

Given the importance of the issue, it was no surprise that the question soon came up for judicial decision. *Re MC Bacon Ltd (No. 2)*,[152] a first instance decision by Mr Justice Millett (later Lord Millett), is the sequel to a case which we encountered twice in chapter 2 in relation to preferences.[153] The sequel concerned the costs of the case and, as a preliminary question, the destination of the recoveries from successful applications under s. 239 IA (preference) and under s. 214 IA (wrongful trading). After having found that *Re Yagerphone* continued to apply to preferences under the new law, so that the proceeds of such an application were not assets of the company subject to a floating charge, the judge went on to consider the wrongful trading point:

> In my judgment, the same reasoning applies with even greater force to a claim brought under section 214 of the Act, which can be brought only by a liquidator not an administrator and in the absence of an insolvent liquidation cannot be brought at all. In any case, I do not see how an application for such an order under the section can properly be described as an attempt to realise or get in an asset of the company. This must, in my view, mean an existing asset and, until the order has been made and complied with, there is no such asset.[154]

Ever since *Re MC Bacon* it has been the orthodox view that a claim brought under s. 214 IA, and the proceeds thereof, are not assets of the company.[155] But the putative advantage for unsecured creditors soon turned into a Pyrrhic victory. *Re MC Bacon* was a paradigmatic case for the conflict between secured and unsecured creditors. The liquidator had brought proceedings against the company's bank with a view to (i) having the bank's floating charge set aside as a voidable preference under s. 239 IA, and (ii) holding the bank liable for wrongful trading as a shadow director. Both claims failed and left the liquidator with a heavy bill in costs. The liquidator then sought to have his costs reimbursed out of the assets of the company, all of which were subject to the floating charge. This would have had the paradoxical consequence that the bank, albeit victorious against the liquidator, would have to bear the entire

[152] [1991] Ch. 127 (where it is reported only as '*Re MC Bacon Ltd*', because the official reports did not carry the first case).

[153] *Re MC Bacon Ltd* [1990] BCC 78; chapter 2 C.1 (separation between transaction at an undervalue and preference) and D.1 (subjective element of 'desire' in s. 239 IA).

[154] [1991] Ch. 127, at 138.

[155] *Goode* (fn. 102), para. 12–46; *Stephen Griffin*, Personal Liability and Disqualification of Company Directors (1999), 81.

litigation costs – an open invitation to liquidators in future cases to challenge floating charges with a guaranteed 100 per cent risk for costs on the part of the secured creditor. Years later, after Lord Millett had arrived in the House of Lords, he said of *Re MC Bacon*: 'A more absurd and unjust outcome could hardly be imagined. The court was able to avoid it only by finding a way to disallow the costs of the action as recoverable expenses of the liquidation.'[156] Thus, on the facts of the case, the judge's reasoning to deny claims under s. 239 IA and s. 214 IA the quality of being 'assets of the company' served a limited purpose – defeating the liquidator's attempt to offload the expenses incurred by his unsuccessful actions onto the winning side. But the conceptual framework employed for that purpose had much wider ramifications.

The consequences for litigation funding in insolvency

The liquidator's main argument in *Re MC Bacon* rested on a statutory provision in the Insolvency Rules 1986.[157] As originally enacted, the provision read:

> 4.218 General rule as to priority
>
> (1) The expenses of the liquidation are payable out of the assets in the following order of priority –
>
> (a) expenses properly chargeable or incurred by the official receiver or the liquidator in preserving, realising or getting in any of the assets of the company . . .

The words 'realising or getting in any of the assets of the company' were critical, and the distinction established in *Re Yagerphone* between 'property of the company' and 'property received by the liquidators impressed in their hands with a trust for [the general body of] creditors'[158] reared its head. It explains Millett J's words: 'I do not see how an application for such an order under [s. 214 IA] can properly be described as an attempt to realise or get in an asset of the company.'[159]

However, this reasoning prevented liquidators from having their costs reimbursed out of the company's assets in all cases where the application failed, irrespective of whether the defendant director or shadow director happened to be the holder of a floating charge over the company's assets (as was the case in *Re MC Bacon*) or not. Coupled with the widespread practice of all-encompassing floating charges, it left liquidators with

[156] *Buchler v Talbot* [2004] UKHL 9 = [2004] 2 AC 298, para. 86. [157] SI 1986/1925.
[158] Above, fn. 148. [159] Above, fn. 154.

no incentive to pursue wrongful trading actions against company directors – perhaps the single most important cause why so few applications were made under s. 214 IA. The messy situation called for an ingenious solution.

In *Re Oasis Merchandising Services Ltd*[160] the liquidator sought to employ the services of a litigation support company which would provide funding for a wrongful trading application in exchange for an equitable assignment of a share in the proceeds of any successful outcome. The risk of the application being unsuccessful would be borne by the litigation support company, not the liquidator. The defendant directors raised an objection to this mode of litigation funding, and once again the argument turned on whether or not the claim under s. 214 IA could be called 'property of the company'. Schedule 4 to the Insolvency Act 1986 sets out the powers conferred on the liquidator, and by virtue of paragraph 6 of Schedule 4 the liquidator has the power 'to sell any of the company's property'. The Court of Appeal accepted the argument put forward on behalf of the directors that, on the basis of *Re MC Bacon*, the fruits of litigation brought by the liquidator under s. 214 IA could not be called 'property of the company'. It followed that the liquidator lacked power to sell a share of them to a litigation support company. Hence the funding scheme was struck down.[161]

This conclusion has subsequently been doubted,[162] but in *Re Floor Fourteen Ltd, Lewis v Inland Revenue Commissioners*[163] the Court of Appeal felt bound, as a matter of precedent, by the authority of *Re Oasis Merchandising Services Ltd.* After that, only the House of Lords or the legislature could remedy the situation. As of 1 January 2003, an amendment to the Insolvency Rules[164] replaced the previous rule 4.218 (1) (a) with the following text:

> 4.218 General rule as to priority
>
> (1) The expenses of the liquidation are payable out of the assets in the following order of priority –
> (a) expenses or costs which –
> (i) are properly chargeable or incurred by the official receiver or the liquidator in preserving, realising or getting in any of the assets of

160 [1998] Ch. 170. 161 Ibid., 186.

162 *Re Exchange Travel (Holdings) Ltd (No. 3), Katz v McNally* [1997] BCC 784, at 791 (Phillips LJ) and 798–799 (Morritt LJ).

163 [2001] 3 All ER 499.

164 By virtue of the Insolvency (Amendment) (No. 2) Rules 2002, SI 2002/2712.

> the company or otherwise relating to the conduct of any legal proceedings which he has power to bring or defend whether in his own name or the name of the company . . .

The extension of rule 4.218 (1) (a) to 'any legal proceedings which [the liquidator] has power to bring or defend whether in his own name or the name of the company' was obviously designed to bring proceedings under provisions such as s. 214 IA or ss. 238, 239 IA within the notion of 'expenses of the liquidation', supposedly allowing the liquidator reimbursement 'out of the assets', i.e. the company's assets, thus reversing the judicial rule emanating from *Re MC Bacon*. But history does not end there.

Early in 2004 the House of Lords decided *Buchler v Talbot* (also known as *Re Leyland Daf Ltd*),[165] a case where the liquidators had not brought any action under s. 214 IA or ss. 238, 239 IA, but had nevertheless incurred substantial costs which they sought to recoup out of the assets of the company which were subject to a floating charge. Lord Millett gave the leading speech, in which he declared that costs of the general liquidation would in no circumstances fall upon the charged assets because these assets were, in a legal sense, property of the chargee (creditor), not property of the company.[166] Against this reasoning, whether the liquidator's expenses are incurred 'in preserving, realising or getting in any of the assets of the company' ceases to be a relevant consideration. In its reaction the insolvency community immediately showed itself fully aware how far this decision would turn back the clock on wrongful trading:

> We have also returned to the debate which ensued following the *Floor Fourteen* decision. Given that only a liquidator can bring wrongful trading proceedings, is there a sufficiently effective financial sanction against delinquent directors if there is no fund earmarked to meet a liquidator's expenses in doing so? Perhaps the legislature thought they were responding to this issue when amending *rule 4.218*. Their Lordships' decision in *Leyland Daf* has shown them that they have not.[167]

There is an argument that *Buchler v Talbot* impliedly overruled the Court of Appeal's decision in *Re Oasis Merchandising Services Ltd*, removing the need for conceptual contortions and paving the way for

[165] [2004] UKHL 9 = [2004] 2 AC 298. [166] At para. 51.

[167] *Anon.*, 'Editorial: Chargeholders floating, but liquidators sinking' (2004) 20 IL&P 45, at 46.

classifying office-holder recoveries under s. 214 IA and ss. 238, 239 IA as 'assets of the company' administered by the office-holder for the benefit of the general creditors, as opposed to the charged assets which, for the purposes of insolvency proceedings, are not assets of the company. If this analysis is correct, it would open up the route towards external financing mechanisms for office-holder actions prevented by the *Oasis* decision.[168] But the *Buchler* decision also drew criticism on conceptual grounds[169] and prompted a controversial debate as to whether the legislature should reverse the ruling by the House of Lords.[170]

The outcome of this debate is a fitting tribute to the tenacity with which the whole saga was fought out over many years: one new section in the Insolvency Act[171] and no fewer than five new provisions in secondary legislation.[172] The key points of the new law can be summarised as follows:

- The liquidation expenses, so far as the assets of the company available for payment of general creditors are insufficient to meet them, have priority over any claims to property comprised in or subject to any floating charge created by the company and shall be paid out of any such property accordingly.[173] This provision is intended to reverse *Buchler v Talbot*.[174]
- The expenses of the liquidation are payable out of 'assets of the company available for the payment of general creditors, which shall be taken to include proceeds of any legal action which the liquidator has power to bring in his own name or in the name of the company'.[175] Whereas the expression 'legal proceedings which [the liquidator] has

[168] *John Armour/Adrian Walters*, 'Funding Liquidation: A Functional View' (2006) 122 LQR 295, at 323–324.
[169] *Rizwaan Mokal*, 'Liquidation expenses and floating charges – the separate funds fallacy' [2004] LMCLQ 387.
[170] Cf. the proposed clause 868 of the Company Law Reform Bill as introduced in the House of Lords on 1 November 2005, the critique of this proposal in a letter from the Financial Law Committee of the City of London Law Society to the Insolvency Service, published in (2006) 22 IL&P 3, the reply from the Insolvency Service, (2006) 22 IL&P 43, and the memorandum from the Insolvency Law Committee of the City of London Law Society in support of the proposal, (2006) 22 IL&P 46.
[171] Insolvency Act 1986, s. 176ZA, inserted by virtue of s. 1282 of the Companies Act 2006.
[172] Insolvency Rules 1986, rr. 4.218A to 4.218E, inserted, together with an amendment of r. 4.218, by virtue of the Insolvency (Amendment) Rules 2008, SI 2008/737.
[173] Insolvency Act, s. 176ZA (1).
[174] Explanatory notes to the Companies Act 2006, para. 1699.
[175] Insolvency Rules, r. 4.218 (2) (a) (i).

power to bring ... whether in his own name or the name of the company' was already used in the 2002 amendment to the Insolvency Rules[176] with the intention of reversing the effects of *Re Oasis Merchandising Services Ltd*, the new wording expressly declares the proceeds of any such action to be included in the 'assets of the company available for the payment of general creditors'. It follows that the words 'to make [a] contribution to the company's assets' in s. 214 (1) IA, which have been the root of so much confusion among German observers, must now be read in this sense. But there remains a need to distinguish the use of 'the company's assets' in s. 214 (1) IA from the use of the same words in s. 212 (3) (b) IA, because the latter term refers to 'assets' which may be subject to a floating charge, in which case they are not 'available for the payment of general creditors', although they may now be available for the payment of liquidation expenses.

– As regards the narrower category of litigation expenses incurred by the liquidator in the preparation or conduct of any legal proceedings, the new provisions in the Insolvency Rules restrict the general rule that liquidation expenses have priority over any claims of the secured creditor to property comprised in or subject to any floating charge. If the liquidator is unable to fund litigation from the assets of the company available for payment of general creditors, but cannot obtain prior approval or subsequent authorisation from the secured creditor for having recourse to the charged property, the court is given a wide discretion to 'approve or authorise such amount of litigation expenses as it thinks fit'.[177] Yet the express clarification that the proceeds of office-holder actions form part of the 'assets of the company' should finally permit the development of mechanisms for external litigation funding,[178] reducing the need to have recourse to the charged property in the first place.[179]

What can be learnt from this sequence of events for the purpose of this book? In the first place, it lends support to an understanding of the law as an evolutionary process. To be sure, the legislature has the power to

[176] Above, fn. 164. [177] Insolvency Rules, r. 4.218E (1). [178] *Armour / Walters* (fn. 168).

[179] In addition, financial support for office-holder actions may be available in consequence of s. 176A, inserted into the Insolvency Act 1986 by virtue of the Enterprise Act 2002 and in force since 15 September 2003. This provision curtails the rights of secured creditors by setting aside a share of the realisations of property subject to a floating charge for the satisfaction of unsecured creditors ahead of the charge holder; for details as to the calculation of that share see the Insolvency Act 1986 (Prescribed Part) Order 2003, SI 2003/2097.

adopt rules which may not be ignored. But even the legislature cannot decree an end to a doctrinal debate in which lawyers may find arguments subverting the legislature's intentions and creating the need for further legislative intervention in order to achieve the intended result. This is exactly what happened after the 2002 amendment to the Insolvency Rules. One can only hope that s. 176ZA IA and the 2008 amendment to the Insolvency Rules have now laid the matter to rest.

From an outsider's perspective, such a process cannot be properly understood without a comprehensive knowledge of the legal framework in which it takes place and the forces of legal argument which keep it moving. Scholars intent on identifying the common 'principles' underlying different legal systems may be tempted to disregard a mundane matter such as litigation costs. Surely this can be left to the practitioners? The discourse on wrongful trading provides a perfect example of litigation costs holding the key to the practical impact of a remedy. A more specific insight is that a claim under s. 214 IA differs in its legal nature from a claim against a director for breach of duty, while it shares certain features of transaction avoidance remedies. It is this background which is needed to fully appreciate how English lawyers conceptualise wrongful trading. To them what matters is not the German concern with internal and external liability; it is something that might be viewed as a subdivision within internal liability, but whose relevance cannot be understood without knowledge of the wider legal context in which it operates. German lawyers writing on wrongful trading were often content to identify wrongful trading as a case of internal liability. Some saw that there was a further issue as to whether or not the proceeds of an action would benefit the holder of a floating charge or the unsecured creditors,[180] but even these writers have shown themselves unwilling or unable to penetrate the complex interrelationship between the nature of the claim against the director and the consequential restrictions on the funding of litigation. As far as I can see, no German writer has to date offered an exposition of the subject which would enable a German readership to follow the English debate on a par with their English colleagues in a genuinely European legal discourse.

On a final note, the story of wrongful trading and whether or not the proceeds of such an action constitute an 'asset of the company'

[180] *Höfling* (fn. 115), 230, 232; *Habersack / Verse* (fn. 115), 196, 201; *Redeker* (fn. 115), 161–162, 182 (each with an account of the different outcomes of claims brought under s. 214 IA and s. 212 IA).

illustrates the power of legal language to 'reconstruct' real life situations in the imaginary world of law, as Gunter Teubner has pointed out in his article 'On the Surplus Value of the Twelfth Camel'.[181] The relationship of doctrinal legal language and ordinary language is captured marvellously in an anecdote from another case, *Re Ayala Holdings*.[182] The proceedings in this case were brought not by the liquidator but by one of the company's creditors, a Mr Menzies, whom the judge politely described as 'a litigant who is not a lawyer experienced in insolvency matters'.[183] Mr Menzies sued on the basis of an assignment by the liquidator, the idea behind this assignment being to save on costs because the liquidator would have been required to retain counsel, whereas Mr Menzies could appear in court as a litigant in person.[184] It is not difficult to see that the case turned on the same issue as the later case of *Re Oasis Merchandising Services Ltd*,[185] namely whether causes of action arising under the provisions of the Insolvency Act, and purportedly assigned to Mr Menzies by the liquidator, came within the liquidator's power as specified in para. 6 of Schedule 4 of the Insolvency Act, i.e. the 'power to sell any of the company's property'. Mr Menzies contended that they did, and he had armed himself with a number of authorities from Halsbury's Laws of England and from reported cases in the House of Lords for the proposition that 'where a statute is unambiguous in its terms the court's duty is to give effect to it'. To this the judge replied drily: 'Those [authorities] are not in doubt; the question is, what does para. 6 of Schedule 4 to the 1986 Act mean when it uses the expression, which it does, "property of the company"?'[186]

Can there be a better illustration of the importance of doctrinal language, as opposed to everyday language? All those German writers

[181] *Gunther Teubner*, 'Alienating Justice: On the Surplus Value of the Twelfth Camel', in: *Jiří Přibáň / David Nelken* (eds.), Law's New Boundaries – The Consequences of Legal Autopoiesis (2001), 21 at 25–26; chapter 1, fn. 113.

[182] *Re Ayala Holdings* [1993] BCLC 256; *Re Ayala Holdings (No. 2)* [1996] 1 BCLC 467.

[183] [1993] BCLC 256, at 261.

[184] Under English law, an individual is entitled to act as a litigant in person irrespective of the amount in dispute, and even at the appeal stage of his case. In the *Bairstow* case ([2001] EWCA Civ 712 = [2002] BCC 91) two of the directors appeared as litigants in person in the Court of Appeal, notwithstanding that the total sum in dispute was well over £90 million. In contrast, German law requires every party to the litigation to be represented by an attorney-at-law even at first instance before the Landgericht (§ 78 ZPO, with limited exceptions, e.g. in family law matters) and in all cases on appeal.

[185] Above, fn. 160. [186] *Re Ayala Holdings (No. 2)* [1996] 1 BCLC 467, at 480.

who, without deeper reflection, assumed a claim against a director under s. 214 IA to be an asset of the company appear to have fallen into the same trap as Mr Menzies. Let us pause for a moment and think of what the multi-lingual European legislator would make of this.

3. Wrongful trading and directors' duty to exercise reasonable care, skill and diligence

Directors' duties of care, skill and diligence had long been a problematic aspect of English company law. In chapter 4 we noted the decisive influence of equity on the early development of company law. Equity has traditionally been conceptualised as 'acting upon the conscience' of a person,[187] hence equity is preoccupied with the honesty of a person's conduct. Nineteenth-century chancery judges seemed happy to proceed on the basis that there was no need to impose legal duties over and above the fiduciary duties to combat fraud and dishonesty, because the shareholders had appointed whomsoever they thought fit to be a director. In *Turquand v Marshall*, the report of the decision by the Lord Chancellor, Lord Hatherley, puts this philosophy in drastic words: 'However ridiculous and absurd their conduct might seem, it was the misfortune of the company that they chose such unwise directors; but as long as they kept within the powers of [the company's constitution], the Court could not interfere with the discretion exercised by them.'[188] The low point was reached with the decision in *Re Cardiff Savings Bank*, which exemplifies how in those days directors were often no more than prominent figureheads who were not expected to take an active part in the management of the company. The bank had been established under the auspices of the late Marquis of Bute. Upon the death of the Marquis, his son, then at the tender age of six months, was nominated to succeed his father as president of the bank, only attended a single board meeting in 38 years, yet was acquitted of liability for negligence.[189]

[187] This metaphor is still very much alive; see *Westdeutsche Landesbank Girozentrale v Islington LBC* [1996] AC 669, at 705 (Lord Browne-Wilkinson: 'Equity operates on the conscience of the owner of the legal interest') and *Bank of Credit and Commerce International (Overseas) Ltd v Akindele* [2001] Ch. 437, at 455 (Nourse LJ: 'the recipient's state of knowledge [is] such as to make it unconscionable for him to retain the benefit of the receipt') (chapter 4 at fn. 122).

[188] (1869) LR 4 Ch.App. 376, at 386. [189] [1892] 2 Ch. 100.

For much of the twentieth century, the leading case was *Re City Equitable Fire Insurance Co Ltd*[190] The case combined an objective standard of care and diligence ('reasonable care')[191] with a subjective standard of skills ('may reasonably be expected from a person of *his* knowledge and experience'). This resulted in 'incompetence [being] its own defence',[192] as a suitably qualified but careless director would be held liable where an ignorant director could successfully plead his lack of understanding. Some argue that the subjectivity of *Re City Equitable Fire Insurance* may have been misrepresented by subsequent writers and that, given the state of the law at the time, the decision was quite advanced.[193] But the received wisdom about the case through many decades appears to have deterred potential claimants from relying on negligence to sue directors, as liquidators were not sufficiently confident to sue directors in respect of errors of judgment, with the law either uncertain or unable to supply an adequate remedy.[194]

This forms the background to a number of contributions throughout the 1980s and 1990s arguing in favour of an objective standard of care and skill,[195] or sometimes against it.[196] It also forms the background to the legislator's creation of the wrongful trading remedy in s. 214 IA. As explained before, its introduction was recommended by the Cork Committee in its 1982 report[197] as a means of protecting creditors against honest, but unreasonable behaviour of company directors.[198] It is tempting, and perhaps even more so when one approaches the matter from a German perspective, to see wrongful trading as the legislator's reaction to the – real or perceived – weaknesses of the common law in relation to the duty of care and skill. As we have seen, however, such a

[190] [1925] Ch. 407; building on *Lagunas Nitrate Co v Lagunas Syndicate* [1899] 2 Ch. 392; *Re Brazilian Rubber Plantations and Estates Ltd* [1911] 1 Ch. 425.

[191] This is stressed by *Sarah Worthington*, 'The Duty to Monitor: A Modern View of the Director's Duty of Care', in: *Fiona Patfield* (ed.), Perspectives on Company Law 2 (1997), 181 at 190.

[192] *Eilís Ferran*, Company Law and Corporate Finance (1999) 213.

[193] *Andrew Hicks*, 'Directors' Liability for Management Errors', (1994) 110 LQR 390, at 392; *Adrian Walters*, 'Directors' duties: the impact of the Company Directors Disqualification Act 1986' (2000) 21 CoLaw 110, at 111–112.

[194] *Hicks* (fn. 193) 391 (in a case note on *Norman v Theodore Goddard* and *Re D'Jan of London Ltd*, below fn. 201 and 202).

[195] *Vanessa Finch*, 'Company Directors: Who Cares about Skill and Care?', (1992) 55 MLR 179, at 202–203; *Sarah Worthington* (fn. 191), 190–194.

[196] *C.A. Riley*, 'The Company Director's Duty of Care and Skill: The Case for an Onerous but Subjective Standard', (1999) 62 MLR 697.

[197] Cork Report (fn. 113), ch. 44.

[198] See in particular para. 1782–1783 of the report.

categorisation seems to be a lot less clear-cut to English lawyers. In any case, once wrongful trading had been enacted, it produced a kind of rebound effect on the common law.

Under s. 214 IA directors are judged by an objective standard of care, skill and diligence – s. 214 (4) (a) – which can only be heightened, not lowered by the personal knowledge, skills and experience of the director concerned – s. 214 (4) (b). The Cork Report makes it clear that the concept of wrongful trading was created specifically with a view to introducing an objective standard of directors' conduct,[199] and for that reason the arrival of wrongful trading was welcomed to counteract the general perception of common law duties of care and skill as one of too much subjectivity and lenience for directors to secure any effective protection of creditor interests.[200] It did not take long before the courts seized the opportunity to borrow from s. 214 with a view to shifting the general law on directors' duties towards objective and more rigorous standards of conduct. The turning point came with two first-instance judgments delivered by Mr Justice Hoffmann (later Lord Hoffmann) in *Norman v Theodore Goddard*[201] and, even more forcefully, in *Re D'Jan of London Ltd*, where he held that 'the duty of care owed by a director at common law is accurately stated in s. 214 (4) of the Insolvency Act 1986'.[202] His reasoning was subsequently applied in *Re Westlowe Storage & Distribution Ltd*,[203] and it was endorsed by the Court of Appeal in *Cohen v Selby*.[204] One is thus led to conclude that, immediately before the Companies Act 2006, the standards for the conduct of directors were taken to be the same under the common law and under s. 214 of the Insolvency Act. The Companies Act 2006 confirms this by using the same words, in s. 174, to define the general duty to exercise reasonable care, skill and diligence as are used in s. 214 of the Insolvency Act to define the standard of conduct a director must comply with in order to avoid wrongful trading.

Welcome though this development may be in other respects, especially when it comes to strengthening directors' accountability to shareholders, it creates a significant overlap between the wrongful trading remedy, on the one hand, and claims against directors for breach of duty, which the liquidator may also pursue under s. 212 IA. Both types of claim were advanced in *Re Continental Assurance Company of London plc*, where Park J related them in these words: 'As an alternative

[199] At para. 1783. [200] See above, fn. 114. [201] [1992] BCC 14.
[202] [1993] BCC 646, at 648. [203] [2000] BCC 851, at 870. [204] [2002] BCC 82, para. 21.

to the wrongful trading claim the liquidators contend that they are entitled to recover damages from the directors for the same alleged loss – the increase in net deficiency – but in the case of this claim on the footing that it was caused by a different kind of wrongful conduct on the part of the directors.'[205]

If this contention is valid, then any detriment of the company in the sense of increasing the net deficiency[206] caused by mismanagement after the time when any reasonable prospect of the company avoiding insolvent liquidation had ceased could, in principle, give rise to both a claim for wrongful trading and one for directors' breach of duty. That this is possible has been demonstrated not just by *Re Continental Assurance*, but also by two other cases whose fact patterns were very similar: in each case the directors had entered into a contract about a large investment (incidentally, both cases concerned ships to be built) without proper financing arrangements in place so that the company could not afford to honour its commitments. In *Re Howard Holdings Inc*[207] this was argued as the basis for an application under s. 214 IA, whereas in *Stocznia Gdanska SA v Latreefers Inc* the Court of Appeal thought that there was a real prospect of a claim for 'misfeasance', i.e. breach of duty.[208]

Such concurrent claims for wrongful trading and for breach of the general duty to exercise reasonable care, skill and diligence may, however, differ in three respects: first, the question has been raised whether principles of causation have the same role to play in establishing the quantum for either cause of action. So far the Court of Appeal has not had an opportunity to decide on the quantum of an application under s. 214 IA. Lord Justice Chadwick explored the issue in *Cohen v Selby*,[209] a case on breach of the duty of care brought to court as an application under s. 212 IA. The judge at first instance had held that the court's discretion to grant a summary remedy under the latter section was not restricted by considerations of causation. The Court of Appeal rejected this proposition and made it clear that a claim against a director for breach of the duty of care, equally if brought to court as an application under s. 212 IA based on such a breach, must establish causation between the negligent act and the loss for which compensation is sought.[210] However, Lord Justice Chadwick left open whether the same

[205] [2001] BPIR 733, para. 392. [206] Above, B.2 (text accompanying fn. 37).
[207] [1998] BCC 549. [208] [2001] BCC 174, para. 34 and 36. [209] [2002] BCC 82.
[210] At para. 20.

applied in a case of wrongful trading, saying that he was 'content to assume (without so deciding) that, on an application under s. 214 of the Insolvency Act 1986, it may not be necessary to establish a causal link between the wrongful trading and any particular loss'.[211]

The legislature, in s. 214 (1) IA, confines itself to saying that the court may declare the director to be liable 'to make such contribution (if any) to the company's assets as the court thinks proper'. It appears to confer the widest possible discretion on the court. The Act itself does not relate the amount of contribution either to any particular period of trading or to the loss suffered by the company or creditors.[212] Despite this, the courts have constantly held that the provision is compensatory rather than penal,[213] and this is seen as a key consideration in determining quantum. Prima facie, the appropriate amount that a director is liable to contribute is the amount by which the company's assets have been depleted by the director's conduct.[214]

But the courts have been remarkably reluctant to commit themselves more firmly to principles of causation. In *Re Continental Assurance Company of London plc*, a very elaborate judgment hailed as 'perhaps the most significant pronouncement on section 214 to date',[215] the judge relied on the dictum in *Cohen v Selby* and declined to say whether he had to import principles of causation into s. 214 IA.[216] However, looking around further in his judgment, it becomes obvious how much counsel and the judge himself were concerned with minute details about particular transactions,[217] which hardly suggests that establishing a causal link between the directors' failure to act properly and the compensation payable by them under s. 214 IA is irrelevant in practice.

The second point of discrepancy concerns the availability of discretionary relief from liability. A claim for breach of the general duty to exercise reasonable care, skill and diligence is susceptible to relief under s. 1157 CA 2006,[218] notwithstanding the conceptual difficulty surrounding the test of reasonableness in this section.[219] If a claim for

211 At para. 21. 212 *Sealy / Milman*, Insolvency Legislation (10th edn 2007), vol. I, 233.

213 Although it would appear that it is open to a court to include a punitive element: *Sealy* (fn. 114), 76.

214 *Re Produce Marketing Consortium Ltd (No. 2)* [1989] BCC 569, at 597.

215 *Adrian Walters*, 'Wrongful trading: two recent cases' [2001] Insolvency Lawyer 211.

216 [2001] BPIR 733, para. 377. 217 See, for instance, para. 348 ff.

218 Which restates s. 727 CA 1985 without substantive amendment: chapter 4 B.3.

219 *Re D'Jan of London Ltd* [1993] BCC 646; chapter 4, text accompanying fn. 106 to 108.

breach of duty is pursued by way of the summary remedy procedure in s. 212 IA, the latter section provides the court with a further discretion to grant relief from liability, which may be exercised differently from the discretion under s. 1157 CA 2006.[220] Contrariwise, it has been decided that relief under this section is not available to the respondents in an application under s. 214 IA.[221] However, s. 214 IA confers such a wide discretion on the judge that it is difficult to see what difference the additional availability of s. 1157 CA 2006 would make in practice.[222] In particular, the court may use its discretion under s. 214 IA to reduce a director's liability to a level below what a stringent application of rules on causation would produce, achieving in effect a partial relief for a minor degree of fault of a director in relation to the requisite standard of care and skill under s. 214 (4) IA.[223] Such practice is evidenced by the case of *Re Brian D Pierson (Contractors) Ltd*,[224] which can be contrasted with very similar considerations (one director unable to form a fully independent judgment and to resist the influence of another person with whom he had a close family relationship) expressed in *Cohen v Selby*, a case concerned with relief under s. 727 of the Companies Act 1985.[225] There remains a risk, however, that a discretionary reduction of the compensation payable under s. 214 IA leaves the director exposed to proceedings brought by a creditor under s. 212 (3) IA, unless the court is prepared to grant relief under s. 1157 CA 2006 on the same grounds as under s. 214 IA.

Leaving both types of discretionary relief aside, and assuming that the IND-measure under s. 214 IA[226] corresponds to what the company may claim for breach of the duty to exercise reasonable care, skill and diligence under s. 174 CA 2006, the trickiest problem still lies ahead: given the different application of the proceeds from these two sources in the case of a floating charge it appears difficult to devise any sensible rule as to the application of any payment obtained under s. 214, because it would necessarily be subsumed in a claim for breach of duty based on

[220] *Inland Revenue Commissioners v Richmond, Re Loquitur Ltd* [2003] EWHC 999 (Ch) = [2003] 2 BCLC 442, para. 245 ff.

[221] *Re Produce Marketing Consortium Ltd, Halls v David* [1989] 1 WLR 745.

[222] *Prentice* (fn. 110), at 270 in fn. 33.

[223] *Stephen Griffin*, Personal Liability and Disqualification of Company Directors (1999), 83–84.

[224] [1999] BCC 26, at 57.

[225] The first instance judgment is not reported, but the passage is cited in the decision of the Court of Appeal [2002] BCC 82, para. 17; on appeal the issue of relief under s. 727 CA ceased to be relevant and the Court refrained from expressing any opinion (para. 33).

[226] Above, text accompanying fn. 37.

the same incident of 'trading while insolvent' (to avoid the technical term 'wrongful trading'). It is no solution if the court simply uses its discretion under ss. 212 and 214 IA to decree that payments made pursuant to an order under s. 212 IA 'are to be taken as satisfying the order under s. 214 as well',[227] because that begs the question rather than answers it. Rebecca Parry discusses the issue briefly and suggests that global recoveries 'should be earmarked as far as possible'.[228] That may work if there is, say, one claim for wrongful trading based on the continuance of a loss-making business and another for a preferential payment to a creditor.[229] But it will not work if the very same conduct of the directors has given rise to both claims. A liquidator may be able to avoid the problem by making only an application under s. 214 IA (*sed quaere* whether he may do so without incurring a breach of duty on his part for failure to get in an asset of the company). But s. 212 IA also allows any creditor of a company to bring an application; thus the holder of a floating charge who hopes to benefit from the proceeds of a claim against a director for breach of duty may take matters into his own hands.[230]

At the end of the day, in the absence of any guiding principle, the court may use its discretion under ss. 212 and 214 IA to impose an arbitrary apportionment as between the secured and the unsecured creditors. In terms of principle, that solution is far from satisfactory.

4. *Wrongful trading and directors' fiduciary duty to consider the interests of creditors*

As if the ambivalent relationship between wrongful trading and the directors' general duty to exercise reasonable care, skill and diligence did not put enough strain on the coherence of English law in this field, yet more complexity is added by a special duty which requires directors to have regard to the interests of creditors as the company nears insolvency. The duty represents a situation-specific variation of the directors'

227 As in *Re DKG Contractors Ltd* [1990] BCC 903, at 912 (a case where there appear to have been only unsecured creditors).

228 *Rebecca Parry*, 'The destination of proceeds of insolvency litigation' (2002) 23 CoLaw 49, at 56.

229 See below, section 4.

230 Subject to the right of the unsecured creditors to share in the proceeds of such a realisation in accordance with s. 176A of the Insolvency Act; see above, fn. 179.

general duty to act in the best interests of the company.[231] During the Company Law Review and thereafter this general duty proved one of the most contentious and politically sensitive issues. Eventually, the duty was transposed in s. 172 of the Companies Act 2006 as the 'duty to promote the success of the company for the benefit of its members as a whole', coupled with a long list of considerations intended to 'enshrine in statute' the government's idea of 'enlightened shareholder value'.[232] Before the Act, the duty to act in the interests of the company was widely regarded as an instance of directors' fiduciary duties, as opposed to their duties of care and skill,[233] and this classification is now confirmed by s. 178 (2) of the Companies Act 2006.[234]

For present purposes, however, s. 172 is less interesting for what it says in relation to 'enlightened shareholder value' than for what it refuses to say. Its subsection (3) provides:

> The duty imposed by this section has effect subject to any enactment or rule of law requiring directors, in certain circumstances, to consider or act in the interests of creditors of the company.

This unspecific reference marks the waypoint, for the time being, for a protracted debate, in which the legislature, apparently, did not see fit to take up a stance. The explanatory notes shed more light on the provision:

> Subsection (3) recognises that the duty to promote the success of the company is displaced when the company is insolvent. Section 214 of the Insolvency Act 1986 provides a mechanism under which the liquidator can require the directors to contribute towards the funds available to creditors in an insolvent winding up, where they ought to have recognised that the company had no reasonable prospect of avoiding insolvent liquidation and then failed to take all reasonable steps to minimise the loss to creditors.
>
> It has been suggested that the duty to promote the success of the company may also be modified by an obligation to have regard to the interests of creditors as the company nears insolvency. Subsection (3) will leave the law to develop in this area.[235]

231 *Re Smith & Fawcett Ltd* [1942] Ch. 304; *Howard Smith Ltd v Ampol Petroleum Ltd* [1974] AC 821.

232 Explanatory notes to the Companies Act 2006, para. 325.

233 *Gower & Davies*' Company Law (7th edn 2003), 381; *Brenda Hannigan*, Company Law (2003), 191.

234 Chapter 4 B.1 and D.

235 Explanatory notes to the Companies Act 2006, para. 331–332.

Whereas it is obvious that the word 'enactment' in s. 172 (3) CA relates to s. 214 IA, the expression 'rule of law', given the context, must be taken to refer to a line of cases that began to take shape during the 1980s. It can be traced to precedents in New Zealand[236] and Australia[237] and soon reached England with the decision of the Court of Appeal in *West Mercia Safetywear Ltd v Dodd.*[238] In this case, the defendant, in his capacity as director of the claimant company, had caused the company to pay a debt of £4,000 due to its parent company, thereby reducing the parent company's bank overdraft, for which the same director was personally liable under a guarantee. The transfer was held to be a 'fraudulent preference',[239] and the court concluded that 'there was misfeasance on the part of [the director] who owed a fiduciary duty to the West Mercia company'.[240] The director was held liable to repay the sum of £4,000.

In his speech in *West Mercia*, Lord Justice Dillon expressly approved a dictum in the Australian case of *Kinsela v Russell Kinsela Pty Ltd*, where Chief Justice Street had said:

> In a solvent company the proprietary interests of the shareholders entitle them as a general body to be regarded as the company when questions of the duty of directors arise. . . . But where a company is insolvent the interests of the creditors intrude. They become prospectively entitled, through the mechanism of liquidation, to displace the power of the shareholders and directors to deal with the company's assets. It is in a practical sense their assets and not the shareholders' assets that, through the medium of the company, are under the management of the directors.[241]

The important insight from these cases is that the company's creditors are protected through the concept of a fiduciary duty in an indirect manner, by arguing that where a company has become insolvent, the interests of the company, to which directors as fiduciaries must have regard, are essentially the interests of the creditors. As a consequence, the remedy to bring the delinquent director to account lies with the company, not with individual creditors, and during insolvency

[236] *Nicholson v Permakraft (NZ) Ltd* [1985] 1 NZLR 242 (New Zealand Court of Appeal).
[237] *Kinsela v Russell Kinsela Pty Ltd* (1986) 4 NSWLR 722 (New South Wales Court of Appeal).
[238] [1988] BCC 30.
[239] Although after the Insolvency Act 1986, this older terminology should have been replaced by the simple word 'preference' (s. 239 IA).
[240] [1998] BCC 32.
[241] (1986) 4 NSWLR 722, at 730A-B; cited [1988] BCC 30, at 33.

proceedings the office-holder, in his capacity as representative of the company, can realise this asset by way of a summary action under s. 212 IA. These principles have since been confirmed and applied in a number of English cases.[242]

The rationale for this protection of creditors is arguably the same that underlies wrongful trading.[243] However, the practice of the English courts under s. 214 IA has been to intervene at a rather late stage in the company's demise.[244] By contrast, the *West Mercia* duty to take account of creditor interests may well become operative at an earlier stage; in the words of Andrew Keay, a declared supporter of the doctrine:

> While wrongful trading cannot occur until there is an end to all reasonable hope of the company's recovery, liquidators are able to take action against directors for breach of duty, and claim for amounts lost at an early point of time, namely when the company's solvency is questionable, there is a risk of insolvency or even if there is financial instability. These are likely to precede that time when the directors knew or ought to have concluded that there was no reasonable prospect of the company avoiding going into insolvent liquidation.[245]

The controversy surrounding the *West Mercia* doctrine centres on the considerable uncertainty about the timing of the duty's intervention,[246] as it is by no means settled at what precise point in a company's financial crisis the duty becomes operative. The cases suggest that, at the latest, the duty springs into life as soon as the company has become insolvent on a balance sheet basis, i.e. has an excess of liabilities over assets,[247] or on either of the two tests of insolvency.[248] But there is some authority that the duty may already arise when the company is

[242] *Yukong Line Ltd of Korea v Rendsburg Investments Corporation of Liberia (No. 2)* [1998] 1 WLR 294; *Facia Footwear Ltd v Hinchliffe* [1998] 1 BCLC 218; *Re Pantone 485 Ltd, Miller v Bain* [2002] 1 BCLC 266; *Colin Gwyer & Associates Ltd v London Wharf (Limehouse) Ltd* [2002] EWHC 2748 (Ch) = [2003] BCC 885.

[243] Cf. *Rizwaan Mokal*, 'An Agency Cost Analysis of the Wrongful Trading Provisions: Redistribution, Perverse Incentives and the Creditors' Bargain' [2000] CLJ 335; above, text accompanying fn. 3.

[244] See the analysis of the decided cases in *Thomas Bachner* (fn. 8), at 300–309.

[245] *Andrew Keay*, 'The Duty of Directors to Take Account of Creditors' Interests: Has It Any Role to Play?' [2002] JBL 379, at 388.

[246] A point raised by commentators immediately after the *West Mercia* decision: *Vanessa Finch*, 'Directors' duties towards creditors' (1989) 10 CoLaw 23, at 24.

[247] *Nicholson v Permakraft (NZ) Ltd* [1985] 1 NZLR 242, at 254 (Richardson J) and 255 (Somers J).

[248] *West Mercia Safetywear Ltd v Dodd* [1988] BCC 30, at 32 (unspecified insolvency).

'doubtfully solvent'[249] or where a company is 'insolvent, or near insolvent, or of doubtful solvency, or if a contemplated payment or other course of action would jeopardise its solvency'.[250] In the *Kinsela* case Chief Justice Street hesitated to formulate a general test of the degree of financial instability which would impose upon directors an obligation to consider the interests of creditors, but he went on to express what may be termed a sliding scale: 'the plainer it is that it is the creditors' money that is at risk, the lower may be the risk to which the directors ... can justifiably expose the company'.[251]

This vagueness has prompted forceful criticism of the *West Mercia* doctrine, notably by Jonathan Rickford.[252] It must be said, however, that the provision on wrongful trading has equally been criticised for being 'singularly imprecise [as to] just what conduct on the part of a director will bring him within its scope'.[253] Andrew Keay, in turn, concedes in his recent book that the courts have failed to arrive at a consistent approach in relation to the point in time from which the duty to consider the interests of creditors operates, with problematic consequences for both directors and office-holders.[254] This may well explain the ambivalent discussion amongst the Company Law Review Steering Group on whether to incorporate the duty in the proposed codification of directors' duties.[255] Whereas the Steering Group ultimately decided the point in favour of including a clause to this effect in its proposed statement of directors' duties,[256] the point was dropped from the subsequent White Paper 'Modernising Company Law',[257] and the legislature left it to the courts to develop the law in this area.[258]

The scope of the doctrine – transaction avoidance and wrongful trading revisited

The *West Mercia* case[259] is direct authority that a payment in the nature of a preference within s. 239 IA may constitute a misapplication of

249 *Brady v Brady* [1987] BCC 535, at 552 (Nourse LJ); the decision was overturned in the House of Lords, [1989] AC 755, but not on grounds material to this debate.
250 *Nicholson v Permakraft (NZ) Ltd* [1985] 1 NZLR 242, at 249 (Cooke J).
251 (1986) 4 NSWLR 722, at 733A, C.
252 *Jonathan Rickford* (ed.), 'Reforming Capital – Report of the Interdisciplinary Group on Capital Maintenance' [2004] EBLR 919, at 985.
253 *Sealy/Milman* (fn. 212), vol. I, 233. 254 *Keay* (fn. 111), 220.
255 Final Report (2001), para. 3.12–3.20.
256 Final Report (2001), vol. II, Schedule 2, para. 8.
257 Cm. 5553-II, Schedule 2 (July 2002). 258 Fn. 235.
259 *West Mercia Safetywear Ltd v Dodd* [1988] BCC 30.

company property in breach of the director's fiduciary duty. The *Kinsela* case[260] concerned a transaction which, in England, would come within s. 238 IA as a transaction at an undervalue. Thus, together, the two cases cover the most important grounds for transaction avoidance under the Insolvency Act.

Incidentally, this overlap between the statutory remedies for transaction avoidance and directors' fiduciary duties creates the same sort of conflict in respect of the distribution of the recoveries as the overlap between wrongful trading and the directors' duty to exercise reasonable care, skill and diligence discussed in the previous section of this chapter. On the one hand, the recipient may be subject to an order under s. 241 IA to restore to the company the property, or its value, which has been the subject of a voidable transaction within s. 238 or s. 239 IA. On the authority of *Re Yagerphone Ltd*[261] and *Re MC Bacon Ltd (No. 2)*[262] the proceeds of a successful avoidance action are not 'assets of the company' and cannot be caught by a floating charge, but go towards satisfying the company's general creditors.[263] On the other hand, the same defendant, as recipient of the assets given away by the directors in breach of their fiduciary duty, may be subject to a claim for knowing receipt under the general principles of equity.[264] This will depend on the recipient's knowledge, however defined, of the breach of duty, which, in the present context, requires his knowledge of the company's precarious financial situation (an interesting cross-link to the principles underpinning transaction avoidance in Germany[265]). Within a group of companies or amongst otherwise connected persons[266] such knowledge may not be too difficult to establish. As the claim for knowing receipt arises under the general law, it is difficult to see how it could not be an asset of the company and therefore subject to an appropriately drafted floating charge in the same manner as the claim against the director for his breach of duty. It follows that a secured creditor may rely on his standing to commence proceedings under s. 212 IA with a view to realising this company asset in its ultimate favour, notwithstanding that the liquidator may bring concurrent proceedings under s. 241 IA. The recipient, undoubtedly, cannot be made to restore the property twice. It follows that the recoveries obtained from the defendant need to be apportioned between the two claims in a manner similar to the

[260] *Kinsela v Russell Kinsela Pty Ltd* (1986) 4 NSWLR 722.
[261] [1935] Ch. 392. [262] [1991] Ch. 127. [263] Above, C.2. [264] Chapter 4 C.
[265] Chapter 2 D.2. [266] Chapter 2 E.

apportionment between a claim for breach of duty brought under s. 212 IA and a wrongful trading application under s. 214 IA – without any real guiding principles as to how this apportionment can be implemented rationally.

Whereas it appears settled that acts committed by directors in violation of ss. 238, 239 IA may constitute breaches of their fiduciary duty to consider the interests of creditors, the duty seems capable of even wider application. After all, controllers of a limited liability company may harm creditors' interests not only by according preferential treatment to some creditors in violation of the *pari passu* principle, or by siphoning off assets from the company into their hands, but also by continuing the loss-making business with a view to gambling their way out of a crisis.[267] This, of course, is the realm of wrongful trading. But there seems to be no argument why such a conduct could not, in principle, also constitute a breach of the directors' fiduciary duty to consider the interests of creditors. In *Facia Footwear Ltd v Hinchliffe* the argument turned ostensibly on preferential payments. But the impeached payments were a reflection of the company's continued trading and of the directors' attempts to implement a rescue strategy. The only alternative would have been to close down the business forthwith. The judge accepted that determining whether the directors had acted in breach of their fiduciary duty to take into account the interests of creditors included a judgment on which of the two strategies would best serve the interests of the creditors.[268] Once it is accepted that, in certain situations, the duty to consider the interests of creditors requires a business judgment, the overlap with wrongful trading and with the general duty to exercise reasonable care, skill and diligence becomes obvious.

The subjective side of the duty

With this last observation, our analysis returns to the general framework of directors' duties explored in chapter 4, where we encountered the German concept of *Sorgfaltspflicht* as the directors' general duty to act with due diligence in carrying out all those specific duties to which directors are submitted.[269] It does not come as a big surprise that German observers apply this familiar domestic concept to their analysis of English law, and in some instances this has happened specifically in relation to the *West Mercia* doctrine.[270]

[267] Chapter 1 B.2. [268] [1998] 1 BCLC 218, at 228. [269] Chapter 4 B.2.
[270] *Höfling* (fn. 115), 231; *Pernice* (fn. 115), 201–202.

Contrast this with the doctoral thesis by Boris Kasolowsky, published in Germany, but written in English.[271] His analysis is based on the traditional premise that fiduciary duties and duties of care are distinct and that liability for breach of a fiduciary duty does not depend on whether the defendant has acted intentionally, negligently, or innocently.[272] Towards the end of his work the author comments on the Company Law Review's approach to incorporate the *West Mercia* doctrine in the draft statement of directors' duties, where paragraph 8 defined the circumstances in which the duty would arise in the following terms:

> At a time when a director of a company knows, or would know but for a failure of his to exercise due care and skill, that it is more likely than not that the company will at some point be unable to pay its debts as they fall due.[273]

The author seizes on the duty being tied to a director's exercise of due care and skill, and for that reason he concludes: 'The duty envisaged is thus a duty of care, rather than a fiduciary duty.'[274] And he further disagrees with the notes to this clause which state that the duty is meant to codify the *West Mercia* doctrine, arguing that:

> acting in the interests of a particular person or group of persons is one of the characteristics of a fiduciary duty. It is not, however, one of the elements or even characteristics of any tortious duty of care. Thus, Paragraph 8 does not, it is submitted, codify the *West Mercia* principle.[275]

This analysis demonstrates how deeply engrained the thinking is among English lawyers that fiduciary duties and duties of care are two distinct, and even mutually exclusive, categories, whereas, on the other hand, German lawyers take it for granted that whatever duties are incumbent on company directors are to be judged against a yardstick of due diligence and can therefore be labelled '*Sorgfaltspflichten*'. Perhaps these contributions epitomise, more than anything else uncovered in this book, just how much of a risk there is at present that lawyers from England and Germany are talking past each other.

But there is a further twist. Perhaps unwittingly, the German analysis stumbles over a point of English law where English lawyers may easily

[271] *Boris Kasolowsky*, Fiduciary Duties in Company Law (2003).

[272] Ibid., 76–77 (with a critique of Millett LJ's analysis in *Bristol & West Building Society v Mothew* [1998] Ch. 1, at 19–20, demanding an intentional conduct).

[273] Final Report (2001), vol. II, Schedule 2, p. 414. [274] Fn. 271, 298. [275] Ibid.

become the victim of their own preconceptions. Is it really a necessary characteristic of fiduciary duties that they are incommensurable with a standard of due care or diligence?

As we saw in the preceding chapter, there has long existed one pocket of the law on directors' duties where liability, though conceptualised as an instance of the fiduciary duty not to misapply company property, is based on fault. This concerns cases where directors have paid unlawful dividends to shareholders in contravention of the prohibition on the return of capital or the statutory scheme to determine the amount of lawful distributions.[276] Since *West Mercia*, similar considerations have appeared in cases on the duty of directors to consider the interests of creditors. *Facia Footwear Ltd v Hinchliffe* was a case involving financial arrangements within a group of companies and an ex ante assessment of the prospects of a rescue effort. The alternative of closing down the business immediately might well have led to an even greater loss to the creditors. The judge found that whether or not the directors were guilty of 'misfeasance', i.e. breach of duty, depended on 'the boundary between an acceptable risk that an entrepreneur may properly take and an unacceptable risk'.[277] Yet such an assessment requires a yardstick, and the only yardstick that comes to mind is the professional standard of reasonable care, skill and diligence. The same idea also appears in *Re Pantone 485 Ltd, Miller v Bain*, where the director had interests in two companies and caused one of them to enter into obligations under a hire-purchase contract, although the equipment which was the subject of the contract had been transferred to the other company. The judge held that 'it is not a breach of fiduciary duty for a director of company A to advance moneys for the benefit of a related company B, if the director honestly and reasonably believed that company B would repay the moneys so advanced.'[278] The words 'honestly and reasonably' are reminiscent of s. 727 CA 1985 (now s. 1157 CA 2006), but as far as the report goes, that section was not in argument. The judge was clearly talking of whether or not a breach of duty had occurred in the first place.

[276] *Re Kingston Cotton Mill Co (No. 2)* [1896] 1 Ch. 331 (reversed on other grounds [1896] 2 Ch. 279); *Dovey v Cory* [1901] AC 477; *Precision Dippings Ltd v Precision Dippings Marketing Ltd* [1986] Ch. 447; *Bairstow v Queens Moat Houses plc* [2000] BCC 1025 (reversed on other grounds [2001] EWCA Civ 712 = [2002] BCC 91); chapter 4 B.3. (text accompanying fn. 94 to 98).

[277] [1998] 1 BCLC 218, at 228. [278] [2002] 1 BCLC 266, para. 46.

If the ratio of these two cases – that in some situations the duty to consider the interests of creditors can only be complied with by making a business judgment as to the companies financial prospects – is correct, it follows that – contrary to Kasolowsky's opinion – the Company Law Review was right in formulating its restatement of the *West Mercia* doctrine with reference to a standard of due care and skill. This tempts one to reflect on whether English law has not reached a point where the categorical distinction between fiduciary duties and duties of care may be about to break down. Strict liability may still be appropriate within Lord Millet's core duty of loyalty, notably the no-conflict and no-profit rules,[279] whereas other duties which have traditionally been categorised as fiduciary duties cannot always operate without recourse to notions of due care and skill. In practice, the courts may have achieved workable solutions by applying s. 727 CA 1985. Recent cases seem to go further and introduce a notion of fault into the heart of the fiduciary duty to consider and act in the interests of creditors when the company operates in the vicinity of insolvency.

D. Summary and outlook

In a recent article, John Armour and Adrian Walters write that 'insolvency law has developed in the haphazard manner of a medieval building, with new parts being added to existing ones without much concern for the coherence of the resulting edifice or whether the foundations will take the weight.'[280] At the end of this chapter, it is hard to escape the conclusion that the present state of English law on directors' personal liability for conduct in the vicinity of insolvency fits in well with this illustration. Some commentators have gone much further in their criticism and denounce 'the absence of any coherent policy'[281] or call the present state of affairs 'ludicrous' and 'bizarre'.[282] The differing characteristics of directors' liability for wrongful trading, for breach of their general duty to exercise reasonable care, skill and diligence, as well as for breach of their fiduciary duty to take into account the interests of creditors as the company is nearing insolvency, notably as regards the differences as to when the critical time has come for the directors to act and with the attendant complications in relation to the

[279] *Bristol & West Building Society v Mothew* [1998] Ch. 1, at 18; chapter 4 B.1.
[280] *Armour / Walters* (fn. 168), at 295. [281] *Oditah* (fn. 65), at 217.
[282] *Griffin* (fn. 223), 92.

destination of recoveries, present a colourful picture of variety. But they obviously create a host of additional problems compared to the situation of having only a single purpose-built rule, which may be just what the original framers of the wrongful trading provision of s. 214 IA had in mind.

In many ways, the present situation is a tribute to the evolutionary processes which continually shape the law without being guided by one great master-plan. The introduction of the objective standard of care and skill in relation to wrongful trading had major repercussions on the law of directors' general duties, which were greeted almost with a sense of relief among company lawyers. But the increased confidence in dealing with the directors' duty to exercise reasonable care, skill and diligence may be about to produce a rebound effect in that it causes company law doctrines such as directors' duties, in the strict sense of the term, to encroach on the traditional domain of insolvency law. To resolve this conflict and knit together the various strands of the existing law into one solid thread would require a spirited intervention from the legislature even beyond the ambit of the Companies Act 2006. But the right time for this intervention may not yet have come.

The reason for this is another source of friction in the present law which comes to light in the observation that the concept of due care and skill may be about to creep into the directors' fiduciary duty to take account of the interests of creditors as the company is nearing insolvency. This observation takes us back to the concluding remarks in chapter 4 that English law may have reached a point where the traditional doctrinal separation of directors' fiduciary duties and their duty to exercise reasonable care, skill and diligence, which is itself the result of the evolutionary development of company law out of the law of trusts, may be called into question. Besides the duty not to misapply company property in contravention of capital maintenance rules, the duty to take account of the interests of creditors as the company is nearing insolvency provides a further instance of a duty that sits uneasily with the idea of fiduciary duties being strict rather than based on fault. Chapter 4 concluded with my opinion that it would be a pity if the new Companies Act had the effect of cutting short the debate among English lawyers as to whether the concept of strict fiduciary duties should be applied more narrowly so as to include only the duty to act in good faith and the no-conflict and no-profit rules as constituting the core obligation of loyalty owed by a fiduciary. This proposition has the potential to explain why other duties traditionally defined as 'fiduciary', notably the duty to consider and act in the best interests of the creditors as well as the duty not to make unlawful distributions, are in fact duties that can only be exercised to a reasonable standard of care. That the legislature excluded the supposedly fiduciary *West Mercia* duty to take account of the interests of creditors from the scope of the codification exercise and allow the courts to develop the law in this field may have left open a door, albeit a fairly small one, for this debate to continue, despite s. 178 (2) CA 2006. It lies well beyond the ambit of this book to forecast what the future holds for English law in this respect. But it proves the point that law – whether domestic or foreign – should always be understood as a dynamic phenomenon.

Returning to the comparative perspective, the introduction to this chapter set out with the proposition that German liability for delayed filing for insolvency (*Insolvenzverschleppung*) and English liability for wrongful trading or for the breach of a fiduciary duty to protect creditors' interests may be seen as functional equivalents. Indeed, the entire law discussed in this chapter may be understood as a response to one and the same functional problem, viz. to discourage those in control of a financially distressed company to gamble their way out of the crisis on the back of the creditors who are burdened with all the added risk. A study along the lines of the functional method of comparative law would place its emphasis on these functional similarities and might well conclude that the law is ripe for European harmonisation with a view to ironing out remaining divergences. Yet this study has shown that, apart from the functional problem serving as the common reference point, the responses to the problem developed by English law and German law have virtually nothing in common.

This holds true even for the most sensitive point of policy that lies at the heart of the matter: when should the law intervene? The German concept of liability for delayed filing for insolvency tries to pin down the point in time when the hand-over of the company's reins from the directors must happen as the point where either of the two tests of insolvency, illiquidity (*Zahlungsunfähigkeit*, § 17 InsO) or over-indebtedness (*Überschuldung*, § 19 InsO), is triggered. However, the overall effect of this approach appears to have been less than satisfactory given the sizeable number of asset-starved insolvencies, although the Insolvency Code may have brought about a marked improvement in this respect. Before the new law had become operative, the Forum Europaeum Corporate Group Law, whose steering committee was largely made up of academics with a German background, saw British-style wrongful trading as the better alternative to German-style liability for delayed filing for insolvency, because it was thought to apply 'to conduct prior to the point at which the company is in the condition requiring to be wound up'.[283] I have demonstrated elsewhere that this assumption should be treated with caution.[284] However, if German scholars were seeking inspiration on how to trigger directors' personal liability for mismanaging a company's financial crisis at an earlier point in time, they may have been right in looking to English law – only were they looking in the wrong place. They picked wrongful trading as the object of their inquiry because it had become widely known in Germany,[285] whereas the *West Mercia* line of cases was more or less an unknown quantity in comparative law circles at that time. Some judicial authority supports the conclusion that the *West Mercia* principle imposes creditor-regarding duties prior to insolvency on either of the two tests of cash flow insolvency or balance sheet insolvency. Yet this is precisely the reason why the doctrine is treated with caution in the United Kingdom, where the government expressed reservations against early legal intervention on the grounds that it would be likely to chill entrepreneurial activity and thus jeopardise the 'rescue culture', which the government seeks to promote.[286]

Finally, any sense of similarities between English law and German law vanishes as soon as we look at the diverse structural environments of the respective rules on directors' conduct in the vicinity of insolvency, which range from insolvency law to company law and right through to the general law of delict, resulting in an equally broad range of peculiar consequential problems, not all of which have been solved in a satisfactory manner. The evolutionary nature of the process which created these structural interrelations makes it highly unlikely that we shall ever see spontaneous convergence in this respect. This point about legal rules being inextricably linked with their doctrinal context takes us to the bigger picture of our analysis regarding the protection of creditors in limited liability companies and to some wider conclusions for the future of a European legal discourse in this or any other field of private law.

[283] *Forum Europaeum Konzernrecht*, Konzernrecht für Europa, ZGR 1998, 672 at 754; *Forum Europaeum Corporate Group Law*, Corporate Group Law for Europe (2000) 1 EBOR 165, at 247.

[284] *Bachner* (fn. 8). [285] See the references in fn. 115.

[286] DTI White Paper 'Modernising Company Law' (Cm. 5553, July 2002), para. 3.11.

CONCLUSIONS

At this point, after so much detailed analysis, some might expect a straightforward judgment as to which of the two legal systems, that of England or Germany, does better in protecting creditors of limited liability companies. Yet this book has not been written to answer such a question. Any comparison on a scale of 'better or worse' presupposes commensurability. But the price to be paid in order to achieve this commensurability is a reductionism which has a tendency to gloss over the law's inherent indeterminacy, its scope for argument, and its potential for evolution driven by the legal discourse itself. This book has looked at some of the most topical issues in the contemporary European discourse on creditor protection with a view to presenting the issues from the respective internal vantage points of English and German law in order to achieve a more fine-grained, vivid and dynamic picture than has hitherto been presented in comparative legal writing. The preceding chapters have analysed several components or pillars of creditor protection that are shared by English law and German law: the avoidance of pre-insolvency acts that are detrimental to creditors, the reversal of unlawful distributions amounting to a contravention of capital maintenance rules, as well as directors' personal liability for contraventions of capital maintenance rules and for conduct in the vicinity of insolvency. At a general level, it is neither surprising that both legal systems use all these components, nor that they can be applied in broadly similar ways to deal with the functional problems which have been identified in the introductory chapter, viz. the controllers of the company (i) carrying on the business to gamble their way out of the crisis, (ii) siphoning off assets from the company under their control, or (iii) making payments to certain creditors (especially themselves) in preference over other creditors. However, as the analysis has progressed, a more detailed picture has revealed that in each of the systems these pillars carry different weight and that the components are joined together in complex ways which are highly idiosyncratic to each legal system.

For some purposes the components need to be separated, notably with regard to the conflict of laws. Notwithstanding that, for instance, the avoidance of transactions at an undervalue and the reversal of unlawful distributions under capital maintenance principles may serve equivalent functions, the legal regime now in place at EU level forces lawyers to distinguish between matters of insolvency law and matters of company law. For most purposes, though, any such separation has an element of artificiality about it. It is still the case that the vast majority of legal disputes arise in a purely domestic context, and this allows lawyers to apply their domestic law as one coherent body of rules, indeed one system of law. Within this system, evolution is inevitable. But with every evolutionary development factors of continuity are necessary to ensure the cohesion of the system. One particular concern in this book has been to carve out some of the distinctive features that have shaped, and continue to shape, English and German law, respectively, in the area of creditor protection.

Legal evolution as a pattern of change and continuity

In every legal system we observe changes in the law through legislative intervention and, more gradually though no less important, through the decisions of the courts and through doctrinal writing. Yet all these changes, even those emanating from the legislature, will be moulded into existing doctrinal structures so as to preserve the stability of the overall framework. Legal systems have a built-in resistance to root-and-branch reconstruction. A tricky question in every law reform project is where to draw its boundaries. Within a given legal system there are only so many rules that can be changed in one step, yet their interconnectedness is almost unlimited. This book has come across examples from two major law reform projects of recent years, viz. the German Insolvency Code 1994 and the UK Companies Act 2006. Both have brought important structural changes, but neither has attempted to recreate the law from scratch.

In Germany, the rectification of defects in the law on the avoidance of pre-insolvency acts was a stated aim of the reform process leading to the new Insolvency Code. But at a deeper structural level the important role of subjective elements for the balancing of creditor protection and commercial certainty was preserved. If anything, this proves how much German lawyers are convinced of the merits of this principle in avoidance law. Yet the preservation of this feature of avoidance law goes hand in hand, and perhaps is only possible at all, because of the largely objective solution to the problem of value transfers from the company to one of its shareholders, or a person connected to a shareholder, in the realm of capital maintenance, notwithstanding that it has led German law into a convoluted debate about how to extend capital maintenance rules to receipts by persons connected to shareholders. Neither the agitated debate in the literature on English-registered private companies breaking into the German business landscape nor the profound discussion at the Juristentag in 2006 have created sufficient impetus for the MoMiG to shift the balance between capital maintenance and avoidance remedies in this respect, even though such a move from company law to insolvency law could hold gains in terms of applying German law to foreign-registered companies operating from a centre of main interests (COMI) within Germany. One may see the wholesale abolition of the law on equity-substituting shareholder credit and the creation of a new mandatory subordination rule in the Insolvency Code as an example to the contrary, but the situation in this area is no doubt a special one given the evolution of this body of law in the past.

In England, the statement of directors' duties was a centrepiece of the Company Law Review process that culminated in the Companies Act 2006. Easily the most intriguing aspect for civilian observers in this context is the preservation of the distinction between common law rules and equitable principles. The obvious reason for this conservatism lies in the entrenchment of this structural feature in many fields of English private law. Any fundamental change in this respect would have profound implications well beyond company law. A functional comparison of directors' duties may pass over these connections without paying much attention to them. But the law is never static, and for its evolution these structural interrelations matter in two ways. On the one hand, change and innovation are constrained by the need to maintain the coherence of the legal system and cannot easily depart from a given evolutionary path. On the other hand, new problems and solutions may initially come to light in a neighbouring field of law, before being applied more widely throughout the system. The explanatory notes to the Companies Act 2006 capture this insight succinctly: 'In the company law field, the principles being applied will frequently be taken from other areas, in particular trusts and agency. It is important that these connections are not lost and that company law may continue to reflect developments elsewhere.'[1] For anyone interested in this dynamic dimension of the law, a thorough understanding of its complexity is indispensable.

[1] Explanatory notes to the Companies Act 2006, para. 305.

Europeanisation of private law and EU legislation

Once the analysis has proceeded to this point, a provocative implication for European harmonisation efforts becomes obvious. At its heart, the European Union spurns the complexity of national legal systems as the antithesis of the European integration effort. But because Brussels can never hope to replace the entire legal system of all its Member States in one fell swoop, its interventions are limited to enacting solutions for discrete problems – or so it seems. The corollary of this approach is that, in the European legislative process, both the problem and the solution are defined in purely functional terms, thereby suffering from the same inevitable reductionism that is pervasive in the functional methodology of comparative law as such. The result is then parachuted into the legal systems of twenty-seven Member States in the slender hope that the changes brought about in each of the legal systems will miraculously lead to a uniform result. This approach by the legislature is bound to store up problems for the subsequent application of the supposedly harmonised law. Predictably, a European directive on wrongful trading would have been no exception in this regard.

One of the weaknesses of the process of drafting European legislation is that it stands more or less aloof from the evolutionary logic that is intrinsic to every legal system. For simple practical as well as political reasons, large-scale projects similar to the MoMiG, let alone the Company Law Review, are out of the question at EU level. What the European Commission proposed in its May 2003 action plan was a discrete number of small-scale projects, such as a directive on wrongful trading. In purely functional terms, this may seem a laudable idea. But the narrow scope of any such measure brings the issue of complexity to the fore even more forcefully. How would it fit into the framework of existing law in each of the Member States? Looking only at English wrongful trading and German liability for delayed filing for insolvency (*Insolvenzverschleppungshaftung*), we can identify a host of potential friction points. From an English perspective, a sensible European rule would have to take into account the effects of a floating charge, notwithstanding that other Member States do not recognise anything like it in their national laws. Conversely, many German lawyers would probably expect to find a distinction between old and new creditors (*Altgläubiger / Neugläubiger*), given the difficulties they see with enforcing any liability rule based solely on the diminution of the quota (*Quotenverringerung*). English lawyers would perhaps object to such a proposal on the strong ground that it violates the *pari passu* principle.

German lawyers, in turn, may argue that the *pari passu* principle is of less concern given the problem of asset-starved insolvencies (*massearme Insolvenzen*) where no formal insolvency proceedings take place. To this, English lawyers could reply that their law does provide for the possibility of formal insolvency proceedings even where the company has no assets, if there are reasons to investigate the conduct of directors and others responsible for the company's collapse. In the end, it would seem that a decision, no matter which way, whether a European rule on directors' liability for conduct in the vicinity of insolvency should provide for a differential treatment of old and new creditors, would require extending the scope of the EU measure to harmonise also the law on asset-starved insolvencies, and with it the institutional infrastructure of insolvency law, which in turn builds on different national perceptions about the public function of insolvency law. One does wonder whether these consequences had really been thought through before the European Commission proposed a directive on 'wrongful trading' in its action plan. This study highlights the complexity of legal systems, an issue all too often underestimated when it comes to well-intentioned European harmonisation projects. Its main thrust in this respect is to advocate caution and to demand a thorough preliminary inquiry into how any proposed European legislation is likely to coexist with national laws.

Towards a genuine European legal discourse

This leads over to some final observations about the future potential for what I have termed a European legal discourse and which I take to be broadly synonymous with the German idea of '*Europäische Rechtswissenschaft*'.[2] Every lawyer in Europe today is bound to be more familiar with his or her home legal system. This affects not only the way in which we all understand European laws once they have been adopted, but it also influences their genesis, because the drafters in Brussels (or elsewhere) will invariably be lawyers of a particular national origin and with the roots of their legal thinking firmly anchored in one system. Moreover, the experience with official bodies such as the Commission's Company Law Experts Group and the Council Working Party[3] shows that there is only so much that can be achieved in a dialogue between lawyers from different jurisdictions, because each of them will start from the debate

[2] Chapter 1 B.1.

[3] In this respect I may draw upon personal experience as a member of both groups.

within his or her home jurisdiction. This might well lead to a situation where the participants talk past each other in what the French aptly call a *dialogue de sourds*, a 'dialogue of the deaf', who speak at cross-purposes and are unable to pick up what the other side is aiming at.

Does this mean that a European legal discourse is bound to fail? Some, like Pierre Legrand, seem to think so.[4] Personally, I beg to disagree. Yet the potential for such a discourse to bear fruit hinges critically on our ability to understand foreign legal systems and to communicate effectively with lawyers steeped in their respective doctrinal language. As lawyers we are bound to use human language as our means of communication. The dominance of English as the first foreign language among the nations of Europe means that for the foreseeable future only the English language will be capable of supporting a European legal discourse that transcends the boundaries of national laws.

From this seemingly self-evident observation follow two consequences which in fact are two sides of the same coin. In the past, English as a language of law evolved in tandem with the common law, today split up into dozens of jurisdictions across the world, but still with a high degree of structural and conceptual uniformity between them, especially within the narrower group of jurisdictions belonging to the British Commonwealth. With its use as the language for a European legal discourse, English is suddenly called upon to accommodate legal concepts that are alien to the common law, and for which a new terminology must be shaped out of the richness of the general language to the point where it acquires, as far as practicable, the specific qualities of doctrinal legal language in terms of regularity and precision, or else the discourse will ineluctably, though perhaps unwittingly, be tilted in favour of the common law. The other side of the coin means a serious challenge for civilian writers using English to explain their domestic law to a non-domestic audience. The potential confusion resulting from the willingness of German lawyers to equate '*Treuepflichten*' with 'fiduciary duties' provides a striking example.

Leaving aside issues of legal language and terminology, the crucial concern for a European legal discourse is how to obtain knowledge about the laws in the different Member States. The obvious way to discover the contents of a foreign legal system is through the publications of lawyers. For good reasons, these publications tend to focus on

[4] 'European Legal Systems are not Converging' (1996) 45 ICLQ 52; 'The Impossibility of "Legal Transplants"' (1997) 4 Maastricht Journal of European and Comparative Law 111.

those aspects where the law in their respective jurisdiction is evolving. Every legal system has this 'frontier' where the courts, practising lawyers and academic writers work to clarify the law and develop it further. This is the realm of heated discussion about new doctrinal concepts and of long-running disputes awaiting judicial resolve. Many, if not most publications by lawyers seek to contribute to this process. But observers from a foreign legal system are likely to miss out on much of the substance of this writing unless they understand these contributions as answers to specific questions, as reactions to a certain state of affairs or events in the past. The true challenge of a future '*Europäische Rechtswissenschaft*', a genuinely European legal discourse, is the mastery of foreign legal systems that enables lawyers to follow this discourse at a fairly advanced doctrinal level in more than one jurisdiction.

This approach is guided by a methodological concern that differs profoundly from the functional conception of a comparative investigation, which Zweigert and Kötz sum up in these words:

> [T]he negative aspect of the principle of functionality [is] that the comparatist must eradicate the preconceptions of his native legal system; the positive aspect tells us which areas of the foreign legal system to investigate in order to find the analogue to the solution which interests him.[5]

Crucially, 'the solution which interests him' must be defined in strictly non-legal terms, without reference to any legal system. If the preconceptions of one's native legal system are to be eradicated, the preconceptions of the foreign legal system do not even figure in the above equation at all. In sharp contrast, the approach applied in this book embraces the preconceptions of one's native legal system and of the foreign legal system as the key to understanding how the lawyers in each system reconstruct reality in the world of law. At its best, this approach can eradicate the antithesis between 'one's native law' and 'foreign law' without the need to warp the analysis into an extra-legal, functional reconstruction of reality, thereby renouncing legal thought as such and the possibilities offered by the techniques of doctrinal argument.

If successful, this approach has the added advantage of being able to connect effortlessly with the domestic discourse in both legal systems. It does, however, have a downside, too. Clearly, the attempt to master a second, or even a third, legal system in similar depth as one's 'first' law requires a considerable amount of time and effort at a personal level,

[5] *Zweigert / Kötz*, Comparative Law (3rd edn 1998) 35.

seemingly forbidding any idea of EU-wide studies. However, the practice of such wide-ranging comparative enquiries has long been to commission a country report from an author based within the respective jurisdiction, which reports are often presented in a largely isolated manner and only linked together by a fairly general comparison at the beginning or end. If these studies were to adopt a method such as has been applied here, a network of bilateral or trilateral studies should eventually be able to provide much more information than has hitherto been available and to present it in a manner that will be more appealing to traditional doctrinally oriented lawyers.

In a traditional way of looking at the differences between the common law and the civil law, one might object that the fundamental character of this process of discourse, clarification and gradual development of the law is precisely what sets the two worlds apart. The common law, it is thought, evolves gradually, but largely through judicial lawmaking, with English judges showing great reluctance to give credit to academic writing. German law, on the other hand, is thought to be the creation of the law professors, who have cast it in codes and statutes and now continue to shape it through their legal opinions. My own experience with both legal systems has led me to conclude that a real process of convergence is underway in this respect, although it would be unwise to ignore the manifold continuing differences. If they are honest, German lawyers cannot possibly deny the importance of judicial lawmaking. There is hardly a better showpiece than the 1994 decision from the Bundesgerichtshof on the liability of company directors towards new creditors,[6] which is widely referred to in Germany as the '*Wendeentscheidung*' (literally the 'turnabout decision'), and the ongoing debate it has sparked. On the other hand, there is now a visible trend in English judgments, not only in the House of Lords, but also in the Court of Appeal, to cite academic literature. The judges thus acknowledge that lawyers of all professional descriptions are ultimately working on the same project, that is understanding the law. This project has been singularly well characterised by Lord Goff in the Postscript to his speech in *The Spiliada*:

> I feel that I cannot conclude without paying tribute to the writings of jurists which have assisted me in the preparation of this opinion. Although it may be invidious to do so, I wish to single out for special

[6] BGH 6.6.1994, BGHZ 126, 181 = NJW 1994, 2220.

> mention articles by Mr Adrian Briggs in (1983) 3 Legal Studies 74 and in [1984] L.M.C.L.Q. 227, and the article by Miss Rhona Schuz in (1986) 35 I.C.L.Q. 374. They will observe that I have not agreed with them on all points; but even when I have disagreed with them, I have found their work to be of assistance. For jurists are pilgrims with us on the endless road to unattainable perfection; and we have it on the excellent authority of Geoffrey Chaucer that conversations among pilgrims can be most rewarding.[7]

We have it on the excellent authority of Lord Goff that this extends to conversations between lawyers from England and Germany.

[7] *Spiliada Maritime Corporation v Cansulex Ltd (The Spiliada)* [1987] AC 460, at 488.

APPENDIX: STATUTORY PROVISIONS

Companies Act 2006

Section 170. Scope and nature of general duties

(1) The general duties specified in sections 171 to 177 are owed by a director of a company to the company.
(2) A person who ceases to be a director continues to be subject . . .
(3) The general duties are based on certain common law rules and equitable principles as they apply in relation to directors and have effect in place of those rules and principles as regards the duties owed to a company by a director.
(4) The general duties shall be interpreted and applied in the same way as common law rules or equitable principles, and regard shall be had to the corresponding common law rules and equitable principles in interpreting and applying the general duties.
(5) The general duties apply to shadow directors where, and to the extent that, the corresponding common law rules or equitable principles so apply.

Section 171. Duty to act within powers

A director of a company must –

(a) act in accordance with the company's constitution, and
(b) only exercise powers for the purposes for which they are conferred.

Section 172. Duty to promote the success of the company

(1) A director of a company must act in the way he considers, in good faith, would be most likely to promote the success of the company for the benefit of its members as a whole, and in doing so have regard (amongst other matters) to –
    (a) the likely consequences of any decision in the long term,
    (b) the interests of the company's employees,

(c) the need to foster the company's business relationships with suppliers, customers and others,
(d) the impact of the company's operations on the community and the environment,
(e) the desirability of the company maintaining a reputation for high standards of business conduct, and
(f) the need to act fairly as between members of the company.

(2) Where or to the extent that the purposes of the company consist of or include purposes other than the benefit of its members, subsection (1) has effect as if the reference to promoting the success of the company for the benefit of it members were to achieving those purposes.
(3) The duty imposed by this section has effect subject to any enactment or rule of law requiring directors, in certain circumstances, to consider or act in the interests of creditors of the company.

Section 174. Duty to exercise reasonable care, skill and diligence

(1) A director of a company must exercise reasonable care, skill and diligence.
(2) This means the care, skill and diligence that would be exercised by a reasonably diligent person with –
   (a) the general knowledge, skill and experience that may reasonably be expected of a person carrying out the functions carried out by the director in relation to the company, and
   (b) the general knowledge, skill and experience that the director has.

Section 178. Civil consequences of breach of general duties

(1) The consequences of breach (or threatened breach) of sections 171 to 177 are the same as would apply if the corresponding common law rule or equitable principle applied.
(2) The duties in those sections (with the exception of section 174 (duty to exercise reasonable care, skill and diligence)) are, accordingly, enforceable in the same way as any other fiduciary duty owed to a company by its directors.

Section 829. Meaning of 'distribution'

(1) In this Part 'distribution' means every description of distribution of a company's assets to its members, whether in cash or otherwise, subject to the following exceptions.
(2) The following are not distributions for the purposes of this Part –

(a) an issue of shares as fully or partly paid bonus shares;
(b) the reduction of share capital –
  (i) by extinguishing or reducing the liability of any of the members on any of the company's shares in respect of share capital not paid up, or
  (ii) by repaying paid-up share capital;
(c) the redemption or purchase of any of the company's own shares out of capital (including the proceeds of any fresh issue of shares) or out of unrealised profits in accordance with Chapter 3, 4 or 5 of Part 18;
(d) a distribution of assets to members of the company on its winding up.

Section 830. Distributions to be made only out of profits available for the purpose

(1) A company may only make a distribution out of profits available for the purpose.
(2) A company's profits available for distribution are its accumulated, realised profits, so far as not previously utilised by distribution or capitalisation, less its accumulated, realised losses, so far as not previously written off in a reduction or reorganisation of capital duly made.
(3) Subsection (2) has effect subject to sections 832 and 835 (investment companies etc: distributions out of accumulated revenue profits).

Section 836. Justification of distribution by reference to relevant accounts

(1) Whether a distribution may be made by a company without contravening this Part is determined by reference to the following items as stated in the relevant accounts –
  (a) profits, losses, assets and liabilities;
  (b) provisions of the following kinds –
    (i) where the relevant accounts are Companies Act accounts, provisions of a kind specified for the purposes of this subsection by regulations under section 396;
    (ii) where the relevant accounts are IAS accounts, provisions of any kind;
  (c) share capital and reserves (including undistributable reserves).
(2) The relevant accounts are the company's last annual accounts, except that –
  (a) where the distribution would be found to contravene this Part by reference to the company's last annual accounts, it may be justified by reference to interim accounts, and

(b) where the distribution is proposed to be declared during the company's first accounting reference period, or before any accounts have been circulated in respect of that period, it may be justified by reference to initial accounts.

(3) The requirements of –
section 837 (as regards the company's last annual accounts),
section 838 (as regards interim accounts), and
section 839 (as regards initial accounts),
must be complied with, as and where applicable.

(4) If any applicable requirement of those sections is not complied with, the accounts may not be relied on for the purposes of this Part and the distribution is accordingly treated as contravening this Part.

Section 847. Consequences of unlawful distribution

(1) This section applies where a distribution, or part of one, made by a company to one of its members is made in contravention of this Part.

(2) If at the time of the distribution the member knows or has reasonable grounds for believing that it is so made, he is liable –
(a) to repay it (or that part of it, as the case may be) to the company, or
(b) in the case of a distribution made otherwise than in cash, to pay the company a sum equal to the value of the distribution (or part) at that time.

(3) This is without prejudice to any obligation imposed apart from this section on a member of a company to repay a distribution unlawfully made to him.

(4) . . .

Section 1157. Power of court to grant relief in certain cases

(1) If in proceedings for negligence, default, breach of duty or breach of trust against –
(a) an officer of a company, or
(b) a person employed by a company as auditor (whether he is or is not an officer of the company),
it appears to the court hearing the case that the officer or person is or may be liable but that he acted honestly and reasonably, and that having regard to all the circumstances of the case (including those connected with his appointment) he ought fairly to be excused, the court may relieve him, either wholly or in part, from his liability on such terms as it thinks fit.

(2), (3) . . .

Insolvency Act 1986

Section 122. Circumstances in which company may be wound up by the court

(1) A company may be wound up by the court if –
   (a) the company has by special resolution resolved that the company be wound up by the court,
   (b) being a public company which was registered as such on its original incorporation, the company has not been issued with a trading certificate under section 761 of the Companies Act 2006 (requirement as to minimum share capital) and more than a year has expired since it was so registered,
   (c) it is an old public company, within the meaning of the Consequential Provisions Act,
   (d) the company does not commence its business within a year from its incorporation or suspends its business for a whole year,
   (e) except in the case of a private company limited by shares or by guarantee, the number of members is reduced below 2,
   (f) the company is unable to pay its debts,
   (fa) at the time at which a moratorium for the company under section 1A comes to an end, no voluntary arrangement approved under Part I has effect in relation to the company,
   (g) the court is of the opinion that it is just and equitable that the company should be wound up.

(2) . . . [Scotland]

Section 123. Definition of inability to pay debts

(1) A company is deemed unable to pay its debts –
   (a) if a creditor (by assignment or otherwise) to whom the company is indebted in a sum exceeding £750 then due has served on the company, by leaving it at the company's registered office, a written demand (in the prescribed form) requiring the company to pay the sum so due and the company has for 3 weeks thereafter neglected to pay the sum or to secure or compound for it to the reasonable satisfaction of the creditor, or
   (b) if, in England and Wales, execution or other process issued on a judgment, decree or order of any court in favour of a creditor of the company is returned unsatisfied in whole or in part, or
   (c), (d) . . . [Scotland, Northern Ireland]
   (e) if it is proved to the satisfaction of the court that the company is unable to pay its debts as they fall due.

(2) A company is also deemed unable to pay its debts if it is proved to the satisfaction of the court that the value of the company's assets is less than the amount of its liabilities, taking into account its contingent and prospective liabilities.
(3) The money sum for the time being specified in subsection (1)(a) is subject to increase or reduction by order under section 416 in Part XV.

Section 212. Summary remedy against delinquent directors, liquidators, etc.

(1) This section applies if in the course of the winding up of a company it appears that a person who –
    (a) is or has been an officer of the company,
    (b) has acted as liquidator or administrative receiver of the company, or
    (c) not being a person falling within paragraph (a) or (b), is or has been concerned, or has taken part, in the promotion, formation or management of the company, has misapplied or retained, or become accountable for, any money or other property of the company, or been guilty of any misfeasance or breach of any fiduciary or other duty in relation to the company.
(2) The reference in subsection (1) to any misfeasance or breach of any fiduciary or other duty in relation to the company includes, in the case of a person who has acted as liquidator of the company, any misfeasance or breach of any fiduciary or other duty in connection with the carrying out of his functions as liquidator of the company.
(3) The court may, on the application of the official receiver or the liquidator, or of any creditor or contributory, examine into the conduct of the person falling within subsection (1) and compel him –
    (a) to repay, restore or account for the money or property or any part of it, with interest at such rate as the court thinks just, or
    (b) to contribute such sum to the company's assets by way of compensation in respect of the misfeasance or breach of fiduciary or other duty as the court thinks just.
(4) The power to make an application under subsection (3) in relation to a person who has acted as liquidator of the company is not exercisable, except with the leave of the court, after he has had his release.
(5) The power of a contributory to make an application under subsection (3) is not exercisable except with the leave of the court, but is exercisable notwithstanding that he will not benefit from any order the court may make on the application.

Section 213. Fraudulent trading

(1) If in the course of the winding up of a company it appears that any business of the company has been carried on with intent to defraud creditors of the company or creditors of any other person, or for any fraudulent purpose, the following has effect.

(2) The court, on the application of the liquidator may declare that any persons who were knowingly parties to the carrying on of the business in the manner above-mentioned are to be liable to make such contributions (if any) to the company's assets as the court thinks proper.

Section 214. Wrongful trading

(1) Subject to subsection (3) below, if in the course of the winding up of a company it appears that subsection (2) of this section applies in relation to a person who is or has been a director of the company, the court, on the application of the liquidator, may declare that that person is to be liable to make such contribution (if any) to the company's assets as the court thinks proper.

(2) This subsection applies in relation to a person if –

(a) the company has gone into insolvent liquidation,

(b) at some time before the commencement of the winding up of the company, that person knew or ought to have concluded that there was no reasonable prospect that the company would avoid going into insolvent liquidation, and

(c) that person was a director of the company at that time;

but the court shall not make a declaration under this section in any case where the time mentioned in paragraph (b) above was before 28th April 1986.

(3) The court shall not make a declaration under this section with respect to any person if it is satisfied that after the condition specified in subsection (2)(b) was first satisfied in relation to him that person took every step with a view to minimising the potential loss to the company's creditors as (assuming him to have known that there was no reasonable prospect that the company would avoid going into insolvent liquidation) he ought to have taken.

(4) For the purposes of subsections (2) and (3), the facts which a director of a company ought to know or ascertain, the conclusions which he ought to reach and the steps which he ought to take are those which would be known or ascertained, or reached or taken, by a reasonably diligent person having both –

(a) the general knowledge, skill and experience that may reasonably be expected of a person carrying out the same functions as are carried out by that director in relation to the company, and

(b) the general knowledge, skill and experience that that director has.

(5) The reference in subsection (4) to the functions carried out in relation to a company by a director of the company includes any functions which he does not carry out but which have been entrusted to him.

(6) For the purposes of this section a company goes into insolvent liquidation if it goes into liquidation at a time when its assets are insufficient for the payment of its debts and other liabilities and the expenses of the winding up.

(7) In this section 'director' includes a shadow director.

(8) This section is without prejudice to section 213.

Section 238. Transactions at an undervalue (England and Wales)

(1) This section applies in the case of a company where –

(a) the company enters administration, or

(b) the company goes into liquidation;

and 'the office-holder' means the administrator or the liquidator, as the case may be.

(2) Where the company has at a relevant time (defined in section 240) entered into a transaction with any person at an undervalue, the office-holder may apply to the court for an order under this section.

(3) Subject as follows, the court shall, on such an application, make such order as it thinks fit for restoring the position to what it would have been if the company had not entered into that transaction.

(4) For the purposes of this section and section 241, a company enters into a transaction with a person at an undervalue if –

(a) the company makes a gift to that person or otherwise enters into a transaction with that person on terms that provide for the company to receive no consideration, or

(b) the company enters into a transaction with that person for a consideration the value of which, in money or money's worth, is significantly less than the value, in money or money's worth, of the consideration provided by the company.

(5) The court shall not make an order under this section in respect of a transaction at an undervalue if it is satisfied –

(a) that the company which entered into the transaction did so in good faith and for the purpose of carrying on its business, and

(b) that at the time it did so there were reasonable grounds for believing that the transaction would benefit the company.

Section 239. Preferences (England and Wales)

(1) This section applies as does section 238.

(2) Where the company has at a relevant time (defined in the next section) given a preference to any person, the office-holder may apply to the court for an order under this section.

(3) Subject as follows, the court shall, on such an application, make such order as it thinks fit for restoring the position to what it would have been if the company had not given that preference.

(4) For the purposes of this section and section 241, a company gives a preference to a person if –

  (a) that person is one of the company's creditors or a surety or guarantor for any of the company's debts or other liabilities, and

  (b) the company does anything or suffers anything to be done which (in either case) has the effect of putting that person into a position which, in the event of the company going into insolvent liquidation, will be better than the position he would have been in if that thing had not been done.

(5) The court shall not make an order under this section in respect of a preference given to any person unless the company which gave the preference was influenced in deciding to give it by a desire to produce in relation to that person the effect mentioned in subsection (4)(b).

(6) A company which has given a preference to a person connected with the company (otherwise than by reason only of being its employee) at the time the preference was given is presumed, unless the contrary is shown, to have been influenced in deciding to give it by such a desire as is mentioned in subsection (5).

(7) The fact that something has been done in pursuance of the order of a court does not, without more, prevent the doing or suffering of that thing from constituting the giving of a preference.

Section 240. 'Relevant time' under ss. 238, 239

(1) Subject to the next subsection, the time at which a company enters into a transaction at an undervalue or gives a preference is a relevant time if the transaction is entered into, or the preference given –

  (a) in the case of a transaction at an undervalue or of a preference which is given to a person who is connected with the company (otherwise than by reason only of being its employee), at a time in the period of 2 years ending with the onset of insolvency (which expression is defined below),

(b) in the case of a preference which is not such a transaction and is not so given, at a time in the period of 6 months ending with the onset of insolvency,
(c) in either case, at a time between the making of an administration application in respect of the company and the making of an administration order on that application, and
(d) in either case, at a time between the filing with the court of a copy of notice of intention to appoint an administrator under paragraph 14 or 22 of Schedule B1 and the making of an appointment under that paragraph.

(2) Where a company enters into a transaction at an undervalue or gives a preference at a time mentioned in subsection (1)(a) or (b), that time is not a relevant time for the purpose of section 238 or 239 unless the company –
(a) is at that time unable to pay its debts within the meaning of section 123 in Chapter VI of Part IV, or
(b) becomes unable to pay its debts within the meaning of that section in consequence of the transaction or preference;

but the requirements of this subsection are presumed to be satisfied, unless the contrary is shown, in relation to any transaction at an undervalue which is entered into by a company with a person who is connected with the company.

(3) For the purposes of subsection (1), the onset of insolvency is –
(a) in a case where section 238 or 239 applies by reason of an administrator of a company being appointed by administration order, the date on which the administration application is made,
(b) in a case where section 238 or 239 applies by reason of an administrator of a company being appointed under paragraph 14 or 22 of Schedule B1 following filing with the court of a copy of a notice of intention to appoint under that paragraph, the date on which the copy of the notice is filed,
(c) in a case where section 238 or 239 applies by reason of an administrator of a company being appointed otherwise than as mentioned in paragraph (a) or (b), the date on which the appointment takes effect,
(d) in a case where section 238 or 239 applies by reason of a company going into liquidation either following conversion of administration into winding up by virtue of Article 37 of the EC Regulation or at the time when the appointment of an administrator ceases to have effect, the date on which the company entered administration (or, if relevant, the date on which the application for the administration order was made or a copy of the notice of intention to appoint was filed), and
(e) in a case where section 238 or 239 applies by reason of a company going into liquidation at any other time, the date of the commencement of the winding up.

Section 245. Avoidance of certain floating charges

(1) This section applies as does section 238, but applies to Scotland as well as to England and Wales.

(2) Subject as follows, a floating charge on the company's undertaking or property created at a relevant time is invalid except to the extent of the aggregate of –

(a) the value of so much of the consideration for the creation of the charge as consists of money paid, or goods or services supplied, to the company at the same time as, or after, the creation of the charge,

(b) the value of so much of that consideration as consists of the discharge or reduction, at the same time as, or after, the creation of the charge, of any debt of the company, and

(c) the amount of such interest (if any) as is payable on the amount falling within paragraph (a) or (b) in pursuance of any agreement under which the money was so paid, the goods or services were so supplied or the debt was so discharged or reduced.

(3) Subject to the next subsection, the time at which a floating charge is created by a company is a relevant time for the purposes of this section if the charge is created –

(a) in the case of a charge which is created in favour of a person who is connected with the company, at a time in the period of 2 years ending with the onset of insolvency,

(b) in the case of a charge which is created in favour of any other person, at a time in the period of 12 months ending with the onset of insolvency,

(c) in either case, at a time between the making of an administration application in respect of the company and the making of an administration order on that application, or

(d) in either case, at a time between the filing with the court of a copy of notice of intention to appoint an administrator under paragraph 14 or 22 of Schedule B1 and the making of an appointment under that paragraph.

(4) Where a company creates a floating charge at a time mentioned in subsection (3)(b) and the person in favour of whom the charge is created is not connected with the company, that time is not a relevant time for the purposes of this section unless the company –

(a) is at that time unable to pay its debts within the meaning of section 123 in Chapter VI of Part IV, or

(b) becomes unable to pay its debts within the meaning of that section in consequence of the transaction under which the charge is created.

(5) For the purposes of subsection (3), the onset of insolvency is –

(a) in a case where this section applies by reason of an administrator of a company being appointed by administration order, the date on which the administration application is made,

(b) in a case where this section applies by reason of an administrator of a company being appointed under paragraph 14 or 22 of Schedule B1 following filing with the court of a copy of notice of intention to appoint under that paragraph, the date on which the copy of the notice is filed,

(c) in a case where this section applies by reason of an administrator of a company being appointed otherwise than as mentioned in paragraph (a) or (b), the date on which the appointment takes effect, and

(d) in a case where this section applies by reason of a company going into liquidation, the date of the commencement of the winding up.

(6) For the purposes of subsection (2)(a) the value of any goods or services supplied by way of consideration for a floating charge is the amount in money which at the time they were supplied could reasonably have been expected to be obtained for supplying the goods or services in the ordinary course of business and on the same terms (apart from the consideration) as those on which they were supplied to the company.

Section 423. Transactions defrauding creditors

(1) This section relates to transactions entered into at an undervalue; and a person enters into such a transaction with another person if –

(a) he makes a gift to the other person or he otherwise enters into a transaction with the other on terms that provide for him to receive no consideration;

(b) he enters into a transaction with the other in consideration of marriage or the formation of a civil partnership; or

(c) he enters into a transaction with the other for a consideration the value of which, in money or money's worth, is significantly less than the value, in money or money's worth, of the consideration provided by himself.

(2) Where a person has entered into such a transaction, the court may, if satisfied under the next subsection, make such order as it thinks fit for –

(a) restoring the position to what it would have been if the transaction had not been entered into, and

(b) protecting the interests of persons who are victims of the transaction.

(3) In the case of a person entering into such a transaction, an order shall only be made if the court is satisfied that it was entered into by him for the purpose –

(a) of putting assets beyond the reach of a person who is making, or may at some time make, a claim against him, or

(b) of otherwise prejudicing the interests of such a person in relation to the claim which he is making or may make.

(4) . . . [relevant court]

(5) . . . [references to a victim of the transaction are to a person who is, or is capable of being, prejudiced by it]

German Act on Limited Liability Companies (GmbHG)

Translation by the author. Alternative translation: *Martin Peltzer / Jermyn P. Brooks / Terry Hopcroft / Elizabeth A. Voight*, GmbH-Gesetz – German Law Pertaining to Companies with Limited Liability (Cologne: Otto Schmidt, 4th rev. edn 2000).

§ 29. Ergebnisverwendung

(1) Die Gesellschafter haben Anspruch auf den Jahresüberschuß zuzüglich eines Gewinnvortrags und abzüglich eines Verlustvortrags, soweit der sich ergebende Betrag nicht nach Gesetz oder Gesellschaftsvertrag, durch Beschluß nach Absatz 2 oder als zusätzlicher Aufwand auf Grund des Beschlusses über die Verwendung des Ergebnisses von der Verteilung unter die Gesellschafter ausgeschlossen ist. . . .
(2) Im Beschluß über die Verwendung des Ergebnisses können die Gesellschafter, wenn der Gesellschaftsvertrag nichts anderes bestimmt, Beträge in Gewinnrücklagen einstellen oder als Gewinn vortragen.
(3), (4) . . .

§ 29. Appropriation of profit

(1) The shareholders have a right to the annual surplus (*Jahresüberschuss*) plus any profit carried over and less any loss carried over, to the extent that the resulting amount is not excluded from distribution among the shareholders by law, by the company's constitution, by a resolution under subparagraph 2, or as further expense by virtue of the resolution concerning the appropriation of the profit. . . .
(2) In the resolution on the application of the profit, the shareholders can apply amounts to profit reserves or carry them forward as profit, unless the company's constitution provides otherwise.
(3), (4) . . .

§ 30. Kapitalerhaltung

(1) Das zur Erhaltung des Stammkapitals erforderliche Vermögen der Gesellschaft darf an die Gesellschafter nicht ausgezahlt werden. . . .
(2) . . .

§ 30. Capital maintenance

(1) The assets of the company necessary to maintain the share capital must not be paid over to the shareholders. . . .[1]
(2) . . .

§ 31. Erstattung verbotener Rückzahlungen

(1) Zahlungen, welche den Vorschriften des § 30 zuwider geleistet sind, müssen der Gesellschaft erstattet werden.
(2) War der Empfänger in gutem Glauben, so kann die Erstattung nur insoweit verlangt werden, als sie zur Befriedigung der Gesellschaftsgläubiger erforderlich ist.
(3) Ist die Erstattung von dem Empfänger nicht zu erlangen, so haften für den zu erstattenden Betrag, soweit er zur Befriedigung der Gesellschaftsgläubiger erforderlich ist, die übrigen Gesellschafter nach Verhältnis ihrer Geschäftsanteile. Beiträge, welche von einzelnen Gesellschaftern nicht zu erlangen sind, werden nach dem bezeichneten Verhältnis auf die übrigen verteilt.
(4) Zahlungen, welche auf Grund der vorstehenden Bestimmungen zu leisten sind, können den Verpflichteten nicht erlassen werden.
(5) Die Ansprüche der Gesellschaft verjähren in den Fällen des Absatzes 1 in zehn Jahren sowie in den Fällen des Absatzes 3 in fünf Jahren. Die Verjährung beginnt mit dem Ablauf des Tages, an welchem die Zahlung, deren Erstattung beansprucht wird, geleistet ist. . . .
(6) Für die in den Fällen des Absatzes 3 geleistete Erstattung einer Zahlung sind den Gesellschaftern die Geschäftsführer, welchen in betreff der geleisteten Zahlung ein Verschulden zur Last fällt, solidarisch zum Ersatz verpflichtet. Die Bestimmungen in § 43 Abs. 1 und 4 finden entsprechende Anwendung.

§ 31. Restoration of forbidden repayments

(1) Payments which have been made in contravention of § 30 must be restored to the company.
(2) If the recipient has acted in good faith, restoration can only be demanded to the extent necessary for the satisfaction of the company's creditors.

[1] The MoMiG inserted two further sentences in § 30 (1); the new second sentence lies beyond the scope of this study; the new third sentence relates to the repeal of the existing law on equity-substituting shareholder credit, see the excursus in chapter 3 E.

(3) If restoration cannot be obtained from the recipient, the other shareholders are liable for the amount to be restored, insofar as it is required for the satisfaction of the company's creditors, in proportion to their shares. Contributions which cannot be obtained from particular shareholders will be divided among the others in the designated proportion.
(4) Payments due under the foregoing provisions cannot be waived in favour of the liable parties.
(5) The company's claims are subject to a limitation period of ten years in the circumstances of sub-paragraph 1 and five years in the circumstances of sub-paragraph 3. The period starts with the end of the day on which the payment whose restoration is claimed has been made. . . .
(6) For the restoration of a payment made in the circumstances of sub-paragraph 3, the directors who have acted culpably in relation to the payment are liable to compensate the shareholders jointly and severally. The provisions in § 43 (1) and (4) shall apply mutatis mutandis.

§ 32. Rückzahlung von Gewinn

Liegt die in § 31 Abs. 1 bezeichnete Voraussetzung nicht vor, so sind die Gesellschafter in keinem Fall verpflichtet, Beträge, welche sie in gutem Glauben als Gewinnanteile bezogen haben, zurückzuzahlen.

§ 32. Repayment of dividends

Unless the condition specified in § 31 (1) is satisfied, the shareholders are in no case liable to repay sums which they have received in good faith as dividends.

§ 43. Haftung der Geschäftsführer

(1) Die Geschäftsführer haben in den Angelegenheiten der Gesellschaft die Sorgfalt eines ordentlichen Geschäftsmannes anzuwenden.
(2) Geschäftsführer, welche ihre Obliegenheiten verletzen, haften der Gesellschaft solidarisch für den entstandenen Schaden.
(3) Insbesondere sind sie zum Ersatz verpflichtet, wenn den Besimmungen des § 30 zuwider Zahlungen aus dem zur Erhaltung des Stammkapitals erforderlichen Vermögen der Gesellschaft gemacht oder den Bestimmungen des § 33 zuwider eigene Geschäftsanteile der Gesellschaft erworben worden sind. Auf den Ersatzanspruch finden die Bestimmungen in § 9b Abs. 1 entsprechende Anwendung. Soweit der Ersatz zur Befriedigung der Gläubiger der Gesellschaft erforderlich ist, wird die Verpflichtung der Geschäftsführer

nicht dadurch aufgehoben, daß dieselben in Befolgung eines Beschlusses der Gesellschafter gehandelt haben.
(4) Die Ansprüche aufgrund der vorstehenden Bestimmungen verjähren in fünf Jahren.

§ 43. Liability of the directors

(1) The directors, in attending to the affairs of the company, must apply the diligence of a prudent businessman.
(2) Directors who offend against their duties are jointly and severally liable to the company for the resulting damage.
(3) In particular they are liable for compensation if, in contravention of the provisions of § 30, payments have been made out of the assets of the company necessary to maintain the share capital or if, in contravention of the provisions of § 33, own shares of the company have been acquired. The provisions in § 9b (1) shall apply mutatis mutandis to the claim for compensation. Insofar as the compensation is necessary for the satisfaction of the creditors of the company the obligation of the directors is not excluded by the fact that they have acted pursuant to a shareholder resolution.
(4) The claims arising from the preceding provisions are subject to a limitation period of five years.

Vor dem MoMiG:

§ 64. Insolvenzantragspflicht; Haftung

(1) Wird die Gesellschaft zahlungsunfähig, so haben die Geschäftsführer ohne schuldhaftes Zögern, spätestens aber drei Wochen nach Eintritt der Zahlungsunfähigkeit, dic Eröffnung des Insolvenzverfahrens zu beantragen. Dies gilt sinngemäß, wenn sich eine Überschuldung der Gesellschaft ergibt.
(2) Die Geschäftsführer sind der Gesellschaft zum Ersatz von Zahlungen verpflichtet, die nach Eintritt der Zahlungsunfähigkeit der Gesellschaft oder nach Feststellung ihrer Überschuldung geleistet werden. Dies gilt nicht von Zahlungen, die auch nach diesem Zeitpunkt mit der Sorgfalt eines ordentlichen Geschäftsmanns vereinbar sind. Auf den Ersatzanspruch finden die Bestimmungen in § 43 Abs. 3 und 4 entsprechende Anwendung.

Before the MoMiG:

§ 64. Duty to file for insolvency; liability

(1) When the company becomes illiquid, the directors must request the opening of insolvency proceedings without culpable delay, but not later than

three weeks after the occurrence of the illiquidity. The same applies mutatis mutandis, when an over-indebtedness of the company emerges.
(2) The directors are liable to compensate the company for any payments made after the occurrence of the company's illiquidity or after the ascertainment of its over-indebtedness. This does not apply to payments that are compatible with the diligence of a prudent businessman even after this time. The provisions in § 43 (3) and (4) shall apply mutatis mutandis to the claim for compensation.

Nach dem MoMiG:

§ 64. Haftung für Zahlungen nach Zahlungsunfähigkeit oder Überschuldung

Die Geschäftsführer sind der Gesellschaft zum Ersatz von Zahlungen verpflichtet, die nach Eintritt der Zahlungsunfähigkeit der Gesellschaft oder nach Feststellung ihrer Überschuldung geleistet werden. Dies gilt nicht von Zahlungen, die auch nach diesem Zeitpunkt mit der Sorgfalt eines ordentlichen Geschäftsmanns vereinbar sind. Die gleiche Verpflichtung trifft die Geschäftsführer für Zahlungen an Gesellschafter, soweit diese zur Zahlungsunfähigkeit der Gesellschaft führen mussten, es sei denn, dies war auch bei Beachtung der in Satz 2 bezeichneten Sorgfalt nicht erkennbar. Auf den Ersatzanspruch finden die Bestimmungen in § 43 Abs. 3 und 4 entsprechende Anwendung.

After the MoMiG:

§ 64. Liability for payments after illiquidity or over-indebtedness

The directors are liable to compensate the company for any payments made after the occurrence of the company's illiquidity or after the ascertainment of its over-indebtedness. This does not apply to payments that are compatible with the diligence of a prudent businessman even after this time. The same liability is incurred by the directors in respect of payments to shareholders insofar as these payments could only lead to the company's illiquidity, unless this was unknowable even by adhering to the diligence specified in the second sentence. The provisions in § 43 (3) and (4) shall apply mutatis mutandis to the claim for compensation.

German Insolvency Act (Insolvenzordnung, InsO)

Translation by the author. Alternative translations: *Charles E. Stewart*, Insolvenzordnung – Insolvency Code: German–English Edition with an Introduction to the German Law (Frankfurt/Main: Fritz Knapp-Verlag,

1997); *Eberhard Braun* (ed.), Commentary on the German Insolvency Code (Düsseldorf: IDW-Verlag, 2006); *Frank Kebekus / Oliver Sabel / Ursula Schlegel*, Cross-Border Insolvencies: Germany (Cologne: RWS Verlag, 2007); online at www.iuscomp.org/gla/ (current as of 1 January 2004).

§ 15a. Antragspflicht bei juristischen Personen . . .

(1) Wird eine juristische Person zahlungsunfähig oder überschuldet, haben die Mitglieder des Vertretungsorgans . . . ohne schuldhaftes Zögern, spätestens aber drei Wochen nach Eintritt der Zahlungsunfähigkeit oder Überschuldung, einen Insolvenzantrag zu stellen. . . .
(2) – (4) . . .

§ 15a. Duty to file a request on behalf of legal persons . . .

(1) When a legal person becomes illiquid or over-indebted, the members of the representative organ . . . must request the opening of insolvency proceedings without culpable delay, but not later than three weeks after the occurrence of the illiquidity or the over-indebtedness. . . .
(2) – (4) . . .

§ 16. Eröffnungsgrund

Die Eröffnung des Insolvenzverfahrens setzt voraus, dass ein Eröffnungsgrund gegeben ist.

§ 16. Opening ground

The opening of insolvency proceedings presupposes an opening ground.

§ 17. Zahlungsunfähigkeit

(1) Allgemeiner Eröffnungsgrund ist die Zahlungsunfähigkeit.
(2) Der Schuldner ist zahlungsunfähig, wenn er nicht in der Lage ist, die fälligen Zahlungspflichten zu erfüllen. Zahlungsunfähigkeit ist in der Regel anzunehmen, wenn der Schuldner seine Zahlungen eingestellt hat.

§ 17. Illiquidity

(1) Illiquidity constitutes a general opening ground.
(2) The debtor is illiquid if he is not in a position to honour the payment obligations as they fall due. As a rule illiquidity is to be assumed if the debtor has ceased payment.

§ 19. Überschuldung

(1) Bei einer juristischen Person ist auch die Überschuldung Eröffnungsgrund.
(2) Überschuldung liegt vor, wenn das Vermögen des Schuldners die bestehenden Verbindlichkeiten nicht mehr deckt. Bei der Bewertung des Vermögens des Schuldners ist jedoch die Fortführung des Unternehmens zugrunde zu legen, wenn diese nach den Umständen überwiegend wahrscheinlich ist. . . .
(3) . . .

§ 19. Over-indebtedness

(1) With a legal person over-indebtedness also constitutes an opening ground.
(2) Over-indebtedness occurs if the debtor's assets no longer cover the existing debts. However, the valuation of the debtor's assets is to be based on the continuance of the business if this is predominantly likely in the circumstances. . . .[2]
(3) . . .

§ 129. Grundsatz

(1) Rechtshandlungen, die vor der Eröffnung des Insolvenzverfahrens vorgenommen worden sind und die Insolvenzgläubiger benachteiligen, kann der Insolvenzverwalter nach Maßgabe der §§ 130 bis 146 anfechten.
(2) Eine Unterlassung steht einer Rechtshandlung gleich.

§ 129. Principle

(1) Legal acts which have been committed prior to the opening of insolvency proceedings and are detrimental to the insolvency creditors[3] may be avoided by the insolvency administrator as provided in §§ 130 to 146.
(2) An omission is equal to a legal act.

[2] As part of the emergency legislation adopted in response to the crisis on the financial markets (Finanzmarktstabilisierungsgesetz vom 17. Oktober 2008, BGBl. 2008, Part I, p. 1982), § 19 (2) InsO has been temporarily amended. The provision, as it is in force between 18 October 2008 and 31 December 2010, reads: 'Überschuldung liegt vor, wenn das Vermögen des Schuldners die bestehenden Verbindlichkeiten nicht mehr deckt, es sei denn, die Fortführung des Unternehmens ist nach den Umständen überwiegend wahrscheinlich.' (Over-indebtedness occurs if the debtor's assets no longer cover the existing debts unless the continuance of the business is predominantly likely in the circumstances.)

[3] Defined in § 38 InsO as the personal creditors who have a pecuniary claim against the debtor existing at the time when insolvency proceedings are opened.

§ 130. Kongruente Deckung

(1) Anfechtbar ist eine Rechtshandlung, die einem Insolvenzgläubiger eine Sicherung oder Befriedigung gewährt oder ermöglicht hat,

1. wenn sie in den letzten drei Monaten vor dem Antrag auf Eröffnung des Insolvenzverfahrens vorgenommen worden ist, wenn zur Zeit der Handlung der Schuldner zahlungsunfähig war und wenn der Gläubiger zu dieser Zeit die Zahlungsunfähigkeit kannte oder
2. wenn sie nach dem Eröffnungsantrag vorgenommen worden ist und wenn der Gläubiger zur Zeit der Handlung die Zahlungsunfähigkeit oder den Eröffnungsantrag kannte.

. . .

(2) Der Kenntnis der Zahlungsunfähigkeit oder des Eröffnungsantrags steht die Kenntnis von Umständen gleich, die zwingend auf die Zahlungsunfähigkeit oder den Eröffnungsantrag schließen lassen.
(3) Gegenüber einer Person, die dem Schuldner zur Zeit der Handlung nahestand (§ 138), wird vermutet, daß sie die Zahlungsunfähigkeit oder den Eröffnungsantrag kannte.

§ 130. Congruent cover

(1) Voidability attaches to a legal act which has accorded to, or made possible for, an insolvency creditor any security or satisfaction,

1. if the act has been committed in the last three months prior to the request for opening insolvency proceedings, provided that, at the time of the act, the debtor was illiquid and the creditor knew of the illiquidity at this time, or
2. if the act has been committed after the opening request and, at the time of the act, the creditor knew of the illiquidity or of the opening request.

. . .

(2) Equated to knowledge of the illiquidity or of the opening request is knowledge of circumstances which compellingly bespeak the existence of the illiquidity or of the opening request.
(3) As against a person who, at the time of the act, was connected with the debtor (§ 138), it shall be presumed that the person knew of the illiquidity or the opening request.

§ 131. Inkongruente Deckung

(1) Anfechtbar ist eine Rechtshandlung, die einem Insolvenzgläubiger eine Sicherung oder Befriedigung gewährt oder ermöglicht hat, die er nicht oder nicht in der Art oder nicht zu der Zeit zu beanspruchen hatte,

1. wenn die Handlung im letzten Monat vor dem Antrag auf Eröffnung des Insolvenzverfahrens oder nach diesem Antrag vorgenommen worden ist,
2. wenn die Handlung innerhalb des zweiten oder dritten Monats vor dem Eröffnungsantrag vorgenommen worden ist und der Schuldner zur Zeit der Handlung zahlungsunfähig war oder
3. wenn die Handlung innerhalb des zweiten oder dritten Monats vor dem Eröffnungsantrag vorgenommen worden ist und dem Gläubiger zur Zeit der Handlung bekannt war, daß sie die Insolvenzgläubiger benachteiligte.

(2) Für die Anwendung des Absatzes 1 Nr. 3 steht der Kenntnis der Benachteiligung der Insolvenzgläubiger die Kenntnis von Umständen gleich, die zwingend auf die Benachteiligung schließen lassen. Gegenüber einer Person, die dem Schuldner zur Zeit der Handlung nahestand (§ 138), wird vermutet, daß sie die Benachteiligung der Insolvenzgläubiger kannte.

§ 131. Incongruent cover

(1) Voidability attaches to a legal act which has accorded to, or made possible for, an insolvency creditor any security or satisfaction to which he was not entitled or not entitled in the manner or at the time,

1. if the act has been committed in the last month prior to the request for opening insolvency proceedings or after that request,
2. if the act has been committed within the second or third month prior to the request for opening insolvency proceedings and, at the time of the act, the debtor was illiquid, or
3. if the act has been committed within the second or third month prior to the request for opening insolvency proceedings and, at the time of the act, the creditor knew that the act was detrimental to the insolvency creditors.

(2) For the application of sub-paragraph 1 n. 3 it is to be equated to knowledge of the detriment to the insolvency creditors where there is knowledge of circumstances which compellingly bespeak such a detriment. As against a person who, at the time of the act, was connected with the debtor (§ 138), it shall be presumed that the person knew of the detriment to the insolvency creditors.

§ 132. Unmittelbar nachteilige Rechtshandlungen

(1) Anfechtbar ist ein Rechtsgeschäft des Schuldners, das die Insolvenzgläubiger unmittelbar benachteiligt,

1. wenn es in den letzten drei Monaten vor dem Antrag auf Eröffnung des Insolvenzverfahrens vorgenommen worden ist, wenn zur Zeit des

Rechtsgeschäfts der Schuldner zahlungsunfähig war und wenn der andere Teil zu dieser Zeit die Zahlungsunfähigkeit kannte oder
2. wenn es nach dem Eröffnungsantrag vorgenommen worden ist und wenn der andere Teil zur Zeit des Rechtsgeschäfts die Zahlungsunfähigkeit oder den Eröffnungsantrag kannte.

(2) Einem Rechtsgeschäft, das die Insolvenzgläubiger unmittelbar benachteiligt, steht eine andere Rechtshandlung des Schuldners gleich, durch die der Schuldner ein Recht verliert oder nicht mehr geltend machen kann oder durch die ein vermögensrechtlicher Anspruch gegen ihn erhalten oder durchsetzbar ist.
(3) § 130 Abs. 2 und 3 gilt entsprechend.

§ 132. Directly detrimental legal acts

(1) Voidability attaches to a debtor's legal transaction which is directly detrimental to the insolvency creditors,

1. if it has been entered into in the last three months prior to the request for opening insolvency proceedings, provided that, at the time of the transaction, the debtor was illiquid and the other party knew of the illiquidity at this time, or
2. if it has been entered into after the opening request and, at the time of the transaction, the other party knew of the illiquidity or of the opening request.

(2) Equated to a legal transaction, which is directly detrimental to the insolvency creditors, is any another legal act of the debtor whereby the debtor loses a right, or can no longer enforce it, or whereby a pecuniary claim against him is upheld or enforceable.
(3) § 130 (2) and (3) shall apply mutatis mutandis.

§ 133. Vorsätzliche Benachteiligung

(1) Anfechtbar ist eine Rechtshandlung, die der Schuldner in den letzten zehn Jahren vor dem Antrag auf Eröffnung des Insolvenzverfahrens oder nach diesem Antrag mit dem Vorsatz, seine Gläubiger zu benachteiligen, vorgenommen hat, wenn der andere Teil zur Zeit der Handlung den Vorsatz des Schuldners kannte. Diese Kenntnis wird vermutet, wenn der andere Teil wußte, daß die Zahlungsunfähigkeit des Schuldners drohte und daß die Handlung die Gläubiger benachteiligte.
(2) Anfechtbar ist ein vom Schuldner mit einer nahestehenden Person (§ 138) geschlossener entgeltlicher Vertrag, durch den die Insolvenzgläubiger

unmittelbar benachteiligt werden. Die Anfechtung ist ausgeschlossen, wenn der Vertrag früher als zwei Jahre vor dem Eröffnungsantrag geschlossen worden ist oder wenn dem anderen Teil zur Zeit des Vertragsschlusses ein Vorsatz des Schuldners, die Gläubiger zu benachteiligen, nicht bekannt war.

§ 133. Intentional prejudice

(1) Voidability attaches to a legal act which the debtor has committed in the last ten years prior to the request for opening insolvency proceedings or after this request with intent to prejudice its creditors if the other party knew of this intent at the time of the act. This knowledge is presumed if the other party knew that the debtor's illiquidity was threatening and that the act was detrimental to the creditors.
(2) Voidability attaches to a contract for consideration concluded by the debtor with a connected person (§ 138) through which the insolvency creditors suffer a direct detriment. The avoidance is precluded if the contract was concluded more than two years prior to the opening request, or if, at the time of concluding the contract, the other party did not know of the debtor's intent to prejudice the creditors.

§ 134. Unentgeltliche Leistung

(1) Anfechtbar ist eine unentgeltliche Leistung des Schuldners, es sei denn, sie ist früher als vier Jahre vor dem Antrag auf Eröffnung des Insolvenzverfahrens vorgenommen worden.
(2) Richtet sich die Leistung auf ein gebräuchliches Gelegenheitsgeschenk geringen Werts, so ist sie nicht anfechtbar.

§ 134. Transfer without consideration

(1) Voidability attaches to a transfer by the debtor without consideration, unless it has been effected more than four years prior to the request for opening insolvency proceedings.
(2) The transfer is not voidable if it concerns a usual conventional gift of little value.

EDITORIAL NOTE ON GERMAN SOURCES

1. Statutes: The symbol § (denoting '*Paragraph*') is the equivalent of a section in an English statute. A sub-paragraph (*Absatz*) will be indicated by brackets. In some cases, a sub-paragraph is further divided and this will be indicated by 'n.' for 'number' (*Nummer*).

> Example: '§ 131 (1) n. 1 InsO' should be read as: 'paragraph 131 sub-paragraph 1 number 1 of the German Insolvenzordnung'.

A full list of abbreviations of statutes can be found in the Table of abbreviations.

2. Cases: Cases in Germany do not normally have case names. They are instead cited by giving the court, the date of the decision, the court file number (optional), and one or several case reports. Law journals in Germany also function as case reports. Where, exceptionally, a case is known by a name, that name will be added in brackets.

In the footnotes of this book, German cases are cited by reference to the official case reports 'BGHZ' (where applicable) and to the '*Neue Juristische Wochenschrift*' (NJW, perhaps the most widely read law journal in Germany). References to the '*Zeitschrift für Wirtschaftsrecht*' (ZIP) or any other law journal are only given if a case has been reported neither in BGHZ nor in NJW. Further references are given in the table of cases.

> Example: BGH 6.6.1994, BGHZ 126, 181 = NJW 1994, 2220. In the case of BGHZ the first number indicates the volume, whereas in the case of NJW or all other law journals the first number indicates the year. The second number always indicates the page.

3. Commentaries: In Germany, commentaries are a very important form of legal literature and are frequently cited by judges and academic writers. In a commentary, a statute is analysed section by section (i.e. paragraph by paragraph in the German terminology). Due to the frequency of citation a highly abbreviated notation has developed. A commentary is not normally cited by reference to a page, but to the relevant section (paragraph), and within it by using marginal numbers.

Example: *Karsten Schmidt* in *Scholz*, GmbHG[9] § 64 mn. 13 – meaning: *Karsten Schmidt* writing in the ninth edition of the commentary on the GmbH-Gesetz which is known under the name of its (first) editor (*Franz Scholz*), in a passage to be found at paragraph 64 marginal number 13.

The following is a list of German commentaries cited in this book with their respective styles of citation:

Bibliographical data	*Style of citation*
Baumbach, Adolf (†) / Hueck, Afred (†); GmbH-Gesetz (Munich: Beck, 18th edn 2006)	[*Author*] in *Baumbach / Hueck*, GmbHG[18]
Braun, Eberhard (ed.); Insolvenzordnung (InsO) – Kommentar (Munich: Beck, 3rd edn 2007)	[*Author*] in *Braun*, InsO[3]
Braun, Eberhard (ed.); Commentary on the German Insolvency Code (Düsseldorf: IDW-Verlag, 2006)	[*Author*] in *Braun*, German Insolvency Code
Hachenburg, Max (†); Gesetz betreffend die Gesellschaften mit beschränkter Haftung (GmbHG) – Großkommentar (Berlin: De Gruyter, 6th edn 1956/1959, 7th edn 1975/1979, 8th edn 1992/1997)	[*Author*] in *Hachenburg*, GmbHG[edn]
Lutter, Marcus / Hommelhoff, Peter et al.; GmbH-Gesetz Kommentar (Köln: Otto Schmidt, 16th edn 2004)	[*Author*] in *Lutter / Hommelhoff*, GmbHG[16]
Michalski, Lutz (ed.); Kommentar zum Gesetz betreffend die Gesellschaften mit beschränkter Haftung (GmbHG) (Munich: Beck, 2002)	[*Author*] in *Michalski*, GmbHG
Münchener Kommentar zum Bürgerlichen Gesetzbuch (Munich: Beck, 5th edn 2006 ff.)	[*Author*] in Münchener Kommentar BGB[5]
Münchener Kommentar zur Insolvenzordnung (Munich: Beck, 2nd edn 2007 ff.)	[*Author*] in Münchener Kommentar InsO[2]
Roth, Günter H. / Altmeppen, Holger; Gesetz betreffend die Gesellschaften mit beschränkter Haftung (GmbHG) – Kommentar (Munich: Beck, 5th edn 2005)	[*Author*] in *Roth / Altmeppen*, GmbHG[5]
Rowedder, Heinz et al.; Gesetz betreffend die Gesellschaften mit beschränkter Haftung (GmbHG) – Kommentar (Munich: Vahlen, 3rd edn 1997)	[*Author*] in *Rowedder*, GmbHG[3]

(*cont.*)

Bibliographical data	*Style of citation*
Rowedder, Heinz / Schmidt-Leithoff, Christian (eds.); Gesetz betreffend die Gesellschaften mit beschränkter Haftung (GmbHG) – Kommentar (Munich: Vahlen, 4th edn 2002)	[*Author*] in *Rowedder / Schmidt-Leithoff*, GmbHG^{4}
Scholz, Franz (†); Kommentar zum GmbH-Gesetz (Cologne: Otto Schmidt, 6th edn 1978/1983, 7th edn 1986/1988, 8th edn 1993/1995, 9th edn 2000/2002, 10th edn 2006 ff.)	[*Author*] in *Scholz*, GmbHG$^{[edn]}$
Uhlenbruck, Wilhelm (ed.); Insolvenzordnung – Kommentar (Munich: Vahlen, 12th edn 2003)	[*Author*] in *Uhlenbruck*, InsO^{12}
Ulmer, Peter / Habersack, Matthias / Winter, Martin (eds.); Gesetz betreffend die Gesellschaften mit beschränkter Haftung (GmbHG) – Großkommentar (Tübingen: Mohr Siebeck, 2005 ff.)	[Author] in *Ulmer / Habersack / Winter*, GmbHG

BIBLIOGRAPHY

Anon., Editorial: Chargeholders floating, but liquidators sinking (2004) 20 IL&P 45–46

Abeltshauser, Thomas, Leitungshaftung im Kapitalgesellschaftsrecht – Zu den Sorgfalts- und Loyalitätspflichten von Unternehmensleitern im deutschen und im US-amerikanischen Kapitalgesellschaftsrecht (Cologne: Heymanns, 1998)

Allen, William T., The Corporate Director's Fiduciary Duty of Care and the Business Judgment Rule Under U.S. Corporate Law, in: Klaus J. Hopt / Hideki Kanda / Mark J. Roe / Eddy Wymeersch / Stefan Prigge (eds.), Comparative Corporate Governance – The State of the Art and Emerging Research (Oxford: OUP, 1998) 307–331

Altmeppen, Holger, Haftung der Geschäftsleiter einer Kapitalgesellschaft für die Verletzung von Verkehrssicherungspflichten, ZIP 1995, 881–891

'Dritte' als Adressaten der Kapitalerhaltungs- und Kapitalersatzregeln in der GmbH, in: Karl-Heinz Forster et al. (eds.), Festschrift für Bruno Kropff (Düsseldorf: IDW-Verlag, 1997) 641–667

Probleme der Konkursverschleppungshaftung, ZIP 1997, 1173–1185

Schutz vor 'europäischen' Kapitalgesellschaften, NJW 2004, 97–104

Armour, John, Share Capital and Creditor Protection: Efficient Rules for a Modern Company Law (2000) 63 MLR 355–378

Transactions at an Undervalue (Chapter 2), in: John Armour / Howard Bennett (eds.), Vulnerable Transactions in Corporate Insolvency (Oxford: Hart, 2003) 37–93

Transactions Defrauding Creditors (Chapter 3), in: John Armour / Howard Bennett (eds.), Vulnerable Transactions in Corporate Insolvency (Oxford: Hart, 2003) 95–121

Avoidance of Transactions as a 'Fraud on Creditors' at Common Law (Chapter 7), in: John Armour / Howard Bennett (eds.), Vulnerable Transactions in Corporate Insolvency (Oxford: Hart, 2003) 281–329

Who Should Make Corporate Law? EU Legislation versus Regulatory Competition (2005) 58 Current Legal Problems 369–413

Legal Capital: An Outdated Concept? [2006] EBOR 5–27, reprinted in: Horst Eidenmüller / Wolfgang Schön (eds.), The Law and Economics of Creditor

Protection – A Transatlantic Perspective (The Hague: T.M.C. Asser Press, 2008) 3–25

Armour, John / Bennett, Howard (eds.), Vulnerable Transactions in Corporate Insolvency (Oxford: Hart, 2003)

Armour, John / Walters, Adrian, Funding Liquidation: A Functional View (2006) 122 LQR 295–326

Assmann, Heinz-Dieter, The Impact of Insider Trading Rules on Company Law, in: Klaus Hopt / Eddy Wymeersch (eds.), Capital Markets and Company Law (Oxford: OUP, 2003) 529–547

Bachner, Thomas, Freedom of Establishment for Companies: A Great Leap Forward [2003] CLJ 47–50

Wrongful Trading before the English High Court: *Re Continental Assurance Company of London plc (Singer v. Beckett)* [2004] EBOR 195–200

Wrongful Trading – A New European Model for Creditor Protection? [2004] EBOR 293–319

The Battle over Jurisdiction in European Insolvency Law [2006] ECFR 310–329

Creditor protection through insolvency law in England, in: Marcus Lutter (ed.), Legal Capital in Europe (Berlin: De Gruyter, 2006) 427–479 = Gläubigerschutz durch Insolvenzrecht in England, in: Marcus Lutter (ed.), Das Kapital der Aktiengesellschaft in Europa (Berlin: De Gruyter, 2006) 526–574

Die Limited in der Insolvenz (Vienna: LexisNexis ARD Orac, 2007)

Baird, Douglas G., Legal Approaches to Restricting Distributions to Shareholders: The Role of Fraudulent Transfer Law, [2006] EBOR 199–215, reprinted in: Horst Eidenmüller / Wolfgang Schön (eds.), The Law and Economics of Creditor Protection – A Transatlantic Perspective (The Hague: T.M.C. Asser Press, 2008) 199–215

Barkehall-Thomas, Susan, 'Goodbye' Knowing Receipt. 'Hello' Unconscientious Receipt, (2001) 21 OJLS 239–265

Baur, Fritz / Stürner, Rolf, Zwangsvollstreckungs-, Konkurs- und Vergleichsrecht (Heidelberg: Müller, 12th edn 1990)

Bayer, Walter, Moderner Kapitalschutz, ZGR 2007, 220–240

Bebchuk, Lucian A., Federalism and the Corporation: The Desirable Limits on State Competition in Corporate Law, 105 Harvard Law Review 1435–1510 (1992)

Becht, Marco / Mayer, Colin / Wagner, Hannes F., Where Do Firms Incorporate?, ECGI-Working Paper No. 70/2006 (revised August 2007), available at http://papers.ssrn.com/sol3/papers.cfm?abstract_id=906066

Behrens, Peter, Niederlassungsfreiheit und Internationales Gesellschaftsrecht, RabelsZ 52 (1988) 498–525

Sind Gesellschaften Niederlassungsberechtigte minderen Rechts?, EuZW 1991, 97

Behrens, Peter (ed.), Die Gesellschaft mit beschränkter Haftung im internationalen und europäischen Recht (Berlin: De Gruyter, 2nd edn 1997)

Beissenhirtz, Volker, Die Insolvenzanfechtung in Deutschland und England – Eine rechtsvergleichende Betrachtung (Frankfurt/Main: Peter Lang, 2003)

Bennion, Francis, Statutory Interpretation (London: LexisNexis Butterworths, 5th edn 2008)

Bicker, Eike Th., Gläubigerschutz in der grenzüberschreitenden Konzerngesellschaft – Eine international-privatrechtliche Untersuchung am Beispiel der abhängigen englischen Kapitalgesellschaft mit Verwaltungssitz in Deutschland (Berlin: Duncker & Humblot, 2007)

Biehl, Kristof, Insider im Insolvenzverfahren (Berlin: Verlag für die Rechts- und Anwaltspraxis, 2000)

Birks, Peter, Trusts in the Recovery of Misapplied Assets: Tracing, Trusts, and Restitution, in: Ewan McKendrick (ed.), Commercial Aspects of Trusts and Fiduciary Duties (Oxford: Clarendon, 1992) 149–166

What are Law Schools For? (Oxford: OUP, 1996)

Bloß, Henning, Die Unternehmensgruppe im englischen und deutschen Recht der Kapitalgesellschaften (Frankfurt/Main: Peter Lang, 1999)

Böckmann, Tobias, Gläubigerschutz bei GmbH und close corporation (Cologne: Heymanns, 2005)

Bödecker, Carsten, Die Kapitalerhaltung im englischen Gesellschaftsrecht (Frankfurt/Main: Peter Lang, 1994)

Bork, Reinhard, Haftung des GmbH-Geschäftsführers wegen verspäteten Konkursantrags – Besprechung der Entscheidung BGHZ 126, 181, ZGR 1995, 505–528

Einführung in das neue Insolvenzrecht (Tübingen: Mohr Siebeck, 4th edn 2005)

Bork, Reinhard (ed.), Handbuch des Insolvenzanfechtungsrechts (Cologne: RWS-Verlag, 2006)

Kapitel 1: Grundgedanke, Geschichte, Bedeutung, in: Reinhard Bork (ed.), Handbuch des Insolvenzanfechtungsrechts (Cologne: RWS-Verlag, 2006) 1–20

Kapitel 5: Vorsätzliche Gläubigerbenachteiligung (§ 133 InsO), in: Reinhard Bork (ed.), Handbuch des Insolvenzanfechtungsrechts (Cologne: RWS-Verlag, 2006) 99–129

Kapitel 6: Unentgeltliche Leistung (§ 134 InsO), in: Reinhard Bork (ed.), Handbuch des Insolvenzanfechtungsrechts (Cologne: RWS Verlag, 2006) 131–174

Böttcher, Oliver, Gesellschafter- und Gläubigerschutz beim Formwechsel aus der Personen- in die Kapitalgesellschaft (Baden-Baden: Nomos, 2006)

Birds, John et al. (eds.), Boyle & Birds' Company Law (Bristol: Jordans, 5th edn 2004)

Brandner, Hans Erich, Wegfall oder Beständigkeit des Erstattungsanspruchs aus § 31 GmbHG bei anderweitiger Wiederherstellung des Stammkapitals?, in: Reinhard Goerdeler et al. (eds.), Festschrift für Hans-Joachim Fleck zum 70. Geburtstag (Berlin: De Gruyter, 1988) 23–34

Bridge, Michael, Collectivity, Management of Estates and the *Pari Passu* Rule in Winding-up (Chapter 1), in: John Armour / Howard Bennett (eds.), Vulnerable Transactions in Corporate Insolvency (Oxford: Hart, 2003) 1–36

Brougham, Chris, Limitation periods and section 423 explained: MC Bacon questioned [2006] Insolvency Intelligence 135–137

Brüggemeier, Gert, Organisationshaftung – Deliktsrechtliche Aspekte innerorganisatorischer Funktionsdifferenzierung, AcP 191 (1991) 33–68

Buchmann, Thomas, Die Insolvenz der englischen Limited in Deutschland – De lege lata sowie im Gefüge der Modernisierung des europäischen Gesellschaftsrechts (Baden-Baden: Nomos, 2007)

Burrows, Andrew, Understanding the Law of Obligations – Essays on Contract, Tort and Restitution (Oxford: Hart, 1998)

Bydlinski, Franz, System und Prinzipien des Privatrechts (Wien: Springer, 1996)

Cahn, Andreas, Kapitalerhaltung im Konzern (Cologne: Heymann, 1998)

Calnan, Richard J., Corporate Gifts and Creditors' Rights (1990) 11 CoLaw 91–96

Canaris, Claus-Wilhelm, Die Rückgewähr von Gesellschaftereinlagen durch Zuwendungen an Dritte, in: Marcus Lutter et al. (eds.), Festschrift für Robert Fischer (Berlin: De Gruyter, 1979) 31–64

Die Haftung für fahrlässige Verletzungen der Konkursantragspflicht nach § 64 GmbHG, JZ 1993, 649–652

Cary, William, Federalism and Corporate Law: Reflections Upon Delaware, 83 Yale Law Journal 663–705 (1974)

Cheffins, Brian, Company Law – Theory Structure and Operation (Oxford: Clarendon Press, 1997)

Clark, Robert C., Corporate Law (New York: Aspen Publishers, 1986)

Coing, Helmut, Europäisierung der Rechtswissenschaft, NJW 1990, 937–941

Curti, Arthur, Die Englische Aktien-Gesellschaft nach neuem Recht – Systematische Darstellung und Gesetz vom 10. Mai 1929 (Berlin: Springer, 1929)

Davies, Paul, Legal Capital in Private Companies in Great Britain, AG 1998, 346–354

Board Structure in the UK and Germany – Convergence or Continuing Divergence? (2000) 2 ICCLJ 435–456

Introduction to Company Law (Oxford: OUP, 2002)

Gower and Davies' Principles of Modern Company Law (London: Sweet & Maxwell, 7th edn 2003, 8th edn 2008)

Directors' Creditor-Regarding Duties in Respect of Trading Decisions Taken in the Vicinity of Insolvency [2006] EBOR 301–337, reprinted in: Horst Eidenmüller / Wolfgang Schön (eds.), The Law and Economics of Creditor Protection – A Transatlantic Perspective (The Hague: T.M.C. Asser Press, 2008) 303–339

Deakin, Simon, Regulatory Competition versus Harmonization in European Company Law, in: Daniel C. Esty / Damien Geradin (eds.), Regulatory Competition and Economic Integration – Comparative Perspectives (Oxford: OUP, 2001) 190–217

Deakin, Simon / Johnston, Angus / Markesinis, Basil, Markesinis and Deakin's Tort Law (Oxford: OUP, 6th edn 2007)

Degeling, Simone, Restitution for Vulnerable Transactions (Chapter 9), in: John Armour / Howard Bennett (eds.), Vulnerable Transactions in Corporate Insolvency (Oxford: Hart, 2003) 385–426

Dicey, Morris & Collins on The Conflict of Laws (ed. Lawrence Collins) (London: Sweet & Maxwell, 14th edn 2006)

Di Marco, Giuseppe, Der Vorschlag der Kommission für eine 14. Richtlinie, ZGR 1999, 3–12

Donald, David C., Shareholder Voice and its Opponents [2005] JCLS 305–361

Doran, Nigel, Transactions at an Undervalue and the Maintenance of Capital Principle (1991) 12 CoLaw 169–175

Drenckhan, Helke, Gläubigerschutz in der Krise der GmbH (Baden-Baden: Nomos, 2005)

Drury, Robert, A European Look at the American Experience of the Delaware Syndrome [2005] JCLS 1–35

Drury, Robert R. / Xuereb, Peter G. (eds.), European Company Laws: A Comparative Approach (Aldershot: Dartmouth, 1991)

Drygala, Tim, Directors Liability in the Member States of the European Union, in: Marcus Lutter (ed.), Legal Capital in Europe (Berlin: De Gruyter, 2006) 232–253 = Haftung der Geschäftsleiter in den Mitgliedstaaten der Europäischen Union, in: Marcus Lutter (ed.), Das Kapital der Aktiengesellschaft in Europa (Berlin: De Gruyter, 2006) 277–300

Drygala, Tim / Kremer, Thomas, Alles neu macht der Mai – Zur Neuregelung der Kapitalerhaltungsvorschriften im MoMiG, ZIP 2007, 1289–1296

Easterbrook, Frank H. / Fischel, Daniel R., The Corporate Contract, 89 Columbia Law Review 1416–1448 (1989)

Ebert, Sabine / Levedag, Christian, England, in: Rembert Süß / Thomas Wachter (eds.), Handbuch des internationalen GmbH-Rechts (Angelbachtal: Zerb, 2006) 573–728

Ebke, Werner F., *Centros* – Some Realities and Some Mysteries, 48 American Journal of Comparative Law 623–660 (2000)

Edwards, Vanessa, EC Company Law (Oxford: Clarendon Press, 1999)

Ehricke, Ulrich, Das abhängige Konzernunternehmen in der Insolvenz – Wege zur Vergrößerung der Haftungsmasse abhängiger Konzernunternehmen im Konkurs und Verfahrensfragen. Eine rechtsvergleichende Analyse (Tübingen: Mohr Siebeck, 1998)

Kapitel 3: Rechtshandlung, in: Reinhard Bork (ed.), Handbuch des Insolvenzanfechtungsrechts (Cologne: RWS-Verlag, 2006) 51–77

Kapitel 4: Gläubigerbenachteiligung, in: Reinhard Bork (ed.), Handbuch des Insolvenzanfechtungsrechts (Cologne: RWS-Verlag, 2006) 79–98

Eidenmüller, Horst, Wettbewerb der Gesellschaftsrechte in Europa, ZIP 2002, 2233–2245

Free Choice in International Company Insolvency Law in Europe [2005] EBOR 423–447

Eidenmüller, Horst, Die GmbH im Wettbewerb der Rechtsformen, ZGR 2007, 168–211

Eidenmüller, Horst (ed.), Ausländische Kapitalgesellschaften im deutschen Recht (Munich: Beck, 2004)

Eidenmüller, Horst / Grunewald, Barbara / Noack, Ulrich, Minimum Capital in the System of Legal Capital, in: Marcus Lutter (ed.), Legal Capital in Europe (Berlin: De Gruyter, 2006) 17–41 = Das Mindestkapital im System des festen Kapitals, in: Marcus Lutter (ed.), Das Kapital der Aktiengesellschaft in Europa (Berlin: De Gruyter, 2006) 17–41

Eisenberg, Melvin A., The Duty of Good Faith in American Corporate Law [2006] ECFR 1–44

Enriques, Luca / Gelter, Martin, Regulatory Competition in European Company Law and Creditor Protection [2006] EBOR 417–453, reprinted in: Horst Eidenmüller / Wolfgang Schön (eds.), The Law and Economics of Creditor Protection – A Transatlantic Perspective (The Hague: T.M.C. Asser Press, 2008) 421–457

Enriques, Luca / Macey, Jonathan R., Creditors Versus Capital Formation: The Case Against the European Legal Capital Rules, 86 Cornell Law Review 1165–1204 (2001)

Esty, Daniel C. / Geradin, Damien (eds.), Regulatory Competition and Economic Integration – Comparative Perspectives (Oxford: OUP, 2001)

Farrar, John H. / Hannigan, Brenda M., Farrar's Company Law (London: Butterworths, 4th edn 1998)

Ferran, Eilís, Company Law and Corporate Finance (Oxford: OUP, 1999)

The Place for Creditor Protection on the Agenda for Modernisation of Company Law in the European Union [2006] ECFR 178–221

Principles of Corporate Finance Law (Oxford: OUP, 2008)

Finch, Vanessa, Directors' duties towards creditors (1989) 10 CoLaw 23–25

Company Directors: Who Cares about Skill and Care? (1992) 55 MLR 179–214

Corporate Insolvency Law – Perspectives and Principles (Cambridge: CUP, 2002)

Fischer, Michael, Die Verlagerung des Gläubigerschutzes vom Gesellschafts- in das Insolvenzrecht nach 'Inspire Art', ZIP 2004, 1477–1486

Flannigan, Robert, Fiduciary Duties of Shareholders and Directors [2004] JBL 277–302

The Adulteration of Fiduciary Doctrine in Corporate Law (2006) 122 LQR 449–468

Fleck, Hans-Joachim, book review on Tries, Verdeckte Gewinnausschüttungen im GmbH-Recht, ZHR 156 (1992) 81–85

Der Grundsatz der Kapitalerhaltung – seine Ausweitung und seine Grenzen, in: Marcus Lutter et al. (eds.), Festschrift 100 Jahre GmbH-Gesetz (Cologne: Otto Schmidt, 1992) 391–419

Fleischer, Holger, Neue Entwicklungen im englischen Konzernrecht, AG 1999, 350–362

Deliktische Geschäftsführerhaftung gegenüber außenstehenden Dritten im englischen Gesellschaftsrecht – Vergleichende Betrachtungen zu einer aktuellen Grundsatzentscheidung des House of Lords, ZGR 2000, 152–165

Gläubigerschutz in der kleinen Kapitalgesellschaft: Deutsche GmbH versus englische private limited company, DStR 2000, 1015–1021

Zur organschaftlichen Treuepflicht der Geschäftsleiter im Aktien- und GmbH-Recht, WM 2003, 1045–1058

Erweiterte Außenhaftung der Organmitglieder im Europäischen Gesellschafts- und Kapitalmarktrecht – Insolvenzverschleppung, fehlerhafte Kapitalmarktinformation, Tätigkeitsverbote, ZGR 2004, 437–479

The Responsibility of the Management and Its Enforcement, in: Guido Ferrarini / Klaus J. Hopt / Jaap Winter / Eddy Wymeersch (eds.), Reforming Company and Takeover Law in Europe (Oxford: OUP, 2004) 373–416

Legal Transplants in European Company Law – The Case of Fiduciary Duties [2005] ECFR 378–397

Disguised Distributions and Capital Maintenance in European Company Law, in: Marcus Lutter (ed.), Legal Capital in Europe (Berlin: De Gruyter, 2006) 94–111 = Verdeckte Gewinnausschüttung und Kapitalschutz im Europäischen Gesellschaftsrecht, in: Marcus Lutter (ed.), Das Kapital der Aktiengesellschaft in Europa (Berlin: De Gruyter, 2006) 114–133

Fletcher, Ian F., 'Voidable preference' judicially explained [1991] JBL 71–74

Voidable Transactions in Bankruptcy, in: Jacob S. Ziegel (ed.), Current Developments in International and Corporate Insolvency Law (Oxford: Clarendon Press, 1992) 297–376

Florian, Matthias, Das englische internationale Insolvenzrecht (Heidelberg: Verlag Recht und Wirtschaft, 1989)

Flume, Werner, Der Gesellschafter und das Vermögen der Kapitalgesellschaft und die Problematik der verdeckten Gewinnausschüttung, ZHR 144 (1980) 18–33

Die Haftung des GmbH-Geschäftsführers bei Geschäften nach Konkursreife der GmbH, ZIP 1994, 337–342

Forsthoff, Ulrich / Schulz, Martin, Gläubigerschutz bei EU-Auslandsgesellschaften, in: Heribert Hirte / Thomas Bücker (eds.), Grenzüberschreitende Gesellschaften – Praxishandbuch für ausländische Kapitalgesellschaften mit Sitz im Inland (Cologne: Heymanns, 2nd edn 2006) 518–559

Forum Europaeum Corporate Group Law, Corporate Group Law for Europe, [2000] EBOR 165–264

Forum Europaeum Konzernrecht, Konzernrecht für Europa, ZGR 1998, 672–772

Franken, Lars, Gläubigerschutz durch Rechnungslegung nach US-GAAP – Eine ökonomische Analyse (Frankfurt/Main: Peter Lang, 2001)

Gelter, Martin, The Structure of Regulatory Competition in European Corporate Law [2005] JCLS 247–284

Geßler, Ernst, Zur handelsrechtlichen verdeckten Gewinnausschüttung, in: Marcus Lutter et al. (eds.), Festschrift für Robert Fischer (Berlin: De Gruyter, 1979) 131–148

Gilles, Peter / Baumgart, Michael, Schadensersatzpflicht des GmbH-Geschäftsführers nach § 823 II BGB i.V. mit § 64 I GmbHG (Schutzbereichsproblematik), JuS 1974, 226–229

Gloger, Christian, Haftungsbeschränkung versus Gläubigerschutz in der GmbH – Rechtsvergleichende Studie zum deutschen und brasilianischen Recht (Cologne: Heymanns, 2007)

Goette, Wulf, Leitung, Aufsicht, Haftung – zur Rolle der Rechtsprechung bei der Sicherung einer modernen Unternehmensführung, in: Karlmann Geiß / Kay Nehm / Hans Erich Brandner / Horst Hagen (eds.), Festschrift aus Anlaß des fünzigjährigen Bestehens von Bundesgerichtshof, Bundesanwaltschaft und Rechtsanwaltschaft beim Bundesgerichtshof (Cologne: Heymanns, 2000) 123–142

Goode, Roy M., The Secured Creditor and Insolvency Under English Law, RabelsZ 44 (1980) 674–712

Principles of Corporate Insolvency Law (London: Sweet & Maxwell, 3rd edn 2005)

Grantham, Ross, The Judicial Extension of Directors' Duties to Creditors [1991] JBL 1–18

Graziadei, Michele, The functionalist heritage, in: Pierre Legrand / Roderick Munday (eds.), Comparative Legal Studies: Traditions and Transitions (Cambridge: CUP, 2003) 100–127

Griffin, Stephen, Personal Liability and Disqualification of Company Directors (Oxford: Hart, 1999)

Grunewald, Barbara, Die Haftung von Organmitgliedern nach Deliktsrecht, ZHR 157 (1993) 451–463

Grunsky, Wolfgang, Grundzüge des Zwangsvollstreckungs- und Insolvenzrechts (Tübingen: Mohr Siebeck, 5th edn 1996)

Haas, Ulrich, Geschäftsführerhaftung und Gläubigerschutz – Unternehmerische Verhaltenspflichten des GmbH-Geschäftsführers zum Schutz Dritter (Munich: Beck, 1997)

Der Erstattungsanspruch nach § 64 II GmbHG, NZG 2004, 737–745

Reform des gesellschaftsrechtlichen Gläubigerschutzes – Gutachten E zum 66. Deutschen Juristentag Stuttgart 2006 (Munich: Beck, 2006)

Habersack, Mathias / Verse, Dirk A., Wrongful Trading – Grundlage einer europäischen Insolvenzverschleppungshaftung?, ZHR 168 (2004) 174–215

Halbhuber, Harald, Limited Company statt GmbH? – Europarechtlicher Rahmen und deutscher Widerstand (Baden-Baden: Nomos, 2001)

Halen, Curt Christian von, Das Gesellschaftsstatut nach der Centros-Entscheidung des EuGH (Heidelberg: Recht und Wirtschaft, 2001)

Hanisch, Hans, Report for Germany, in: Ian F. Fletcher (ed.), Cross-Border Insolvency: National and Comparative Studies (Tübingen: Mohr Siebeck, 1992) 104–127

Hannigan, Brenda, Company Law (London: LexisNexis UK, 2003)

Hannigan, Brenda / Prentice, Dan (eds.), Hannigan and Prentice: The Companies Act 2006 – A Commentary (London: LexisNexis Butterworths, 2007)

Hayton, D.J., The Law of Trusts (London: Sweet & Maxwell, 4th edn 2003)

Hebrant, Truls, Beihilferechtswidrige Gesellschaftsbeteiligungen und Gläubigerschutz (Frankfurt/Main: Peter Lang, 2006)

Henckel, Wolfram, Die Gläubigeranfechtung – ein taugliches Mittel zur Beseitigung von Verkürzungen der Konkursmasse?, ZIP 1982, 391–399

Hicks, Andrew, Directors' Liability for Management Errors (1994) 110 LQR 390–393

Hicks, Andrew, Director Disqualification: Can it Deliver? [2001] JBL 433–460

Hirt, Hans C., The Wrongful Trading Remedy in UK Law: Classification, Application and Practical Significance [2004] ECFR 71–120

Hirte, Heribert, Kapitalgesellschaftsrecht (Cologne: RWS-Verlag, 5th edn 2006)

Reform des gesellschaftsrechtlichen Gläubigerschutzes, Referat am 66. Deutschen Juristentag Stuttgart 2006, in: Verhandlungen des 66. Deutschen Juristentages, vol. II/1 (Munich: Beck, 2006)

Hirte, Heribert / Bücker, Thomas (eds.), Grenzüberschreitende Gesellschaften – Praxishandbuch für ausländische Kapitalgesellschaften mit Sitz im Inland (Cologne: Heymanns, 2nd edn 2006)

Höfling, Barbara, Das englische internationale Gesellschaftsrecht (Heidelberg: Verlag Recht und Wirtschaft, 2002)

Hommelhoff, Peter, Zum Wegfall des Erstattungsanspruchs aus § 31 GmbHG, in: Reinhard Goerdeler et al. (eds.), Festschrift für Alfred Kellermann zum 70. Geburtstag (Berlin: De Gruyter, 1991) 165–179

Hopt, Klaus J., Self-Dealing and Use of Corporate Opportunity and Information: Regulating Directors' Conflict of Interest, in: Klaus J. Hopt / Gunther Teubner (eds.), Corporate Governance and Directors' Liabilities – Legal, Economic and Sociological Analyses on Corporate Social Responsibility (Berlin: De Gruyter 1985) 285–326

Directors' Duties to Shareholders, Employees, and Other Creditors: A View from the Continent, in: Ewan McKendrick (ed.), Commercial Aspects of Trusts and Fiduciary Duties (Oxford: Clarendon Press, 1992) 115–132

Huber, Ulrich / Habersack, Mathias, Special Rules for Shareholder Loans: Which Consequences Would Arise for Shareholder Loans if the System of Legal Capital Should be Abolished? in: Marcus Lutter (ed.), Legal Capital in Europe (Berlin: De Gruyter, 2006) 308–324 = Zur Reform des Rechts der kapitalersetzenden Gesellschafterdarlehen, in: Marcus Lutter (ed.), Das Kapital der Aktiengesellschaft in Europa (Berlin: De Gruyter, 2006) 370–433 [the German version includes further reflections on the reform of German law]

Husa, Jaakko, Farewell to Functionalism or Methodological Tolerance?, RabelsZ 67 (2003) 419–447

Jackson, Thomas H., Avoiding Powers in Bankruptcy, 36 Stanford Law Review 725–787 (1984)

Jansen, Justus, Der gesellschaftsrechtliche Kapitalschutz in Deutschland, England und Frankreich – Eine rechtsvergleichende Untersuchung zur Ermittlung gemeinsamer gesellschaftsrechtlicher Prinzipien (Frankfurt/Main: Peter Lang, 2007)

Jauernig, Othmar / Berger, Christian, Zwangsvollstreckungs- und Insolvenzrecht (Munich: Beck, 22nd edn 2006)

Joost, Detlev, Kapitalbegriff und Reichweite der Bindung des aufgebrachten Vermögens in der GmbH, GmbHR 1983, 285–290

Entscheidungsanmerkung (case note), EWiR 1990, 481–482

Jugeli, George, Der Gläubigerschutz bei der Umwandlung juristischer Personen – Eine vergleichende Untersuchung zum deutschen und georgischen Recht (Frankfurt/Main: Peter Lang, 2006)

Just, Clemens, Die englische Limited in der Praxis (Munich: Beck, 2nd edn 2006)

Kahan, Marcel, Legal Capital Rules and the Structure of Corporate Law: Some Observations on the Differences Between European and U.S. Approaches, in: Klaus J. Hopt / Eddy Wymeersch (eds.), Capital Markets and Company Law (Oxford: OUP, 2003) 145–149

Kalss, Susanne / Adensamer, Nikolaus / Oelkers, Janine, Director's Duties in the Vicinity of Insolvency – a comparative analysis with reports from Germany, Austria, Belgium, Denmark, England, Finland, France, Italy, the Netherlands, Norway, Spain and Sweden, in: Marcus Lutter (ed.), Legal Capital in Europe (Berlin: De Gruyter, 2006) 112–143 = Die Rechtspflichten der Geschäftsleiter in der Krise der Gesellschaft sowie damit verbundene Rechtsfolgen im Rechtsvergleich, in: Marcus Lutter (ed.), Das Kapital der Aktiengesellschaft in Europa (Berlin: De Gruyter, 2006) 134–187

Kamlah, Klaus, Die Anfechtung in der Insolvenz von Unternehmen – dargestellt am deutschen und englischen Recht (Frankfurt/Main: Peter Lang, 1995)

Kasolowsky, Boris, Fiduciary Duties in Company Law (Baden-Baden: Nomos, 2003)

Kasolowsky, Boris / Schall, Alexander, Die Private Limited Company – England und Wales, in: Heribert Hirte / Thomas Bücker (eds.), Grenzüberschreitende Gesellschaften – Praxishandbuch für ausländische Kapitalgesellschaften mit Sitz im Inland (Cologne: Heymanns, 2nd edn 2006) 140–184

Keay, Andrew, Preferences in Liquidation Law: A Time for a Change [1998] CFILR 198–216

The Duty of Directors to Take Account of Creditors' Interests: Has It Any Role to Play? [2002] JBL 379–410

Transactions Defrauding Creditors: the Problem of Purpose under Section 423 of the Insolvency Act [2003] Conveyancer 272–288

Company Directors' Responsibilities to Creditors (Abingdon: Routledge-Cavendish, 2007)

Keay, Andrew / Walton, Peter, Insolvency Law: Corporate and Personal (Harlow: Pearson, 2003)

Kegel, Gerhard, Es ist was faul im Staate Dänemark . . ., EWS 1999, issue 8 (editorial)

Kieninger, Eva-Maria, Wettbewerb der Privatrechtsordnungen im Binnenmarkt (Tübingen: Mohr Siebeck, 2002)

The Legal Framework of Regulatory Competition Based on Company Mobility: EU and US Compared, 6 German Law Journal 741–770 (2005), available at www.germanlawjournal.com/article.php?id=590

Killinger, Johann, Insolvenzanfechtung gegen Insider (Berlin: Duncker & Humblot, 1991)

Kindler, Peter, Niederlassungsfreiheit für Scheinauslandsgesellschaften? – Die 'Centros'-Entscheidung des EuGH und das internationale Privatrecht, NJW 1999, 1993–2000

Auf dem Weg zur Europäischen Briefkastengesellschaft? – Die 'Überseering'-Entscheidung des EuGH und das internationale Privatrecht, NJW 2003, 1073–1079

Kleindiek, Detlef, Deliktshaftung und juristische Person – Zugleich zur Eigenhaftung von Unternehmensleitern (Tübingen: Mohr Siebeck, 1997)

Knight, W. J. L., Capital Maintenance, in: Fiona Patfield (ed.), Perspectives on Company Law 1 (London: Kluwer, 1995) 49–62

Knobbe-Keuk, Brigitte, Umzug von Gesellschaften in Europa, ZHR 154 (1990) 325–336

Koll-Möllenhoff, Rainer, Das Prinzip des festen Grundkapitals im europäischen Gesellschaftsrecht – Kapitalaufbringung und -erhaltung im EU-Recht und in den Rechten Deutschlands, Frankreichs und Englands (Baden-Baden: Nomos, 2005)

Koziol, Helmut, Grundlagen und Streitfragen der Gläubigeranfechtung (Wien: Springer, 1991)

Kraakman, Reinier / Davies, Paul / Hansmann, Henry / Hertig, Gérard / Hopt, Klaus J. / Kanda, Hideki / Rock, Edward B., The Anatomy of Corporate Law – A Comparative and Functional Approach (Oxford / New York: OUP, 2004)

Krecek, Thomas / Weber-Rey, Daniela, Germany: Company Law – Liability of Managing Directors [1996] ICCLR C192–194

Krüger, Markus E., Mindestkapital und Gläubigerschutz (Baden-Baden: Nomos, 2005)

Kübler, Bruno M., Die Konkursverschleppungshaftung nach der 'Wende' des Bundesgerichtshofes – Bedeutung für die Praxis – Besprechung der Entscheidung BGHZ 126, 181, ZGR 1995, 481–504

Kübler, Friedrich, Erwerbschancen und Organpflichten – Überlegungen zur Entwicklung der Lehre von den 'corporate opportunities', in: Festschrift für Winfried Werner (Berlin: De Gruyter, 1984) 437–448

Kübler, Friedrich / Assmann, Heinz-Dieter, Gesellschaftsrecht – Die privatrechtlichen Ordnungsstrukturen und Regelungsprobleme von Verbänden und Unternehmen (Heidelberg: Müller, 6th edn 2006)

Kühn, Günter, Gläubigerschutz nach § 823 Abs. 2 BGB bei Überschuldung einer GmbH, NJW 1970, 589–593

Lambsdorff (Graf), Hans Georg / Gilles, Peter, Zur Haftung der GmbH-Geschäftsführer bei unterlassenem oder verzögertem Konkursantrag, NJW 1966, 1551–1552

Langenbucher, Katja, Argument by Analogy in European Law [1998] CLJ 481–521

Larenz, Karl, Methodenlehre der Rechtswissenschaft (Berlin: Springer, 6th edn 1991)

Lasser, Mitchel de S.-O.-l'E., The question of understanding, in: Pierre Legrand / Roderick Munday (eds.), Comparative Legal Studies: Traditions and Transitions (Cambridge: CUP, 2003) 197–239

Lawson, F. H. / Rudden, Bernard, The Law of Property (Oxford: OUP, 3rd edn 2002)

Legrand, Pierre, European Legal Systems are not Converging (1996) 45 ICLQ 52–81

Legrand, Pierre, The Impossibility of 'Legal Transplants' (1997) 4 Maastricht Journal of European and Comparative Law 111–124

Lehmann, Julius, Soll bei einer zukünftigen Reform des Aktienrechts eine Annäherung an das englisch-amerikanische Recht in grundlegenden Fragen stattfinden? – Gutachten zum 34. Deutschen Juristentag Köln 1926 (Berlin: de Gruyter, 1926)

Leible, Stefan / Hoffmann, Jochen, 'Überseering' und das (vermeintliche) Ende der Sitztheorie, RIW 2002, 925–936

Lenz, Andreas, Gesellschafter- und Gläubigerschutz bei dem Formwechsel einer OHG in eine GmbH (Berlin: Spitz-Verlag, 2000)

Lindacher, Walter F., Direkte Haftung der AG-Vorstandsmitglieder und GmbH-Geschäftsführer gegenüber Gesellschaftsgläubigern bei unterlassenem oder verzögertem Konkursantrag, DB 1972, 1424–1425

Lipstein, Kurt, The Law relating to the movement of companies in the European Community, in: Festschrift für Erik Jayme (Munich: Sellier, 2004) 527–531

Lutter, Marcus, Zur persönlichen Haftung des Geschäftsführers aus deliktischen Schäden im Unternehmen, ZHR 157 (1993) 464–482

Gefahren persönlicher Haftung für Gesellschafter und Geschäftsführer einer GmbH, DB 1994, 129–135

Gesetzliches Garantiekapital als Problem europäischer und deutscher Rechtspolitik, AG 1998, 375–377

Lutter, Marcus (ed.), Europäische Auslandsgesellschaften in Deutschland (Cologne: Otto Schmidt, 2005)

Legal Capital in Europe (Berlin: De Gruyter, 2006) = Das Kapital der Aktiengesellschaft in Europa (Berlin: De Gruyter, 2006)

Mänhardt, Franz / Posch, Willibald, Internationales Privatrecht – Privatrechtsvergleichung – Einheitsprivatrecht. Eine Einführung in die internationalen Dimensionen des Privatrechts (Wien / New York: Springer, 2nd edn 1999)

Markesinis, Basil, Judicial Style and Judicial Reasoning in England and Germany, [2000] CLJ 294–309

Unity or Division: The Search for Similarities in Contemporary European Law (2001) 54 Current Legal Problems 591–617

Zur Lehre des Rechts anhand von Fällen: Einige bescheidene Vorschläge zur Verbesserung der deutschen Juristenausbildung, in: Festschrift für Peter Schlechtriem (Tübingen: Mohr Siebeck, 2003) 119–140

Markesinis, Basil S. / Unberath, Hannes, The German Law of Torts – A Comparative Treatise (Oxford: Hart, 4th edn 2002)

Markesinis, Basil S. / Unberath, Hannes / Johnston, Angus, The German Law of Contract – A Comparative Treatise (Oxford: Hart, 2nd edn 2006)

Mattei, Ugo, Comparative Law and Economics (Ann Arbor: University of Michigan Press, 1997)

McCormack, Gerard, Swelling Corporate Assets: Changing What Is on the Menu [2006] JCLS 39–69

Medicus, Dieter, Zur deliktischen Eigenhaftung von Organpersonen, in: Festschrift für Werner Lorenz (Tübingen: Mohr Siebeck, 1991) 155–169

Die Außenhaftung des GmbH-Geschäftsführers, GmbHR 1993, 533–540

Meilicke, Wienand, Entscheidungsanmerkung (case note), DB 1999, 627

Merkt, Hanno, Das europäische Gesellschaftsrecht und die Idee des 'Wettbewerbs der Gesetzgeber', RabelsZ 59 (1995) 545–568

Michaels, Ralf, Im Westen nichts Neues? 100 Jahre Pariser Kongreß für Rechtsvergleichung – Gedanken anläßlich einer Jubiläumskonferenz in New Orleans, RabelsZ 66 (2002) 97–115

The Functional Method of Comparative Law, in: Mathias Reimann / Reinhard Zimmermann (eds.), The Oxford Handbook of Comparative Law (Oxford / New York: OUP, 2006) 339–382

Micheler, Eva / Prentice, D. D. (eds.), Joint Ventures in English and German Law – Papers presented to the first Oxford Anglo-German Law Conference Autumn 1999 (Oxford: Hart, 2000)

Milman, David / Parry, Rebecca, A Study of the Operation of Transactional Avoidance Mechanisms in Corporate Insolvency Practice (Wallingford, Oxon.: GTI Specialist Publishing, for the Insolvency Lawyers' Association, 1998)

Mock, Sebastian / Schildt, Charlotte, Insolvenz ausländischer Kapitalgesellschaften mit Sitz in Deutschland, in: Heribert Hirte / Thomas Bücker (eds.), Grenzüberschreitende Gesellschaften – Praxishandbuch für ausländische Kapitalgesellschaften mit Sitz im Inland (Cologne: Heymanns, 2nd edn 2006) 560–609

Mokal, Rizwaan J., An Agency Cost Analysis of the Wrongful Trading Provisions: Redistribution, Perverse Incentives and the Creditors' Bargain [2000] CLJ 335–369

Liquidation expenses and floating charges – the separate funds fallacy [2004] LMCLQ 387–404

Corporate Insolvency Law – Theory and Application (Oxford: OUP, 2005)

Mokal, Rizwaan Jameel / Ho, Look Chan, Consideration, Characterisation, Evaluation: Transactions at an Undervalue after *Phillips v Brewin Dolphin* [2001] JCLS 359–379

Moss, Gabriel / Fletcher, Ian F. / Isaacs, Stuart (eds.), The EC Regulation on Insolvency Proceedings: A Commentary and Annotated Guide (Oxford: OUP, 2002)

Mössle, Claus M., Gläubigerschutz beim Zuzug ausländischer Gesellschaften aus der Sicht des englischen Rechts (Frankfurt/Main: Peter Lang, 2006)

Müller, Alexander, Gläubigerschutzkonzepte bei Sachgründung und Umwandlungsgründung einer GmbH (Munich: Meidenbauer, 2005)

Müller, Gerd, Zur Haftung des Gesellschafter-Geschäftsführers aus culpa in contrahendo und aus § 64 Abs. 1 GmbHG, ZIP 1993, 1531–1538

Nicholls (Lord), Knowing Receipt: The Need for a New Landmark, in: William R. Cornish / Richard Nolan / Janet O'Sullivan / Graham Virgo (eds.), Restitution – Past, Present and Future (Oxford: Hart, 1998) 231–245

Nikoleyczik, Tobias, Gläubigerschutz zwischen Gesetz und Vertrag – Alternativen zum System eines festen Nennkapitals (Cologne: Josef Eul Verlag, 2007)

Nobel, Peter, Unternehmensfinanzierung und gesetzliches Garantiekapital in der Schweiz, AG 1998, 354–358

Nolan, Richard, How Knowing Is Knowing Receipt? [2000] CLJ 447–450

Nölle, Jens-Uwe, Die Eigenhaftung des GmbH-Geschäftsführers für Organisationspflichtverletzungen (Regensburg: Roderer, 1995)

Oditah, Fidelis, Wrongful trading [1990] LMCLQ 205–222

Misfeasance proceedings against company directors [1992] LMCLQ 207–226

Omar, Paul J., European Insolvency Law (Aldershot: Ashgate, 2004)

Oplustil, Krzysztof, Gläubigerschutz durch reale Kapitalaufbringung im deutschen und polnischen Recht der Kapitalgesellschaften (Frankfurt: Peter Lang, 2001)

Otte, Sabine, Das Kapitalschutzsystem der englischen private limited company im Vergleich zur deutschen GmbH (Hamburg: Verlag Dr Kovač, 2006)

Parmentier, Miriam A., Gläubigerschutz in öffentlichen Unternehmen – Die Haftung der Gebietskörperschaft für die Verbindlichkeiten ihrer Eigengesellschaft (Berlin: Berliner Wissenschafts-Verlag, 2000)

Parry, Rebecca, Transaction Avoidance in Insolvencies (Oxford: OUP, 2001)

Case Comentary on *Phillips (Liquidator of AJ Bekhor & Co) v Brewin Dolphin Bell Lawrie Ltd* [2001] Insolvency Lawyer 58–63

The destination of proceeds of insolvency litigation (2002) 23 CoLaw 49–57

Paulus, Christoph G., Entscheidungsanmerkung (case note), EWiR 2000, 947–948

Claw-back Rules and Creditors' Protection, in: Marcus Lutter (ed.), Legal Capital in Europe (Berlin: De Gruyter, 2006) 325–340 = Das Recht der Insolvenzanfechtung und Gläubigerschutz, in: Marcus Lutter (ed.), Das Kapital der Aktiengesellschaft in Europa (Berlin: De Gruyter, 2006) 434–450

Paulus, Christoph G. / Schröder, Wolfgang, Über die Verschärfungen des Rechts der Insolvenzanfechtung, WM 1999, 253–257

Payne, Jennifer, Unjust Enrichment, Trusts and Recipient Liability for Unlawful Dividends (2003) 119 LQR 583–607

Recipient Liability for Unlawful Dividends [2007] LMCLQ 7–14

Payne, Jennifer (ed.), Takeovers in English and German Law (Oxford: Hart, 2002)

Pearce, Robert / Stevens, John, The Law of Trusts and Equitable Obligations (Oxford: OUP, 4th edn 2006)

Pennington, Robert R., Pennington's Company Law (London: Butterworths, 8th edn 2001)

Pennington's Corporate Insolvency Law (London: Butterworths, 2nd edn 1997)

The Genesis of the Floating Charge (1960) 23 MLR 630–646

Perker, Susanne, Das Reorganisationsverfahren im englischen Insolvenzrecht im Vergleich zur geplanten deutschen Insolvenzordnung (Munich: Florentz, 1994)

Pernice, Christina, Die Insolvenzverschleppung durch das Geschäftsführungsorgan der kleinen Kapitalgesellschaft im deutschen, französischen und englischen Recht (Frankfurt/Main: Peter Lang, 2002)

Petersen, Jens, Der Gläubigerschutz im Umwandlungsrecht (Munich: Beck, 2001)

Pettet, Ben, Company Law (Harlow: Pearson, 2nd edn 2005)

Poertzgen, Christoph, Organhaftung wegen Insolvenzverschleppung (Baden-Baden: Nomos, 2006)

Prentice, Dan, The Effect of Insolvency on Pre-Liquidation Transactions, in: B. G. Pettet (ed.), Company Law in Change (London: Stevens, 1987) 69–89

Creditor's Interests and Director's Duties (1990) 10 OJLS 265–277

The Incorporation Theory – The United Kingdom [2003] EBLR 631–641

Prentice, Dan / Payne, Jenny, Directors' Fiduciary Duties (2006) 122 LQR 558–565

Rajak, Harry, The English Limited Company as an Alternative Legal Form for German Enterprise, EWS 2005, 539–545

Redeker, Rouven, Die Haftung für wrongful trading im englischen Recht – Eine vergleichende Betrachtung der deutschen und der englischen Geschäftsleiterhaftung für Insolvenzverschleppung (Cologne: Heymanns, 2007)

Rehm, Gebhard, Die Private Company Limited by Shares (Ltd.) nach englischem Recht, in: Horst Eidenmüller (ed.), Ausländische Kapitalgesellschaften im deutschen Recht (Munich: Beck, 2004) 327–351

Reiff, Peter / Arnold, Arnd, Unbeschränkte Konkursverschleppungshaftung des Geschäftsführers einer GmbH auch gegenüber gesetzlichen Neugläubigern? ZIP 1998, 1893–1899

Reinbach, Ellen, Gläubigerschutz gegen den Mißbrauch einer private limited company – Eine Darstellung anhand einer Gesellschaft des englischen Rechts mit Sitz in Deutschland nach Inspire Art (Frankfurt/Main: Peter Lang, 2005)

Reinhart, Stefan, Germany's Insolvency Bill and its Cross-Border Provisions (1993) 2 IIR 187–214

Remien, Oliver, Europäische Rechtswissenschaft – Voraussetzung oder Folge europäischer Rechtsangleichung?, in: Klaus J. Hopt (ed.), Europäische Integration als Herausforderung des Rechts (Essen: MA Akademie-Verlag 1991) 124–138

Renger, Edward, Gläubigerschutz durch § 32a GmbH – Ein Beitrag zur ökonomischen Analyse des Eigenkapitalersatzrechts unter Einbeziehung US-amerikanischer Regelungskonzepte (Frankfurt/Main: Peter Lang, 2004)

Rickford, Jonathan (ed.), Reforming Capital – Report of the Interdisciplinary Group on Capital Maintenance [2004] EBLR 919–1027

Rieckers, Oliver, Treuepflichten versus Vertragsfreiheit – Neues zur Wirksamkeit von Deal-Protection-Klauseln in der Rechtsprechung Delawares, RIW 2003, 668–676

Riedel, Jens, Unzulässige Vermögenszuwendungen und ihre Rechtsfolgen im Recht der Aktiengesellschaft (Jena: Jenaer Wissenschaftliche Verlagsgesellschaft, 2004)

Riley, C. A., The Company Director's Duty of Care and Skill: The Case for an Onerous but Subjective Standard (1999) 62 MLR 697–724

Robins, Stephen, Knowledge, ignorance, and unlawful dividends [2007] Insolvency Intelligence 33–36

Röhricht, Volker, Insolvenzrechtliche Aspekte im Gesellschaftsrecht, ZIP 2005, 505–516

Rojo, Angel, Unternehmensfinanzierung und gesetzliches Garantiekapital in Spanien, AG 1998, 358–363

Röpke, Katarina, Gläubigerschutzregime im europäischen Wettbewerb der Gesellschaftsrechte (Berlin: De Gruyter, 2007)

Roth, Marcus, Unternehmerisches Ermessen und Haftung des Vorstands (Munich: Beck, 2001)

Rust, Brigitte, Verdeckte Einlagenrückgewähr durch Leistung an Dritte in der Kapitalgesellschaft (Baden-Baden: Nomos, 2000)

Sacco, Rodolfo, Souvenirs d'un vieux comparatiste, ZEuP 2002, 727–736

Samuel, Geoffrey, Law of Obligations and Legal Remedies (London: Cavendish, 2nd edn 2001)

Sandberger, Andreas, Die Außenhaftung des GmbH-Geschäftsführers (Baden-Baden: Nomos, 1998)

Sandrock, Otto, Sitztheorie, Überlagerungstheorie und der EWG-Vertrag: Wasser, Öl und Feuer, RIW 1989, 505–513

Scanlan, Gary / Harvey, Andrew / Prime, Terence / Ogowewo, Tunde, Companies Act 2006 – A Guide to the New Law (London: Law Society, 2007)

Schall, Alexander, Englischer Gläubigerschutz bei der Limited in Deutschland; ZIP 2005, 965–975

The UK Limited Company Abroad – How Foreign Creditors are Protected after Inspire Art (Including a Comparison of UK and German Creditor Protection Rules) [2005] EBLR 1534–1554

Schanze, Erich, Directors' duties in Germany [1999] CFILR 286–298

Schilling, Simon, Insolvenz einer englischen Limited mit Verwaltungssitz in Deutschland (Frankfurt/Main: Peter Peter Lang, 2006)

Schmidt, Karsten, Konkursantragspflichten bei der GmbH und bürgerliches Deliktsrecht, JZ 1978, 661–666

Insolvenzrisiko und gesellschaftsrechtliche Haftung, JZ 1985, 301–308

Wege zum Insolvenzrecht der Unternehmen (Cologne: RWS-Verlag, 1990)

Entscheidungsanmerkung (case note), NJW 1993, 2934–2935

Gesellschaftsrecht (Cologne: Heymanns, 3rd edn 1997, 4th edn 2002)

Insolvenzordnung und Gesellschaftsrecht, ZGR 1998, 633–671

Entscheidungsanmerkung (case note), ZIP 2003, 1715–1716

Verbotene Zahlungen in der Krise von Handelsgesellschaften und die daraus resultierenden Ersatzpflichten – Insolvenzrechtliche Brotvermehrung durch Klagen nach § 64 Abs. 2 GmbHG (§§ 92 AktG, 130a, 177a HGB, 99 GenG)? ZHR 168 (2004) 637–672

Grounds for Insolvency and Liability for Delays in Filing for Insolvency Proceedings – Necessary Supplement to Capital Protection, in: Marcus Lutter (ed.), Legal Capital in Europe (Berlin: De Gruyter, 2006) 144–165 = Insolvenzgründe und Haftung für Insolvenzverschleppung – Notwendige Ergänzung des Kapitalschutzes, in: Marcus Lutter (ed.), Das Kapital der Aktiengesellschaft in Europa (Berlin: De Gruyter, 2006) 188–206

GmbH-Reform, Solvenzgewährleistung und Insolvenzpraxis – Gedanken zum MoMiG-Entwurf, GmbHR 2007, 1–11

Reform der Kapitalsicherung und Haftung in der Krise nach dem Regierungsentwurf des MoMiG – Sechs Leitsätze zu § 30 GmbHG-E, § 64 GmbHG-E und § 15a InsO-E, GmbHR 2007, 1072–1080

Schmidt, Karsten / Uhlenbruck, Wilhelm (eds.), Die GmbH in Krise, Sanierung und Insolvenz (Cologne: Otto Schmidt, 3rd edn 2003)

Schön, Wolfgang, Wer schützt den Kapitalschutz?, ZHR 166 (2002) 1–5

Schönbeck, Tobias, Bankenrechnungslegung nach IAS/IFRS – Gläubigerschutz durch Information? Ein kritischer Vergleich mit den Regeln des deutschen Rechts (Frankfurt/Main: Peter Lang, 2004)

Schoppmeyer, Heinrich, Kapitel 8: Inkongruente Deckung (§ 131 InsO), in: Reinhard Bork (ed.), Handbuch des Insolvenzanfechtungsrechts (Cologne: RWS-Verlag, 2006) 249–322

Schuberth, Ernst-Markus, Konzernrelevante Regelungen im britischen Recht – Ein Beispiel für die Bewältigung konzernrechtlicher Fragestellungen durch Regeln des allgemeinen Gesellschafts-, Kapitalmarkt und Insolvenzrechts (Munich: Beck, 1997)

Schumann, Heribert, Criminal Law, in: Mathias Reimann / Joachim Zekoll (eds.), Introduction to German Law (The Hague: Kluwer, 2nd edn 2005) 387–418

Schüppen, Matthias, Aktuelle Fragen der Konkursverschleppungshaftung durch den GmbH-Geschäftsführer; DB 1994, 197–204

Sealy, Len, Fiduciary Relationships [1962] CLJ 69–81

Some Principles of Fiduciary Obligation [1963] CLJ 199–140

Directors' 'Wider' Responsibilities – Problems Conceptual, Practical and Procedural (1987) 13 Monash Univ. Law Review 164–188

Directors' Duties – An Unnecessary Gloss [1988] CLJ 175–177

Disqualification and Personal Liability of Directors (Kingston upon Thames: CCH New Law, 5th edn 2000)

Cases and Materials in Company Law (London: Butterworths, 7th edn 2001)

Sealy, Len / Milman, David, Annotated Guide to the Insolvency Legislation, 2 vols. (London: Sweet & Maxwell, 10th edn 2007)

Sealy, Len / Worthington, Sarah, Cases and Materials in Company Law (Oxford: OUP, 8th edn 2007)

Seeberg, Holger, Der Gläubigerschutz bei (Schein-)Auslandsgesellschaften mit Verwaltungssitz in Deutschland am Beispiel der Private Limited Company by Shares aus Irland (Berlin: Logos, 2007)

Seibert, Ulrich, Close Corporations – Reforming Private Company Law: European and International Perspectives [2007] EBOR 83–92

Shapiro, Fred R., The Most-Cited Articles from *The Yale Law Journal*, 100 Yale Law Journal 1449–1514 (1991)

Spindler, Gerald, Unternehmensorganisationspflichten – Zivilrechtliche und öffentlich-rechtliche Regelungskonzepte (Cologne: Heymanns, 2001)

Spindler, Gerald / Berner, Olaf, Der Gläubigerschutz im Gesellschaftsrecht nach Inspire Art, RIW 2004, 7–16

Spolidoro, Marco Saverio, The legal capital and the raising of funds through the issuance of securities in Italy, AG 1998, 363–368

Stanton, K.M., Breach of Statutory Duty in Tort (London: Sweet & Maxwell, 1986)

Stapelfeld, Ait, Die Haftung des GmbH-Geschäftsführers für Fehlverhalten in der Gesellschaftskrise (Cologne: Müller Botermann, 1990)

Steffek, Felix, Geschäftsleiterpflichten im englischen Kapitalgesellschaftsrecht – Kodifizierung der directors' duties im Companies Act 2006, GmbHR 2007, 810–815

Das englische Recht der Insolvenzanfechtung – ein funktionaler Vergleich unter besonderer Berücksichtigung kapitalgesellschaftsrechtlicher Aspekte, KTS 2007, 451–483

Steinfeld, Alan / Mann, Martin / Ritchie, Richard / Weaver, Elizabeth / Galley, Helen / Adair, Stuart / McLarnon, Neil / Cloherty, Adam, Blackstone's Guide to The Companies Act 2006 (Oxford: OUP, 2007)

Stirtz, Beate, Gläubigerschutz bei der englischen Limited im Vergleich zur GmbH (Bremen: CT Salzwasser-Verlag, 2007)

Stoll, Andreas, Garantiekapital und konzernspezifischer Gläubigerschutz (Cologne: Heymanns, 2007)

Strüve, Anja, Deutscher Juristentag 2006, Legal Latitudes – Newsletter for the Transatlantic Business and Law Community, vol. 1 no. 1 (2007) 4–6

Teubner, Gunther, Alienating Justice: On the Surplus Value of the Twelfth Camel, in: Jiří Přibáň / David Nelken (eds.), Law's New Boundaries – The Consequences of Legal Autopoiesis (Aldershot: Ashgate Dartmouth, 2001) 21–44

Tham, Chee Ho, Unjust Enrichment and Unlawful Distributions: A Step too Far? [2005] CLJ 177–211

Theißen, Thomas, Gläubigerschutz bei der Spaltung von Gesellschaften nach dem Umwandlungsgesetz (Hamburg: Verlag Dr Kovač, 2001)

Tries, Hermann-Josef, Verdeckte Gewinnausschüttungen im GmbH-Recht (Cologne: Otto Schmidt, 1991)

Ulmer, Peter, Gesellschafterhaftung gegenüber der GmbH bei Vorteilsgewährung unter Verstoß gegen § 30 Abs. 1 GmbHG, in: Marcus Lutter et al. (eds.), Festschrift 100 Jahre GmbH-Gesetz (Cologne: Otto Schmidt, 1992) 363–389

Entscheidungsanmerkung (case note), ZIP 1993, 769–772

van Gerven, Walter et al. (eds.), Tort Law (Casebooks on the Common Law of Europe) (Oxford: Hart, 2000)

Veil, Rüdiger, Capital Maintenance – The regime of the Capital Directive versus Alternative Systems, in: Marcus Lutter (ed.), Legal Capital in Europe (Berlin: De Gruyter, 2006) 75–93 = Kapitalerhaltung – Das System der

Kapitalrichtlinie versus situative Ausschüttungssperren, in: Marcus Lutter (ed.), Das Kapital der Aktiengesellschaft in Europa (Berlin: De Gruyter, 2006) 91–113

Veith, Alexander, Der Gläubigerschutz beim Formwechsel nach dem Umwandlungsgesetz (Frankfurt/Main: Peter Lang, 2003)

Vella, John, Departing from the Legal Substance of Transactions in the Corporate Field: the Ramsay Approach beyond the Tax Sphere [2007] JCLS 243–283

Virgo, Graham, The Principles of the Law of Restitution (Oxford: OUP, 2nd edn 2006)

Volhard, Rüdiger / Taschke, Jürgen, Managing Directors and Authorized Representatives, in: Rüdiger Volhard / Arndt Stengel (eds.), German Limited Liability Company (Chichester: John Wiley & Sons, 1997) 137–176

Vogenauer, Stefan, Die Auslegung von Gesetzen in England und auf dem Kontinent – eine vergleichende Untersuchung der Rechtsprechung und ihrer historischen Grundlagen (Tübingen: Mohr Siebeck, 2001)

Vogenauer, Stefan, An Empire of Light? Learning and Lawmaking in the History of German Law [2005] CLJ 481–500

Wagner, Gerhard, Distributions to Shareholders and Fraudulent Transfer Law [2006] EBOR 217–231, reprinted in: Horst Eidenmüller / Wolfgang Schön (eds.), The Law and Economics of Creditor Protection – A Transatlantic Perspective (The Hague: T.M.C. Asser Press, 2008) 217–231

Walters, Adrian, Directors' duties: the impact of the Company Directors Disqualification Act 1986 (2000) 21 CoLaw 110–119

Wrongful trading: two recent cases [2001] Insolvency Lawyer 211

Preferences (Chapter 4), in: John Armour / Howard Bennett (eds.), Vulnerable Transactions in Corporate Insolvency (Oxford: Hart, 2003) 123–181

Walters, Adrian / Davis-White, Malcolm, Directors' Disqualification & Bankruptcy Restrictions (London: Sweet & Maxwell, 2005)

Watson, Alan, Legal Transplants – An Approach to Comparative Law (Athens, Ga. and London: University of Georgia Press, 2nd edn 1993)

Weber-Rey, Daniela, Effects of the Better Regulation Approach on European Company Law and Corporate Governance [2007] ECFR 370–416

Wedderburn (Lord Wedderburn of Charlton), The Legal Development of Corporate Responsibility – For Whom Will Corporate Managers Be Trustees? in: Klaus J. Hopt / Gunther Teubner (eds.), Corporate Governance and Directors' Liabilities – Legal, Economic and Sociological Analyses on Corporate Social Responsibility (Berlin: De Gruyter 1985) 3–54

Weiß, Stefan, Aktionärs- und Gläubigerschutz im System der echten nennwertlosen (Stück-)Aktie; (Munich: Sellier, 2007)

Wheeler, Sally, Swelling the Assets for Distribution in Corporate Insolvency [1993] JBL 256–269

Wiedemann, Herbert, Gesellschaftsrecht – Ein Lehrbuch des Unternehmens- und Verbandsrechts, Band I: Grundlagen (Munich: Beck, 1980)
Entscheidungsanmerkung (case note), EWiR 1993, 583–584
Wilhelm, Jan, Die Vermögensbindung bei der Aktiengesellschaft und der GmbH und das Problem der Unterkapitalisierung, in: Horst Heinrich Jakobs et al. (eds.), Festschrift für Werner Flume zum 70. Geburtstag (Cologne: Otto Schmidt, 1978) vol. II, 337–397
Konkursantragspflicht des GmbH-Geschäftsführers und Quotenschaden, ZIP 1993, 1833–1837
Wilms, Tobias, Die englische Ltd. in deutscher Insolvenz – Nach Centros, Überseering und Inspire Art (Baden-Baden: Nomos, 2006)
Wimmer-Leonhardt, Susanne, Konzernhaftungsrecht – Die Haftung der Konzernmuttergesellschaft für die Tochtergesellschaften im deutschen und englischen Recht (Tübingen: Mohr Siebeck, 2004)
Winkler, Eberhard, Zum Schutzumfang des § 64 Abs. 1 GmbH-Gesetz, MDR 1960, 185–187
Winter, Martin, Verdeckte Gewinnausschüttungen im GmbH-Recht, ZHR 148 (1984) 579–602
Wolf, Martin, Konzernhaftung in Frankreich und England (Cologne: Heymann, 1995)
Wooldridge, Frank, Aspects of German Law Governing Private Limited Liability Companies, in: David Feldman / Frank Meisel (eds.), Corporate and Commercial Law: Modern Developments – Published in Honour of Professor R.R. Pennington (London: Lloyd's of London Press, 1996) 33–56
Duty of Care and Liabilities of Members of the Two Boards of German Public Companies [2006] EBLR 109–120
Worthington, Sarah, The Duty to Monitor: A Modern View of the Director's Duty of Care, in: Fiona Patfield (ed.), Perspectives on Company Law 2 (London: Kluwer, 1997) 181–202
Fiduciaries: When is Self-Denial Obligatory? [1999] CLJ 500–508
Corporate Governance: Remedying and Ratifying Directors' Breaches (2000) 116 LQR 638–675
Reforming Directors' Duties (2001) 64 MLR 439–458
Equity (Oxford: OUP, 2nd edn 2006)
Zander, Michael, The Law-Making Process (Cambridge: CUP, 6th edn 2004)
Zeeck, Sebastian, Das Internationale Anfechtungsrecht in der Insolvenz – Die Anknüpfung der Involvenzanfechtung (Tübingen: Mohr Siebeck, 2003)
Zimmer, Daniel, Wie es Euch gefällt? Offene Fragen nach dem Überseering-Urteil des EuGH, BB 2003, 1–7
Zimmermann, Reinhard, The Law of Obligations – Roman Foundation of the Civilian Tradition (Oxford: Clarendon Press, 1996 [paperback edition])

The New German Law of Obligations – Historical and Comparative Perspectives (Oxford: OUP, 2005)

Zweigert, Konrad / Kötz, Hein, Einführung in die Rechtsvergleichung (Tübingen: Mohr Siebeck, 3rd edn 1996) – English translation by Tony Weir: Introduction to Comparative Law (Oxford: Clarendon Press, 3rd edn 1998)

COMPANY LAW REVIEW CONSULTATION DOCUMENTS

Document	Publication	Reference
Modern Company Law for a Competitive Economy	March 1998	–
Modern Company Law for a Competitive Economy: The Strategic Framework	February 1999	URN 99/654
Modern Company Law for a Competitive Economy: Company General Meetings & Shareholder Communication	October 1999	URN 99/1144
Modern Company Law for a Competitive Economy: Company Formation & Capital Maintenance	October 1999	URN 99/1145
Modern Company Law for a Competitive Economy: Reforming the Law Concerning Overseas Companies	October 1999	URN 99/1146
Modern Company Law for a Competitive Economy: Developing the Framework	March 2000	URN 00/656
Modern Company Law for a Competitive Economy: Capital Maintenance: Other Issues	June 2000	–
Modern Company Law for a Competitive Economy: Trading Disclosures	October 2000	–
Modern Company Law for a Competitive Economy: Registration of Company Charges	October 2000	–
Modern Company Law for a Competitive Economy: Completing the Structure	November 2000	URN 00/1335

(*cont.*)

Document	Publication	Reference
Modern Company Law for a Competitive Economy: Final Report (2 vols.)	June 2001	URN 01/942 URN 01/943
White Paper 'Modernising Company Law' (2 vols.)	July 2002	Cm. 5553
White Paper 'Company Law Reform'	March 2005	Cm. 6456

INDEX